Youth in Superdiverse Societies

Youth in Superdiverse Societies brings together theoretical, methodological, and international approaches to the study of globalization, diversity, and acculturation in adolescence. It examines vital issues including migration, integration, cultural identities, ethnic minorities, and the interplay of ethnic and cultural diversity with experiences of growing up as an adolescent. This important volume focuses on understanding the experiences and consequences of multicultural societies and offers valuable new insights in the field of intergroup relations and the complexity of growingly heterogeneous societies.

The book comprises four parts. The first includes fresh theoretical perspectives for studying youth development in multicultural societies, exploring topics such as superdiversity, globalization, bicultural identity development, polyculturalism, the interplay of acculturation and development, as well as developmental-ecological approaches. The second part highlights innovative methods in studying multicultural societies. It contains innovative dynamic concepts (e.g. experience-based sampling), methods for studying the nested structure of acculturative contexts, and suggestions for cross-comparative research to differentiate universal and context-specific processes. The third part examines social relations and social networks in diverse societies and features developmentally crucial contexts (e.g. family, peers, schools) and contributions on interethnic interactions in real-life contexts. The final part presents applications in natural settings and includes contributions on participatory action research and teachers' dealings with ethnic diversity. Each chapter provides a thorough overview of current research trends and findings, followed by detailed recommendations for future research, suggesting how the approaches can be cited, applied, and improved.

Youth in Superdiverse Societies is valuable reading for students studying adolescent acculturation and development in psychology, sociology, education, anthropology, linguistics, and political science. It will also be of interest to scholars and researchers in social and developmental psychology, and related disciplines, as well as professionals in the field of migration.

Peter F. Titzmann is Professor for Developmental Psychology at the Leibniz University Hannover, Germany. In his research he investigates the interplay between normative development and migration-related adaptation among adolescents with immigrant backgrounds. He studied this interplay in developmental outcomes, such as acculturative stress, delinquency, family interactions, autonomy, and self-efficacy.

Philipp Jugert is Professor of Intercultural Psychology – Migration and Integration at the University of Duisburg-Essen, Germany. His major research interests include social development in the context of ethnic diversity, group processes and intergroup relations, and civic engagement.

Studies in Adolescent Development
Series Editor: Susan Branje

The *Studies in Adolescent Development* series is published in conjunction with the European Association for Research on Adolescence and is committed to publishing and promoting the highest quality of writing in the field of adolescent development.

The series aims to respond to the recent shifts in the social and ecological environment of adolescents and in the new theoretical perspectives within the social science by providing a range of books, each of which deals in-depth with an aspect of current interest within the field of adolescent development.

Each book focuses on a specific aspect of adolescence and provides either a clear picture of the research endeavours which are currently serving to extend the boundaries of our knowledge and understanding of the field, or an insightful theoretical perspective of adolescent development. The editors encourage publications which represent original contributions to the field.

Also available in this series:

Siblings in Adolescence
Emerging individuals, lasting bonds
Angela Ittel and Aiden Sisler

Autonomy in Adolescent Development
Towards Conceptual Clarity
Bart Soenens, Maarten Vansteenkiste and Stijn Van Petegem

Psychosocial Development in Adolescence
Insights from the Dynamic Systems Approach
E. Saskia Kunnen, Naomi M. P. de Ruiter, Bertus F. Jeronimus, Mandy A. E. van der Gaag

Youth in Superdiverse Societies
Growing up with globalization, diversity, and acculturation
Peter F. Titzmann and Philipp Jugert

Youth in Superdiverse Societies

Growing up with Globalization, Diversity, and Acculturation

Edited by Peter F. Titzmann and Philipp Jugert

LONDON AND NEW YORK

First published 2020
by Routledge
2 Park Square, Milton Park, Abingdon, Oxon OX14 4RN

and by Routledge
52 Vanderbilt Avenue, New York, NY 10017

Routledge is an imprint of the Taylor & Francis Group, an informa business

© 2020 selection and editorial matter, Peter F. Titzmann and Philipp Jugert; individual chapters, the contributors

The right of Peter F. Titzmann and Philipp Jugert to be identified as the authors of the editorial material, and of the authors for their individual chapters, has been asserted in accordance with sections 77 and 78 of the Copyright, Designs and Patents Act 1988.

All rights reserved. No part of this book may be reprinted or reproduced or utilised in any form or by any electronic, mechanical, or other means, now known or hereafter invented, including photocopying and recording, or in any information storage or retrieval system, without permission in writing from the publishers.

Trademark notice: Product or corporate names may be trademarks or registered trademarks, and are used only for identification and explanation without intent to infringe.

British Library Cataloguing-in-Publication Data
A catalogue record for this book is available from the British Library

Library of Congress Cataloging-in-Publication Data
A catalog record has been requested for this book

ISBN: 978-1-138-48838-0 (hbk)
ISBN: 978-1-138-48839-7 (pbk)
ISBN: 978-1-351-04026-6 (ebk)

Typeset in Garamond
by Swales & Willis, Exeter, Devon, UK

Contents

List of contributors	x
Introduction PETER F. TITZMANN AND PHILIPP JUGERT	1

PART I
Conceptual considerations   5

1 Growing up with difference: superdiversity as a habitual frame of reference   7
FRAN MEISSNER

2 Globalization and the proliferation of complex acculturation processes   23
SIMON OZER

3 Biculturalism and bicultural identity development: a relational model of bicultural systems   41
ALAN MECA, KYLE EICHAS, SETH J. SCHWARTZ, AND RACHEL J. DAVIS

4 Polyculturalism: current evidence, future directions, and implementation possibilities for diverse youth   58
LISA ROSENTHAL, MARYBETH APRICENO, AND SHERI R. LEVY

5 Towards a more dynamic perspective on acculturation research   74
RICHARD M. LEE, PETER F. TITZMANN, AND PHILIPP JUGERT

6 Development in context: the importance of country and school level factors for the mental health of immigrant adolescents 92
GONNEKE W.J.M. STEVENS AND SOPHIE D. WALSH

PART II
Innovative methods 109

7 Applying experience-sampling methods to investigate the impact of school diversity on youth development in multicultural contexts 111
TIFFANY YIP, YUEN MI CHEON, AND ALEXANDRA EHRHARDT

8 Immigrant youth adaptation in a multilevel context: conceptual and statistical considerations 129
JENS B. ASENDORPF AND FROSSO MOTTI-STEFANIDI

9 The role of comparative research in understanding the diversity of immigrant youth 144
ALISON E. F. BENBOW AND LARA AUMANN

PART III
Adolescents' diverse social worlds 161

10 Adolescent language brokers: developmental and familial considerations 163
ROBERT S. WEISSKIRCH

11 Ethnic majority and minority youth in multicultural societies 177
SABAHAT CIGDEM BAGCI AND ADAM RUTLAND

12 A new agenda for examining interethnic interactions amongst youth in diverse settings 196
SHELLEY MCKEOWN, AMANDA WILLIAMS, THIA SAGHERIAN-DICKEY, AND KATARZYNA KUCABA

13 Bridging contexts: the interplay between parents, peers, and schools in explaining youth reactions to growing diversity 213
MARTA MIKLIKOWSKA AND ANDREA BOHMAN

14 Understanding the causes and consequences of segregation
in youth's friendship networks: opportunities and challenges
for research 233
LARS LESZCZENSKY AND TOBIAS STARK

PART IV
Preparing multicultural societies for dealing with diversity inside and outside of schools **249**

15 Participatory approaches to youth civic development in
multicultural societies 251
PARISSA J. BALLARD, AHNA SULEIMAN, LINDSAY TILL HOYT, ALISON K. COHEN,
METSEHATE AYENEKULU, AND GENET EBUY

16 Teachers' dealings with ethnic diversity 268
JOCHEM THIJS AND ROSELIEN VERVAET

17 How to best prepare teachers for multicultural schools:
challenges and perspectives 285
SAURO CIVITILLO AND LINDA P. JUANG

Index 302

Contributors

MaryBeth Apriceno is a graduate student in Social and Health Psychology at Stony Brook University. She earned her BA in Forensic Psychology from John Jay College of Criminal Justice (CUNY) and her MA in Social and Health Psychology from Stony Brook University. Her research interests include prejudice and prejudice reduction.

Jens B. Asendorpf is a retired professor of personality psychology at Humboldt University Berlin, Germany. His major research interests include personality development over the lifespan, and also from an intercultural perspective, and statistical methods for longitudinal and multilevel data.

Genet Ebuy Assefa is Assistant Lecturer in Mekelle University's Department of Psychology. She earned her Bachelors of Art degree in psychology and sociology from Mekelle University. Currently she is enrolled in a Masters of Early Childhood Care and Development program.

Lara Aumann is a PhD student at the Leibniz University Hanover, Germany. Her major research interest is the acculturation process of migrant adolescents and their families. In particular she is interested in (migrant) family interactions and dynamics in different contexts and cultures.

Metsehate Ayenekulu, MS, is a public health and gender expert. She is currently an Adolescent Youth Family Planning Program Director at PSI/Ethiopia.

Sabahat Cigdem Bagci, PhD, is Associate Professor of Psychology at Sabanci University, Turkey. She is interested in various intergroup processes among both majority and minority group status children and adults. Her main research areas include intergroup contact and cross-group friendships, prejudice and discrimination, social identity, and psychological well-being.

Parissa J. Ballard is an assistant professor of Family & Community Medicine in the Wake Forest School of Medicine. In her research she draws on multiple methods and perspectives to investigate how diverse young people engage with their communities and she is specifically interested in the role of civic engagement in promoting health, wellbeing, and equity for youth and communities.

Alison E. F. Benbow, PhD, is a social and developmental psychologist currently working at the Institute of Psychology of the Leibniz University Hannover, Germany. She researches the psychosocial adaptation of migrant adolescents, their bi- and multiculturalism, more general consequences of living in highly diverse contexts, and (positive) intergroup relations.

Andrea Bohman is a researcher at the Department of Sociology, Umeå University. Her research interests lie in how anti-immigrant prejudice develops under different social and societal circumstances.

Yuen Mi Cheon is Postdoctoral Fellow in the Department of Psychology at Fordham University. Her major research interests include the family environment and identity development during adolescence, the role of ethnicity/race and socioeconomic status in health and academic outcomes, within-person changes, and individual differences.

Sauro Civitillo is Postdoctoral Researcher in the Intercultural Psychology – Migration and Integration research group at the University of Duisburg-Essen, Germany. His work lies at the interface of psychology and education. His research interests include teacher cultural diversity beliefs, teacher discrimination, culturally responsive teaching, and initial teaching preparation.

Alison K. Cohen is an assistant professor of public and nonprofit administration at the University of San Francisco. Trained in epidemiology and education, she does quantitative social science research related to issues of educational and health equity, including doing community-based participatory research and policy and program evaluation.

Rachel Davis is doctorate student in the Developmental Program at Virginia Commonwealth University. Her research interests include identity development as it pertains to positive youth development and academic outcomes among ethnic/racial minority youth.

Alexandra Ehrhardt, MS, is a graduate of Fordham University. Her research interests include how contextual variations in stress, biology, and sleep affect long-term developmental outcomes as well as exploring protective factors that influence positive adolescent development.

Kyle Eichas is Associate Professor in the Department of Psychological Sciences at Tarleton State University in Waco, Texas, USA. His research interests include using outreach science to build community-supported interventions that help marginalized young people develop a sense of possibility, connection, and direction in their lives.

Lindsay Till Hoyt is Assistant Professor of Applied Developmental Psychology at Fordham University. She applies theory and methods from multiple perspectives to study complex developmental processes and racial, ethnic, and socioeconomic disparities across adolescence and youth adulthood.

Linda Juang is Professor in the Department of Inclusive Education at the University of Potsdam, Germany. Her research focuses on how experiences of immigration relate to adolescents' and young adults' development and adjustment in family, school, and community contexts.

Philipp Jugert is Professor of Intercultural Psychology – Migration and Integration at the University of Duisburg-Essen, Germany. His major research interests include social development in the context of ethnic diversity, group processes and intergroup relations, and civic engagement.

Katarzyna Kucaba is Research Associate in the Faculty of Education and Health at the University of Greenwich, London. Her research interests include the well-being and mental health of young people and adults, as well as educational aspirations and behavioral disorders of young people in diverse environments.

Richard M. Lee, PhD, is Distinguished McKnight University Professor in the Department of Psychology at the University of Minnesota, Twin Cities. He examines the psychological aspects of culture, ethnicity, and race, including acculturation/enculturation, ethnic-racial socialization, ethnic-racial identity development, perceived discrimination, and health disparities in immigrants and minority youth.

Lars Leszczensky is a postdoctoral research fellow at the Mannheim Centre for European Social Research (MZES) at the University of Mannheim, Germany. His research interests include intergroup relations, friendship formation, ethnic/religious identities, and social network analysis.

Sheri R. Levy is Professor of Psychology at Stony Brook University, New York, USA. Her research investigates factors that cause and maintain prejudice and stigmatization and that can be harnessed to reduce bias, marginalization, and discrimination. Her research considers the potential intersectionality of ageism, heterosexism, racism, and sexism.

Shelley McKeown Jones is Senior Lecturer in Social Psychology at the University of Bristol. Her research focuses on examining the everyday nature of intergroup interactions, approaches to reducing prejudice, and strategies to promote pro-social behaviors and positive outcomes, particularly for youth in conflict and ethnically diverse settings.

Alan Meca is Assistant Professor in the Department of Psychology at Old Dominion University. His research focuses on identity development across various domains and on the links between identity and psychosocial functioning. The majority of his work has focused on cultural identity and how ethnic/racial minorities navigate their cultural environments.

Fran Meissner is Marie Skłodowska Curie Fellow in Urban Studies at the TU Delft in the Netherlands. Her interdisciplinary research profile is focused on contemporary urban social configurations and on how these are transformed through international migration.

Marta Miklikowska is Researcher in Social-Developmental Psychology at Umeå University, Sweden and Visiting Scholar at Utrecht University, the Netherlands. She studies youth ethnic relations and the development of anti-immigrant prejudice. To that end, she looks at the role of social contexts (parents, peers, school), cross-ethnic friendships, and empathy.

Frosso Motti-Stefanidi is Professor of Psychology at the National and Kapodistrian University of Athens, Greece. Her research focuses on the study of immigrant youth adaptation, development, and acculturation. She has developed the Athena Studies of Resilient Adaptation (AStRA) project, which is framed within a risk and resilience developmental perspective and addresses the research question: "Who among immigrant youth do well, and why?"

Simon Ozer is a postdoctoral researcher at the Department of Psychology and Behavioural Sciences, Aarhus University, Denmark. His research interests concern the psychological processes of cultural globalization in regard to acculturation, identity development, and extremism.

Lisa Rosenthal is Associate Professor of Psychology at Pace University in New York City. Her research focuses on intersectional stigma, social justice, and intergroup relations. This includes seeking to understand how experiences with different forms of discrimination, stereotyping, and inequality contribute to health disparities, as well as factors that contribute to positive intergroup dynamics.

Adam Rutland, PhD, is Professor of Psychology at the University of Exeter and Visiting Research Fellow at Goldsmiths, University of London. His research focuses on social, cognitive, and moral development, especially how children think about social exclusion, group dynamics, friendships, pro-social behavior, acculturation, and science within intergroup contexts.

Thia Sagherian-Dickey is a social psychologist and a postdoctoral researcher in "Political Apologies across Cultures" at Tilburg University. Her research interests also include intergroup relations in challenging contexts, with particular focus on trust and contact.

Seth J. Schwartz is Professor of Public Health Sciences at the University of Miami Leonard M. Miller School of Medicine. His research interests include identity, acculturation, family relationships, and substance use. His recent work is in crisis migration or migration driven by natural disasters, violence, and other important push factors.

Tobias H. Stark is an assistant professor in the department of Interdisciplinary Social Science at Utrecht University, the Netherlands. His research focuses on the intersection of prejudice and interethnic relations in social networks. He also conducts methodological studies on how to measure prejudice and social networks.

Gonneke Stevens is Associate Professor at Utrecht University, the Netherlands. Using different research methods, she investigates the mechanisms behind the association between immigration and adolescent wellbeing in different contexts.

Ahna Suleiman, DrPH, is a transdisciplinary independent consultant based in Northern California. Her work integrates best practices from public health, effective youth engagement, and development science to inform policies and practices that support positive sexual and reproductive health trajectories for young people across the globe.

Jochem Thijs is an associate professor at the department of Interdisciplinary Social Science and the European Research Center on Migration and Ethnic Relations at Utrecht University, The Netherlands. His research interests include children's group relations in educational contexts, and the educational adjustment of ethnic minority children and adolescents.

Peter F. Titzmann is Professor for Developmental Psychology at the Leibniz University Hannover, Germany. In his research he investigates the interplay between normative development and migration-related adaptation among adolescents with immigrant backgrounds. He studies this interplay in developmental outcomes, such as acculturative stress, delinquency, family interactions, autonomy, and self-efficacy.

Roselien Vervaet did a PhD in the research team CuDOS (Cultural Diversity: Opportunities and Socialisation) at the Department of Sociology at Ghent University (Belgium). Her core topics are the determinants of ethnic prejudice among Flemish teachers and pupils against Turkish, Moroccan, and Eastern European minority students.

Sophie D. Walsh is Associate Professor in the Criminology Department at Bar Ilan University. She is a clinical psychologist and her research focuses on psychological mechanisms related to adolescent involvement in risk behaviors, substance use, and delinquency. In particular, she examines mediating and moderating processes of the relationship between discrimination and risk among immigrant adolescents.

Robert S. Weisskirch, MSW, PhD, is Professor of Human Development in the Liberal Studies Department at California State University, Monterey Bay. His research has focused on language brokering among children, adolescents, emerging adults, and adults; ethnic identity; acculturation and immigrant issues; how technology affects relationships; and the pedagogy of human development.

Amanda Williams is Lecturer of Psychology at the University of Bristol. Her research focuses on the development of implicit prejudice and the consequences this has on intergroup relations.

Tiffany Yip, PhD, is Professor of Psychology at Fordham University. Her research on ethnic identity, discrimination, and sleep among ethnic/racial minority adolescents and young adults employs multilevel longitudinal methods to investigate the role of physical, social, and institutional contexts on development.

Introduction

Peter F. Titzmann and Philipp Jugert

> We were a pretty cool class, I think. It was then already quite mixed, but that was nothing one would have noticed a lot ... And also in secondary school it was very mixed, many nationalities ... All my close friends were born here; they don't have a migration background. Okay, one friend is from Bulgaria, another one from Poland, that's also a migration background ... today this is so normal that you have all these cultures together ... If I notice at all, it is when they dress differently.
>
> (Schneider, 2018, p. 67)

This is a quote from a former student who had attended a school in a small town in South-West Germany. It exemplifies the experiences of youths today of ethnic and cultural diversity. It also shows that having a migration background is becoming increasingly normal – to the extent that adolescents are not aware anymore what a migration background really means. Having non-German relatives is simply part of many adolescents' and their peers' everyday lives – so much so that they may find it difficult to answer questions about their peers' ethnicities. The dominant conceptual approach in research on migration and integration, however, is still focused on two groups in contact (immigrants vs. natives; Turks vs. Germans, etc.), the immigrant group and the group representing the receiving society (e.g. Berry, 1997; Tajfel & Turner, 2001). The reality is, however, that there is not AN immigrant. The anecdotal example given above as well as recent societal trends seriously put the simple ingroup–outgroup distinction into question. Today's societies are confronted with rising levels of ethnic diversity leading to intergroup contact between many different ethnic groups. London, for example, accommodates individuals from as many as 179 countries, which led, together with many other factors of diversity, to the term "super-diversity" in modern polycultural societies (Vertovec, 2007). In addition, media (Indian Bollywood movies, Jamaican reggae music, or American advertisements) and a globalized world transport cultures into adolescents' worlds without them ever having direct contact with members of those cultures. This means that many adolescents do not face the question of heritage vs. host orientation, but instead have to deal with multiple cultural identities that are present in a given society. This mismatch between common bi-dimensional acculturation models and multi-dimensional adolescents' daily experiences convinced us that the time was ripe for a book that brings together new perspectives on research on intergroup relations. The rising complexity of ethnically diverse societies, which also include rising numbers of multi-ethnic youth (who do not fit easily into dichotomous categories like ethnic majority or ethnic minority) necessitates that we conceptualize and measure diversity in more complex ways (Brown & Juvonen, 2018; Graham, 2018). It is our hope that the chapters in this book fulfill this promise. Our major aim was to bring together authors that have a novel and innovative perspective on the experiences of adolescents with diverse ethnic and cultural backgrounds. These aspects comprise four broader categories: Conceptual Approaches for Studying Multicultural Societies, Development in Context in Multicultural Societies, Social Relations in Multicultural Societies, and Preparing Multicultural Societies for Dealing with Diversity Inside and Outside of Schools.

First, and in line with our initial motivation for this book, we identified conceptual approaches that allow us to overcome the intergroup host vs. heritage culture view in acculturation. This part includes chapters offering fresh theoretical perspectives for studying youth development in multicultural societies. The chapter by Meissner (Chapter 1) introduces the concept of superdiversity and describes how a superdiversity lens challenges traditional concepts and approaches in studying youth in multicultural societies. Ozer (Chapter 2) describes how globalization processes necessitate a more complex perspective on acculturation processes that go beyond bi-dimensional frameworks. Meca et al. (Chapter 3) delve into the latest developments with regard to bicultural identity development by focusing on the multifaceted, interrelated, and dynamic nature of bicultural identities. Rosenthal et al. (Chapter 4) introduce the concept of polyculturalism as an individual difference belief that acknowledges that all cultures are the product of many different cultural influences. Benbow and Aumann (Chapter 9) discuss the need to disentangle unique from universal processes of immigrant youth adaptation and provide theoretical and methodological considerations of cross-comparative research that can help in this disentangling.

The common denominator of the second part is an innovative developmental-contextual view on acculturative processes, which allows a better understanding of acculturative changes over time. This part includes chapters that describe approaches for studying youth development in particular contexts. Lee et al. (Chapter 5) highlight the dynamic nature of acculturation processes by introducing the concepts of acculturative timing, tempo, pace, and synchrony as a means to study the interplay of acculturation and development. Yip et al. (Chapter 7) discuss a program of research that uses experience-based sampling methods to examine how variations in daily life experiences contribute to minority youth development. Asendorpf and Motti-Stefanidi (Chapter 8) explain how multi-level frameworks can inform our understanding of immigrant youth embedded in multiple developmental contexts. Weisskirch (Chapter 10) considers developmental and familial aspects of adolescent language brokering. Stevens and Walsh (Chapter 10) explain why it is important to consider country and school-level factors for explaining the mental health of immigrant adolescents. All these chapters together not only show the complexity of studying an adolescent with diverse ethnic or cultural backgrounds but also offer methodological advice on how this could be done.

The third part focuses on relationships in diverse societies. Bagci and Rutland (Chapter 11) explore the extent to which youth transform their multicultural experiences into an asset or a hindrance and investigate underlying situational and personal factors. McKeown et al. (Chapter 12) delineate a new research agenda for studying interethnic interactions in diverse environments by focusing on behavior in real life contexts. Miklikowska and Bohman (Chapter 13) describe how ethnic majority youth react to growing ethnic diversity and, more specifically, show the role that proximal social contexts (parents, peers, schools and the interplay between these contexts) play in shaping youth's intergroup attitudes. Leszczensky and Stark (Chapter 14) show how social network analysis advances our knowledge of the causes and consequences of segregation in youth's friendship networks.

The fourth and final part is more applied. It brings together extant findings and approaches of how multicultural societies can be prepared for dealing with diversity inside and outside of schools. Ballard and colleagues (Chapter 15) highlight two different participatory approaches designed to teach youth civic engagement through authentic civic experiences. Thijs and Vervaet (Chapter 16) examine research on teachers' approaches to teaching ethnically diverse classrooms and its effects on students' intergroup relations. Civitillo and Juang (Chapter 17) discuss how to prepare future teachers to teach in multicultural classrooms by considering the cognitive, emotional, and pedagogical components.

We are very grateful to all the authors who contributed to this book. We think that research has already made important contributions to the understanding of immigrant and minority youth, but our multicultural societies are changing at an unprecedented pace. All the chapters in this book can add new insights into the challenges these societies face. This book brings together approaches that can help us to better understand how societies deal with heterogeneity, the complexity of various ethnicities and cultures living together, and the dynamics of change that these new circumstances bring about. Although many articles, chapters, and books in the field of immigration end with recommendations for future research, we have brought together an entire book on these potentially research-stimulating ideas. In our book, these ideas are not just mentioned as a next step, but are spelled out so that they can be cited, applied, and improved in future research.

We hope this book will stimulate advanced undergraduate or postgraduate students and investigators of the social and behavioral sciences. It should also be relevant for professionals in the field of migration because it addresses their everyday experience of dealing with cooperation, tension, or coalition between various ethnic groups. These are not frequently addressed in the immigration literature – and if they are addressed then not in a comprehensive multifaceted approach as in our book. The interdisciplinary scope that is necessary for addressing the topic of immigration and acculturation in adolescence has also implications for the readership, as the book will be attractive to a variety of disciplines, such as sociologists, psychologists, linguists, and political scientists.

References

Berry, J. W. (1997). Immigration, acculturation, and adaptation. *Applied Psychology: an International Review*, 46(1), 5–68.

Brown, C. S., & Juvonen, J. (2018). Insights about the effects of diversity: When does diversity promote inclusion and for whom? *Journal of Applied Developmental Psychology*, 59, 75–81.

Graham, S. (2018). Race/ethnicity and social adjustment of adolescents: How (not if) school diversity matters. *Educational Psychologist*, 53(2), 64–77.

Schneider, J. (2018). "Ausländer" (foreigners), migrants, or new Germans? Identity-building processes and school socialization among adolescents from immigrant backgrounds in Germany. *New Directions in Child and Adolescent Development*, 160, 59–73.

Tajfel, H., & Turner, J. (2001). An integrative theory of intergroup conflict. In M. A. Hogg & D. Abrams (Eds.), *Intergroup relations: Essential readings* (pp. 94–109). New York, NY: Psychology Press.

Vertovec, S. (2007). Super-diversity and its implications. *Ethnic and Racial Studies*, 29(6), 1024–1054.

Part I

Conceptual considerations

Chapter 1

Growing up with difference

Superdiversity as a habitual frame of reference[1]

Fran Meissner

Today many young people are diversity natives as much as they are digital natives. They have to be able to use various registers to make sense of and engage with how migration-driven diversity is impacting on their lives. It is not surprising that generational specificities of experiencing living in contexts of diversity are gaining in academic interest. Today urban and increasingly also rural youth grow up in social contexts that are so imbued with the implications of international migration that migration-driven diversity has become a habitual frame of reference – a fact of everyday life. Socio-demographic changes are no longer just evident at the margins of society, they are perceived as central to our social fabrics.

Rapid changes in the prevalence of migration have gone hand in hand with a complexification of diversity. This is due to changing migration patterns, with migrants moving from more origins to fewer destinations (Czaika & Haas, 2014). More importantly those trends are tightly intertwined with new ways of regulating migration, migrants, and migration-driven diversity itself. The term superdiversity was coined to better make sense of the simultaneity of those changes (Vertovec, 2007). Superdiversity was 'to encapsulate a range of […] changing variables surrounding migration patterns – and, significantly, their interlinkages – which amount to a recognition of complexities that *super*sede previous patterns and perceptions' (Meissner & Vertovec, 2015, p. 542: emphasis added). Superdiversity challenges reductionist approaches to studying the implications of international migration (Vertovec, 2017b). The term is not about how 'super' diversity is. Instead, it presents a complexity-sensitive notion of diversity and diversification processes. Adopting a superdiversity lens poses a number of challenges for studying youth in multicultural societies – including how to approach and theorise research and who or what is made the focus of research. Further, comparatively thinking with superdiversity can shed light on both contextual and broader patterns of how difference comes to matter for young people, both those settled in place and those on the move.

The notion of superdiversity is not always used in-line with the above given definition. In fact, over the past decade, the word has been so frequently invoked that its meanings and adaptations proliferated beyond original intentions (Vertovec, 2017a). Superdiversity – concertedly applied – however, is an important intervention for studying youth in multicultural societies. The aim of this chapter is to substantiate this argument. I will first discuss how superdiversity has come to be a central anchor in the migration and ethnic studies literature. In doing so, I will comment both on the sea changes in the literature that accompanied the consolidation of superdiversity as a research field and on a number of recent criticisms leveraged against the notion. I then briefly expand on why superdiversity should be of central importance for studying youth and negotiations of difference. I specifically highlight why a focus on youth exposes the need to be vigilant about equating diversity as a habitual frame of reference with overly positively connoted ideas about diversity as the new normal. In conclusion, I will comment on the relevance of this chapter to the collection of essays in this book.

Superdiversity as a malleable concept for studying emergent social configurations

Like previous concepts that posed a significant challenge to how international migration and its implications are researched and thought about, superdiversity is omnipresent in the recent literature. As Alba and Duyvendak note:

> Today, any European scholar addressing issues of migration, integration, and (ethnic) diversity who does not explicitly take into account the notion of super-diversity runs the risk of being reproached for neglecting the 'new multicultural condition of the 21st century'.
>
> (2017, pp. 1–2)

To offer a flip-side to this statement, when I am presented with work that claims to use superdiversity, I often find that it has little if anything to add to better understanding the challenges posed by superdiversity as defined in the introduction. In other words, I often voice the opposite reproach from the one Alba and Duyvendak suggest. If I see the term used as only a meagre complexification of an otherwise very conventional ethnofocal analysis, I ask authors why they use superdiversity – and I encourage students of migration-driven diversity to do the same. While superdiversity's prominence leads to (sometimes productive) criticisms, its omnipresence also fosters confusions about what superdiversity refers to and how it can add to our debates. I here see the attention paid to the term as an invitation to explore the potency of thinking through and with superdiversity to spur on innovative research.

To explain what I mean by thinking through and with superdiversity, it is necessary to trace the development of the term since its inception. As I note elsewhere (Meissner, 2015), superdiversity was introduced to debates about the implications of international migration at a very specific juncture in the migration and ethnic studies literature. That juncture was marked by a stalemate: authors in the field came to realise that research conclusions too frequently amounted to not much more than saying that 'things were more complex'. This lead some scholars to note that 'we need to do better than that [...] it is necessary to specify in which ways "things are more complex"' (Hylland Eriksen, 2007, p. 1059). This very particular juncture is often forgotten when superdiversity is used to refer to a 'new multi-cultural condition of the 21st century' and when the notion is employed as a descriptive term that itself merely indexes that things are more complex or varied. This cannot suffice if the overarching goal of superdiversity research is precisely to move beyond seeking simple explanations and conclusions (Vertovec, 2017b).

In the now more than ten years since the publication of the original article introducing superdiversity to the scholarly debate (Vertovec, 2007), much has changed in the research landscape. Multiple special issues have been published that revolve around the term (Androutsopoulos & Juffermans, 2014; Arnaut, Blommaert, Rampton, & Spotti, 2012; Foner, Duyvendak, & Kasinitz, 2017; Geerts, Withaeckx, & van den Brandt, 2018; Grzymala-Kazlowska & Phillimore, 2017; Meissner & Vertovec, 2016; Phillimore, Sigona, & Tonkiss, 2017). The original superdiversity article has – according to google scholar – been cited over 3000 times, making it one of the youngest seminal articles in the field. Significant research time (and money) has been invested in projects that adopted some version of a superdiversity lens and entire research centres are devoted to uniting work on superdiversity.[2] The resulting research has significantly impacted on how the term is used and how it is empirically made sense of. Superdiversity is a malleable concept (Meissner, 2015) that is filled with more concrete meaning through research and through critically reflecting on the developments that research points to. Such an empirically substantiated and critically reflected agenda setting, with frequent reviews of its own subject matter, is at the heart of what thinking through and with superdiversity is about. It is also at the heart of what sets superdiversity apart from the many 'isms' that otherwise dominate research agendas.[3]

But what does superdiversity in very basic terms refer to? In his article originally coining the term, Vertovec (2007) emphasised various blind spots in how migration was diversifying social contexts. Specific focus was on 'a dynamic interplay of variables [relating to] [1] multiple-origin, [2] transnationally connected, [3] socio-economically differentiated and [4] legally stratified immigrants' (Vertovec, 2007, p. 1024). In the same article Vertovec adds [5] differentiated gender and age patterns of migrant cohorts as another important aspect. Subsequent work has noted further blind-spots and often emphasises the role of the spatiality of diversity, the temporalities of change, and the interplay between legal stratification and other instruments of migrant control (e.g. access to social support services). Notably many of these aspects are changeable and sometimes difficult to anchor in hard and fast categories of difference. Growing up with difference viewed through a superdiversity lens is not only about making sense of an expanded taxonomy of difference. It is not about devising more and more detailed categories. Superdiversity provides us with a concept that calls for better connecting of the multiple dimensions of differentiation by moving beyond simply stating that things are more complex.

This basic definition shows that superdiversity was never a theory. This means that the word itself was never meant to give insights into how the dynamic interplay of those different aspects works – nor how it ought to work. One of the initial aims of introducing superdiversity was to move beyond a then pervasive and mono-focal *ethnic lens*. Noting that superdiversity was never a theory (Vertovec, 2017b) counters one recurring criticism, namely that the term suggests a rigid and necessarily positive picture of diversity (Makoni, 2012). Rather than precluding theoretical pluralism, which is another criticism (Ndhlovu, 2015), thinking through superdiversity invites multiple ways of addressing, poking at, and questioning the riddles that arise when thinking about multidimensional differentiations – and most importantly about how these come about, transmute, and co-evolve within multilateral and temporally shifting regulatory regimes (Hall, 2017; Nieswand, 2018).

Superdiversity has been used in many ways. In a recent article Vertovec (2017a) presents a typology that points to no less than seven ways of using the term. If we agree with his assessment that what should propel the use of superdiversity is finding 'better ways to describe and analyse new social patterns, forms and identities arising from migration-driven diversification' (Vertovec, 2017a, p. 1) we can focus on the domains that contribute towards this goal.

Three waves of superdiversity research

To more clearly delineate uses of superdiversity we can note that the term, over the past ten years, has mostly engaged with three domains – descriptive work documenting a diversification of diversity, practical applications that engage with the 'So what?' and the 'What next?' once a diversified diversity has been recognised, and finally theoretical and methodological innovation which allow looking at diversification processes with novel tools or data (Meissner & Vertovec, 2015). To situate these domains, I here use the analogy of a set of waves that are entangled and intertwined but distinctly evident.

Encounters in diversifying contexts are a central theme of what we might call the first wave of superdiversity research. Often this work is focussing on the increasing everydayness of migration-driven diversity in primarily urban settings (Neal, Bennett, Jones, Cochrane, & Mohan, 2015; e.g. Wessendorf, 2014; Wise & Velayutham, 2009; Ye, 2016). This focus was particularly strong in early work referring to superdiversity, but it continues to be relevant. Criticisms that gesture towards an insufficiently critical or ahistorical presentation of superdiversity (Back & Sinha, 2016; Sealy, 2018) tend to focus on this wave. One of the goals of this work is to make sense of how and when diversity works – an important and necessary exercise that provides a needed balance to research and public discourse focused on instances when the implications of migration are characterised as an obstacle to social cohesion. This specific focus sought out positively or ambivalently connoted examples of how people muddle through in light of tremendous differentiations. One of the most prominent and most cited examples of this work is Wessendorf's (2014) ethnographic study in the London borough of Hackney where she notes that migration-driven diversity in this setting was not out of the ordinary but very much a 'commonplace' aspect of her respondents' lives. She thus presents a counter-narrative to ideas about diversity anxieties and pitfalls (Putnam, 2000) then fiercely debated. What is more, parts of this first-wave research also point to accompanying ruptures and inequalities. Researching encounters in contexts of superdiversity thus does not only paint a positive picture of what it means when diversity (seems) to work (Piekut, Rees, Valentine, & Kupiszewski, 2012; Ye, 2018). For example Ye (2018), also employing ethnographic techniques, but focussing on the context of Singapore, notes how observing everyday practices of diversity highlights a number of presuppositions we maintain about the disconnection of those practices from, for instance, politics of migrant labour integration.

A 'second wave', which certainly overlaps with the first, both in terms of authors and in terms of timing, devotes its focus to practical challenges that are highlighted if shifting from a uni- to a multi-focal research lens. They moved specifically policy focused research from addressing ethnic or country of origin diversity to addressing migration-driven diversity as a more multi-faceted phenomenon. Doing so posed the challenge of simultaneously considering overlapping differentiations, shifting ideas about how in practice diversity is made sense of and, in terms of policy, how migration-driven change could be better responded to. Previously targeted migrant groups can no longer be taken for granted as subjects of policy interventions (Van Breugel & Scholten, 2017), service providers have to adjust to the 'novelty and newness' that thinking through superdiversity on the ground entails (Boccagni, 2015; Phillimore, 2015). This research has progressed work on unpacking and evaluating approaches to policy making and what kinds of institutional adaptations might be necessary in light of recognising a diversified diversity and on how to move beyond imaginaries implicit in measuring the 'success' of multiculturalism (Schinkel, 2017). For example, building primarily on the analysis of policy documents and interviews with policy makers, Scholten and colleagues (2018) show how in superdiverse contexts it becomes more important to think about immigrant policies as a multi-level policy challenge – meaning as a concern that matters to local, national, and supranational rules and regulations that are developed as a response to migration.

I here certainly only point to some authors. There is a much larger range of articles falling into these two waves and ongoing research is still just starting to fill some of the empirical voids that are fundamental to making sense of the observable dynamics of diversity – including temporal and spatial changes in 'where, how and with whom people live' (Vertovec, 2007, p. 1025).

What has now been noted repeatedly is that change does not always come about through linear progression but also through the momentary salience of some aspects of superdiversity over others. For example, Magazzini in speaking about the case of Roma migrants in Italy points to how in her research:

> a group of people who had been acknowledged solely on the basis of their ethnicity [came] to be seen as people experiencing severe housing deprivation, in a way that did not negate their ethnicity but that did not make their ethnicity the only possible lens to construct narratives and policies about them.
> (Magazzini, 2017, p. 537)

At a more macro-level we can see that, following increased refugee migrations to Europe in 2015 and a subsequent surge in restricting migration, legal-status stratification seems to have surpassed the attention previously payed to ethnic diversity and this can be recognised and made the subject of research by working with a superdiversity lens (Meissner, 2017). Yet, as for example Aptekar (2017) reminds us, in drawing on superdiversity, it is important not to forget about 'old' categories of difference and what role they play. This is part of concertedly applying superdiversity. As Nieswand (2017) shows in his analysis of social service provision targeting youth in two German cities – diversity may need to be rethought in settings where new person-related differences, that seem to have little to do with migration-related differentiations, are enmeshed with the experiences of migrants, particularly racialized migrants. Nieswand, in describing the case of a single mother of African descent, very clearly shows how a situation that is not in principle structured around migration-related differences often cannot escape the relevance of those differences. An untethering of the role of migration in such processes is not in itself possible without contextually recognising how the relevance of migration unfolds and emerges in the activation of power differentials and structures that allow for shielding a recognition of the work those differentials do. Multidimensional differentiations do not only focus on less researched aspects – but on the complex, multi-variate interplay of many aspects that can be linked to the social changes migration entails.

Sticking with the theme of tightly entangled waves, we can thus point to a third wave, one that uses superdiversity as a departing point to theorise and to popularise and develop new methodological approaches. This work shines a light on under-researched connections and on systematic holes in the availability or use of social science data (Blommaert, 2013; Meissner, 2016; Nieswand, 2017). While the first two waves are more about thinking through superdiversity, such theorising and methodological adjustments are crucial for thinking *with* superdiversity. This work is also pertinent to ensure that superdiversity does not stand still in a continuously changing world, where the question 'How are the implications of international migration complex?' is subject to both patterns of repetition and patterns of change – subject to continuity, social slippage, feedback loops, and ruptures.

Superdiversity casts diversity as necessarily dynamic and superdiversity research and reasoning has to reflect and trace those dynamics of how migration-driven diversity comes to matter in time and place. The third wave importantly stands in opposition to those claiming that superdiversity is tied to an individualist tradition (Sealy, 2018). Superdiversity can be used to introduce notions such as relational diversity. In my own work introducing the idea of relational diversity (Meissner, 2016) the starting point is not how individuals are different from each other but how multiple migration-related aspects shape and condition how we can describe the social networks of my respondents as highly differentiated. Further, the work that is done through and with superdiversity evidences that superdiversity research goes much beyond the notion, being a mere slogan as some authors maintain (Pavlenko, forthcoming). Indeed, in my eyes, surveying research that does rigorously use superdiversity as a thinking tool, also shows why superdiversity fares better as a research term and thinking tool than as an applied policy term. Still it has to be acknowledged that the term has found its way into applied policy circles. As I noted at the start of this section it remains important to ask: What does using a superdiversity lens add to the proposed or conducted analysis?

For new scholars entering the field, it may be difficult to imagine that previously many of the aspects considered under the umbrella of superdiversity research were only marginally part of debates in migration and ethnic studies. If they were, they were analysed solely side by side rather than focusing on their interconnections. Recognising this shift highlights a move away from thinking about ethnic diversity to studying migration-driven diversity. Clearly this shift is not one of blanket coverage (nor should it be). Pointing very explicitly to this shift does expose the fact that some of the research tools we work with and much of the data available are still the product of a more prevalent focus on putatively cohesive ethnic or religious groups. Further, in moving my elaborations towards why superdiversity is relevant for studying youth in multicultural societies, it needs to be recognised that previous approaches were also driven by a research focus on large and assumed to be stable and settled groups of post-Second World War migrants (De Bock, 2014). Migrants that were thought of as embedded in national (much less than local) contexts of destination. This also had the effect that a still prevailing origin and destination dichotomy often implicitly suggested relatively homogeneous contexts of departure and arrival in theorising different national models of migrant incorporation (Scholten, 2016). Many of those considerations can no longer be taken for granted as easily. At the same time, diversity today is intimately entangled with those historical migrations (Vertovec, 2015) – not least when a mythical time before them is alluded to in talking about current migration as a societal challenge.

Although there is still research that takes ethnic groups as its starting point – unreflective groupism (Brubaker, 2003) is by far less prominent – and although it was not superdiversity alone propelling those changes, superdiversity has been a success in evoking the kind of reflexivity that was needed in making this shift. Important work on groupism (Brubaker, 2003), methodological nationalism (Amelina, Nergiz, Faist, & Glick Schiller, 2012; Wimmer & Glick Schiller, 2002), on questions of boundary making (Kroneberg & Wimmer, 2012), and a higher prominence of a local turn (Scholten, 2018) clearly have to be read alongside ideas about the relevance of superdiversity. Further new methodologies and data sources became available at the time that superdiversity became a popular starting point for conducting research into the implications of international migration. These included, for example, network analytic approaches and more visually oriented ways of doing research and presenting its results. Those methods produced new data that needed new approaches amenable to being formulated by thinking with superdiversity. A pressing question still to be answered is how new media data or big data will come to play a role in how migration-driven diversity is regulated but also made sense of.

To sum up this review of what superdiversity means and how it has been used, we can note that using superdiversity as a short-hand for a new multicultural condition of the 21st century falls short of the analytical potential of the term. What is needed to spur on a continued productive use of superdiversity that goes beyond this flattened interpretation is a reflexivity-driven research approach (Bourdieu, 1990) that continuously reviews and debates how we study the implication of international migration, who the subjects of our research need to be, and how we may need to adjust our preconceptions in light of changes in migratory patterns and related patterns of global interconnectedness. While this assessment is broadly applicable it is, as I will be discussing in the following sections, of specific relevance to the study of youth in contexts of migration-driven diversities.

Youth and superdiversity

Youth, for the purpose of this chapter, is broadly defined. In relation to superdiversity there is the noted question of different migrant cohorts showing different age and gender patterns. It is also relevant that specifically if we speak about youth in contemporary Europe, but likely also beyond, we speak about a generation that is growing up with migration repeatedly being a major topic of debate, not in a distant sense, but for many as an everyday experience. For example, many young people born in the late 1990s have only known a post-multicultural politics that followed the denouncement of multicultural policies by various European leaders (cf. Schinkel, 2017). Youth in relation to superdiversity increasingly also involves the question of disrupted biographies – as migration plays a vastly different role in propelling given types of biographies given different migration trajectories. These processes and the resulting patterns of experiencing youth add to differentiations difficult to cast in hard and fast categories. The implications of this will certainly play into future dynamics of diversity.

A basic search on google scholar as well as on the web of knowledge suggests that published work combining an *explicit* focus on 'super(-)diversity' and 'youth' is still limited and often falls in the realm of social linguistics. The latter is not surprising as linguistics most quickly and voraciously employed superdiversity.[4] It is surprising, however, that superdiversity research focused on youth remains, it seems, in its infancy. We do have a large literature on migrant youth but its lack of explicit links to superdiversity is at odds with the fact that youth are overrepresented in most migrant populations and that multidimensional differentiations shape how young migrants and youth affected by migration experience living in contexts of migration-driven diversity (United Nations, 2013). This filters down to everyday experiences as for example Iqbal, Neal, and Vincent (2017) show with their research in highly mixed London primary schools. For their study they analyse interviews and pictorial data from 78 children between the ages of eight and nine. They use this to assess how children make, manage, or avoid friendships and can show that children engage multiple dimensions of difference in their friendship choices. This sheds a more differentiated light on previous studies that looked at such friendship patterns primarily in terms of race segregation. Such practices that highlight the importance of paying attention to multiple dimensions of difference have been shown to continue to play a role during adolescence and beyond (Harris, 2015; Schönwälder et al., 2016). In thinking with and through superdiversity there is always an interplay of demographic changes, regulatory changes, and perception changes that play into the complexities being investigated. As more and more people grow up in post-migration contexts and view them as habitual frames of reference (Foroutan, 2015), it is about time to become more serious about exploring what it means to think through and with superdiversity in addressing the experiences of young people and their active role in shaping the dynamics of diversity through their involvement as place makers rather than just passive consumers of future diversities (Çağlar & Glick Schiller, 2018).

Changed migration patterns have resulted in more and more young people being on the move. Capital regions in Europe tend to have both high shares of foreign born residents and they are also home to more young people (Eurostat, 2017). Patterns are by no means equal across European contexts as for example Germany attracts more younger migrants than other European countries. These movement dynamics are in part the result of policies encouraging the movement of young people but also an effect of selection bias in who gets to migrate internationally. Diversity dynamics however are not limited to these demographic shifts, they are also subject to responses to those shifts. While we lack analysis from a superdiversity perspective, in terms of country of origin and religious diversity we have some insights. For example, in 2016 the Pew Foundation surveyed individuals in ten European countries about their opinions on migration-driven diversity. Using this data, Stokes (2017) shows that opinions about who gets to belong in a country differ starkly by age. For example just 23 percent of younger respondents (18–34 years of age) thought that it was necessary to have been 'born in a country' to be from that country. For those older than 50 years of age almost twice as many (41 percent) thought this was of high importance (Stokes, 2017, p. 5). Differences in opinion between age groups are also noted in the other country contexts considered by the report (Japan, the USA, Canada, and Australia). Collectively, the report notes that if birth right is not a necessary condition for belonging, a host of other markers are relevant. Language competence is amongst the most prevalent factors the report looks into although then the data is no longer differentiated by age cohorts. In light of these variations it remains to be better understood why younger people, on balance, seem to have a more inclusive notion of belonging. A large study, focused on how Muslims are perceived in Germany, comes to similar results and makes the argument that there is something about growing up at a time when the prevalence of migration-driven diversity is high which helps to make sense of generational differences and that diversity for younger people is a normal part of their everyday lives (Foroutan, 2015). Those are certainly arguments that deserve further investigation especially if we consider how they stand in relation to a diversification of diversity and diversity dynamics as I discussed them earlier.

Taking into account how I presented superdiversity as a thinking tool in the previous section and pointing to the broad range of research that takes inspiration from superdiversity, we can for example query the idea that diversity, if it becomes a habitual frame of reference, results in diversity as the new (and improved?) normal. What does it mean if diversity is normal at times when authors such as Hall alert us to the necessity to moor superdiversity to brutal migration regimes by recognising 'a zeitgeist in which migrants are actively displaced, sorted and segregated' (Hall, 2017, p. 1564). There is a disconnect that becomes bluntly evident in thinking specifically about youth through superdiversity. This disconnect between an inhumane governance of migration and an experienced everydayness of difference urgently needs to be addressed. The idea of normalisation would not only embrace more inclusive perceptions, but also a further entrenching of inequalities that thus become part of the new normal. In asking questions, as some of the following chapters do, about adaptation and context relevance, for example, it is then necessary to widen the purview of how ideas about describing contexts are shaped by the interplay of different aspects of migration-driven diversity. As is also noted in the chapters that follow, doing so requires diligent work in terms of methodological innovation, defining who is included in research and why (Römhild, 2014). How continued changes in migration-driven diversity can be made sense of in accessible ways takes centre stage in repeatedly asking how what is being researched is complex. In doing so focusing in on youth will prove to be illuminating and will potentially also provide more nuanced ideas of how in various different contexts it is necessary to think through and with superdiversity about youth.

Towards conclusions

The book that this chapter contributes to shows well that there are many different means by which the study of youth in multicultural societies can be approached – superdiversity is by no means the only one. With this chapter I have introduced the notion of superdiversity to show that much can be learned from taking up a multidimensional and complexity-sensitive notion such as superdiversity. It is surprising that the role of youth as one aspect of difference and diversification has not yet more clearly moved into the focus of superdiversity research – or for that matter that superdiversity still seems mostly absent from research on youth living in multicultural societies. The different 'waves' of superdiversity research, that I referred to, would certainly benefit from a more balanced focus on youth and young people, especially since this would also better reflect the composition of many migrant cohorts and it would likely shine an even clearer light on the dynamics of diversity. Old ideas about relatively settled and stable migrant populations have to be rethought in light of much more dynamic movement patterns with young people moving through various different migration trajectories and legal statuses that have been shown to impact on their outcomes and participation opportunities (Söhn, 2014).

As I noted in the introduction to this chapter, superdiversity poses a number of challenges for studying youth in multicultural societies – including how we approach and theorise research and who or what is the focus of the research. I also noted how comparative thinking with superdiversity can shed light on both contextual and broader patterns of how migration-driven diversity comes to matter for young people, both those settled in place and those on the move. I have so far not commented on this last point but it allows me, by way of conclusion, to address a final criticism leveraged against superdiversity: that the notion is only able to respond to the situation in European cities. Superdiversity is certainly most prevalent in research focused on European contexts but the basic challenge, to consider the co-development of migration and the changes it introduces to different social contexts, remains relevant if we move into non-European contexts. For that matter, it also remains relevant if our aim is to draw contrasts between urban and rural youth experiences. Superdiversity is not about identifying more diversity; translating insights gained from thinking through and with superdiversity in many contexts ultimately enriches the registers with which we as researchers are able to speak about diversifying diversity and its implications. Doing so with reference to chiselling out the role youth play in those dynamics deserves further attention. Keeping this in mind and considering that not all chapters in this book have been written with superdiversity in mind, I encourage readers of this book to consider what might be gained (or lost) in thinking about the following work through and with superdiversity. How would suggestions made travel to different (non-European/urban-rural) contexts? Reviewing work in this way means taking up the challenge of moving on from reductionist approaches to making sense of migration-driven diversity.

Notes

1 I thank Tilmann Heil (https://valueddifference.info) for comments on an earlier draft of this chapter. This work was made possible by funding from the European Union's Marie Skłodowska-Curie Actions Grant Agreement No. 707,124.

2 E.g. www.birmingham.ac.uk/research/activity/superdiversity-institute/index.aspx [accessed 20 June 2018].
3 Superdiversity has in the past been called a post-multiculturalism concept. At the same time it has been criticised for being "old multicultural wine in new bottles." I see a clear difference in thematic focus. Superdiversity points us towards the interplay between socio-demographic, socio-legal, and migration governance aspects. I further propose that the notion calls for an explicit engagement less with group focused approaches and more with social complexities and migration-driven diversity. Given those distinctions, I here do not further expand on the difference between superdiversity and multi-cultural approaches.
4 Compare special issues referred to earlier.

References

Alba, R., & Duyvendak, J. W. (2017). What about the mainstream? Assimilation in super-diverse times. *Ethnic and Racial Studies*, *81*, 1–20. 10.1080/01419870.2017.1406127.

Amelina, A., Nergiz, D. D., Faist, T., & Glick Schiller, N. (2012). *Beyond methodological nationalism: Research methodologies for cross-border studies/edited by Anna Amelina ... {et al.}. Routledge research in transnationalism: Vol. 24*. New York: Routledge.

Androutsopoulos, J., & Juffermans, K. (2014). Digital language practices in superdiversity: Introduction. *Discourse, Context & Media*, *4–5*, 1–6. 10.1016/j.dcm.2014.08.002.

Aptekar, S. (2017). Super-diversity as a methodological lens: Re-centring power and inequality. *Ethnic and Racial Studies*, *13*(1), 1–18. 10.1080/01419870.2017.1406124.

Arnaut, K., Blommaert, J., Rampton, B., & Spotti, M. (Eds.). (2012). *Language and superdiversities II*. Paris. Retrieved from http://unesdoc.unesco.org/images/0022/002223/222319e.pdf

Back, L., & Sinha, S. (2016). Multicultural conviviality in the midst of racism's ruins. *Journal of Intercultural Studies*, *37*(5), 517–532. 10.1080/07256868.2016.1211625.

Blommaert, J. (2013). *Ethnography, superdiversity and linguistic landscapes: Chronicles of complexity. Critical language and literacy studies: Vol. 18*. Bristol, Buffalo: Multilingual Matters.

Boccagni, P. (2015). (Super)diversity and the migration–social work nexus: A new lens on the field of access and inclusion? *Ethnic and Racial Studies*, *38*(4), 608–620. 10.1080/01419870.2015.980291.

Bourdieu, P. (1990). *In other words: Essays towards a reflexive sociology*. Stanford, CA: Stanford University Press.

Brubaker, R. (2003). Neither individualism nor 'groupism': A reply to Craig Calhoun. *Ethnicities*, *3*(4), 553–557. 10.1177/1468796803003004006.

Çağlar, A., & Glick Schiller, N. (2018). *Migrants and city-making: Dispossession, displacement, and urban regeneration*. Durham: Duke University Press.

Czaika, M., & Haas, H. de. (2014). The globalization of migration: Has the world become more migratory? *International Migration Review*, *48*(2), 283–323. 10.1111/imre.12095.

De Bock, J. (2014). Not all the same after all? Superdiversity as a lens for the study of past migrations. *Ethnic and Racial Studies*, 38(4), 583–595. 10.1080/01419870.2015.980290.

Eurostat (2017). *Eurostat regional yearbook: 2017 edition. Eurostat statistical books*. Luxembourg: Publications Office of the European Union.

Foner, N., Duyvendak, J. W., & Kasinitz, P. (2017). Introduction: Super-diversity in everyday life. *Ethnic and Racial Studies, Online First*, 1–16. 10.1080/01419870.2017.1406969.

Foroutan, N. (2015). *Deutschland postmigrantischn2*. Berlin: BIM Berliner Institut für Empirische Integrations- und Migrationsforschung.

Geerts, E., Withaeckx, S., & van den Brandt, N. (2018). Editorial. *Tijdschrift Voor Genderstudies*, 21(1), 1–5. 10.5117/TVGN2018.1.EDIT.

Grzymala-Kazlowska, A., & Phillimore, J. (2017). Introduction: Rethinking integration. New perspectives on adaptation and settlement in the era of super-diversity. *Journal of Ethnic and Migration Studies*, 20(169), 1–18. 10.1080/1369183X.2017.1341706.

Hall, S. M. (2017). Mooring "super-diversity" to a brutal migration milieu. *Ethnic and Racial Studies*, 40(9), 1562–1573.

Harris, A. (2015). Belonging and the uses of difference: Young people in Australian urban multiculture. *Social Identities*, 22(4), 359–375. 10.1080/13504630.2015.1113128.

Hylland Eriksen, T. (2007). Complexity in social and cultural integration: Some analytical dimensions. *Ethnic and Racial Studies*, 30(6), 1055–1069. 10.1080/01419870701599481.

Iqbal, H., Neal, S., & Vincent, C. (2017). Children's friendships in super-diverse localities: Encounters with social and ethnic difference. *Childhood*, 24(1), 128–142. 10.1177/0907568216633741.

Kroneberg, C., & Wimmer, A. (2012). Struggling over the boundaries of belonging: A formal model of nation building, ethnic closure, and populism 1. *American Journal of Sociology*, 118(1), 176–230. 10.1086/666671.

Magazzini, T. (2017). Making the most of super-diversity: Notes on the potential of a new approach. *Policy & Politics*, 45(4), 527–545. 10.1332/030557317X14972819300753.

Makoni, S. (2012). A critique of language, languaging and supervernacular. *Muitas Vozes*, 1(2), 189–199. 10.5212/MuitasVozes.v.1i2.0003.

Meissner, F. (2015). Migration in migration-related diversity? The nexus between superdiversity and migration studies. *Ethnic and Racial Studies*, 38(4), 556–567. 10.1080/01419870.2015.970209.

Meissner, F. (2016). *Socialising with diversity: Relational diversity through a superdiversity lens*. London: Palgrave Macmillan UK.

Meissner, F. (2017). Legal status diversity: Regulating to control and everyday contingencies. *Journal of Ethnic and Migration Studies*, 44(2), 287–306. 10.1080/1369183X.2017.1341718.

Meissner, F., & Vertovec, S. (2015). Comparing super-diversity. *Ethnic and Racial Studies*, 38(4), 541–555. 10.1080/01419870.2015.980295.

Meissner, F., & Vertovec, S. (Eds.). (2016). *Comparing super-diversity. Ethnic and racial studies*. London: Routledge.

Ndhlovu, F. (2015). A decolonial critique of diaspora identity theories and the notion of superdiversity. *Diaspora Studies*, 9(1), 28–40. 10.1080/09739572.2015.1088612.

Neal, S., Bennett, K., Jones, H., Cochrane, A., & Mohan, G. (2015). Multiculture and public parks: Researching super-diversity and attachment in public green space. *Population, Space and Place*, 21(5), 463–475. 10.1002/psp.1910.

Nieswand, B. (2017). Towards a theorisation of diversity: Configurations of person-related differences in the context of youth welfare practices. *Journal of Ethnic and Migration Studies*, 43(10), 1714–1730. 10.1080/1369183X.2017.1293593.

Nieswand, B. (2018). Problematisierung und Emergenz.: Die Regimeperspektive in der Migrationsforschung. In A. Pott, C. Rass, & F. Wolff (Eds.), *Migrationsgesellschaften. Was ist ein Migrationsregime? What is a migration regime?* (pp. 81–106). Wiesbaden: Springer VS.

Pavlenko, A. (forthcoming). Superdiversity and why it isn't: Reflections on terminological innovation and academic branding. In S. Breidbach, L. Küster, & B. Schmenk (Eds.), *Sloganizations in language education discourse*. Bristol: Multilingual Matters.

Phillimore, J. (2015). Delivering maternity services in an era of superdiversity: The challenges of novelty and newness. *Ethnic and Racial Studies*, 38(4), 568–582. 10.1080/01419870.2015.980288.

Phillimore, J., Sigona, N., & Tonkiss, K. (2017). Introduction: Superdiversity, policy and governance in Europe. *Policy & Politics*, 45(4), 487–491. 10.1332/030557317X15076320392001.

Piekut, A., Rees, P., Valentine, G., & Kupiszewski, M. (2012). Multidimensional diversity in two European cities: Thinking beyond ethnicity. *Environment and Planning A*, 44(12), 2988–3009. 10.1068/a4512.

Putnam, R. D. (2000). *Bowling alone: The collapse and revival of American community*. New York: Simon & Schuster.

Römhild, R. (2014). Diversität?! Postethnische Perspektiven für eine reflexive Migrationsforschung. In B. Nieswand & H. Drotbohm (Eds.), *Kultur, gesellschaft, migration* (pp. 255–270). Wiesbaden: Springer Fachmedien Wiesbaden. 10.1007/978-3-658-03626-3_10.

Schinkel, W. (2017). *Imagined societies*. Cambridge: Cambridge University Press.

Scholten, P. (2016). Between national models and multi-level decoupling: The pursuit of multi-level governance in Dutch and UK policies towards migrant incorporation. *Journal of International Migration and Integration/Revue De L'integration Et De La Migration Internationale*, 17(4), 973–994. 10.1007/s12134-015-0438-9.

Scholten, P., & van Breugel, I. (Eds.). (2018). *Mainstreaming integration governance: New trends in migrant integration policies in Europe*. Basingstoke: Palgrave Macmillan.

Scholten, P. W. A. (2018). Beyond migrant integration policies: Rethinking the urban governance of migration-related diversity. *Croatian and Comparative Public Administration*, 18(1), 7–30.

Schönwälder, K., Petermann, S., Hüttermann, J., Vertovec, S., Hewstone, M., Stolle, D., ... Schmitt, T. (2016). *Diversity and contact*. London: Palgrave Macmillan UK.

Sealy, T. (2018). Multiculturalism, interculturalism, 'multiculture' and super-diversity: Of zombies, shadows and other ways of being. *Ethnicities*, *16*(3), 146879681775157. 10.1177/1468796817751575.

Söhn, J. (2014). How legal status contributes to differential integration opportunities. *Migration Studies*, *2*(3), 369–391. 10.1093/migration/mnu022.

Stokes, B. (2017). *What it takes to truly be 'one of us': In U.S., Canada, Europe, Australia and Japan, publics say language matters more to national identity than birthplace*. Washington, DC.

United Nations (2013). *Youth and migration: World youth report. World report youth: Vol. 2011*. New York: United Nations Publications.

Van Breugel, I., & Scholten, P. (2017). Mainstreaming in response to superdiversity? The governance of migration-related diversity in France, the UK and the Netherlands. *Policy & Politics*, *45*(4), 511–526. 10.1332/030557317X14849132401769.

Vertovec, S. (2007). Super-diversity and its implications. *Ethnic and Racial Studies*, *30*(6), 1024–1054. 10.1080/01419870701599465.

Vertovec, S. (2015). Introduction: Migration, cities, diversities 'old' and 'new'. In S. Vertovec (Ed.), *Diversities old and new* (pp. 1–22). London: Palgrave Macmillan UK.

Vertovec, S. (2017a). Talking around super-diversity. *Ethnic and Racial Studies*, *14*(2), 1–15. 10.1080/01419870.2017.1406128.

Vertovec, S. (2017b). Mooring, migration milieus and complex explanations. *Ethnic and Racial Studies*, *40*(9), 1574–1581. 10.1080/01419870.2017.1308534.

Wessendorf, S. (2014). *Commonplace diversity: Social relations in a super-diverse context. Global diversities*. Basingstoke: Palgrave Macmillan.

Wimmer, A., & Glick Schiller, N. (2002). Methodological nationalism and beyond: Nation-state building, migration and the social sciences. *Global Networks*, *2*(4), 301–334. 10.1111/1471-0374.00043.

Wise, A., & Velayutham, S. (Eds.). (2009). *Everyday multiculturalism*. Houndmills, Basingstoke, Hampshire, New York: Palgrave Macmillan.

Ye, J. (2016). The ambivalence of familiarity: Understanding breathable diversity through fleeting encounters in Singapore's Jurong West. *Area*, *48*(1), 77–83. 10.1111/area.12237.

Ye, J. (2018). Re-orienting geographies of urban diversity and coexistence. *Progress in Human Geography*, 030913251876840. 10.1177/0309132518768405.

Chapter 2

Globalization and the proliferation of complex acculturation processes

Simon Ozer

Globalization has emerged as a defining feature of the 21st century affecting the majority of the world's population. Elucidating the psychological effects of embracive cultural globalization, theories of acculturation psychology have been developed to comprehend the complexity of such increased cultural connectivity. Cultural globalization, understood as complex cultural interconnectivity and interaction across geographical distance (Tomlinson, 1999), has made new cultural streams accessible for most of the world's population, both through the technological advancement of media such as entertainment and the Internet and through means of transportation boosting tourism and trade. With such interconnectivity and interaction, multidirectional flows of goods, people, and ideas have emerged as salient phenomena (Jensen, Arnett, & McKenzie, 2011). Such multidirectional flows of cultural elements include not only the apparent spread of Western cultural influences, but likewise the spread of global cultural elements originating from various parts of the world, for example the spread of the Kawaii-culture of cuteness originating from Japan (Nittono, Fukushima, Yano, & Moriya, 2012). The importance of cultural globalization has been apprehended within recent developments in acculturation psychology conceptualizing acculturation processes initiated by globalization mechanisms (Chen, Benet-Martínez, & Bond, 2008; Ferguson & Bornstein, 2012).

As a consequence of cultural globalization, acculturation processes among immigrants have been additionally complexified. Furthermore, people who are not relocating to another country are likewise confronted with new cultural values, practices, and identifications that must be negotiated in regard to peers, significant others, and society, and then integrated within the individual. With cultural globalization, cultural rootedness is no longer something inherited by birth or limited to national boundaries but rather a gravitation that is developed and dynamically changing throughout life as a process of cultural amalgamation. Indeed, such processes of multiple cultural amalgamations warrant a developmental process of individual selectivity and reflection to embrace the opportunities and divert the risks of multiple cultural possibilities.

Globalization and the complexification of acculturation

Acculturation has widely been defined as "those phenomena which result when groups of individuals having different cultures come into continuous first-hand contact with subsequent changes in the original culture patterns of either or both groups" (Redfield, Linton, & Herskovits, 1936). Based on this definition, the classical bidimensional acculturation framework was spearheaded by Berry (1997) to examine psychological processes of adapting to cultural transition. This approach has been applied universally in studies of diverse acculturating groups such as immigrants, refugees, sojourners, and indigenous people (Sam & Berry, 2006). The bidimensional framework theory has at its core the examination of the acculturating individual's orientation toward heritage and new cultural streams comprising the domains of attitude and behavior. These two independent cultural orientations can be related to each other suggesting four ways of maintaining or discharging the cultural streams in question. These ways of handling intercultural processes have often been designated acculturation strategies or acculturation orientations. Within this conception, the acculturating individual can endorse the heritage rather than the new cultural stream (*separation*), or conversely, endorse the new rather than the heritage cultural stream (*assimilation*). Alternatively, the individual can endorse both the heritage and the new cultural steam (*integration*) or neither of the cultural streams in question (*marginalization*; Berry, 1997). The original conception deliniates the orientation toward a new cultural stream as interaction with other cultures, with the description of culture being unspecified (Berry, 1997). However, to a great degree, operationalizations within acculturation research have widely examined the new cultural stream as a uniform national culture (Nguyen & Benet-Martínez, 2013). Such a conception of interaction between two predominantly homogeneous cultural streams might not be applicable regarding globalization-initiated acculturation processes that comprise a multitude of interacting cultural streams within contemporary multicultural and globalized societies (Ferguson & Bornstein, 2012; Ozer & Schwartz, 2016). Globalization involves intercultural contact, which constitutes the starting point for acculturation processes to emerge (Berry, 2008); all four acculturation orientations have been previously applied and exemplified in various globalizing contexts (Jensen et al., 2011). However, recent advancements within acculturation psychology have addressed the particularity of globalization-initiated acculturation processes.

The theoretical advancements of remote and globalization-based acculturation

Recent developments in remote (Ferguson & Bornstein, 2012; Ferguson, Tran, Mendez, & van de Vijver, 2017) and globalization-based acculturation theory (Chen et al., 2008, 2016) examine the phenomenon of cultural globalization through either a multidimensional culture-specific or a more generic approach. Both theories discuss how and why acculturation processes alluding to globalization differ from immigration-based acculturation, which has been the prevalent focus within classical acculturation psychology. Within the new conceptual framework examining cultural globalization, acculturation can be defined as "what happens when groups of individuals of different cultures come into contact – whether continuous or intermittent, firsthand or indirect – with subsequent changes in the original culture patterns of one or more parties" (Ferguson, 2013, p. 249). This definition emphasizes the intermittent and mediated character of contemporary intercultural contact pertaining to several processes of cultural globalization. For example, the mass media provides popular cultural products from foreign countries without exposing the remotely acculturating individual to direct contact with other individuals from that remote cultural context. Likewise, people traveling to popular tourist destinations are usually limited by the tourist season and the intercultural contact is clearly demarcated by their length of stay. Especially consequential from the new definition is the widening of the scope of individuals exposed to acculturation. From focusing on immigrants who are internationally relocating, it now comprises both immigrants and non-immigrants who are exposed to new cultural influences through mechanisms of globalization within the context of their homeland. Thus, individuals can develop biculturalism (endorsement of two cultural streams) and bicultural identities through direct and mediated cultural contact while remaining in their home country (Chen, Benet-Martínez, Wu, Lam, & Bond, 2013). This can take the form of an acculturating individual being rooted in the culture of origin while adopting a global identity related to a global cultural stream (Arnett, 2002). Furthermore, the new definition broadens the range of cultural influences originating from various cultural streams. This spectrum of intercultural interaction influencing cultural practices, values, and identities is captured by the theory of remote acculturation which expands the classical conception of the acculturation phenomena to include indirect and/or intermittent contact between distinct cultural groups across geographical distance (Ferguson & Bornstein, 2012). This theory specifies the cultural content of the globalized acculturation process. Indeed, such specification includes various cultural levels such as the national level exemplified in one study as American, British, and South African cultural influences on Zambian adolescents (Ferguson, Ferguson, & Ferguson, 2015) and the ethno-cultural level exemplified in another study as South African emerging adults gravitating to various ethnic South African cultural streams along with European-American and African American culture (Ferguson & Adams, 2016). Through such remote cultural influences, individuals can significantly endorse cultural streams reflecting a sociocultural context they have never lived in.

Approaching the complexified acculturation processes: generic and culture-specific approaches

With globalization expanding contemporary acculturation processes from a two-cultural interaction to include multiple cultural influences determined by both the context and the individual, the globalization-initiated acculturation process becomes severely complex (Doucerain, Dere, & Ryder, 2013). Thus, approaching the acculturative processes of cultural globalization warrants flexibility, with multiple levels of cultural delineation summing across great cultural variation. As indicated, such levels can include the global, the national, the regional, the ethnic or even the subcultural level (Ozer & Schwartz, 2016).

The theory of globalization-based acculturation has approached the question of cultural delineation on a superordinate level. The theory examines how individuals may identify with several cultural elements through globalized multicultural exposure (Chen et al., 2016). Such an approach builds on the conception of globalized individuals being rooted in their local culture while adopting the global cultural stream and consequently developing a global identity relative to their local identity (Arnett, 2002; Chen et al., 2016). In operationalization, the local culture has been examined as national culture and the global cultural stream has been examined as Western culture in Eastern contexts (Chen et al., 2008, 2013). This operationalization corresponds to the bidimensional model in acculturation psychology (Berry, 1997). Recent developments within globalization-based acculturation have operationalized and examined the globalized individual in regard to their global orientation. Such orientation encompasses the proactive, deliberate, and integrative reactions to cultural globalization entitled "multicultural acquisition" and the defensive, reflexive, and exclusionary reactions termed "ethnic protection" (Chen et al., 2016). Indeed, such a generic approach acknowledges how individuals may endorse several elements of different globalized cultural streams along with or as an alternative to their ethnic rooting. Such global and local cultural orientations apply to majority as well as minority groups and likewise to both immigrants and non-immigrants exposed to cultural globalization (Chen et al., 2016).

Remote acculturation approaches the question of cultural delineation with greater sensitivity to the specificity of cultural content and context.

Much of the literature within acculturation psychology has recently emphasized the importance of the contextual specificity affecting the acculturative process, thus highlighting the variations among present day unique intercultural interactions (Bornstein, 2017). The inclusion of specific cultural streams within remote acculturation allows for a particular focus on what is relevant to examine in a given context – for example, examining mainstream US cultural endorsement in regard to nutritional patterns within Jamaican families (Ferguson, Muzaffar, Iturbide, Chu, & Meeks Gardner, 2018). In order to elucidate more of the complexity pertaining to globalized acculturation processes, remote acculturation has operationalized examinations that expand beyond the classical bidimensional model of acculturation psychology. Acknowledging that some globalized contexts comprise more than two cultural streams interacting within the individual, additional cultural dimensions have been added to capture the context-specific multitude of interacting cultural streams. For example, examining cultural gravitation toward more than two cultures in a globalized context is seen in the study of Ferguson and Adams (2016) where they investigated emerging adults with orientations toward (1) black South African, (2) white South African, (3) colored South African, (4) Indian South African, (5) European American, and (6) African American culture. These cultural dimensions were chosen based on antecedent ethnographic information describing urban contexts in South Africa. Furthermore, such an addendum of cultural dimensions expands the conception of understanding heritage and new cultural streams as homogeneous entities in order to understand the multicultural conglomerate they constitute (Ferguson, Tran et al., 2017). This can be achieved, for example, by differentiating the effects of endorsing European-American culture vis-à-vis African American culture among Jamaican Islanders (Ferguson & Bornstein, 2012). Research indicates that an addendum of cultural dimensions is applicable for investigating unique acculturation processes in certain globalized contexts (Ozer & Schwartz, 2016).

The multidimensional perspective of acculturation processes applies, furthermore, to national and international immigrants who are also affected by cultural globalization. National migrants relocating from local rural regions to globalized urban contexts might find themselves negotiating their cultural orientation toward local, national, and global cultural streams (Jensen & Arnett, 2012; Ozer, Bertelsen, Singla, & Schwartz, 2017). Furthermore, immigrants relocating to a new national context might be gravitating to not only the heritage and the new contextual cultural streams but, additionally, to globalized cultural streams remotely influential in the given new cultural context. For example, young second generation immigrants will have to negotiate endorsement of their parents heritage culture, the local culture, and the global youth cultural streams. An ecology of peer influence is manifest in globalized youth culture where young people share a common set of values, lifestyles, or a meaning system which is distinguishable from superordinate cultural streams (Brown, 1999). Such negotiation requires flexibility in behavior, values, and identifications in order to be able to move in and out of dissimilar (sub)cultural contexts. Additionally, research within acculturation psychology has emphasized the notion of including the importance of transnational intercultural contact (Van Oudenhoven, Ward, & Masgoret, 2006). Within this line of thought, transnationalism designates the multiple ties and interactions that link people across borders. The notion of transnationalism can add a third dimension to the classical bidimensional model for international migration relating to the involvement in transnational contact. Such transnational contact can provide immigrants with alternative cultural life possibilities within their new societal context, enhancing contact with their country of origin and, consequently, strengthening the maintenance of their heritage cultural connectivity (Van Oudenhoven et al., 2006). Indeed, such transnationalism could foster processes of remote acculturation (Ferguson et al., 2017) that create enduring influences from the heritage cultural stream (Schwartz, Birman, Benet-Martínez, & Unger, 2017).

As the acculturative phenomena of cultural globalization comprise both general processes on the global level as well as culture-specific processes on the local level, generic and culture-specific approaches generate valuable contributions to understanding the general aspects along with the complexity characterizing such globalized acculturative processes. Each approach comprises various advantages and limitations. That is, while the generic approach allows for cross-cultural comparison and broader generalizations, it also includes an unclear delineation of the cultural elements comprising multicultural acquisition, thus summing across great diversity in its conception of culture. In comparison, the culture-specific approach captures more of the complexity and details pertaining to the particularity of the globalized acculturation phenomena, while it consequently is more challenging to relate findings and implications to other studies that include dissimilar assessments of cultural gravitation.

Processes of cultural integration and amalgamation

In contemporary globalized societies, youth are dynamically engaging and disengaging with dissimilar and sometimes remote sociocultural and subcultural contexts. The globalization-initiated processes of endorsing multiple cultural streams encompass continuous and dynamic negotiations among the individual, other members of society, and the global context, representing a multitude of cultural positions (Hermans & Dimaggio, 2007). Such processes evolve unique cultural amalgamations combining and blending various cultural elements toward an intercultural unification.

Approaching such complexity of cultural globalization necessitates a shift away from an essentialist and categorical conception of culture as being static and bounded, toward more of a dynamic network perspective of how individuals are influenced from multiple cultural streams making their cultural endorsements partial and plural (Morris, Chiu, & Liu, 2015). Such a polycultural approach underlines the dynamics of individual differences in how people during globalization gravitate toward various cultural streams in regard to cultural practices, values, and identifications (Schwartz et al., 2017). With such an understanding of intercultural processes related to cultural globalization, the conception of cultural endorsement becomes more complex, dynamic, and malleable as compared to previous acculturation approaches (Morris et al., 2015). This emphasizes individual processes of cultural amalgamation in which cultural elements from various cultural streams are combined and integrated in accordance with the individual's current situation and context, reflecting how intrapersonal processes are embedded within interpersonal and societal conditions.

On the intrapersonal level, the globalized individual needs to integrate cultural positions and meaning systems representing the various internalized cultural streams. This is done by either synthesizing one's cultural streams and affiliated cultural identities so they are experienced as a single, harmonized new cultural position or by shifting between sustained cultural positions according to the social context and situational cues. Such integration can result in conflicting cultural ways of living that can constrain the process of cultural amalgamation (Ozer et al., 2017). The successful integration of local and global cultural streams has been associated with higher levels of self-esteem and lower levels of anxiety and depression (Chen et al., 2008). The risk of a cultural conflict within the individual can, to some degree, be avoided by employing a careful metacognitive selectivity of compatible cultural elements (Ozer et al., 2017). The acculturative process of cultural globalization is said to include a more agentic approach to cultural amalgamation as compared to immigration-based acculturation. This is done by actively attaining knowledge of, identifying with, and internalizing several cultural streams. In the case of immigration, the new culture surrounds the acculturating individual with expectations of cultural integration present among the majority society. On the other hand, gravitation toward globalized cultural streams is usually more of a voluntary process characterized by a high degree of selectivity (Chen et al., 2008; Ozer & Schwartz, 2016), yet embedded in specific interpersonal processes and societal norms.

Regarding the interpersonal level, cultural amalgamation within the individual is largely inspired and shaped by the people surrounding the individual in everyday life. New innovative constellations of integrating cultural elements are mediated by the ways in which friends and family are integrating and encouraging specific practices, values, and identifications. That is, family expectations and peer influence are proliferating cultural positions and, consequently, shaping the individual cultural gravitation. Furthermore, acculturation discrepancies between parents and youth affect the cultural globalization process on an interpersonal level in regard to situational dynamics. For example, adolescents in urban globalized Thai communities expressed their cultural hybridity in a compartmentalized way by alternating between local and global practices in relation to their interactional partner (McKenzie, 2018). Moreover, in the context of Zambia, globalized adolescents were grouped by cluster analysis into (1) a traditional endorsement of Zambian cultural orientation, interdependent self, and family obligations and (2) a Westernized category of integrating endorsement of US, UK, and South African cultural streams (Ferguson et al., 2015). Such categories might reflect the diverse trajectories of either adhering to the cultural norms of family and local society or gravitating toward the remote cultural streams possibly influenced by peers. Such interpersonal dynamics indicate that the individual expressions of unique amalgamation of cultural elements have to be recognized and approved of by others providing cultural capital and congruent interaction. Positive reactions from peers and other members of society would encourage and motivate the continuation of such cultural gravitation.

On the societal level, contextual norms and characteristics can facilitate, shape, and constrain processes of cultural amalgamation. For example, the societal expectations of females in Ladakh abiding to cultural traditions and roles impede exploration and integration of new globalized cultural elements (Ozer et al., 2017). However, such affects adhere to cultural specific variation in which more collectivist and "tight" cultural societies or groupings might be strongly influenced by the cultural behavior of others and the societal reactions to such behavior. This suggests that such acculturative processes of cultural amalgamation emerge in dissimilar manners across various collectivist and individualist, as well as "tight" and "loose" sociocultural contexts (Gelfand et al., 2011). Such contextual dynamics play, overall, an immense role in the development of adolescents and emerging adults.

Globalization and youth

Young people – especially – are strongly engaged with and influenced by processes of cultural globalization. This relates to their high use of technology and their openness to new cultural influences (Arnett, 2002; Ferguson & Adams, 2016). As compared to adults, adolescents and emerging adults acquire new cultural elements more easily and fluidly during processes of acculturation. Such quotidian involvement with multiple cultural elements can activate novel and creative thinking (Leung, Maddux, Galinsky, &

Chiu, 2008). However, challenging identity processes affected by the rapid sociocultural changes of globalization are most likely in youth who navigate their local rootedness with global awareness (Arnett, 2002).

The developmental period of adolescence has been characterized as the ascendance period for finding out who one wants to be and what life direction to follow; this involves an experimental phase of *psychosocial moratorium* with the possibility of considering various life choices prior to life commitments (Schwartz, Zamboanga, Meca, & Ritchie, 2012). In Western and a limited segment of non-Western contexts, the period of life exploration and experimentation has been expanded due to demographic, economic, and cultural changes along with the great increase in tertiary education. This prolonged transition to adulthood and life commitments has been entitled "emerging adulthood." Globalization processes might be promoting the global spread of emerging adulthood with the delay of adult commitments until the late 20s (Arnett, 2002). Thus, the globalized phenomenon of emerging adulthood is characterized by a decrease in traditional cultural markers and a proliferation of multiple cultural influences both challenging and facilitating the youth's quest to reach a sense of self and a sense of belonging. Just as globalization might extend the period of life characterized by exploration, it also multiplies the range of suggested life paths and, therefore, the possibilities of exploration through new cultural influences suggesting alternative ways of living (Ferguson & Adams, 2016).

Globalized identity processes

Identity development occurs through interaction between the individual and the surrounding sociocultural context. Thus, contemporary identity processes have been increasingly affected by the dynamics of cultural globalization. One of the major consequences of globalization is that youth experience a growing access to new cultural elements, which complexifies their cultural identity development and sense of belonging (Jensen & Arnett, 2012; Marsella, 2012).

Many adolescents and emerging adults around the world are adapting to a bicultural, multicultural, or hybrid identity of being rooted in a local context with awareness and participation in the globalized world. Such a globalized identity allows interaction with family and friends within a local context as well as participation in a technology driven global cultural stream (Arnett, 2002). During processes of cultural globalization, the cultural identity negotiation of youth appears to be more strongly rooted in the local culture as compared to behavioral components of the acculturation orientation (Ozer et al., 2017). Internalizing multiple cultural identities that involve great cultural distance can be a considerable challenge for globalized adolescents and emerging adults (Hong, Zhan, Morris, &

Benet-Martínez, 2016). Yet, it is possible to develop a cultural identity configuration that is flexible enough to reflect one's interaction in different sociocultural contexts (Jensen & Arnett, 2012). Research has found multicultural acquisition among Hong Kong students to be positively related to integrating dissimilar cultural identities and, conversely, ethnic protection to be negatively associated with the successful experience of integrating more than one cultural identity (Chen et al., 2016).

Personal identity is greatly affected by the sociocultural context. Thus, new cultural interaction has been associated with the explorative aspect of personal identity development, suggesting that acculturation can be an explorative phase introducing alternative lifestyles (Schwartz et al., 2013). In the globalized context of the Himalayan region of Ladakh in India, endorsement of local Ladakhi, national Indian, and global Western cultural streams all facilitate and enable various adaptive identity processes of exploration and reflective commitment. This indicates that personal identity development constitutes a significant aspect of local adaptation to globalization-based acculturation (Ozer, Meca, & Schwartz, 2019).

Central for the relationship between cultural globalization and identity processes is the youth's exploration of the rapidly increasing number of socioculturally embedded life paths. Such exploration of life paths has become more complex as culturally prescribed roles have become less significant, providing the individual with greater personal freedom as well as the responsibility for constructing and negotiating viable and coherent identities (Côté & Levine, 2002). Consequently, the processes of cultural globalization – and specifically the endorsement and integration of multiple cultural streams – can open up a great plurality of developmental paths and culturally embedded self-identifications (Jensen & Arnett, 2012).

Opportunities and risks of cultural globalization

Cultural globalization yields diverse and significant psychological implications through the interplay between risks and opportunities. The generic processes related to attitudes of multicultural acquisition and ethnic protection reveal the general aspects of adapting to new cultural influences. The culture specific dynamics reveal detailed information about how distinct cultural endorsement is combined and integrated as well as how specific cultural cues are associated with cognition and behavior; for example involvement with Japanese Kawaii culture has been found to promote careful behavior and to narrow one's attentional focus (Nittono et al., 2012). Consequently, cultural globalization holds significant psychological ramifications for adolescents and emerging adults who balance their endorsement of and involvement with local and global cultural streams comprising both salutary and adverse facets (Marsella, 2012).

Salutary implications

Adolescents' and emerging adults' involvement with cultural globalization can create great opportunities in regard to personal and societal development. Research has found an orientation toward multicultural acquisition to be significantly and positively correlated with openness to experience, while an orientation toward ethnic protection was significantly and negatively correlated with openness to experience (Chen et al., 2016). The openness to new experiences characterizing youth is facilitated by new cultural endorsement resulting in a myriad of culturally embedded life possibilities. Reaching such hybrid cultural practices and identifications in which various cultural elements are amalgamated can lead to innovative expressions of entirely new cultural concepts and practices (Hermans & Dimaggio, 2007; Jensen & Arnett, 2012). Indeed, such negotiation and integration of diverse cultural elements has been associated with the initiation of creative thinking (Leung et al., 2008) and innovation in regard to the individual expression of one's cultural configuration (Hermans & Dimaggio, 2007). Consequently, such processes of cultural amalgamation can create new cultural expressions and facilitate new customs. Additionally, reactions to cultural globalization can include more psychological consequences than the innovative exploration of cultural life possibilities and identities. The different ways of approaching cultural globalization can relate to the psychological well-being of the acculturating individual. Fluidly integrating multiple cultural identities is generally related to positive psychological functioning (Schwartz et al., 2017). Research with students in Hong Kong have found multicultural acquisition to be significantly, negatively associated with acculturative stress, depression, anxiety, and general stress, and positively related to sociocultural adaptation and psychological adaptation comprising self-esteem and life satisfaction. Conversely, ethnic protection was significantly, positively associated with acculturative stress, depression, anxiety, and stress and negatively associated with sociocultural and psychological adaptation (Chen et al., 2016). Such endorsement and preservation of local cultural streams does not necessarily evolve in a defensive and deleterious character. Among Ladakhi youth, the preservation of Ladakhi traditional culture has been an important aspect of negotiating new cultural influences (Ozer et al., 2017).

Adolescents and emerging adults use globalized means such as social media for civic involvement, for example in establishing and mobilizing political movements that hold the potential to transform the world on a global scale (Jensen & Arnett, 2012). In the Ladakhi cultural context, youth reacting to new cultural influences from the Indian plains and Western societies have engaged actively in preserving traditional cultural practices while at the same time embracing the new cultural possibilities, trying to direct the sociocultural development in a commendable direction (Ozer et al., 2017).

Adverse implications

Just as adaptation to globalization generates salutary processes, it can also cause adverse psychological consequences (Marsella, 2012). Among the many psychological implications and challenges of cultural globalization are the risk of identity confusion and intergenerational conflicts that furthermore can influence individuals' well-being.

The influences of cultural globalization on psychological adaptation and well-being appear to be particularly complex and less clear, as seen within immigrant-based acculturation, especially when examining the endorsement of specific cultural streams. Within immigration-based acculturation, research has found strong support for the assumption that biculturalism, comprising an integration of the new and heritage cultural stream, is the most adaptive way of handling the acculturation process (Nguyen & Benet-Martínez, 2013). Such cultural orientation toward more than one's ethnic culture has also emerged as salutary in globalized contexts (Chen et al., 2016). Conversely, simultaneous exposure to dissimilar globalized cultural streams has been found to enhance essentialist perceptions of cultural differences and incompatibility, which can lead to exclusionary and defensive responses to globalization (Torelli, Chiu, Tam, Au, & Keh, 2011). Addressing the particularity of cultural streams in the globalized context of Mexico, a study found that endorsement of the U.S. cultural stream was associated with a higher positive smoking-related attitude, while endorsement of a Mexican cultural stream might be preventive in regard to such an attitude (Lorenzo-Blanco, Arillo-Santillán, Unger, & Thrasher, 2018). In Ladakh, a quantitative examination of cultural endorsement did not reveal any significant relationship with psychological adaptation even though a qualitative examination related the Western cultural endorsement with detrimental mental health and Ladakhi cultural rootedness with improved psychological health (Ozer, 2015). Such findings challenge the assumption of a direct association between cultural endorsement and psychological adaptation. Likewise, remotely acculturated adolescents in Zambia did not differ across cultural orientation in regard to psychological problems or life satisfaction (Ferguson et al., 2015). Such inconclusive findings could suggest that the relationship between cultural endorsement and psychological well-being is, in some contexts, being mediated and moderated by other related factors, such as identity processes and intergenerational dynamics.

Identity confusion has long been anticipated as a central challenge of cultural globalization (Arnett, 2002). This confusion can relate to various aspects of identity, such as the personal and the cultural level. On the cultural level, globalized youth, as previously described, are challenged in regard to integrating dissimilar cultural streams in their identity configuration; these streams can include great cultural distance and perhaps conflictual positions (Hong et al., 2016; Schwartz et al., 2017). Research has found the integration of one's cultural identities into one's cultural self-concept to be positively and significantly predicting psychological adaptation to processes of globalization-based acculturation in Hong Kong (Chen et al., 2013). Especially challenged are globalized youth in developing societies who are integrating local and global cultural identities across great cultural distance. Consequently, in addition to their local identities being defined by their local circumstances and traditions, youth in such contexts often develop a sense of belonging to a global cultural stream. Such globalized bicultural identity dynamics can result in confusion when global cultural possibilities undermine the values associated with the local cultural identity. For example, this can be seen in youth endorsing media depicted youth culture, which is neither an actually lived lifestyle nor compatible in local cultural traditional contexts (Ozer et al., 2017). Additionally, if global culture appears too foreign and inaccessible, they can experience themselves as excluded and thus entangled in the local and the global while belonging to neither (Arnett, 2002). Such contested negotiations of globalized cultural identities can lead to cultural identity confusion through, for example, unattainable media ideals and devaluation of local traditions as too simplistic (Jensen & Arnett, 2012).

Concerning personal identity confusion, the proliferation of new globalized life possibilities and trajectories could cause some youth to become bewildered in their identity exploration with an overload of identity possibilities. Within such fluid identity exploration, youth can become confused in their identity development, inhibiting them from settling on a choice of commitments (Ozer et al., 2019). Besides the intrapersonal identity processes challenged by globalized cultural dynamics, such cultural complexity also holds implications for interpersonal processes.

Some of the great challenges of cultural globalization concern family coherence and harmony. Research has found that family dynamics are important aspects of intercultural processes (Ferguson et al., 2017). These findings yield that family cohesion leads to positive outcomes while family conflict has negative consequences for young people (Ward & Geeraert, 2016). In general, research has shown that youth acculturate more quickly than their parents. Such findings have been replicated within the context of cultural globalization where Jamaican adolescents were more globalized and endorsed American culture to a higher degree than their parents (Ferguson & Bornstein, 2012). Elders in non-Western countries have often expressed concern about the younger generation being undermined by Western values of individualism, competitiveness, and materialism

(Ozer, 2015). Conflicts between parents and their children due to discrepancy in their acculturative trajectories would be a possible consequence of the accelerating phenomena of cultural globalization. Among remotely acculturated dyads in the context of Jamaica, more intergenerational conflicts were reported among adolescents and parents whose acculturation cluster did not match as compared to dyads with matching acculturative orientation (Ferguson & Bornstein, 2012). Conversely, remotely acculturated adolescents in Zambia did not differ across cultural orientation in regard to parental conflict (Ferguson et al., 2015). However, this could be due to greater alignment between the cultural orientation of the adolescents and their parents. Research from Thailand indicates that globalized urban contexts extend the dyadic gap between parents and youth in regard to morality as compared to rural contexts (McKenzie, 2016), indicating that global cultural influences can shape the conception of proper and improper behavior among youth. In the context of Jamaica, endorsement of American culture was associated with an unhealthy nutrition pattern. Furthermore, the family dynamics appear influential in this regard, as the Jamaican mothers' remote acculturation was related to their daughters' unhealthy lifestyle (Ferguson et al., 2017). These diverse implications of cultural globalization call for more research to develop this new important field of psychology.

Research implications

The complexity of cultural globalization holds several implications for psychological research. First, globalization has proliferated acculturative processes to be salient in most countries worldwide. That is, acculturation psychology has been broadened to include non-immigrants who are exposed to new cultural influences affecting developmental processes and psychological well-being. Second, immigrants are not just exposed to heritage and new cultural streams but likewise to globalized multicultural elements, complexifying the process of cultural negotiation. Third, measurements tapping into more than two distinct cultural streams or generically approaching cultural globalization are needed in order to capture the cultural complexity among both immigrants and non-immigrants. In conclusion, contemporary cultural complexity within both the individual and the group suggests the need for new approaches in psychological research going beyond an essentialist conception of cultural homogeneous and bounded groups and individuals, as cultural globalization affects individuals worldwide.

Conclusion

The bourgeoning field of psychological research on cultural globalization has yielded important theoretical and conceptual developments as well as significant findings regarding youths' negotiation and integration of multiple cultural streams through processes of cultural amalgamation. The new theoretical developments of remote and globalization-based acculturation (Chen et al., 2008; Ferguson & Bornstein, 2012) have paved the way for new psychological studies elucidating the implications of cultural globalization. The complexity of such intercultural processes is especially relevant for young people who are in a life period of immense exploration, reaching for coherent self-identifications and a sense of belonging through interaction and negotiations with peers, family, and the surrounding society.

The outcome of cultural globalization processes among adolescents and emerging adults comprises the interplay between individual factors such as agency and ability to selectively navigate and negotiate cultural complexity and societal influences. Such processes of cultural amalgamation are adapted thorough societal constraints and cultural facilitation of new life possibilities. The ramifications of cultural globalization include the positive implications of enhancement and escalation of culturally prescribed life possibilities and processes of creativity, along with the negative implications of identity confusion in the process of negotiating viable identities without prescriptive identity categories and with intergenerational conflicts reflecting the dissimilar acculturative trajectories of youth and their parents. As a new focus within intercultural psychology, the study of cultural globalization processes reflects a new and promising field of research capturing the current global proliferation of complex acculturation processes.

References

Arnett, J. J. (2002). The psychology of globalization. *American Psychologist*, 57(10), 774–783. doi:10.1037/0003-066X.57.10.774.

Berry, J. W. (1997). Immigration, acculturation, and adaptation. *Applied Psychology: An International Review*, 46(1), 5–34. doi:10.1111/j.1464-0597.1997.tb01087.x.

Berry, J. W. (2008). Globalisation and acculturation. *International Journal of Intercultural Relations*, 32(4), 328–336. doi: 2048/10.1016/j.ijintrel.2008.04.001.

Bornstein, M. H. (2017). The specificity principle in acculturation science. *Perspectives on Psychological Science*, 12(1), 3–45. doi:10.1177/1745691616655997.

Brown, B. B. (1999). Measuring the peer environment of American adolescents. In S. L. Friedman & T. D. Wachs (Eds.), *Measuring environment across the life span: Emerging methods and concepts* (pp. 59–90). Washington, DC: American Psychological Association.

Chen, S. X., Benet-Martínez, V., & Bond, M. H. (2008). Bicultural identity, bilingualism, and psychological adjustment in multicultural societies: Immigration-based and globalization-based acculturation. *Journal of Personality*, 76(4), 803–838. doi:10.1111/j.1467-6494.2008.00505.x.

Chen, S. X., Benet-Martínez, V., Wu, W. C. H., Lam, B. C. P., & Bond, M. H. (2013). The role of dialectical self and bicultural identity integration in psychological adjustment. *Journal of Personality*, *81*(1), 61–75. doi:10.1111/j.1467-6494.2012.00791.x.

Chen, S. X., Lam, B. C. P., Hui, B. P. H., Ng, J. C. K., Mak, W. W. S., Guan, Y., ... Lau, V. C. Y. (2016). Conceptualizing psychological processes in response to globalization: Components, antecedents, and consequences of global orientations. *Journal of Personality and Social Psychology*, *110*(2), 302–331. doi:10.1037/a0039647.

Côté, J. E., & Levine, C. G. (2002). *Identity formation, agency, and culture: A social psychological synthesis*. Mahwah, NJ: Lawrence Erlbaum Associates Publishers.

Doucerain, M., Dere, J., & Ryder, A. G. (2013). Travels in hyper-diversity: Multiculturalism and the contextual assessment of acculturation. *International Journal of Intercultural Relations*, *37*(6), 686–699. doi:10.1016/j.ijintrel.2013.09.007.

Ferguson, G. M. (2013). The big difference a small island can make: How Jamaican adolescents are advancing acculturation science. *Child Development Perspectives*, *7*, 248–254. doi:10.1111/cdep.12051.

Ferguson, G. M., & Adams, B. G. (2016). Americanization in the rainbow nation: Remote acculturation and psychological well-being of South African emerging adults. *Emerging Adulthood*, *4*(2), 104–118. doi:10.1177/2167696815599300.

Ferguson, G. M., & Bornstein, M. H. (2012). Remote acculturation: The "Americanization" of Jamaican islanders. *International Journal of Behavioral Development*, *36*(3), 167–177. doi:10.1177/0165025412437066.

Ferguson, G. M., Muzaffar, H., Iturbide, M. I., Chu, H., & Meeks Gardner, J. M. (2018). Feel American, watch American, eat American? Remote acculturation, TV, and nutrition among adolescent-mother dyads in Jamaica. *Child Development*, Advance online publication. doi:10.1111/cdev.12808.

Ferguson, G. M., Tran, S. P., Mendez, S. N., & van de Vijver, F. J. R. (2017). Remote acculturation: Conceptualization, measurement, and implications for health outcomes. In S. J. Schwartz & J. B. Unger (Eds.), *Oxford handbook of acculturation and health*. (pp. 157–173). New York, NY: Oxford University Press.

Ferguson, Y. L., Ferguson, K. T., & Ferguson, G. M. (2015). I am AmeriBritSouthAfrican-Zambian: Multidimensional remote acculturation and well-being among urban Zambian adolescents. *International Journal of Psychology*, *52*(1), 67–76. doi:10.1002/ijop.12191.

Gelfand, M. J., Raver, J. L., Nishii, L., Leslie, L. M., Lun, J., Lim, B. C., ... Aycan, Z. (2011). Differences between tight and loose cultures: A 33-nation study. *Science*, *332*(6033), 1100–1104.

Hermans, H. J. M., & Dimaggio, G. (2007). Self, identity, and globalization in times of uncertainty: A dialogical analysis. *Review of General Psychology*, *11*(1), 31–61. doi:10.1037/1089-2680.11.1.31.

Hong, Y., Zhan, S., Morris, M. W., & Benet-Martínez, V. (2016). Multicultural identity processes. *Current Opinion in Psychology*, *8*, 49–53. doi:10.1016/j.copsyc.2015.09.020.

Jensen, L. A., & Arnett, J. J. (2012). Going global: New pathways for adolescents and emerging adults in a changing world. *Journal of Social Issues*, *68*(3), 473–492. doi:10.1111/j.1540-4560.2012.01759.x.

Jensen, L. A., Arnett, J. J., & McKenzie, J. (2011). Globalization and cultural identity. In S. J. Schwartz, K. Luyckx, & V. L. Vignoles (Eds.). *Handbook of identity theory and research*. (pp. 285–301). New York: Springer. doi:10.1007/978-1-4419-7988-9_13.

Leung, A. K., Maddux, W. W., Galinsky, A. D., & Chiu, C. (2008). Multicultural experience enhances creativity: The when and how. *American Psychologist*, 63(3), 169–181. doi:10.1037/0003-066X.63.3.169.

Lorenzo-Blanco, E. I., Arillo-Santillán, E., Unger, J. B., & Thrasher, J. (2018). Remote acculturation and cigarette smoking susceptibility among youth in Mexico. *Journal of Cross-Cultural Psychology*. doi:10.1177/0022022118807578.

Marsella, A. (2012). Psychology and globalization: Understanding a complex relationship. *Journal of Social Issues*, 68(3), 454–472. doi:10.1111/j.1540-4560.2012.01758.x.

McKenzie, J. (2016). Globalization and moral personhood: Dyadic perspectives of the moral self in rural and Urban Thai communities. *Journal of Adolescent Research*, 33(2), 209–246. doi:10.1177/0743558416670007.

McKenzie, J. (2018). Shifting practices, shifting selves: Negotiations of local and global cultures among adolescents in Northern Thailand. *Child Development*. doi:10.1111/cdev.13076.

Morris, M. W., Chiu, C., & Liu, Z. (2015). Polycultural psychology. *Annual Review of Psychology*, 66, 631–659. doi:10.1146/annurev-psych-010814-015001.

Nguyen, A. D., & Benet-Martínez, V. (2013). Biculturalism and adjustment: A meta-analysis. *Journal of Cross-Cultural Psychology*, 44(1), 122–159. doi:10.1177/0022022111435097.

Nittono, H., Fukushima, M., Yano, A., & Moriya, H. (2012) The power of Kawaii: Viewing cute images promotes a careful behavior and narrows attentional focus. *PLOS ONE*, 7(9). doi:10.1371/journal.pone.0046362.

Ozer, S. (2015). Acculturation, adaptation, and mental health among Ladakhi college students: A mixed methods study of an indigenous population. *Journal of Cross-Cultural Psychology*, 46(3), 435–453. doi:10.1177/0022022114567195.

Ozer, S., Bertelsen, P., Singla, R., & Schwartz, S. J. (2017). "Grab your culture and walk with the global": Ladakhi students' negotiation of cultural identity in the context of globalization-based acculturation. *Journal of Cross-Cultural Psychology*, 48(3), 294–318. doi:10.1177/0022022116687394.

Ozer, S., Meca, A., & Schwartz, S. J. (2019). Globalization and identity development among emerging adults from Ladakh. *Cultural Diversity and Ethnic Minority Psychology*. doi:10.1037/cdp0000261.

Ozer, S., & Schwartz, S. (2016). Measuring globalization-based acculturation in Ladakh: Investigating possible advantages of a tridimensional acculturation scale. *International Journal of Intercultural Relations*, 53, 1–15. doi:10.1016/j.ijintrel.2016.05.002.

Redfield, R., Linton, R., & Herskovits, M. J. (1936). Memorandum for the study of acculturation. *American Anthropologist*, 38(1), 149–152. doi:10.1111/1467-9450.00213.

Sam, D. L., & Berry, J. W. (Eds). (2006). *The Cambridge handbook of acculturation psychology*. New York, NY: Cambridge University Press.

Schwartz, S. J., Birman, D., Benet-Martínez, V., & Unger, J. (2017). Biculturalism: Negotiating Multiple Cultural Streams. In S. Schwartz & J. Unger (Eds.). *Oxford handbook of acculturation and health.* (pp. 29–47). New York, NY: Oxford University Press.

Schwartz, S. J., Kim, S. Y., Whitbourne, S. K., Zamboanga, B. L., Weisskirch, R. S., Forthun, L. F., ... Luyckx, K. (2013). Converging identities: Dimensions of acculturation and personal identity status among immigrant college students. *Cultural Diversity and Ethnic Minority Psychology, 19*(2), 155–165. doi:10.1037/a0030753.

Schwartz, S. J., Zamboanga, B. L., Meca, A., & Ritchie, R. A. (2012). Identity around the world: An overview. In Schwartz, S. J. (Ed.), *Identity around the world; identity around the world* (pp. 1–18, 152) Jossey-Bass: San Francisco, CA.

Tomlinson, J. (1999). *Globalization and Culture.* Cambridge, UK: Polity Press.

Torelli, C. J., Chiu, C., Tam, K., Au, A. K. C., & Keh, H. T. (2011). Exclusionary reactions to foreign cultures: Effects of simultaneous exposure to cultures in globalized space. *Journal of Social Issues, 67*(4), 716–742. doi:10.1111/j.1540-4560.2011.01724.x.

Van Oudenhoven, J. P., Ward, C., & Masgoret, A. (2006). Patterns of relations between immigrants and host societies. *International Journal of Intercultural Relations, 30*(6), 637–651. doi:10.1016/j.ijintrel.2006.09.001.

Ward, C., & Geeraert, N. (2016). Advancing acculturation theory and research: The acculturation process in its ecological context. *Current Opinion in Psychology, 8,* 98–104. doi: 2048/10.1016/j.copsyc.2015.09.021.

Chapter 3

Biculturalism and bicultural identity development
A relational model of bicultural systems

Alan Meca, Kyle Eichas, Seth J. Schwartz, and Rachel J. Davis

Biculturalism and bicultural identity development

As a result of increases in international migration, there has been a surge in cross-cultural contact across the globe (Jensen, Arnett, & MacKenzie, 2011). Although international migration is not a new phenomenon, the acculturation process, or the cultural change that occurs as a result of contact between two cultural groups (Berry, 1980), has changed in many ways. Since the late 20th century, many migrant-receiving countries have adopted increasingly multiculturalist ideologies that allow, and sometimes even encourage, migrants and their immediate descendants to honor, embrace, and celebrate their heritage (Berry, 2013). The influence of multiculturalist ideologies is enhanced by modern technologies that enable migrants and their immediate descendants to stay in touch with friends and relatives back home (Portes & Rumbaut, 2014) and to access heritage-cultural media (Jensen et al., 2011). For this reason, the influence of immigrants' heritage cultures may be more enduring than in past generations.

Despite these sociocultural changes, immigrants still need to be sufficiently facile in the language and customs of the receiving society so that they can make friends, find work, and otherwise "fit in" with members of the dominant culture (Schwartz, Unger, Zamboanga, & Szapocznik, 2010). At the same time, with international migration reaching an all-time high (United Nations, 2017), non-immigrant members of destination societies (who are usually, but not always, the larger and more dominant group) also need to adapt to life in an increasingly multicultural context. Indeed, it is estimated that by 2044, more than half of all Americans will belong to a minority group (any group other than non-Hispanic White alone) (Colby & Ortman, 2015). As a result, navigating multiple cultural streams will become increasingly prominent in countries around the world.

Although biculturalism research originally adopted an additive approach, where biculturalism was assumed to represent the sum of its parts, more recent work has suggested that bicultural people's identities are multifaceted, interrelated, and dynamic (West, Zhang, Yampolsky, & Sasaki,

2017). Extending current models of biculturalism, we draw on Erikson's (1968) conceptualization of identity development and on relational developmental systems theory (RDST, Lerner & Overton, 2008) to contextualize biculturalism as a developmental process. Towards this end, we begin by defining biculturalism and reviewing traditional and contemporary models of it. Next, we introduce the guiding principles of RDST and propose a relational model of bicultural systems. We then conclude our review by highlighting specific avenues for future research.

Defining biculturalism: what is it and who is bicultural?

For the purposes of this chapter, we use "biculturalism" as an umbrella term to refer to any case in which a person endorses at least one heritage culture and at least one receiving culture. Early models of bicultural identification are rooted in acculturation research (Berry, 1980). Traditional conceptualizations of acculturation grew out of what is termed the "unidimensional" view, which conceptualizes acculturation as a zero-sum experience in which "successful" acculturation involves complete adoption of the receiving culture and forfeiture of one's cultural heritage (Schwartz et al., 2010). In contrast, drawing on Berry's (1980) model, contemporary approaches have conceptualized receiving-culture acquisition and heritage-culture retention as independent dimensions. Within this framework, individuals can acquire some aspects of their receiving culture while still retaining some aspects of their cultural heritage. Working within a bidimensional model of acculturation, Berry (1980) crossed the independent dimensions of receiving-culture acquisition and heritage-culture retention to create four categories: *assimilation* (i.e., acquires the receiving culture and discards the heritage culture), *separation* (i.e., rejects the receiving culture and retains the heritage culture), *marginalization* (i.e., rejects the receiving culture and discards the heritage culture), and *integration* (i.e., acquires the receiving culture and retains the heritage culture). Within this model, integration represents biculturalism, and we use these terms interchangeably here.

Since the introduction of Berry's (1980) model, a substantial literature has emerged focusing on differences between bicultural individuals and other acculturating groups (i.e., assimilation, separation, or marginalization approaches). For the most part, the majority of this research has found that biculturalism is associated with the most favorable psychosocial outcomes among a range of immigrant groups (Nguyen & Benet-Martínez, 2013; Tadmor, Tetlock, & Peng, 2009). However, research conducted with a variety of populations has shown not only that most immigrants are bicultural (Huynh, Nguyen, & Benet-Martínez, 2011), but also that bicultural individuals' identities are multifaceted, interrelated, and dynamic (West et al., 2017). As a result, recent models have attempted to identify heterogeneous groups of bicultural individuals (Nguyen & Benet-Martínez, 2013) and to examine the processes through which bicultural individuals negotiate their cultural identities (Ward, Tseung-Wong, Szabo, Qumeseya, & Bhowon, 2018; West et al., 2017).

Bicultural identity integration

Seeking to explore the degree of heterogeneity among bicultural individuals, Benet-Martínez and colleagues (e.g., Benet-Martínez & Haritatos, 2005; Nguyen & Benet-Martínez, 2013) proposed the construct of bicultural identity integration (BII). According to Benet-Martínez and Haritatos (2005, p. 1019), BII represents "a framework for organizing and understanding individual differences in the way biculturals perceive the intersection between their mainstream and ethnic cultures." BII is operationalized to refer to the degree to which individuals view heritage and receiving cultural identities as compatible and able to be integrated (i.e., blendedness versus compartmentalized) versus oppositional and in conflict (i.e., harmony versus conflict) (see Huynh et al., 2011, for further review). BII goes beyond additive considerations of cultural identification, as two bicultural people whose two cultures are equally important to them can differ on BII depending on how they manage and integrate the two cultural systems.

In essence, blendedness represents a socio-cognitive component (e.g., "I cannot ignore the Mexican or American side of me" vs. "I do not blend Mexican and American cultures") whereas harmony represents an affective component (e.g., "I rarely feel conflicted about being bicultural"). A growing body of research has highlighted the role that blendedness and harmony play in contributing to and defining an integrated identity (Schwartz, Birman, Benet-Martínez, & Unger, 2017). Moreover, subsequent research has indicated that BII predicts success on biculturalism-related tasks. For example, Benet-Martínez, Leu, Lee, and Morris (2002) randomized Chinese American individuals to view either Chinese (e.g., dragon, Great Wall) or U.S. (e.g., bald eagle, Abraham Lincoln) icons and to complete a task indexing individualistic and collectivistic values. They found that individuals high in BII responded to U.S. primes with individualist-oriented reactions, and to Chinese primes with collectivist-oriented reactions. In contrast, low-BII individuals displayed the opposite (i.e., "incorrect") pattern. In sum, BII has emerged as a framework for understanding heteroegenity among bicultural individuals' sense of self and identity.

Transformative theory of biculturalism

Seeking to move beyond additive theories of biculturalism, West and colleagues (2017) proposed a transformative theory of biculturalism positing that "biculturals' characteristics and experiences result not only from the direct influences of each of their cultures but also from the processes they use to negotiate their cultures" (p. 964). Towards this end, West and colleagues (2017) proposed three bicultural negotiation processes that represent the ways in which individuals negotiate with their cultural context.

The first of the three bicultural negotiation processes is *integration*. Integration refers to the weaving and meshing of one's different cultural identities to form a cohesive whole. In integrating, one *actively* reconciles the differences between one's cultural groups by resolving conflicts and discrepancies between them. Further, integrating centers on appreciating the similarities between one's cultural systems (Tadmor & Tetlock, 2006). There are several strategies that individuals may adopt towards achieving integration. For example, one may seek to value the differing perspectives of each of one's cultural groups as equally valid and beneficial (Tadmor et al., 2009). Alternatively, individuals may seek to minimize differences by focusing on the similarities between two cultural systems (Yampolsky, Amiot, & de la Sablonnière, 2016). Still others may achieve integration by identifying with a larger superordinate identity (e.g., European, human) that encompasses both cultural streams (Yampolsky et al., 2016).

Hybridizing, the second strategy, occurs when bicultural individuals are able to fuse two cultural streams to create a mixture that is unique and distinct from the initial cultural streams. Thus, hybridizing involves an active recombination process and is likely to result in the emergence of a third culture that bridges the two initial cultural streams. In this sense, whereas integration involves the resolution in the discrepancies between two cultural streams, hybridizing involves the formation of a new, blended, cultural identity. Hybridizing also differs from Benet-Martínez and Haritatos's (2005) blendedness in that blendedness reflects a perceived compatibility between two cultural streams, whereas hybridizing emphasizes the "individual's active role in fusing their cultures and creating something new" (West et al., 2017, p. 10). Thus, blendedness may serve as a necessary but insufficient condition for an individual's capacity to develop a hybridized fused culture.

Cultural frame switching, the final bicultural negotiation process outlined by West et al. (2017), involves activating culturally relevant cognitive systems in response to situational and cultural cues (e.g., cultural images) (Hong, Morris, Chiu, & Benet-Martínez, 2000). Naturalistic experience sampling has indicated not only that bicultural individuals frame switch in their daily lives (Doucerain, Dere, & Ryder, 2013), but also that frame switching may represent both a conscious and an unconscious process (Zou, Morris, & Benet-Martínez, 2008). In addition, research has indicated that frame switching is affected by the degree to which individuals view their cultural identities as overlapping and compatible (Huynh et al., 2011). Indeed, individuals high in BII tend to activate culturally relevant cognitive systems of the cultural system being primed. In contrast, those low in BII may adopt behavior more characteristic of the culture that is *not* primed. Together, these three processes capture the ways in which bicultural individuals negotiate with their cultural contexts and manage their cultural identity.

Cultural identity styles

Along a similar yet independent line of research, Ward and colleagues (2018) have begun exploring the ways in which individuals manage multiple cultural identities. Specifically, Ward et al. (2018) identified two strategies that individuals use to maintain a bicultural identity: hybridizing and alternating. *Hybridizing*, similar to West et al. (2017), reflects the process by which individuals identify specific elements from two or more cultures and combine them, often in a unique and novel way (e.g., "I am a 'melange' of Mexican and American"). Thus, hybridizing reflects dynamism and flexibility and, at least to some extent, a degree of novelty in the integration process.

In contrast, *alternating* represents a situated identity (Noels & Clément, 2015) and the process by which individuals change and shift depending upon the circumstances (e.g., "I am Hispanic at home and an American at school/work"). To some degree, alternating is conceptually similar to cultural frame switching in that both represent the process by which individuals shift their cultural identity based upon the specific circumstances. However, frame switching largely represents a spontaneous attempt to adapt to changing contextual cues (Doucerain et al., 2013), whereas alternating represents a more conscious attempt to shift one's cultural identity from one situation to another and can result from either contextual cues or from a sense of cultural confusion (Ward et al., 2018).

Within this developing framework, cultural identity styles are activated by a desire to achieve integration. Thus, hybridizing and alternating identity styles are hypothesized to promote cultural identity development. However, evidence from a daily diary study with Hispanic college students has indicated that hybridizing is predicted by BII harmony and blendedness (Schwartz et al., 2019). These findings suggest that perceiving one's cultural identity components as compatible and capable of being integrated may pave the way for a sense of self where the person is comfortable creating an individualized cultural mosaic. Moreover, Schwartz et al. found that hybridizing and alternating cultural identity approaches are weakly correlated. Alternating may therefore be largely orthogonal to hybridizing. Indeed, some highly hybridized people may engage in effective alternation to meet the demands of the specific cultural environment, whereas others may present a hybridized cultural self regardless of the environment. Still other individuals who are unable to develop a hybridized cultural identity may nonetheless be able effectively to shift their cultural identity from one situation to another. In essence, regardless of one's level of hybridization, individuals vary in their capacity for alternation.

Person–environment interactions

In summarizing these theoretical frameworks that have focused on extending the biculturalism literature by identifying heterogeneity among bicultural individuals (Nguyen & Benet-Martínez, 2013) and specifying the processes through which individuals navigate two cultural streams (Ward et al., 2018; West et al., 2017), there is a clear need for integration. Given that cultural adaptation and identity are inherently developmental processes (Schwartz et al., 2010), we propose to draw on RDST (Lerner & Overton, 2008) and Erikson's (1968) conceptualization of identity as a means of clarifying and integrating these three theoretical frameworks within the context of a broader developmental framework.

RDST

In recent years, developmental science has moved towards recognizing that development involves mutually influential relations between the person and multiple levels of their changing context (Lerner & Overton, 2008). Towards this end, contemporary theories have adopted a theoretical framework known as RDST. RDST depicts human development as a property of systematic change in the multiple and integrated levels of organization that comprise human life and its ecology, rather than an exclusive property of the individual or of the environment. Towards this end, RDST adopts a developmental-contextual and relational framework by incorporating not just *multi-linear* developmental relationships, but rather *bidirectional* relationships across multiple levels of organization (e.g., biological, psychological, and social ecological levels) that are structurally and functionally integrated (Lerner & Overton, 2008).

As a result, RDST rejects Cartesian polarities or false dichotomies (e.g., nature vs. nurture), including the dichotomy of *person* versus *context*. Instead, it conceptualizes the unit of development as the embodied *person-in-context* and the unit of analysis as the bidirectional relation between person and context (person ←→ context) (Gestsdóttir & Lerner, 2008). These bidirectional relations between individual and context regulate the course of development and shift the focus from attributes of the individual to attributes of the developmental system. Thus, these "developmental regulations," or the dynamic process of individuals acting on their contexts and contexts acting upon individuals, are the key process of human development (Brandtstädter, 2006).

Within RDST, a distinction has been made between the individual's versus the context's contributions to developmental regulation. The individual contributes to developmental regulation through *self-regulation* (Gestsdóttir & Lerner, 2008). Self-regulation refers to the ability to flexibly activate, monitor, inhibit, preserve, and/or adapt physiological, behavioral, and psychological processes in response to environmental demands and as a way of attaining personally relevant goals. Self-regulation can be further differentiated into organismic versus intentional self-regulation. Unlike organismic self-regulation (which is primarily physiological), intentional self-regulation refers to goal-directed actions-in-contexts that can be actively selected and controlled (Gestsdóttir & Lerner, 2008). In other words, intentional self-regulation represents "contextualized actions that are actively aimed toward harmonizing demand and resources in the context with personal goals" (Gestsdóttir & Lerner, 2008, p. 204).

Erikson's conceptualization of identity development

Erikson described identity development as a structural-organizational integration that occurs both (a) within people as they make choices about goals, roles, and beliefs about the world and (b) within the person's cultural context as the communal group recognizes and affirms these choices. As such, identity development is an inherently relational process that establishes the "identity of those two identities" (Erikson, 1968, p. 22). In experiential terms, the result is psychosocial wholeness – that is, an inner sense of continuity and self-sameness matched by a sense of social continuity and sameness (Erikson, 1968). In this view, identity provides a relatively stable foundation (i.e., level of analysis; Overton, 2015) for conceptualizing the person's subjective sense of the dynamic relation between the self and culture, where self and culture represent levels of the developmental system. Using identity as a standpoint implies that single-level explanations will not provide a sufficient account of biculturalism. Josselson (1994) refined Erikson's ideas by explicitly using relational terms to describe the interplay between self and society that represents identity development. Josselson described identity development as a relational process in which the individual joins society by finding a niche within a group of other people that fosters a sense of belonging to that group. Consistent with Erikson's (1968) theory and RDST, Josselson (1994) described identity development as relational and bidirectional. That is, the individual becomes *embedded* within their social world, and the social world becomes embedded within the individual.

Towards an integrated RDST of biculturalism

Drawing on RDST, and on Erikson's (1968) conceptualization of identity which is consistent with the process-relational worldview underlying

RDST (Overton, 2015), our proposed relational model of bicultural systems seeks to provide a contemporary conceptualization of biculturalism that integrates the theoretical frameworks previously discussed. Drawn from these two frameworks, we conceptualize identity development as something that cannot be coherently divided into self and social components and reflects the embodied person-in-context (Eichas, Meca, Montgomery, & Kurtines, 2015). As such, identity development emerges from the ongoing dynamic relation between self and society and represents a process that occurs both (a) within individuals as they navigate their context to make choices about goals, roles, and beliefs about the world and (b) within a society as it recognizes and affirms these choices, thereby recognizing and affirming the multiple cultural streams from which it is comprised. From the perspective of researchers focused on how individuals navigate two or more cultural streams, the focus turns to how individuals develop an *inner* sense of cultural continuity and self-sameness, matched by a sense of *social* continuity and self-sameness as the individual finds their place in a multicultural society. In turn, this sense of self and identity informs one's dynamic and integrated self-system that regulates the actions individuals use to adapt to changing developmental contexts and functions as a "steering mechanism" for decisions and actions throughout the life course (Eichas et al., 2015).

Individual level of analysis

At the individual level, to conceptualize identity development from a bicultural perspective, we draw on cultural identity literature and Benet-Martinez's BII framework. Drawing from cultural identity literature (see Umaña-Taylor et al., 2014), individuals belonging to two or more cultural groups are tasked with considering the subjective meaning of their membership in these cultural groups (i.e., cultural identity commitment) and developing emotional attachments to both cultural groups (i.e., cultural identity belonging). In addition, as reviewed earlier in this chapter, one's bicultural identity consists of the degree to which one perceives relevant cultural streams as distinct from each other (i.e., judged distance), compatible and intermingled (i.e., BII blendedness), and harmonized (i.e., BII harmony).

Drawing on RDST and identity theory (Eichas et al., 2015), one's bicultural identity represents a self-constructed self-structure that not only provides direction for individuals' intentional self-regulations, functioning as a "steering mechanism" for decisions and actions they take within a particular context, but is also informed by individuals' interaction with their context. Towards this end, we draw on cultural identity literature (see Umaña-Taylor et al., 2014; West et al., 2017; and Ward et al., 2018) to identify four forms of intentional self-regulation that are relevant within the context of biculturalism. In line with West et al. (2017) we refer to these three processes as "bicultural negotiation processes." Although they are consistent with RDST, we conceptualize these processes as an individual's conscious contribution to the person ←→ context, and consistent with Ward et al. (2018) describe cognitive and behavioral strategies that "individuals with multicultural backgrounds construct, revise, and maintain their cultural identities" (p. 4). It should be noted, that although we identify four bicultural negotiation processes, we are not suggesting that these are the only forms of intentional self-regulation that are relevant within the context of biculturalism.

To begin with and drawing on cultural identity literature (Umaña-Taylor et al., 2014), *exploration* represents the process by which individuals consider what it means to belong to a cultural group. Conceptualizations of cultural identity exploration have varied within the literature. Cultural identity exploration may consist of direct participation in events or experiences that teach individuals something about the cultural groups they belong to (e.g., attending social activities, participating in cultural traditions) or may consist of talking to others or thinking about one's ethnicity (Syed et al., 2013). In essence, exploration represents the process by which individuals develop their cultural identity to begin with and represents a foundational step prior to the development of a broader cultural identity.

Consistent with Ward et al. (2018), we propose *alternating* as a second form of intentional self-regulation whereby individuals consciously activate relevant aspects of their bicultural identity in response to their immediate social environment. For example, a Hispanic young adult may initially act in a manner they perceive to be consistent with an "American" identity during an interview (e.g., reserved) but shift to a *more* Hispanic (e.g., talking in Spanglish) way of being upon realizing the interviewer is also Hispanic. Drawing on West et al.'s (2018) framework, we propose integration as a third form of intentional self-regulation. However, we argue that integration naturally arises from a perceived conflict between one's cultural identity and distance within a particular cultural context. In response, individuals may engage in several strategies to either minimize (or accentuate) the differences and/or conflicts between their two cultural identities. Finally, we draw on both West et al.'s (2017) and Ward et al.'s (2018) conceptualization of *hybridizing* to frame the process by which individuals fuse two or more elements of their cultural identities. For example, Cuban Americans may often celebrate "Sangiving" (i.e., Thanksgiving) with traditionally Cuban cuisine. Similarly, reggaeton is a music genre that represents the fusion of hip hop, Latin American, and Caribbean music.

The degree to which individuals engage in *exploration, alternating, integration*, and *hybridizing* is informed not only by one's bicultural identity and by the degree of perceived compatibility and conflict between one's two cultural backgrounds, but also in negotiation with the cultural context. These bicultural negotiation processes therefore inform, and help to construct and revise, one's bicultural identity. At the same time, these negotiation processes provide opportunities for bicultural individuals to shape the way they interact with their environment, and in turn, their cultural environment itself.

Cultural-historical level of analysis

Consistent with an RDST framework, both the individual's bicultural identity and the process by which the individual negotiates with the cultural context are contextually regulated within the broader ecological systems within which the individual is nested (e.g., family, neighborhood, country, historical period). At the most immediate level, bicultural identity and the process by which individuals negotiate with their cultural context is informed by the affordances provided by the person's upbringing and family context. As has been noted in the cultural identity literature, caregivers provide youth with affordances toward the development of an integrated/hybridizing bicultural identity by playing an active role in socializing them towards the values and behaviors of their heritage cultural streams (Umaña-Taylor, Bhanot, & Shin, 2006).

Beyond the context of one's family, bicultural identity and the process by which individuals negotiate with their cultural context are also informed by the affordances provided by the community and society where they reside. Thus, the views and expectations of members in a given society, as they relate to multiculturalism, are important to examine (Berry, 2013). Indeed, biculturalism is facilitated by specific environmental conditions (Mistry & Wu, 2010). These include acceptance of both cultural systems among individuals within the immediate receiving context – for example, acceptance of both Hispanic and U.S. cultural behaviors, values, and ideals in cities such as Miami, Los Angeles, and New York City. As outlined by Berry (2013), multiculturalism represents the joint value placed on cultural diversity and equitable participation. It should be noted that multiculturalism may present in the immediate neighborhood (e.g., Little Havana in Florida), the receiving city (e.g., Miami), and/or at the broader level of the receiving society (e.g., the United States). Within context marked by multiculturalism, bicultural individuals are likely afforded more opportunities to engage in individual-level hybridity. As argued by Schwartz and Zamboanga (2008), biculturalism would not only be more prevalent but most adaptive in a bicultural environment such as large gateway cities (e.g., New York, Toronto, London) as it affords individuals with multiple cultural backgrounds the capacity to interact with people both from the larger society and from the heritage cultural community.

In contrast, more monocultural, culturally disjointed, or conflicted societies/areas would afford fewer opportunities for individual-level hybridity and might be more likely to encourage alternating biculturalism. For example, given the distinction between public and private acculturation proposed by Arends-Tóth and van de Vijver (2007), individuals in less multicultural societies would likely be expected to restrict their heritage-cultural activities to their homes and other private contexts. Regardless of the views a particular society has towards multiculturalism, discrimination and foreigner objectification (i.e., perceptions of being treated as a foreigner) can serve as barriers, challenges, and threats towards the consolidation of a bicultural identity (Schwartz et al., 2010). Finally, it should also be noted that, in highly multicultural societies, bicultural identity development likely applies to all members, not just minorities, as "majority-group members" are also faced with the need to adapt to more than one cultural stream – although majority-group members may lack the skills for negotiating multiple cultures and/or feel threatened by immigrants whom they perceive as either "diluting" or potentially "taking over" the national in-groups (Caldwell, 2008). For example, French people living in Paris likely must adapt to the presence of Muslim immigrants, migrant languages, and Islamic religious attire. At the same time, some French people may consider the presence of veiled women, for example, to be a threat to French national identity (van der Noll, 2010).

It is also important to acknowledge that development is historically contextualized. For example, comparing the histories of two southern states with large Hispanic populations illustrates the importance of historical context for understanding biculturalism in place and time. In the Texas border region, the relation between Mexicans (and, later, Mexican Americans) and the majority White American culture has undergone many changes over a long span of time that has included both periods of economic participation and leadership and periods of widespread land dispossession (Matovina, 1999). These changes occurred in response to a series of social and economic transformations (as well as changing sovereignties), first from Spanish-Mexican hacienda society to Anglo-Mexican ranching society in the 19th century, then to a segregated farm society in the first half of the 20th century, and finally to a pluralistic urban-industrial society by the second half of the 20th century (Montejano, 1987). Because of these changing relations, ethnic identity among Mexican-Americans in Texas is complex, often in flux, and often self-questioning (De León, 2003). In contrast, the influx of Cuban immigrants in the 1960s fundamentally changed Miami into a thriving metropolis (Portes & Stepick, 1993). Since then, not only have Cuban Americans held the majority of political and economic power, but the Hispanic population has diversified to include Central and South Americans (Aranda, Hughes, & Sabogal, 2014). As a result, Miami has come to represent a friendly context for Hispanic immigrants (Stepick, Grenier, Castro, & Dunn, 2003).

Future directions

The primary purpose of this chapter was to extend current models of biculturalism. In so doing, we drew on Erikson's (1968) conceptualization of identity development and RDST (Lerner & Overton, 2008) to contextualize biculturalism as a developmental process. Building on this relational model of bicultural systems, below we outline key directions for future research.

Development of measures capturing bicultural negotiation

Critical for understanding individuals' conscious contribution to the person ⟵⟶ context interplay is essential for developing assessments capable of tapping into individuals' capacity and predisposition to integrate, hybridize, and alternate. As a starting point, Ward et al. (2018) developed the multicultural identity styles scale (MISS), a self-report assessment that seeks to tap into strategies (i.e., hybridizing and alternating) that bicultural individuals activate to manage multiple cultural identities. Although the MISS has been found to be psychometrically valid, the current items vary in the extent to which they capture the *process* involved in managing cultural identities. Additionally, the MISS does not capture the process by which individuals seek to integrate two cultural streams. As previously noted, individuals may engage in several strategies to either minimize (or accentuate) the differences and/or conflicts between their two cultural identities. Additional items are needed to tap into these dimensions and strategies. Although quantitative methodology serves as an important step towards understanding biculturalism, it is also important to emphasize the need for phenomenological approaches given the complicated, multi-faceted, and relational nature of identity (Josselson & Flum, 2015). Thus, qualitative methodology is necessary to capture the "richness" and "complexity" associated with how individuals develop a bicultural identity and navigate their cultural context. In sum, the development of various methods for assessing individuals' engagement in bicultural negotiation processes is fundamental for understanding how these processes impact the development of a bicultural identity and navigating one's context and, as elaborated in our next point, how these processes change and evolve over time.

Understanding the development of bicultural negotiations

Within the ethnic/racial identity literature, there has been a growing recognition of the need to understand the interface of ethnic/racial identity with developmental and contextual issues across the life span and to identify key developmental milestones in cultural identity development

(Umaña-Taylor et al., 2014). Consistently, and within the scope of our relational model of bicultural systems, it is critical to understand how biculturalism and bicultural negotiation processes map onto developmental and contextual issues across the life span. Indeed, the developmental trajectories of these bicultural negotiation processes are likely to vary with age. Whereas alternating may emerge earlier in development as children are tasked with activating relevant identities and behavioral repertoires in response to one's immediate social environment (Spiegler & Leyendecker, 2017), exploration, integration, and hybridizing are likely to be developmentally salient in adolescence as advances in cognitive and socioemotional development enable abstract and counterfactual thinking skills and interpretive and meaning-making capacities necessary to consider identity issues (Cross & Cross, 2008).

The importance of multi-site research

The incorporation of RDST provides further impetus for multi-site research. As has been highlighted in the acculturation literature, many studies have made the often-implicit assumption that each context of reception is equally welcoming and inviting (Schwartz et al., 2010). However, immigration and acculturation are often conceptualized as the interaction between a specific immigrant group and the context in which that group is received (Schwartz, Vignoles, Brown, & Zagefka, 2014). Given the variability in the opportunity structure, degree of openness, hostility, and acceptance across various receiving contexts (both within and across countries), multi-site research is essential for understanding the affordances that various contexts provide individuals to engage in bicultural negotiation processes and develop a consolidated bicultural identity.

Affordances provided by familial context

As previously noted, bicultural identity and the process through which individuals negotiate with their cultural context is informed by the affordances provided by their own upbringing. Indeed, research in the past decade has focused on clarifying the ways in which caregivers encourage children to gravitate toward specific aspects of their cultural heritage and to avoid aspects of the receiving cultural context (Portes & Rumbaut, 2014). Umaña-Taylor et al. (2006) have referred to this phenomenon as *familial ethnic socialization*. Studies have found that the presence of heritage-cultural symbols increases the likelihood that children and adolescents will retain or adopt their heritage culture (Umaña-Taylor et al., 2006). Regarding acquisition of U.S. culture, there is evidence that caregivers' socialization attempts are less effective in shaping youths' adoption of it (Schwartz et al., 2007). Peers, school, and media may play a greater role in shaping U.S. culture acquisition. Additionally, although scholars have emphasized the role of adolescents in transmitting U.S. values and culture (Padilla, 2006), studies have yet to empirically examine whether adolescents have an impact on their caregivers' acquisition/retention of U.S. and heritage cultures. Thus, a critical step for future research is to conceptualize the family as a holistic and constantly evolving system – recognizing that each member within the family system are not only likely engaging in bicultural negotiation processes but are actively working to influence each other's identity.

Conclusion

The relational model of bicultural systems model we put forth in the current chapter not only sought to unify current models of biculturalism but contextualize biculturalism within RDST's metatheoretical discourse (Overton, 2015), providing a perspective by which we can understand and operationalize bicultural identity development. Within our framework, at the individual level of analysis, we proposed four processes that represent individuals' conscious contributions to the (person ⟵⟶ context): exploration, integration, hybridizing, and alternating. Additionally, at the broader cultural-historical level of analysis, we emphasize the affordances that family, context of reception, and the historical era exert on the development of one's bicultural identity. Finally, we concluded with a few avenues of future directions informed by our proposed relational model of bicultural systems. As navigating multiple cultural streams will become increasingly prominent in countries around the world, it will become increasingly critical for researchers to contextualize the study of biculturalism within the framework of a larger developmental model. In doing so, we may further understand the mechanisms underlying bicultural identity development. We hope our chapter serves as an important stepping stone towards that endeavor.

References

Aranda, E., Hughes, S., & Sabogal, E. (2014). *Making a life in multiethnic Miami: Immigration and the rise of a global city*. Boulder, CO: Lynne Rienner.

Arends-Tóth, J., & van de Vijver, F. J. R. (2007). Acculturation attitudes: A comparison of measurement methods. *Journal of Applied Social Psychology*, 37, 1462–1488.

Benet-Martínez, V., & Haritatos, J. (2005). Bicultural identity integration (BII): Components and psycho- social antecedents. *Journal of Personality*, 73, 1015–1050.

Benet-Martínez, V., Leu, J., Lee, F., & Morris, M. W. (2002). Negotiating biculturalism: Cultural frame switching in biculturals with oppositional versus compatible cultural identities. *Journal of Cross-Cultural Psychology*, 33, 492–516.

Berry, J. W. (1980). Acculturation as varieties of adaptation. In A. M. Padilla (Ed.), *Acculturation: Theory, models, and some new findings* (pp. 9–25). Boulder, CO: Westview.
Berry, J. W. (2013). Research on multiculturalism in Canada. *International Journal of Intercultural Relations*, 37, 663–675.
Brandtstädter, J. (2006). Action perspectives on human development. In W. Damon & R. M. Lerner (Eds.), *Handbook of child psychology. Vol. 1: Theoretical models of human development* (6th ed., pp. 516–568). Hoboken, NJ: Wiley.
Caldwell, C. (2008). *Reflections on the revolution in Europe: Immigration, Islam, and the West*. New York, NY: Doubleday.
Colby, S. L., & Ortman, J. M. (2015). *Projections of the size and composition of the U.S. population: 2014 to 2060, current population reports*, P25–1143. Washington, DC: Census Bureau.
Cross, W. E., Jr., & Cross, T. B. (2008). Theory, research, and models. In S. M. Quintana & C. McKown (Eds.), *Handbook of race, racism, and the developing child* (pp. 154–181). Hoboken, NJ: Wiley.
De León, A. (2003). Whither Tejano history: Origins, development, and status. *The Southwestern Historical Quarterly*, 106, 349–364.
Doucerain, M., Dere, J., & Ryder, A. G. (2013). Travels in hyper-diversity: Multiculturalism and the con- textual assessment of acculturation. *International Journal of Intercultural Relations*, 37, 686–699.
Eichas, K., Meca, A., Montgomery, M. J., & Kurtines, W. M. (2015). Identity and positive youth development: Advances in developmental intervention science. In K. McLean & M. Syed (Eds.), *The Oxford handbook of identity development* (pp. 337–354). Oxford, UK: Oxford University Press.
Erikson, E. H. (1968). *Identity: Youth and crisis*. New York, NY: Norton.
Gestsdóttir, S., & Lerner, R. M. (2008). Positive development in adolescence: The development and role of intentional self-regulation. *Human Development*, 51, 202–224.
Hong, Y.-Y., Morris, M. W., Chiu, C., & Benet-Martínez, V. (2000). Multicultural minds: A dynamic constructivist approach to culture and cognition. *American Psychologist*, 55, 709–720.
Huynh, Q.-L., Nguyen, A.-M. T. D., & Benet-Martínez, V. (2011). Bicultural identity integration. In S. J. Schwartz, K. Luyckx, & V. L. Vignoles (Eds.), *Handbook of identity theory and research* (pp. 827–843). New York, NY: Springer.
Jensen, L. A., Arnett, J. J., & MacKenzie, J. (2011). Globalization and cultural identity. In S. J. Schwartz, K. Luyckx, & V. L. Vignoles (Eds.), *Handbook of identity theory and research* (pp. 285–301). New York, NY: Springer.
Josselson, R. (1994). The theory of identity development and the question of intervention: An introduction. In S. L. Archer (Ed.), *Sage focus editions, Vol. 169. Interventions for adolescent identity development* (pp. 12–25). Thousand Oaks, CA: Sage Publications, Inc.
Josselson, R., & Flum, H. (2015). Identity status: On refinding the people. In K. C. McLean & M. Syed (Eds.), *Oxford library of psychology. The Oxford handbook of identity development* (pp. 132–146). New York, NY: Oxford University Press.
Lerner, R. M., & Overton, W. F. (2008). Exemplifying the integrations of the relational developmental system: Synthesizing theory, research, and application to promote positive development and social justice. *Journal of Adolescent Research*, 23, 245–255.

Matovina, T. M. (1999). *Tejano Legacy: Rancheros and Settlers in South Texas, 1734–1900.* Hispanic American Historical Review 79, 539–541.

Mistry, J., & Wu, J. (2010). Navigating cultural worlds and negotiating identities: A conceptual model. *Human Development*, 53, 5–25.

Montejano, D. (1987). *Anglos and Mexicans in the making of Texas, 1836–1986.* Austin, TX: University of Texas Press.

Nguyen, A. M. D., & Benet-Martínez, V. (2013). Biculturalism and adjustment: A meta-analysis. *Journal of Cross-Cultural Psychology*, 44, 122–159.

Noels, K. A., & Clément, R. (2015). Situational variations in ethnic identity across immigration generations: Implications for acculturative change and cross-cultural adaptation. *International Journal of Psychology*, 50, 451–462.

Overton, W. F. (2015). Processes, relations, and relational-developmental-systems. In R. M. Lerner, W. F. Overton, & P. C. M. Molenaar (Eds.), *Theory and method. Volume 1 of the Handbook of child psychology and developmental science* (7th ed., pp. 9–62). Hoboken, NJ: Wiley.

Padilla, A. M. (2006). Bicultural social development. *Hispanic Journal of Behavioral Sciences*, 28, 467–497.

Portes, A., & Rumbaut, R. (2014). *Immigrant America: A portrait.* Oakland, CA: University of California Press.

Portes, A., & Stepick, A. (1993). *City of edge: The transformation of Miami.* Oakland, CA: University of California Press.

Schwartz, S. J., Birman, D., Benet-Martínez, V., & Unger, J. (2017). Biculturalism: Negotiating multiple cultural streams. In S. J. Schwartz & J. Unger (Eds.), *The Oxford handbook of acculturation and health.* (pp. 29–47). Oxford, UK: Oxford University Press.

Schwartz, S. J., Meca, A., Ward, A., Szabo, A., Benet-Martínez, V., Lorenzo-Blanco, E. I., … Zamboanga, B. L. (2019). Biculturalism dynamics: A daily diary study of bicultural identity and psychosocial functioning. *Journal of Applied Developmental Psychology*, 62, 26–37.

Schwartz, S. J., Unger, J. B., Zamboanga, B. L., & Szapocznik, J. (2010). Rethinking the concept of acculturation: Implications for theory and research. *American Psychologist*, 65, 237–251.

Schwartz, S. J., Vignoles, V. L., Brown, R., & Zagefka, H. (2014). The identity dynamics of acculturation and multiculturalism: Situating acculturation in context. In V. Benet-Martínez & Y.-Y. Hong (Eds.), *Oxford library of psychology. The Oxford handbook of multicultural identity* (pp. 57–93). New York, NY: Oxford University Press.

Schwartz, S. J., & Zamboanga, B. L. (2008). Testing Berry's model of acculturation: A confirmatory latent class approach. *Cultural Diversity and Ethnic Minority Psychology*, 14, 275–285.

Schwartz, S. J., Zamboanga, B. L., Rodriguez, L., & Wang, S. C. (2007). The structure of cultural identity in an ethnically diverse sample of emerging adults. *Basic and Applied Social Psychology*, 29, 159–173. doi: 10.1080/01973530701332229

Spiegler, O., & Leyendecker, B. (2017). Balanced cultural identities promote cognitive flexibility among immigrant children. *Frontiers in Psychology*, 8, 1579.

Stepick, A., Grenier, G., Castro, M., & Dunn, M. (2003). *This land is our land: Immigrants and power in Miami.* Berkeley, CA: University of California Press.

Syed, M., Walker, L. H. M., Lee, R. M., Umaña-Taylor, A. J., Zamboanga, B. L., Schwartz, S. J., ... Huynh, Q. L. (2013). A two-factor model of ethnic identity exploration: Implications for identity coherence and well-being. *Cultural Diversity and Ethnic Minority Psychology, 19*, 143–154.

Tadmor, C. T., & Tetlock, P. E. (2006). Biculturalism: A model of the effects of second-culture exposure on acculturation and integrative complexity. *Journal of Cross-Cultural Psychology, 37*, 173–190.

Tadmor, C. T., Tetlock, P. E., & Peng, K. (2009). Acculturation strategies and integrative complexity: The cognitive implications of biculturalism. *Journal of Cross-Cultural Psychology, 40*, 105–139.

Umaña-Taylor, A. J., Bhanot, R., & Shin, N. (2006). Ethnic identity formation during adolescence: The critical role of families. *Journal of Families, 27*, 390–414.

Umaña-Taylor, A. J., Quintana, S. M., Lee, R. M., Cross, W. E., Rivas-Drake, D., & Schwartz, S. J.; Study Group on Ethnic and Racial Identity in the 21st Century. (2014). Ethnic and racial identity revisited: An integrated conceptualization. *Child Development, 85*, 21–39.

United Nations, Department of Economic and Social Affairs, Population Division (2017). International Migration Report 2017: Highlights(ST/ESA/SER.A/404).

van der Noll, J. (2010). Public support for a ban on headscarves: A cross-national perspective. *International Journal of Conflict and Violence, 4*, 191–204.

Ward, C., Tseung-Wong, C. N., Szabo, A., Qumeseya, T., & Bhowon, U. (2018). Hybrid and alternating identity styles as strategies for managing multicultural identities. *Journal of Cross-Cultural Psychology, 49*, 1402–1436.

West, A. L., Zhang, R., Yampolsky, M., & Sasaki, J. Y. (2017). More than the sum of its parts: A transformative theory of biculturalism. *Journal of Cross-Cultural Psychology, 48*, 963–990.

Yampolsky, M. A., Amiot, C. E., & de la Sablonnière, R. (2016). The Multicultural Identity Integration Scale (MULTIIS): Developing a comprehensive measure for configuring one's multiple cultural identities within the self. *Cultural Diversity & Ethnic Minority Psychology, 22*, 166–184.

Zou, X., Morris, M. W., & Benet-Martínez, V. (2008). Identity motives and cultural priming: Cultural (dis)identification in assimilative and contrastive responses. *Journal of Experimental Social Psychology, 44*, 1151–1159.

Chapter 4

Polyculturalism

Current evidence, future directions, and implementation possibilities for diverse youth

Lisa Rosenthal, MaryBeth Apriceno, and Sheri R. Levy

With increasing diversity along with continued prejudice and intergroup conflict both within and across many societies, understanding how people conceptualize and maneuver through diverse environments is critical. For many decades, schools have been thought of as environments that could be structured and contain messages to foster positive intergroup relations among students and thereby society more broadly (e.g., Allport, 1954). Despite continued segregation, in educational settings diverse youth often have contact with each other, which can foster positive intergroup attitudes and behaviors in addition to broader benefits to students, such as greater empathy and feelings of safety at school (e.g., Aboud & Spears Brown, 2013; Juvonen, Kogachi, & Graham, 2017; Killen & Smetana, 2015; Pettigrew & Tropp, 2006). Accordingly, schools possess the opportunity to implement programming, policies, and curricula that communicate how to understand and respond to diversity to promote positive intergroup interactions among their students (e.g., Aboud et al., 2012; Banks, 2013; Banks & Banks, 2013; Zirkel, 2008). Yet, schools vary greatly in the extent to which they aim to and successfully do so (e.g., Hajisoteriou, Karousiou, & Angelides, 2017; Levy, Shin, Lytle, & Rosenthal, 2017; Zirkel, 2008), and students themselves vary in the extent to which they want and take advantage of opportunities for positive intergroup contact with their peers (e.g., Derman-Sparks & Ramsey, 2011; Killen, Mulvey, & Hitti, 2013; Sidanius, Levin, Van Laar, & Sears, 2010).

Polyculturalism – a concept from the discipline of history (Kelley, 1999; Prashad, 2001, 2003) – has recently been studied from a psychological perspective as an individual difference belief, namely the extent to which individuals believe that diverse groups have interacted and exchanged with each other, thus influencing each other's cultures throughout history (Rosenthal & Levy, 2010, 2013). Although polyculturalism has thus far not been studied with youth under the age of 18, growing correlational, longitudinal, and experimental evidence from around the world with adults suggests polyculturalism has important implications for understanding youth's experiences with diversity, including specifically in schools (e.g., Bernardo et al., 2016; Cho, Morris, & Dow, 2018; Healy, Thomas, & Pedersen, 2017; Rosenthal & Levy, 2016; Rosenthal, Levy, London, & Lewis, 2016; Rosenthal, Ramírez, Levy, & Bernardo, 2019; Salanga & Bernardo, 2017). In this chapter, we review existing research on polyculturalism, identify needed future research on polyculturalism, and discuss possibilities for implementation of polyculturalism in school programming, policies, and curricula to support positive intergroup interactions among diverse youth.

Diverse youth in educational settings

Demographic shifts and immigration have increased the diversity of populations in many parts of the world (Vertovec, 2007). In the U.S.A., there have been increases in the percentages of people of color, who are expected to account for 56 percent of the U.S. population by 2060 (Bryant, Triplett, Watson, & Lewis, 2017). Students of color represent an increasing proportion of school-age Americans, making up 50 percent of this age group in the U.S.A. in 2014 (U.S. Census Bureau, 2015). Accordingly, this demographic shift is particularly pronounced in public schools (Bryant et al., 2017). By 2060, children of color are expected to account for 64 percent of school-aged children in the U.S.A. (U.S. Census Bureau, 2015). Despite much continued segregation across the U.S.A., many schools are becoming more integrated (Zirkel, 2008), leading to increasingly diverse educational settings. Similar patterns are projected across Europe, including Austria, Denmark, Germany, Greece, the Netherlands, Norway, Sweden, Switzerland, and the U.K. (Coleman, 2010).

Diverse elementary and middle schools provide for more regular contact among children of different racial and ethnic backgrounds during adolescence, when peers play a particularly central role in students' development (Erikson, 1968). Children begin making social comparisons as early as age three (e.g., Killen & Smetana, 2015) and develop prejudicial attitudes during childhood and adolescence along with the development of social and cognitive skills, including moral reasoning and understanding of group norms (e.g., Raabe & Beelmann, 2011; Rutland & Killen, 2015). Prejudice in children often manifests as discrimination in the form of social exclusion (Brenick & Killen, 2013), and these attitudes and behaviors likely form the basis of similar attitudes and behaviors into adulthood (Abrams & Killen, 2014). Further, because of the tendency of people to avoid information disconfirming prejudiced attitudes (Aboud et al., 2012), efforts to reduce prejudice during childhood and adolescence may be more effective than later in adulthood.

Meanwhile, schools are the most significant non-familial setting for children (Duncan & Raudenbush, 1999). In diverse school environments, children often interact with peers of their own as well as different racial/ethnic backgrounds. Intergroup contact in which individuals have equal status and common goals and their interactions are sanctioned by a mutually respected authority can reduce prejudice and improve intergroup dynamics (e.g., Allport, 1954; Pettigrew & Tropp, 2006; Tropp & Prenovost, 2008). Accordingly, diverse educational environments are uniquely poised to promote positive, proactive, intergroup interactions by providing youth opportunities for intergroup contact along with messaging about how to understand and respond to diversity (e.g., Aboud et al., 2012; Banks, 2013; Banks & Banks, 2013; Zirkel, 2008). Students in diverse school settings show more empathy, tolerance, and perspective taking (Killen & Smetana, 2015). Among Dutch fourth-grade students, more cooperative contact in class with students from different backgrounds (e.g., Moroccan, Surinamese, Turkish) was associated with greater tolerance for Muslim practices (Gieling, Thijs, & Verkuyten, 2014). In a study of over 4000 students across 26 middle schools in California, students in more ethnically and racially diverse classroom settings (averaged across students' math, English, science, and social studies classes) reported feeling safer and less lonely at school, as well as being victimized less often (Juvonen et al., 2017). In this study, students in more diverse classroom settings also reported formation and maintenance of more cross-ethnic friendships (Graham, 2018). A longitudinal study of German middle schools also found students in classrooms that promoted equality, inclusion, and cultural pluralism showed more psychological well-being and fewer behavioral problems (Schachner, Van de Vijver, Noack, & Eckstein, 2016).

Yet, research on what philosophies and programs schools espouse to address diversity is scarce. It is assumed that many schools take a colorblind approach, ignoring or avoiding discussion of diversity, or a multicultural approach, highlighting important group differences and celebrating groups' positive contributions to society (e.g., Levy et al., 2017; Rosenthal & Levy, 2010). In response to growing diversity, multiculturalism has been implemented in educational settings from pre-school through high school and in various countries, including the Netherlands and the U.S.A. (e.g., Banks, 2013; Banks & Banks, 2013; Zirkel, 2008). However, schools rarely implement the full multicultural education model as proposed by Banks and Banks (2013; see Zirkel, 2008). Instead, in practice parts of the multicultural approach are often employed as stand-alone units, for example celebrations of Black History Month or the Chinese New Year, which may increase stereotyping and prejudice by placing too much focus on group differences (e.g., Levy et al., 2017; Rosenthal & Levy, 2010). In schools where both colorblind and multicultural approaches are adopted in part, students report receiving conflicting messages (Hajisoteriou et al., 2017).

In school environments where diversity is not addressed, students do not always view it favorably or utilize opportunities for diverse contacts on their own. Diversity unaccompanied by messages to help frame how to understand and react to that diversity can increase bias, prejudice, and discriminatory beliefs toward out-group members (Killen & Smetana, 2009). Students report being anxious about transitioning to new schools with high levels of racial and ethnic diversity (Benner & Graham, 2009). And, at the start of middle school, students report less anxiety when interacting with racial and ethnic in-group members than with out-group members (Douglass, Yip, & Shelton, 2014). Further, children who experience prejudice are at risk of negative psychological and social consequences, including anxiety, depression, social withdrawal, and disengagement (Rubin, Bukowski, & Parker, 2006; Rutland & Killen, 2015). Taken together, it is important to understand what factors contribute to how youth negotiate their diverse environments as well as what approaches can be implemented by schools to foster positive intergroup dynamics among their students. Although polyculturalism has not been studied in educational settings among youth under the age of 18, research suggests this may be one such factor and approach that can contribute to positive intergroup dynamics among diverse youth.

Existing research on polyculturalism

The concept of polyculturalism originated in the field of history, with the work of Robin D. G. Kelley and Vijay Prashad. Kelley (1999), writing about his own and his family's experiences as well as more broadly about Black Americans, asserted that "our cultural lines of descent are about as mixed up as a pot of gumbo ... What we know as 'black culture' has always been fluid, hybrid, and polycultural." Prashad (2001) wrote *Everybody Was Kung Fu Fighting: Afro-Asian Connections and the Myth of Cultural Purity*, outlining evidence of the many different cultural influences that shaped kung fu in addition to the diverse groups of people who were influenced by it over time. Polyculturalism involves attending to cross-cultural influences both currently and historically, including conceptualizing cultures as fluid and constantly changing due to those influences. In this original conception, polyculturalism was explicitly distinguished from multiculturalism. Kelley (1999) explained his preference for the term *polycultural* over the term *multicultural* because "the latter often implies that cultures are fixed, discrete entities that exist side by side – a kind of zoological approach to culture." Prashad (2003) explained that his interest in kung fu was in its potential to "help us move from a limited multicultural framework into an antiracist, polycultural one" because a multicultural framework leads us "to pretend that our histories are not already overlapping, that the borders of each of our cultures are not porous" (p. 52). This more dynamic understanding of culture has since been adopted in other research in different disciplines, such as documenting multiple cultural influences on medical practices in South Africa (Flint, 2006) and analyzing YouTube videos posted by Black American fans of K-pop music (Oh, 2017). This original work also inspired us to develop a program of research on polyculturalism in psychology (Rosenthal & Levy, 2010, 2013).

From a psychological perspective, polyculturalism has been conceptualized as both an approach to addressing diversity and an individual difference belief focused on the ways that different racial and ethnic groups around the world have always interacted with, learned from, and influenced each other's cultures (Rosenthal & Levy, 2010, 2013). As an approach, polyculturalism can be adopted and implemented by institutions and societies to address diversity and intergroup relations, such as through policies and content/messaging (e.g., in educational curricula) that focus on cross-cultural influences and connections, which can thereby affect intergroup relations in societies broadly and in specific contexts implementing the approach. Some have suggested that interculturalism programs/policies that exist in some countries, which encourage cross-cultural contact, dialogue, and collaboration, reflect polyculturalism (Morris, Chiu, & Liu, 2015). In addition to being an approach, polyculturalism is also conceptualized as an individual difference belief, as individuals agree to varying extents that different cultural groups influence and are connected to each other, which also has implications for intergroup attitudes and dynamics. Psychological research on polyculturalism began with correlational studies of undergraduates and community adults in the U.S.A., using a measure of endorsement of polyculturalism (e.g., "Different racial, ethnic, and cultural groups influence each other") to explore associations of individual differences in this belief with intergroup attitudes and intentions (Rosenthal & Levy, 2012). These initial studies found that people in the U.S.A. do tend to endorse polyculturalism, on average scoring on the "Agree" side of the response scale (Rosenthal & Levy, 2012). Further, the more people endorse polyculturalism, the more positive toward and comfortable with diversity they feel, the more they support social equality, the more they are willing to interact with people from different backgrounds, and the more they support liberal/progressive policies related to immigration and affirmative action; and, these findings were consistent across participants from diverse racial/ethnic groups, including Asian, Black, Latinx, and white Americans (Rosenthal & Levy, 2012).

Psychological research on polyculturalism has since expanded, with growing correlational, longitudinal, and experimental evidence of its implications for a range of intergroup attitudes around the world. In the U.S.A., greater endorsement of polyculturalism has been associated with more positive attitudes and less intergroup anxiety toward greater willingness to interact with, and greater endorsement of policies that support (and do not discriminate against), Muslim Americans (Rosenthal, Levy, Katser, & Bazile, 2015). Across samples from Colombia, the Philippines, and the

U.S.A., greater endorsement of polyculturalism has been associated with more positive attitudes toward people from other countries and greater intentions to become friends with people immigrating from a range of different countries (e.g., Afghanistan, Ecuador, England, North Korea, Spain, Venezuela) to one's own country (Bernardo, Rosenthal, & Levy, 2013; Rosenthal et al., 2019). In Australia, endorsement of polyculturalism has been associated with greater support for Harmony Day, which celebrates diverse cultures, and greater disapproval of discrimination toward a Muslim woman (Pedersen, Paradies, & Barndon, 2015). Also in Australia, endorsement of polyculturalism has been associated with less prejudice toward refugees, and this association was mediated by lower moral exclusion of refugees and greater quality of contact with refugees (Healy et al., 2017). Across samples from Australia and China, endorsement of polyculturalism has been found to be associated with greater cultural intelligence (i.e., effectiveness at interacting with people from diverse cultures) as well as to partially explain country-level differences in cultural intelligence (Bernardo & Presbitero, 2017). In the U.S.A., both correlationally and experimentally polyculturalism has been found to be associated with greater preference for experiences involving cultural mixing, and this association was mediated by less importance placed on cultural purity (i.e., less concern over "contamination" of cultures; Cho, Morris, Slepian, & Tadmor, 2017). In the U.S.A., polyculturalism has also been found correlationally and experimentally to be associated with more positive evaluations of a Chinese business person visiting the U.S.A. and behaving in ways that accommodate U.S. culture (e.g., using a handshake rather than a bow and an English rather than a Chinese name; Cho et al., 2018). Taken together, these findings support that across samples from multiple continents – Asia, Australia, North America, and South America – polyculturalism has positive implications for intergroup attitudes and behaviors, including attitudes and behavioral intentions toward people from diverse backgrounds, immigrants and refugees, diversity-related policies, and cultural exchange. Polyculturalism, then, likely holds promise for promoting positive intergroup relations in a range of settings.

There has also been some research on polyculturalism specifically focused on dynamics in educational settings. Among Filipino university students, endorsement of polyculturalism has been associated with greater cognitive empathy toward a Filipino professor faced with a Korean student who is struggling on a course due to language difficulties (Salanga & Bernardo, 2017). Among undergraduates at a diverse university in the U.S.A., greater endorsement of polyculturalism before the start of college was found to prospectively predict increases in positive intergroup contact and friendships across the first to second years of college in a longitudinal study (Rosenthal & Levy, 2016). This suggests polyculturalism has implications among young adults for intergroup behaviors and relationship formation in educational settings. Also among undergraduates at diverse universities and colleges in the U.S.A., endorsement of polyculturalism has been associated with greater sense of belonging, academic self-efficacy, and less use of alcohol to cope with intergroup anxiety, all through the mechanism of lower intergroup anxiety in cross-sectional and longitudinal studies (Rosenthal et al., 2016). Thus, polyculturalism may have positive implications even for well-being among students in diverse educational settings because it helps them to feel more comfortable interacting with people from different backgrounds.

In addition to having implications for racial, ethnic, and cultural diversity, growing evidence supports that polyculturalism has implications for other intergroup attitudes, particularly related to gender and sexual orientation diversity. In the U.S.A., greater endorsement of polyculturalism has been associated with less sexism and greater support for feminism and women's rights cross-sectionally and longitudinally, and those associations were mediated by greater openness to criticizing one's own culture (Rosenthal, Levy, & Militano, 2014). Across Australia, the Philippines, and the U.S.A., greater endorsement of polyculturalism has been associated with less sexual prejudice, including more positive attitudes toward gay, lesbian, bisexual, transgender, and intersex individuals; these associations were mediated by lower moral exclusion and greater quality of contact in Australia and by greater openness to criticizing one's own culture in the U.S.A. (Bernardo, 2013; Healy et al., 2017; Rosenthal, Levy, & Moss, 2012). Thus, polyculturalism potentially has positive implications for a wide range of intergroup attitudes relevant to multiple forms of diversity and social justice issues.

Across the psychological research on polyculturalism reviewed, findings support that polyculturalism is distinct from and has unique implications when accounting for other diversity-related approaches or beliefs as well as other potentially confounding predictors of intergroup attitudes. In the first studies on polyculturalism in psychology, a factor analysis and multiple regression analyses supported that polyculturalism is distinct from and predicts unique variance in intergroup attitudes while accounting for multiculturalism, colorblindness, and assimilation (Rosenthal & Levy, 2012). Specifically, polyculturalism focuses on cross-cultural influences and connections while still acknowledging the importance of people's cultural identities. Thus, polyculturalism does not focus on highlighting cultural differences and distinctions as multiculturalism does. Polyculturalism also does not suggest ignoring race/ethnicity as colorblindness does. And, polyculturalism does not suggest immigrants or nondominant racial/ethnic groups must adopt the dominant culture as assimilation does. Polyculturalism has been further distinguished from multiculturalism and colorblindness through factor analysis, multiple regression analysis, and experimental manipulation among other samples from Australia, China, Hong Kong, Indonesia, Macau, Malaysia, the Philippines, and the U.S.A. (Bernardo &

Presbitero, 2017; Bernardo et al., 2016; Cho et al., 2017, 2018; Rosenthal & Levy, 2016; Rosenthal et al., 2012, 2014, 2016; Salanga & Bernardo, 2017).

Evidence also supports that polyculturalism explains unique variance in intergroup attitudes among samples from Australia, China, Colombia, the Philippines, and the U.S.A. when accounting for the contributions of other important predictors and potentially confounding variables, including sociodemographic characteristics (age, education, gender, nativity, race/ethnicity, social class), academic achievement, conservatism/liberalism, egalitarianism, essentialism, ethnic identification, gender identification, general social anxiety, mood, national identification, self-esteem, Protestant work ethic, social dominance orientation, and right-wing authoritarianism (Bernardo, 2013; Bernardo et al., 2013; Cho et al., 2017, 2018; Rosenthal & Levy, 2016; Rosenthal et al., 2012, 2014, 2015, 2016, 2019; Salanga & Bernardo, 2017). Taken together, polyculturalism seems to make a unique contribution to intergroup relations. While evidence supports polyculturalism is a unique belief, it has also been found to correlate positively with some measures of multiculturalism in Australia, China, Hong Kong, Indonesia, Macau, Malaysia, the Philippines, and the U.S.A. (Bernardo & Presbitero, 2017; Bernardo et al., 2016; Cho et al., 2017, 2018; Pedersen et al., 2015; Rosenthal & Levy, 2012, 2016; Rosenthal et al., 2012, 2016; Salanga & Bernardo, 2017), as well as more rarely with some measures of colorblindness in Australia and the U.S.A. (Pedersen et al., 2015; Rosenthal & Levy, 2012). Thus, we have suggested that polyculturalism is not necessarily in conflict with and instead can be combined with other approaches and beliefs for intervention (Rosenthal & Levy, 2010).

Needed future research on and possible implementation of polyculturalism

Although the growing body of research on polyculturalism supports its potential to promote positive intergroup relations, no work to date has explored endorsement and the consequences of polyculturalism among youth younger than undergraduate students, which is an important limitation particularly for the purposes of this book. Future research is needed to test implications of this belief for youth of different ages and in different educational settings across different parts of the world. Research with youth could help to identify when and from what sources young people are exposed to and begin to endorse polyculturalism, including the role of educational settings in those processes. As examples, youth who have had more direct or indirect contact with culturally diverse others, such as through attending schools with diverse student bodies, living in neighborhoods with diverse neighbors, having family or friends of diverse backgrounds, consuming media depicting diverse individuals, and enjoying art, music, or other cultural products from diverse groups might endorse polyculturalism more and at younger ages than youth who have had less of that contact. Positive and negative messages that youth have been exposed to while growing up about people from different backgrounds and cross-cultural contact from various sources might also impact their endorsement or openness to polyculturalism, including messages from family, friends, teachers, school curricula and programming, media, community leaders, and political leaders. Current events and the political and economic climates in which youth grow up may also influence endorsement of and reactions to polyculturalism. All of these and other potential influences on youth's endorsement of polyculturalism would be fruitful to explore in future research to better understand polyculturalism from a developmental perspective. It will be particularly important for research to test whether endorsement of polyculturalism has the same positive consequences for young people's intergroup attitudes and behaviors that have been found for adults, including for positive intergroup interactions and friendships, or whether these consequences fluctuate at different developmental stages.

More research is also needed to test the potential for polyculturalism interventions, programs, and educational policies to improve intergroup relations, well-being, and academic outcomes among youth. Recent longitudinal and experimental evidence supports that polyculturalism may lead to improved intergroup attitudes and behaviors (e.g., Cho et al., 2017, 2018; Rosenthal & Levy, 2016), but what the consequences are for intergroup relations over time need attention. Future research should also examine how to increase endorsement of polyculturalism in more enduring ways than through a brief priming manipulation. This future work, ideally conducted in different types of educational settings in different parts of the world, can help to inform implementation of polyculturalism through interventions, programs, and policies in schools and other settings relevant to diverse youth. It is also important for future research to continue exploring mechanisms involved in polyculturalism's links to positive intergroup relations, particularly when thinking from a developmental perspective, to understand processes of change over time that can inform intervention. Future research in all of these areas with youth (in addition to other age groups) should include the use of multiple methodologies. More longitudinal and experimental work is needed, and no published work to date has used qualitative methods to explore polyculturalism, which could contribute uniquely to our understanding of this approach/belief system. Further, community-based participatory methods might engage youth in ways that would be particularly informative for intervention development and assessment.

While more research is needed, evidence to date supports that polyculturalism might be utilized to promote positive intergroup relations, well-being, and academic success for youth from different backgrounds in increasingly diverse settings around the world. Polyculturalism can be used as a guiding framework for school policies aimed at promoting positive intergroup interactions among students and staff, with a wide range of applications from choices about school food (e.g., offering fusion foods) to curricula (e.g., Rosenthal & Levy, 2016; Rosenthal et al., 2016). Polyculturalism can be infused in standard curricula, highlighting different cultural influences on concepts and events being learned about across subject areas, such as math, science, language, and history. Polyculturalism can also be implemented in extra-curricular programming and interventions, having students explore examples of cross-cultural influences historically and currently, including in the creation and evolution of things they particularly enjoy and benefit from, such as music and other forms of art.

We do not suggest that polyculturalism alone is all that is needed to foster positive intergroup relations among youth or that polyculturalism should completely replace other diversity approaches in educational settings, but rather that it may be an important ingredient that can be combined with others to have greater positive impact (e.g., Rosenthal & Levy, 2010). Fostering polyculturalism in schools may help to strengthen and address weaknesses of other existing approaches and intervention models, such as multiculturalism, which has demonstrated positive consequences (e.g., Banks, 2013; Richeson & Nussbaum, 2004; Stephan, Renfro, & Stephan, 2004; Verkuyten, 2009) but has also been critiqued for emphasizing group differences and boundaries as well as promoting stereotyping (e.g., Bigler, 1999; Kelley, 1999; Prashad, 2001; Ryan, Casas, & Thompson, 2010; Wittig & Molina, 2000). By combining polycultural and multicultural messaging, students may be able to benefit from positive aspects of multiculturalism (e.g., promoting appreciation for cultural differences and important contributions of diverse groups) while avoiding its negative aspects because of polyculturalism simultaneously promoting awareness of cross-cultural influences and the dynamic, changing nature of cultures. For example, multicultural programming in schools tends to focus on celebrating one broad racial/ethnic group and that group's distinct experiences, culture, and contributions at a particular time, such as schools celebrating Hispanic Heritage Month in the U.S.A. by highlighting achievements of Hispanic/Latinx Americans and cultural products, like salsa music and dance. Infusing polyculturalism would involve focusing more on cross-cultural connections and contributions of multiple groups to various achievements and cultural products, such as highlighting how salsa music and dance have roots in and influences from African, Indigenous American, and European cultures that have interacted in Latin America and also influenced peoples and cultures all over the world. Further, infusing polyculturalism ideally would involve highlighting the contributions of many different racial, ethnic, and cultural groups to various disciplines and valued products more regularly throughout all courses, curricula, and programming, rather than only dedicating a month to one group.

Additionally combining positive aspects of colorblindness (e.g., acknowledging commonalities across diverse groups and uniqueness of individuals) along with polyculturalism and positive aspects of multiculturalism could also help to avoid known negative consequences of colorblindness (e.g., ignoring racial/ethnic identities and denying racism; e.g., Neville, Awad, Brooks, Flores, & Blumel, 2013) because polyculturalism and multiculturalism highlight the importance of race, ethnicity, and culture (Rosenthal & Levy, 2010). Highlighting that there are commonalities across diverse groups as well as much diversity and individuality within groups while also acknowledging the importance of race, ethnicity, and culture to people's experiences and lives may have a more positive impact than has been found for colorblind messages delivered alone. Polycultural messages could also be combined with and infused into other existing programs and interventions, such as anti-bias education (e.g., Derman-Sparks & Edwards, 2009), the jigsaw classroom (e.g., Aronson & Thibodeau, 1992), and other interventions based in intergroup contact theory (e.g., Davies & Aron, 2016; Pettigrew & Tropp, 2006). There are many possible ways that polyculturalism can be implemented in educational settings to be explored, which may help to promote positive intergroup relations and thriving among diverse youth.

Conclusion

With increasing diversity in many parts of the world, along with sustained intergroup conflict and stigma toward marginalized groups, it is critical to identify ways that educational settings can promote positive intergroup relations and well-being among youth from diverse racial, ethnic, and cultural backgrounds. The growing body of research on polyculturalism – a belief or approach to diversity focused on cross-cultural influences and connections – suggests it holds promise to improve intergroup relations and well-being among youth and adults in diverse societies. More research on polyculturalism focused on youth, exploring mechanisms, and using multiple methodologies is needed to help inform how polyculturalism can be implemented effectively in educational and other settings. Combining polyculturalism with other diversity approaches and interventions may maximize the potential positive impact on intergroup dynamics for diverse youth.

References

Aboud, F. E., & Spears Brown, C. (2013). Positive and negative intergroup contact among children and its effect on attitudes. In G. Hodson & M. Hewstone (Eds.), *Advances in intergroup contact* (pp. 176–199). New York, NY: Psychology Press.

Aboud, F. E., Tredoux, C., Tropp, L. R., Spears Brown, C., Nuens, U., & Noor, N. M. (2012). Interventions to reduce prejudice and enhance inclusion and respect for ethnic differences in early childhood: A systematic review. *Developmental Review*, 32, 307–336. doi:10.1016/j.dr.2012.05.001

Abrams, D., & Killen, M. (2014). Social exclusion of children: Developmental origins of prejudice. *Journal of Social Issues*, 70, 1–11. doi:10.1111/josi.12043

Allport, G. W. (1954). *The nature of prejudice*. Cambridge, MA: Addison-Wesley.

Aronson, E., & Thibodeau, R. (1992). The jigsaw classroom: A cooperative strategy for reducing prejudice. In J. Lynch, C. Modgil, & S. Modgil (Eds.), *Cultural diversity in the schools* (pp. 110–118). London: Falmer Press.

Banks, J. A. (2013). *An introduction to multicultural education* (Fifth edition). Upper Saddle River, NJ: Pearson.

Banks, J. A., & Banks, C. A. M. (2013). *Multicultural education: Issues and perspectives* (Eighth Edition). Hoboken, NJ: Wiley.

Benner, A. D., & Graham, S. (2009). The transition to high school as a developmental process among multiethnic urban youth. *Child Development*, 80, 356–376. doi:10.1111/j.1467-8624.2009.01265.x

Bernardo, A. B. I. (2013). Exploring social cognitive dimensions of sexual prejudice in Filipinos. *Philippine Journal of Psychology*, 46, 19–48.

Bernardo, A. B. I., & Presbitero, A. (2017). Belief in polyculturalism and cultural intelligence: Individual- and country-level differences. *Personality and Individual Differences*, 119, 307–310. doi:10.1016/j.paid.2017.08.006

Bernardo, A. B. I., Rosenthal, L., & Levy, S. R. (2013). Polyculturalism and attitudes toward people from other countries. *International Journal of Intercultural Relations*, 37, 335–344. doi:10.1016/j.ijintrel.2012.12.005

Bernardo, A. B. I., Salanga, M. G. C., Tjipto, S., Hutapea, B., Yeung, S. S., & Khan, A. (2016). Contrasting lay theories of polyculturalism and multiculturalism: Associations with essentialist beliefs of race in six Asian cultural groups. *Cross-Cultural Research*, 50, 231–250. doi:10.1177/1069397116641895

Bigler, R. S. (1999). The use of multicultural curricula and materials to counter racism in children. *Journal of Social Issues*, 55, 687–705. doi:10.1111/0022-4537.00142

Brenick, A., & Killen, M. (2013). Moral judgments about Jewish–Arab intergroup exclusion: The role of cultural identity and contact. *Development Psychology*, 50, 86–99. doi:10.1037/a0034702

Bryant, A. C., Triplett, N. P., Watson, M. J., & Lewis, C. W. (2017). The browning of American Public Schools: Evidence of increasing racial diversity and the implications for policy, practice, and student outcomes. *Urban Review*, 49, 263–278. doi:10.1007/s11256-017-0400-6

Cho, J., Morris, M. W., & Dow, B. (2018). How do the Romans feel when visitors 'do as the Romans do'? Diversity ideologies and trust in evaluations of cultural accommodation. *Academy of Management Discoveries*, 4, 11–31. doi:10.5465/amd.2016.0044

Cho, J., Morris, M. W., Slepian, M. L., & Tadmor, C. T. (2017). Choosing fusion: The effects of diversity ideologies on preference for culturally mixed experiences. *Journal of Experimental Social Psychology*, 69, 163–171. doi:10.1016/j.jesp.2016.06.013

Coleman, D. (2010). Projections of the ethnic minority populations of the United Kingdom 2006–2056. *Population and Development Review*, 36, 441–486. doi:10.1111/j.1728-4457.2010.00342.x

Davies, K., & Aron, A. (2016). Friendship development and intergroup attitudes: The role of interpersonal and intergroup friendship processes. *Journal of Social Issues*, 72, 489–510. doi:10.1111/josi.12178

Derman-Sparks, L., & Edwards, J. O. (2009). *Anti-bias education for young children and ourselves*. Washington, DC: National Association for the Education of Young Children.

Derman-Sparks, L., & Ramsey, P. G. (2011). *What if all the kids are white? Anti-bias multicultural education with young children and families* (Second Editon). New York, NY: Teachers College Press.

Douglass, S., Yip, T., & Shelton, N. (2014). Intragroup contact and anxiety among ethnic minority adolescents: Considering ethnic identity and social diversity transitions. *Journal of Youth and Adolescence*, 43, 1628–1641. doi:10.1007/s10964-014-0144-5

Duncan, G. J., & Raudenbush, S. (1999). Assessing the effects of context in studies of child and youth development. *Educational Psychologist*, 34, 29–41.

Erikson, E. (1968). *Identity youth and crisis*. New York, NY: Norton.

Flint, K. (2006). Indian-African encounters: Polyculturalism and African therapeutics in Natal, South Africa, 1886-1950s. *Journal of Southern African Studies*, 32, 367–385.

Gieling, M., Thijs, J., & Verkuyten, M. (2014). Dutch adolescents' tolerance of Muslim immigrants: The role of assimilation ideology, intergroup contact, and national identification. *Journal of Applied Social Psychology*, 44, 155–165. doi:10.1111/jasp.12220

Graham, S. (2018). Race/ethnicity and social adjustment of adolescents: How (not if) school diversity matters. *Educational Psychologist*, 53, 64–77. doi:10.1080/00461520.2018.1428805

Hajisoteriou, C., Karousiou, C., & Angelides, P. (2017). Mapping cultural diversity through children's voices: From confusion to clear understandings. *British Educational Research Journal*, 43, 330–349. doi:10.1002/berj.3266

Healy, E., Thomas, E., & Pedersen, A. (2017). Prejudice, polyculturalism, and the influence of contact and moral exclusion: A comparison of responses toward LGBI, TI, and refugee groups. *Journal of Applied Social Psychology*, 47, 389–399. doi:10.1111/jasp.12446

Juvonen, J., Kogachi, K., & Graham, S. (2017). When and how do students benefit from ethnic diversity in middle school? *Child Development, epub ahead of print*. doi:10.1111/cdev.12834.

Kelley, R. D. G. (1999). The people in me. *Utne Reader*, 95, 79–81.

Killen, M., Mulvey, K., & Hitti, A. (2013). Social exclusion in childhood: A developmental intergroup perspective. *Child Development*, 84, 772–790. doi:10.1111/cdev.12012

Killen, M., & Smetana, J. G. (2015). Origins and development of morality. In M. Lamb (Ed.), *Handbook of child psychology* (Vol. III, 7th ed., pp. 701–749). Hoboken, NJ: John Wiley & Sons Inc.

Levy, S. R., Shin, E., Lytle, A., & Rosenthal, L. (2017). Systemic approaches to reduce prejudice in schools. In E. C. Lopez, S. G. Nahari, & S. L. Proctor (Eds.),

Handbook of multicultural school psychology: An interdisciplinary perspective (2nd ed., pp. 237–257). London: Routledge.

Morris, M. W., Chiu, C.-Y., & Liu, Z. (2015). Polycultural psychology. *Annual Review of Psychology, 66*, 631–659. doi:10.1146/annurev-psych-010814-015001

Neville, H. A., Awad, G. H., Brooks, J. E., Flores, M. P., & Blumel, J. (2013). Color-blind racial ideology: Theory, training, and measurement implications in psychology. *American Psychologist, 68*, 455–466. doi:10.1037/a0033282

Oh, D. C. (2017). Black K-pop fan videos and polyculturalism. *The International Journal of Media and Culture, 15*, 269–282. doi:10.1080/15405702.2017.1371309

Pedersen, A., Paradies, Y., & Barndon, A. (2015). The consequences of intergroup ideologies and prejudice control for discrimination and harmony. *Journal of Applied Social Psychology, 45*, 684–696. doi:10.1111/jasp.12330

Pettigrew, T. F., & Tropp, L. R. (2006). A meta-analytic test of intergroup contact theory. *Journal of Personality and Social Psychology, 90*, 751–783. doi:10.1037/0022-3514.90.5.751

Prashad, V. (2001). *Everybody was Kung Fu fighting: Afro-Asian connections and the myth of cultural purity*. Boston, MA: Beacon Press.

Prashad, V. (2003). Bruce Lee and the anti-imperialism of Kung Fu: A polycultural adventure. *Positions, 11*, 51–89.

Raabe, T., & Beelmann, A. (2011). Development of ethnic, racial, and national prejudice in childhood and adolescence: A multinational meta-analysis of age differences. *Child Development, 82*, 1715–1737. doi:10.1111/j.1467-8624.2011.01668.x

Richeson, J. A., & Nussbaum, R. J. (2004). The impact of multiculturalism versus color blindness on racial bias. *Journal of Experimental Social Psychology, 40*, 417–423. doi:10.1016/j.jesp.2003.09.002

Rosenthal, L., & Levy, S. R. (2010). The colorblind, multicultural, and polycultural ideological approaches to improving intergroup attitudes and relations. *Social Issues and Policy Review, 4*, 215–246. doi:10.1111/j.1751-2409.2010.01022.x

Rosenthal, L., & Levy, S. R. (2012). The relation between polyculturalism and intergroup attitudes among racially and ethnically diverse adults. *Cultural Diversity and Ethnic Minority Psychology, 18*, 1–16. doi:10.1037/a0026490

Rosenthal, L., & Levy, S. R. (2013). Thinking about mutual influences and connections across cultures relates to more positive intergroup attitudes: An examination of polyculturalism. *Social and Personality Psychology Compass, 7*, 547–558. doi:10.1111/spc3.12043

Rosenthal, L., & Levy, S. R. (2016). Polyculturalism predicts increased positive intergroup contact and friendship across the beginning of college. *Journal of Social Issues, 72*, 472–488. doi:10.1111/josi.12177

Rosenthal, L., Levy, S. R., Katser, M., & Bazile, C. (2015). Polyculturalism and attitudes toward Muslim Americans. *Peace and Conflict: Journal of Peace Psychology, 21*, 535–545. doi:10.1037/pac0000133

Rosenthal, L., Levy, S. R., London, B., & Lewis, M. A. (2016). Polyculturalism among undergraduates at diverse universities: Associations through intergroup anxiety with academic and alcohol outcomes. *Analyses of Social Issues and Public Policy, 16*, 193–226. doi:10.1111/asap.12121

Rosenthal, L., Levy, S. R., & Militano, M. (2014). Polyculturalism and sexist attitudes. *Psychology of Women Quarterly.*, *38*, 519–534. doi:10.1177/0361684313510152

Rosenthal, L., Levy, S. R., & Moss, I. (2012). Polyculturalism and openness about criticizing one's culture: Implications for sexual prejudice. *Group Processes and Intergroup Relations*, *15*, 149–166. doi:10.1177/1368430211412801

Rosenthal, L., Ramírez, L., Levy, S. R., & Bernardo, A. B. I. (2019). Polyculturalism: Viewing cultures as dynamically connected and its implications for intercultural attitudes in Colombia. *Avances en Psicología Latinoamericana*, *37*, 133–151. doi:10.12804/apl

Rubin, K., Bukowski, W., & Parker, J. (2006). Peers, relationships, and interactions. In W. Damon & R. Lerner (Eds.), *Handbook of child psychology* (pp. 571–645). Hoboken, NJ: John Wiley & Sons Inc.

Rutland, A., & Killen, M. (2015). A developmental science approach to reducing prejudice and social exclusion: Intergroup processes, social-cognitive development, and moral reasoning. *Social Issues and Policy Review*, *9*, 121–154. doi:10.1111/sipr.12012

Ryan, C. S., Casas, J. F., & Thompson, B. K. (2010). Interethnic ideology, intergroup perceptions, and cultural orientation. *Journal of Social Issues*, *66*, 29–44. doi:10.1111/j.1540-4560.2009.01631.x

Salanga, M. G. C., & Bernardo, A. B. I. (2017). Cognitive empathy in intercultural interactions: The roles of lay theories of multiculturalism and polyculturalism. *Current Psychology*, epub ahead of print. doi: 10.1007/s12144-017-9599-3.

Schachner, M. K., Van de Vijver, F. J., Noack, P., & Eckstein, K. (2016). Cultural diversity climate and psychological adjustment at school—Equality and inclusion versus cultural pluralism. *Child Development*, *87*, 1175–1191. doi:10.1111/cdev.12536

Sidanius, J., Levin, S., Van Laar, C., & Sears, D. O. (2010). *The diversity challenge: Social identity and intergroup relations on the college campus*. New York, NY: Russell Sage Foundation.

Stephan, C. W., Renfro, L., & Stephan, W. G. (2004). The evaluation of multicultural education programs: Techniques and meta-analysis. In W. G. Stephan & P. G. Vogt (Eds.), *Education programs for improving intergroup relations: Theory, research, and practice* (pp. 227–242). New York, NY: Teachers College Press.

Tropp, L. R., & Prenovost, M. A. (2008). The role of intergroup contact in predicting children's inter- ethnic attitudes: Evidence from meta-analytic and field studies. In S. Levy & M. Killen (Eds.), *Intergroup attitudes and relations in childhood through adulthood* (pp. 236–248). Oxford, UK: Oxford University Press.

U.S. Census Bureau (2015). *Projections of the size and composition of the U.S. population: 2014 to 2060: Estimates and projections*. Washington, DC.

Verkuyten, M. (2009). Self-esteem and multiculturalism: An examination among ethnic minority and majority groups in the Netherlands. *Journal of Research in Personality*, *43*, 419–427. doi:10.1016/j.jrp.2009.01.013

Vertovec, S. (2007). Super-diversity and its implications. *Ethnic and Racial Studies*, *30*, 1024–1054. doi:10.1080/01419870701599465

Wittig, M. A., & Molina, L. E. (2000). Moderators and mediators of prejudice reduction in multicultural education. In S. Oskamp (Ed.), *Reducing prejudice and discrimination* (pp. 295–318). Mahwah, NJ: Lawrence Erlbaum Associates, Publishers.

Zirkel, S. (2008). Creating more effective multiethnic schools. *Social Issues and Policy Review, 2*, 187–241. doi:10.1111/j.1751-2409.2008.00015.x

Chapter 5

Towards a more dynamic perspective on acculturation research

Richard M. Lee, Peter F. Titzmann, and Philipp Jugert

Psychological acculturation has increasingly become the focus of scientific and public debate, as more and more individuals and families worldwide live in a different country or geographic region from where they were born or raised. These migration movements toward living elsewhere may be voluntary or involuntary, as well as permanent or temporary. Regardless of the reasons for migration and duration of resettlement, immigrants undergo some degree of change in their behaviors, values, beliefs, and lifestyles. These changes are due to the inevitable interactions (or intersections) between heritage and host cultures in their daily lives, as well as contact with other cultures that occur when living in culturally diverse societies and through travel and media exposure (Ferguson, Muzaffar, Iturbide, Chu, & Meeks Gardner, 2017; Morris, Chiu, & Liu, 2015). It is important to recognize that these cultural changes also occur among individuals and families from the host culture, as they have more sustained interactions with people from other cultures (Redfield, Linton, & Herskovits, 1936). However, the changes among natives from the host culture may be less apparent and not as sudden given the systemic imbalance in power and privilege between the different cultural groups (Liu et al., 2019).

Living in the host society and culture can offer immigrants a range of psychosocial benefits, from safety, security, and stability to new opportunities for educational, career, and personal development. In this context, immigrants may develop or adopt new behaviors to adapt to their host environment, begin to reshape how they see and present themselves, and change how they interact with people from different cultural backgrounds. At the same time, immigrants are not welcomed and sometimes openly opposed in many host countries (see for instance the refusal of Eastern European countries to accept refugees). When they do emigrate to the country, they are often confronted with numerous societal and social barriers (in the forms of prejudice, discrimination, and racism) that can make them vulnerable to harm, restrict them from opportunities and growth, and lead them to be more reticent or unwilling to change their cultural orientation. Whether immigrants adopt a particular cultural orientation may not even be up to them because the dominant majority in many host countries bars immigrants or people of color from the mainstream (Liu et al., 2019). Thus, acculturation can be a double-edged sword that presents opportunities for change and growth while concurrently reflecting the challenges of living in a society that is not always receptive and often openly hostile to immigrants (Redfield et al., 1936).

Acculturation also is not a unidimensional, one-way process (Berry, Phinney, Sam, & Vedder, 2006). Many elements of the heritage culture may be strongly valued and beneficial to immigrants and families despite pressures to adopt new cultural norms. Immigrants may make a conscious effort to maintain or strengthen their heritage culture by speaking their heritage language, sustaining connections to their homeland, continuing cultural traditions and practices, and building up their ethnic community in the host society. At times, holding on to one's heritage culture may serve as a buffer against stress by stabilizing the self. At other times, it may hinder the ability to gain access to new communities and opportunities. Importantly, these heritage-culture-sustaining behaviors and preferences may occur concurrently with acculturation to the host culture. That is, adoption of new behaviors that align with the host culture does not necessarily require the shedding of behaviors that align with the heritage culture. Empirical research has documented the validity and utility of having a bicultural orientation (Nguyen & Benet-Martínez, 2013).

Beyond these conceptual advances in understanding what is acculturation, theoretical models of acculturation have focused mainly on how it unfolds over time in a broad sense. Some scholars have proposed acculturation to follow an inverted U-shape with an initial honeymoon, a temporary drawback due to acculturative stress, and long-term adaptation and re-established happiness (e.g., Lysgaard, 1955; Oberg, 1960). Other scholars have suggested acculturative change is better described as a coping process after cultural shock due to the relocation into another society (Ward, Bochner, & Furnham, 2001). Ward and colleagues (1998), for example, followed international students over several months after arrival in New Zealand and documented acculturative change that resembled a learning curve rather than a U-curve. By contrast, Hurh and Kim (1990) using a large cross-sectional sample of Korean immigrants documented only moderate support for a J-type learning curve model when examining adjustment by length of residence. Although these studies examine how general change in acculturation occurs over time, they do not address the specific developmental process of acculturation in immigrant populations and mostly ignore the substantial inter-individual differences in intra-individual acculturative change.

Recent advances in methodology have allowed researchers to study developmental processes of acculturation more explicitly. Multi-level modeling, for example, has allowed researchers to study whether (daily, monthly, or yearly) variations in acculturative outcomes over time are associated with variations in predictors (e.g., Chung, Flook, & Fuligni, 2011; Michel, Titzmann, & Silbereisen, 2012). Growth curve models and latent change mixture models (sometimes combined with multi-level approaches) also can be used to differentiate between various longitudinal trajectories and change patterns (Juang & Cookston, 2009; Motti-Stefanidi, Asendorpf, & Masten, 2012; Stoessel, Titzmann, & Silbereisen, 2014). Despite these methodological advancements in the study of how acculturation may explicitly unfold, researchers continue to rely on traditional models and methods of studying it that look at general changes in it over time.

There remains a pressing need to fully take into account the specific developmental processes of acculturation. In particular: When does acculturation begin? How long does it last? How fast does it occur? And how coordinated are these changes across life domains? The aim of this chapter, therefore, is to address the need for greater specificity in the conceptualization of developmental processes of acculturation. We draw upon existing concepts from developmental psychology pertaining to the biological, social, and psychological changes in pubertal development to infer conceptual opportunities for studying acculturation processes in a more dynamic way. We specifically elaborate on the concepts of acculturative timing, tempo, pace, and synchronicity as systematic approaches to describing and measuring acculturative change processes among children, adolescents, and young adults, which were recently introduced (Titzmann & Lee, 2018).

Pubertal development research as a model to describe acculturation processes

When considering acculturation processes, developmental psychology as a discipline can provide important insights. "Developmental psychology deals with the description, explanation, and modification (optimization) of intraindividual change in behavior across the life span and with interindividual differences (and similarities) in intraindividual change" (Baltes, Reese, & Nesselroade, 1988, p. 4). Hence, developmental psychology, as an established discipline focusing on change in individuals, can provide the necessary framework for a dynamic view on developmental processes of acculturation. Within developmental psychology, pubertal development is one of the most dynamic fields of study. It is our contention that there are conceptual similarities between how pubertal development unfolds and how acculturation change occurs. Changes in pubertal development and in acculturation are, for example, both dynamic and multidimensional (Mendle, 2014; Van de Vijver, 2018). The dynamic changes that occur during pubertal development also have cascading effects in other life domains (e.g., cognitive development precedes changes in risk-taking).

Likewise, there are cascading effects that occur with acculturation processes and changes (e.g., changes in cultural practices precede changes in ethnic and national identity, which precede changes in cultural values; Lee et al., 2018).

Research on pubertal development, however, has benefited more from elaborated concepts of change than research on acculturation. Puberty researchers have articulated the importance of documenting when puberty begins (timing), how long it lasts (tempo), how fast it occurs (pace), and how coordinated pubertal changes are across different domains (synchrony). These concepts may be utilized to better describe acculturation processes, as well as to differentiate between various components of acculturative change (Titzmann & Lee, 2018). In this chapter, we elaborate on Titzmann and Lee's (2018) application of pubertal development concepts of timing and tempo (Beltz, Corley, Bricker, Wadsworth, & Berenbaum, 2014; Mendle, Harden, Brooks-Gunn, & Graber, 2010) and pace and synchrony (Caspi, Lynam, Moffitt, & Silva, 1993) to the conceptualization of acculturation processes.

The starting point: acculturation timing

Acculturation timing refers to the beginning of acculturation processes. It is an index for when a person begins to initiate and experience cultural and psychological changes related to the meeting of two or more cultures. These changes are often toward the host culture, but they also may be toward the heritage culture, such as the case of adolescents born or raised for most of their lives in the host culture.

Drawing upon pubertal development literature, we make a distinction between chronological, transition, and relative timing in acculturation. To understand these different forms of acculturation timing, we provide an illustration from pubertal timing research. Researchers may be interested in the age of pubertal onset as measured by hormonal changes. Puberty also can be understood in terms of when physical changes to the body become more visible, such as age of menarche or voice change. Pubertal development in terms of these two types of timing – hormonal changes and physical changes – may not always match or align (Shirtcliff, Dahl, & Pollak, 2009). Additionally, pubertal timing is relative to how individuals perceive their timing in relation to their peers (Mendle, 2014; Weichold, Silbereisen, & Schmitt-Rodermund, 2003). Some may perceive their pubertal development to be early, on-time, or late compared to their peers. We draw upon these different ways of measuring pubertal timing to understand acculturation timing.

Chronological timing is traditionally assumed to start on the day when an adolescent arrives in a new society and, hence, can be measured by the age of immigration. Support for the relevance of this chronological timing for acculturative processes is found in research showing the association between age of immigration and acculturation outcomes. For instance, individuals who immigrate before the onset of adolescence acquire the second language much sooner (Jia & Aaronson, 2003) and identify more strongly with their host country than children who immigrate after the adolescent years (Tsai, Ying, & Lee, 2000). Similarly, Cheung and colleagues showed that the association between time in the new country and identification with the receiving society differs depending on the age of immigration. Whereas individuals increased in their identification with the Canadian culture when they migrated before the age of 15, this identification decreased among those immigrants who arrived after age 30, individuals who arrived between 15 and 30 did not show a general trend (Cheung, Chudek, & Heine, 2011). Nevertheless, chronological timing, such as age of immigration and its corollary length of residence, is at best a proxy for acculturation timing. That is, chronological timing may not always reflect the actual starting point of acculturation.

Adolescents may prepare themselves for the transition and may start to acculturate even before they actually move to the new country. Hence, to be more precise, the actual starting point of acculturation – the *transition timing* – should be assessed, whether it is before, later, or in line with the actual age at immigration. For instance, adolescents may start learning the host language and may study books about the new culture before they immigrate. Preparatory classes are in fact the standard procedure for certain immigrant groups, such as expatriates (Oddou, 1991). Sometimes, acculturation can be found without migrating at all, for example through exposure to media and music, which also transfer cultural values and norms (Ferguson & Bornstein, 2012).

Transition timing also may begin with changes to how people perceive and relate to their own ethnic culture, irrespective of their orientation to the new host culture. Youth may choose to stop speaking in their heritage language or change their diet away from traditional ethnic cuisine. While these cultural shifts may align with the adoption of new attitudes, behaviors, and customs from the host culture, it is not necessarily always the case. Some youth may simply be distancing themselves from their ethnic heritage in anticipation of change. In other situations, transition timing is more complicated and difficult to assess because the host culture may actually be a long-lost home culture. For instance, diaspora migrants often "maintained their own distinct communities and dreamed of one-day returning to their Ancient Home" (Weingrod & Levy, 2006, p. 691) and hence have a connection to the receiving host society (i.e., "Ancient Home") even before they actually (re-)migrated.

In other instances though, the start of acculturation may be delayed far beyond the actual arrival in the new country. Immigrants may be placed in shelters and refugee camps with little contact with the receiving society so that acculturation does not start even though these adolescents have already moved physically to the new society. Figure 5.1 illustrates such differences with two hypothetical individuals. Both these adolescents arrived at age 14, but adolescent A started language acquisition before migrating (at age 12), whereas adolescent B started about two years after arrival (at age 16). For these two adolescents, age at immigration (chronological timing) would not be the best index for assessing the onset of acculturation. Instead, transition timing is a more appropriate measure of actual acculturation timing.

Acculturative processes usually do not take place in a social vacuum. This is particularly likely in the adolescent years, where peers are a crucial source for self-evaluations (Brechwald & Prinstein, 2011; Hergovich, Sirsch, & Felinger, 2002). While chronological timing and transition timing capture acculturation timing from a within-person perspective, there also is a need to look at acculturation timing from a between-person perspective. Similar to pubertal development which may be early, on-time, or late compared to peers (Hill & Lynch, 1983; Savin-Williams & Small, 1986), an adolescent's acculturation may start earlier or later than their immigrating peers'. This between-person difference in timing is referred to as *relative timing*. Relative timing (e.g., comfort level with interacting with

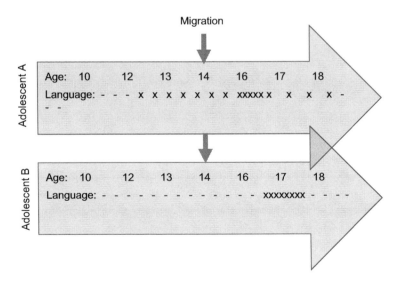

Figure 5.1 The acculturation of two hypothetical adolescents

Notes: "X" refers to cultural change in the particular domain of acculturation; "–" refers to stability in cultural cognitions and behaviors; a shorter space between "X"s indicates a more accelerated rate of change.

peers from the host culture) may affect how youth are treated by parents, peers, and others in their family, school, and community. Parents may place a greater emphasis on ethnic socialization practices if they perceive their child is acculturating too quickly compared to her peers and if they have concerns about the child losing touch with her heritage culture.

Relative timing is rarely directly studied in acculturation research. Some empirical findings suggest that deviations from the norms of the co-ethnic peer groups in a new society may have consequences for the acculturation of adolescents. For instance, there is some evidence to suggest Mexican immigrant girls who acculturate later than their peers (as measured by greater family expectations) and engage in more language brokering for their parents report less depressive symptoms (Love & Buriel, 2007). Another study found that adolescent immigrants reported more daily socio-cultural acculturation hassles and language hassles if they were not oriented towards the majority culture whereas the co-ethnic peers in their school, on average, were (Titzmann & Jugert, 2015).

How long it takes from beginning to end: acculturation tempo

Once the type of acculturation timing is determined, it is necessary to understand the duration of the acculturation process. That is, how long does it last from beginning to end? Drawing upon an operational definition of tempo in pubertal development, *acculturation tempo* can be similarly thought of as "variation in the time taken to pass through the various stages of [acculturative] development" (Marshall & Tanner, 1969, p. 291). Importantly, the tempo concept applied to acculturation requires a definition of the start and the end of acculturation processes. The starting point will usually align with acculturation timing, whether chronological, transition, or relative timing is used as the start. Which of these types of acculturation timing is appropriate may depend on the particular group, the context, or the specific research question being addressed. A more complicated question is how to best define the endpoint or final stage of development in acculturation processes. Acculturation does not always have a clearly defined endpoint as puberty (e.g., menarche, deeper voice, pubic hair). For this reason, we would like to expand a little bit on the ways by which the end of acculturation may be defined and also would like to introduce some caveats in its definition.

Endpoint in uni-dimensional views

One way to define the end of acculturation is the achievement in a predefined area of competence, such as language acquisition, sociocultural knowledge, culturally appropriate behaviors and skills, achievement of a developmental task (e.g., identity commitment), or the significantly reduced risk for maladjustment associated with acculturative stress. In Figure 5.1, the acculturation tempo varies between two hypothetical adolescents. Whereas it takes from age 12 to 18 for adolescent A from start to finish for language acquisition, adolescent B takes only about one year, from age 16 to 17.

The implication of defining the acculturation endpoint in a particular domain is that acculturation models have to be outcome specific. For instance, acculturation tempo may vary between language proficiency and identity development (see also acculturation synchrony). Once the specific outcome is identified, the smallest unit of an acculturation outcome needs to be determined. Language proficiency may vary in listening comprehension, reading comprehension, or correct grammar use (Farhady, 1982). In addition, there may be variability between objective measures and subjective measures. An adolescent who scores high in objective new language acquisition tests may still not feel comfortable and competent in using this language and vice versa.

A disadvantage of uni-dimensional views is that they may reinforce assimilation to the majority culture. Berry (1997) defined assimilation as an acculturation orientation where individuals have a strong association with the host society and a low maintenance of own cultural traditions. To define the endpoint of acculturation solely by competence in the new language may imply that adolescent immigrants lose touch with their heritage culture. For adolescent development, this uni-dimensional view of acculturation is not always beneficial. In fact, past work has found that maintaining ties to one's heritage culture serves as a protective factor during acculturation. For instance, Noh and Kaspar (2003) found that a strong ethnic identity "may compensate for the distress-exacerbating effect of emotion-focused coping" in Korean immigrants residing in Toronto after experiences of discrimination. Similarly, ethnic segregation, which some scholars and politicians assume to be maladaptive, can be protective for immigrants because it provides support, resources, and safety that allow for healthy adaptation. A recent study found ethnic segregation protected pregnant women from risky behaviors, such as smoking (Yang, Shoff, Noah, Black, & Sparks, 2014). A meta-analysis more broadly found that an orientation towards both heritage and host culture (i.e., an integration orientation) seems most beneficial for the mental health of immigrants (Yoon et al., 2013).

Multi-dimensional definitions of endpoints

A more optimal approach to studying acculturation processes is to take into account several acculturation dimensions simultaneously and *not* to define endpoints in a single domain. In the area of language, for example, reaching a certain level of proficiency in both heritage and host language may be an aim (Genesee & Gándara, 1999). In ethnic identity development, reaching an integration of both heritage and host identity seems a beneficial aim (Mok & Morris, 2012; Schwartz et al., 2015). In addition, subjective components may be helpful in defining the endpoint in acculturation. These may be subjective self-reports of psychological variables that are known to fluctuate during the course of acculturation. Self-efficacy, for instance, was found to be weakened after immigration and to be reestablished in the years after (Titzmann & Jugert, 2017). In addition, researchers may start studying differences between real-self and ideal-self known from research on self-concept (Waugh, 2001). Navas and colleagues (2005), for instance, proposed the Relative Acculturation Extended Model to describe the potential difference between the ideal and the real acculturation situation for immigrants. Refugees ideally want to have time and opportunity to learn the host language upon arrival in the host country but the real situation in various countries often requires them to defer learning the host language due to the pressure and demand to work immediately upon arrival as part of their resettlement agreement.

Independent of whether a uni-dimensional or a multi-dimensional view is applied to endpoints, objective measures of an endpoint are also viable, particularly if they focus on particular needs in the new context. A certain competence or skill may be worth assessing if it is decisive for the success in the educational system or the labor market. A difference between puberty and acculturation is, however, that acculturation is potentially a life-long experience without a clearly defined endpoint. Hence, all definitions of an endpoint are likely to be provisional and subject to future change. Figure 5.2 illustrates the differences in a hypothetical endpoint between two variables. In both adolescents (A and B) it is shown that they arrive at the potential endpoint earlier in terms of language than in terms of identity. The figure also shows that acculturation tempo can also vary within individuals. For Adolescent A, the tempo is about six years for language, but only about 2.5 years for identity changes.

In addition, researchers have to be aware of cultural differences in what different ethnic heritage groups see as a successful endpoint in development. Greenfield and colleagues proposed that ethnic groups often differ in their socialization of children (Greenfield, Keller, Fuligni, & Maynard, 2003; Greenfield & Suzuki, 1998). Some families emphasize raising a child into an "autonomous, self-fulfilled individual who enters into social relationships and responsibilities by personal choice" (Greenfield & Suzuki, 1998, p. 1060). Other families emphasize raising a child into a "mature person to be embedded in a network of relationships and responsibilities to others; personal achievements are ideally in the service of a collectivity, most often the family" (Greenfield & Suzuki, 1998, p. 1060). Importantly, assimilation may not be the acculturation endpoint for all families. In fact, many immigrant youth and their families seek to accommodate without

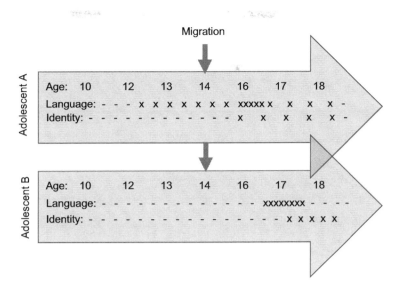

Figure 5.2 The acculturation of two hypothetical adolescents
Notes: "X" refers to change in the particular domain of acculturation; "–" refers to stability in cultural cognitions and behaviors; a shorter space between "X"s indicates a more accelerated rate of change.

assimilating, as Gibson (1988) described Punjabi youth who were encouraged to learn English and follow host culture customs at school but were discouraged from interacting with White peers. Moreover, as our societies become more global and transnational, youth may be expected to be more flexible and adaptive in their acculturation processes to successfully and simultaneously navigate multiple cultural contexts (Morris et al., 2015).

The change across different domains of life: acculturation synchrony

The study of different dimensions and domain endpoints for acculturation tempo leads directly to the need to recognize that acculturation processes may or may not be synchronized across dimensions and domains. *Acculturation synchrony* refers to the coordination of acculturation processes across different dimensions and domains. This concept of synchrony is drawn from puberty research, where pubertal synchrony refers to a variation between different pubertal indicators. As Mendle has noted, "[a] high degree of synchrony indicates that the level of development in one area of puberty 'matches' the level of development in another area" (Mendle, 2014, p. 216). Differentiation in puberty can occur across biological, social, and psychological (e.g., emotional) changes (Archibald, Graber, & Brooks-Gunn, 2003). Synchrony also can occur between biological changes, such as the synchrony in breast development and pubic hair development (Rachel, Yihe, Yukiko, John, & Gertraud, 2011). Similarly, acculturation processes across dimensions and domains may not occur in synchrony.

Because acculturation is a multi-faceted phenomenon without a single indicator for when an adolescent is "well-acculturated", acculturation researchers have differentiated between psychological and socio-cultural domains of adaptation and adjustment (Ataca & Berry, 2002; Ward et al., 1998). More recent works also have elaborated on these differentiations (e.g., Genkova, Trickett, Birman, & Vinokurov, 2014; Schwartz, Unger, Zamboanga, & Szapocznik, 2010). Hence, adolescents may have different views on heritage and host culture acculturation. Furthermore, within host and heritage culture dimensions and domains, differences in the degree of acculturation may exist. An adolescent may be proficient in the host language, but may not necessarily adopt host values and customs in family interactions (Arends-Tóth & van de Vijver, 2004; Noels & Clément, 2015).

Measuring acculturation synchrony becomes a vital component in research on acculturation processes. Stoessel et al. (2014) demonstrated the advantage of combining outcomes by employing a person-oriented and longitudinal study using growth mixture modeling on host and heritage identification of young immigrants from the former Soviet Union in Germany. The analysis revealed three subgroups of specific host and heritage identification change: one group, named Idealists, reported a high and stable identification with their host culture and a low increasing identification with their heritage culture. A second group, named Skeptics, reported a low and stable identification with their host culture and high decreasing identification with their heritage culture. The third group was labeled Realists and was found to have a medium-level and stable identification with both host and heritage cultures (Stoessel et al., 2014). Additional analyses showed that membership in these groups was predicted by pre-migration factors and it was accompanied with specific acculturation-oriented experiences.

The pace of change: acculturation pace

Beyond timing, tempo, and synchrony, the rate or speed of acculturative change is not uniform across groups of immigrants. In pubertal development, some adolescents have an accelerated puberty and others a decelerated puberty, which has been found to be associated with cortisol secretion and maltreatment (Negriff, Saxbe, & Trickett, 2015). Similar to the pace in pubertal development, *acculturation pace* refers to the speed at which acculturation occurs in a given dimension or domain.

This speed can vary between individuals and groups, but also within individuals and groups. A study on diaspora immigrants from the former Soviet Union who moved to Israel or Germany found that they differed in acculturation pace. The rate of change in the share of immigrant friends among all friends decreased by about 1.5 percent per year in Israel, whereas the respective change in Germany was 4 percent (Titzmann, Silbereisen, & Mesch, 2012). This difference was explained by the established Russian-speaking infrastructure in Israel, which prevented adolescents in Israel from quickly establishing interethnic friendships.

Acculturative pace also may vary at the within-person level. Within-person variation is common when looking at acculturation domains that mirror surface and deep structure aspects of culture (Hall, 1976). Surface structures refer to cultural behaviors that change rather easily. Language, food, and music are common examples of surface structures. Somewhat deeper are beliefs, assumptions, or attitudes. These are associated with emotions and change less easily. Even deeper cultural structures are cultural group norms and views that determine purpose in life. Changes in these deep cultural structures can be assumed to be much harder and perhaps not always desirable.

In Figure 5.2, we show a different pace between and within adolescents. The rate of change is depicted as the density of X-marks. The further apart these marks are the slower is the rate of change. The figure shows that the rate of change varies between and within persons. In the identity domain, adolescent A changes at a slower pace than Adolescent B. In the language domain, Adolescent A also changes at a different pace before and after immigration. It may be, for example, that adolescent A learns the new language as an autodidact before the actual migration and speeds up afterwards through direct contact or additional learning classes offered in their school.

Conclusion

The major aim of this chapter was to highlight the developmental dynamics in acculturation processes. Although acculturation process is not a new psychological construct (e.g., Redfield et al., 1936), concepts that describe these changes in acculturation have been surprisingly rare. We introduced concepts originating in the description of pubertal development that can inform acculturation research by making it more meaningful and dynamic. Which of the discussed components (timing, tempo, synchrony, or pace) is a better predictor for which outcome and why remains open for theoretical and empirical research. We are aware that these components may need a critical view and that they may even be accompanied with newer, more acculturation-focused components of change processes. Nevertheless, identifying and operationalizing acculturation timing, tempo, synchrony, and pace are a first start.

In addition, acculturation timing, tempo, synchrony, and pace are not completely independent from one another. The study of acculturation tempo is dependent on the type of acculturation timing of interest. Acculturation tempo and pace similarly may be associated, particularly if pace does not differ intra- and inter-individually. The timing and tempo of different dimensions and domains of acculturation also will affect acculturation synchrony. More research is needed that combines assessments of timing, tempo, pace, and synchrony to better grasp the dynamics of acculturative change across life domains.

To best study the interplay between the dimensions, it will be important to properly identify and document how individuals, families, and communities are situated in their heritage and host cultural contexts. To what extent adolescents experience barriers or rewards as they negotiate developmental tasks associated with acculturation dimensions and domains will greatly impact how these acculturation processes unfold. For example, adolescent immigrants who experience isolation or marginalization from their ethnic heritage community due to early loss of heritage language may have an accelerated acculturation pace toward the host culture across other domains. Which of these other domains are affected first and subsequently affect other domains is not always clear or predictable.

In sum, the use of dynamic assumptions in acculturation research allows us to develop a whole new set of hypotheses regarding the acculturation of adolescents to new cultural environments. Relative acculturative timing, for example, may be more decisive for the psychosocial functioning of adolescents than the actual level of acculturation. Research on pubertal timing discussed, for instance, whether girls are at higher risk of maladjustment if they deviate from their peers' puberty status independently of whether they are early or late (deviance hypothesis) or whether only being early is associated with higher risk (stage termination hypothesis). Empirical results find evidence primarily for the deviance hypothesis (see Weichold et al., 2003 for an overview on short-term and long-term consequences of pubertal timing). Extant findings of acculturation research may also be explained by relative acculturative timing. Ward and colleagues (1998) report that the correlation between psychological and socio-cultural adaptation increased among Japanese students in New Zealand with time in the new country. In the beginning of acculturative processes, being low in socio-cultural adaptation may not be associated with psychological functioning, because all co-ethnic students are low as well and support one another. With time, however, those students who do not adjust may also lose the support (and understanding) of better adjusted co-ethnic students and hence may report lower psychological functioning.

These are just examples of possible hypotheses, but they can highlight the potential of more dynamic views on acculturation processes. Given that acculturation has always been seen as a concept of change, such dynamic concepts are timely and urgently needed. We need to learn more about when, with whom, and with what measures societies can support adolescent immigrants during their journey in the new country. In growing multicultural societies this knowledge will help to create more cohesive and supportive societies.

References

Archibald, A. B., Graber, J. A., & Brooks-Gunn, J. (2003). Pubertal processes and physiological growth in adolescence. In G. R. Adams & M. D. Berzonsky (Eds.), *Blackwell handbook of adolescence* (pp. 24–47). Malden, MA: Blackwell Publishing.

Arends-Tóth, J., & van de Vijver, F. J. R. (2004). Domains and dimensions in acculturation: Implicit theories of Turkish-Dutch. *International Journal of Intercultural Relations*, 28(1), 19–35. doi:10.1016/j.ijintrel.2003.09.001

Ataca, B., & Berry, J. W. (2002). Psychological, sociocultural, and marital adaptation of Turkish immigrant couples in Canada. *International Journal of Psychology*, 37(1), 13–26.

Baltes, P. B., Reese, H. W., & Nesselroade, J. R. (1988). *Life-span developmental psychology: Introduction to research methods.* Hillsdale, NJ: Lawrence Erlbaum Associates, Inc.

Beltz, A. M., Corley, R. P., Bricker, J. B., Wadsworth, S. J., & Berenbaum, S. A. (2014). Modeling pubertal timing and tempo and examining links to behavior problems. *Developmental Psychology*, 50(12), 2715–2726. doi:10.1037/a0038096

Berry, J. W. (1997). Immigration, acculturation, and adaptation. *Applied Psychology: An International Review*, 46(1), 5–68. doi:10.1080/026999497378467

Berry, J. W., Phinney, J. S., Sam, D. L., & Vedder, P. (2006). Immigrant youth: Acculturation, identity, and adaptation. *Applied Psychology: An International Review*, 55(3), 303–332.

Brechwald, W. A., & Prinstein, M. J. (2011). Beyond homophily: A decade of advances in understanding peer influence processes. *Journal of Research on Adolescence*, 21(1), 166–179. doi:10.1111/j.1532-7795.2010.00721.x

Caspi, A., Lynam, D., Moffitt, T. E., & Silva, P. A. (1993). Unraveling girls' delinquency: Biological, dispositional, and contextual contributions to adolescent misbehavior. *Developmental Psychology*, 29(1), 19–30. doi:10.1037/0012-1649.29.1.19

Cheung, B. Y., Chudek, M., & Heine, S. J. (2011). Evidence for a sensitive period for acculturation: Younger immigrants report acculturating at a faster rate. *Psychological Science*, 22(2), 147–152. doi:10.1177/0956797610394661

Chung, G. H., Flook, L., & Fuligni, A. J. (2011). Reciprocal associations between family and peer conflict in adolescents' daily lives. *Child Development*, 82(5), 1390–1396. doi:10.1111/j.1467-8624.2011.01625.x

Farhady, H. (1982). Measures of language proficiency from the learner's perspective. *TESOL Quarterly*, 16(1), 43–59. doi:10.2307/3586562

Ferguson, G. M., & Bornstein, M. H. (2012). Remote acculturation: The 'Americanization' of Jamaican islanders. *International Journal of Behavioral Development*, 36(3), 167–177. doi:10.1177/0165025412437066

Ferguson, G. M., Muzaffar, H., Iturbide, M. I., Chu, H., & Meeks Gardner, J. (2017). Feel american, watch american, eat american? Remote acculturation, tv, and nutrition among adolescent–Mother dyads in jamaica. *Child Development*. doi:10.1111/cdev.12808

Genesee, F., & Gándara, P. (1999). Bilingual education programs: A cross-national perspective. *Journal of Social Issues*, 55(4), 665–685. doi:10.1111/0022-4537.00141

Genkova, A. G., Trickett, E. J., Birman, D., & Vinokurov, A. (2014). Acculturation and adjustment of elderly émigrés from the former Soviet Union: A life domains perspective. *Psychosocial Intervention*, 23(2), 83–93. doi:10.1016/j.psi.2014.07.004

Gibson, M. A. (1988). *Accommodation without assimilation: Sikh immigrants in an American high school*. New York, NY: Cornell University Press.

Greenfield, P. M., Keller, H., Fuligni, A. J., & Maynard, A. (2003). Cultural pathways through universal development. *Annual Review of Psychology*, 54(1), 461–490.

Greenfield, P. M., & Suzuki, L. K. (1998). Culture and human development: Implications for parenting, education, pediatrics and mental health. In W. Damon, I. E. Sigel, & K. A. Renninger (Eds.), *Handbook of child psychology: Child psychology in practice* (pp. 1059–1109). Hoboken, NJ: John Wiley & Sons Inc.

Hall, E. T. (1976). *Beyond culture*. Oxford, England: Anchor.

Hergovich, A., Sirsch, U., & Felinger, M. (2002). Self-appraisals, actual appraisals and reflected appraisals of preadolescent children. *Social Behavior and Personality: an International Journal*, 30(6), 603–611. doi:10.2224/sbp.2002.30.6.603

Hill, J. P., & Lynch, M. E. (1983). The intensification of gender-related role expectations during early adolescence. In J. Brooks-Gunn & A. C. Petersen (Eds.), *Girls at puberty: Biological and psychosocial perspectives* (pp. 201–228). Boston, MA: Springer US.

Hurh, W. M., & Kim, K. C. (1990). Adaptation stages and mental health of Korean male immigrants in the United States. *The International Migration Review*, 24(3), 456–479. doi:10.2307/2546369

Jia, G., & Aaronson, D. (2003). A longitudinal study of Chinese children and adolescents learning English in the United States. *Applied Psycholinguistics*, 24(1), 131–161. doi:10.1017/S0142716403000079

Juang, L. P., & Cookston, J. T. (2009). Acculturation, discrimination, and depressive symptoms among Chinese American adolescents: A longitudinal study. *The Journal of Primary Prevention*, 30(3), 475–496. doi:10.1007/s10935-009-0177-9

Lee, T. K., Meca, A., Unger, J. B., Zamboanga, B. L., Baezconde-Garbanati, L., Gonzales-Backen, M., ... Schwartz, S. J. (2018). Dynamic transition patterns in acculturation among Hispanic adolescents. *Child Dev*. doi:10.1111/cdev.13148

Liu, W. M., Liu, R. Z., Garrison, Y. L., Kim, J. Y. C., Chan, L., Ho, Y. C. S., & Yeung, C. W. (2019). Racial trauma, microaggressions, and becoming racially innocuous: The role of acculturation and white supremacist ideology. *American Psychologist*, 74(1), 143–155.

Love, J. A., & Buriel, R. (2007). Language brokering, autonomy, parent-child bonding, biculturalism, and depression: A study of Mexican American adolescents from immigrant families. *Hispanic Journal of Behavioral Sciences*, 29(4), 472–491.

Lysgaard, S. (1955). Adjustment in a foreign society: Norwegian Fulbright grantees visiting the United States. *Acta Psychologica*, 11, 189–190.

Marshall, W. A., & Tanner, J. M. (1969). Variations in pattern of pubertal changes in girls. *Archives of Disease in Childhood*, 44(235), 291–303.

Mendle, J. (2014). Beyond pubertal timing: New directions for studying individual differences in development. *Current Directions in Psychological Science*, 23(3), 215–219. doi:10.1177/0963721414530144

Mendle, J., Harden, K. P., Brooks-Gunn, J., & Graber, J. A. (2010). Development's tortoise and hare: Pubertal timing, pubertal tempo, and depressive symptoms in boys and girls. *Developmental Psychology*, 46(5), 1341–1353. doi:10.1037/a0020205

Michel, A., Titzmann, P. F., & Silbereisen, R. K. (2012). Language shift among adolescent ethnic German immigrants: Predictors of increasing use of German over time. *International Journal of Intercultural Relations*, 36(2), 248–259. doi:10.1016/j.ijintrel.2011.10.002

Mok, A., & Morris, M. W. (2012). Managing two cultural identities: The malleability of bicultural identity integration as a function of induced global or local processing. *Personality and Social Psychology Bulletin*, 38(2), 233–246. doi:10.1177/0146167211426438

Morris, M. W., Chiu, C.-Y., & Liu, Z. (2015). Polycultural psychology. *Annual Review of Psychology*, 66, 631–659. doi:10.1146/annurev-psych-010814-015001

Motti-Stefanidi, F., Asendorpf, J. B., & Masten, A. S. (2012). The adaptation and well-being of adolescent immigrants in Greek schools: A multilevel, longitudinal study of risks and resources. *Development and Psychopathology*, 24(2), 451–473. doi:10.1017/S0954579412000090

Navas, M., García, M. C., Sánchez, J., Rojas, A. J., Pumares, P., & Fernández, J. S. (2005). Relative Acculturation Extended Model (RAEM): New contributions with regard to the study of acculturation. *International Journal of Intercultural Relations*, 29(1), 21–37. doi:10.1016/j.ijintrel.2005.04.001

Negriff, S., Saxbe, D. E., & Trickett, P. K. (2015). Childhood maltreatment, pubertal development, HPA axis functioning, and psychosocial outcomes: An integrative biopsychosocial model. *Developmental Psychobiology*, 57(8), 984–993. doi:10.1002/dev.21340

Nguyen, A.-M. D., & Benet-Martínez, V. (2013). Biculturalism and adjustment: A meta-analysis. *Journal of Cross-Cultural Psychology*, 44(1), 122–159. doi:10.1177/0022022111435097

Noels, K. A., & Clément, R. (2015). Situational variations in ethnic identity across immigration generations: Implications for acculturative change and cross-cultural adaptation. *International Journal of Psychology*, 50(6), 451–462. doi:10.1002/ijop.12205

Noh, S., & Kaspar, V. (2003). Perceived discrimination and depression: Moderating effects of coping, acculturation, and ethnic support. *American Journal of Public Health*, 93(2), 232–238. doi:10.2105/ajph.93.2.232

Oberg, K. (1960). Cultural shock: Adjustment to new cultural environments. *Practical Anthropology*, 7(4), 177–182.

Oddou, G. R. (1991). Managing your expatriates: What the successful firms do. *Human Resource Planning*, 14(4), 301–308.

Rachel, N., Yihe, D., Yukiko, M., John, S., & Gertraud, M. (2011). Puberty, body fat, and breast density in girls of several ethnic groups. *American Journal of Human Biology*, 23(3), 359–365. doi:doi:10.1002/ajhb.21145

Redfield, R., Linton, R., & Herskovits, M. J. (1936). Memorandum for the study of acculturation. *American Anthropologist*, 38, 149–152.

Savin-Williams, R. C., & Small, S. A. (1986). The timing of puberty and its relationship to adolescent and parent perceptions of family interactions. *Developmental Psychology*, 22(3), 342–347. doi:10.1037/0012-1649.22.3.342

Schwartz, S. J., Unger, J. B., Baezconde-Garbanati, L., Benet-Martínez, V., Meca, A., Zamboanga, B. L., ... Szapocznik, J. (2015). Longitudinal trajectories of bicultural identity integration in recently immigrated Hispanic adolescents: Links with mental health and family functioning. *International Journal of Psychology*, 50(6), 440–450. doi:10.1002/ijop.12196

Schwartz, S. J., Unger, J. B., Zamboanga, B. L., & Szapocznik, J. (2010). Rethinking the concept of acculturation: Implications for theory and research. *American Psychologist*, 65(4), 237–251.

Shirtcliff, E. A., Dahl, R. E., & Pollak, S. D. (2009). Pubertal development: Correspondence between hormonal and physical development. *Child Development*, 80(2), 327–337. doi:10.1111/j.1467-8624.2009.01263.x

Stoessel, K., Titzmann, P. F., & Silbereisen, R. K. (2014). Being "them" and "us" at the same time? subgroups of cultural identification change among adolescent diaspora immigrants. *Journal of Cross-Cultural Psychology*, 45(7), 1089–1109. doi:10.1177/0022022114534770

Titzmann, P. F., & Jugert, P. (2015). Acculturation in context: The moderating effects of immigrant and native peer orientations on the acculturation experiences of immigrants. *Journal of Youth and Adolescence*, 44(11), 2079–2094. doi:10.1007/s10964-015-0314-0

Titzmann, P. F., & Jugert, P. (2017). Transition to a new country: Acculturative and developmental predictors for changes in self-efficacy among adolescent immigrants. *Journal of Youth and Adolescence*, 46(10), 2143–2156. doi:10.1007/s10964-017-0665-9

Titzmann, P. F., & Lee, R. M. (2018). Adaptation of young immigrants: A developmental perspective on acculturation research. *European Psychologist*, 23(1), 72–82. doi:0.1027/1016-9040/a000313

Titzmann, P. F., Silbereisen, R. K., & Mesch, G. S. (2012). Change in friendship homophily: A German Israeli comparison of adolescent immigrants. *Journal of Cross-Cultural Psychology*, 43(3), 410–428. doi:10.1177/0022022111399648

Tsai, J. L., Ying, Y.-W., & Lee, P. A. (2000). The meaning of 'being Chinese' and 'being American': Variation among Chinese American young adults. *Journal of Cross-Cultural Psychology*, 31(3), 302–332. doi:10.1177/0022022100031003002

Van de Vijver, F. (2018). Challenges in the study of adolescent and acculturative changes. *Journal of Adolescence*, 226–229. doi:10.1016/j.adolescence.2017.08.004

Ward, C., Bochner, S., & Furnham, A. (2001). *The psychology of culture shock.* (2nd ed.). New York, NY: Routledge.

Ward, C., Okura, Y., Kennedy, A., & Kojima, T. (1998). The U-curve on trial: A longitudinal study of psychological and sociocultural adjustment during cross-cultural transition. *International Journal of Intercultural Relations, 22*(3), 277–291. doi:10.1016/S0147-1767(98)00008-X

Waugh, R. F. (2001). Measuring ideal and real self-concept on the same scale, based on a multifaceted, hierarchical model of self-concept. *Educational and Psychological Measurement, 61*(1), 85–101. doi:10.1177/00131640121971086

Weichold, K., Silbereisen, R. K., & Schmitt-Rodermund, E. (2003). Short-term and long-term consequences of early versus late physical maturation in adolescents. In C. Hayward & C. Hayward (Eds.), *Gender differences at puberty* (pp. 241–276). New York, NY: Cambridge University Press.

Weingrod, A., & Levy, A. (2006). Social thought and commentary: Paradoxes of homecoming: The Jews and their diasporas. *Anthropological Quarterly, 79*(4), 691–716.

Yang, T.-C., Shoff, C., Noah, A. J., Black, N., & Sparks, C. S. (2014). Racial segregation and maternal smoking during pregnancy: A multilevel analysis using the racial segregation interaction index. *Social Science & Medicine (1982), 107,* 26–36. doi:10.1016/j.socscimed.2014.01.030

Yoon, E., Chang, C.-T., Kim, S., Clawson, A., Cleary, S. E., Hansen, M., ... Gomes, A. M. (2013). A meta-analysis of acculturation/enculturation and mental health. *Journal of Counseling Psychology, 60*(1), 15–30. doi:10.1037/a0030652

Chapter 6

Development in context
The importance of country and school level factors for the mental health of immigrant adolescents

Gonneke W.J.M. Stevens and Sophie D. Walsh

Introduction

Theories on the impact of immigration on the mental health of adolescents have suggested two contradictory perspectives: a risk and a resilience perspective. In this literature, immigrants are often defined as those that are born abroad or have parents that are born abroad, while for mental health problems a distinction is frequently made between internalizing and externalizing problems. Internalizing problems are predominantly harmful for the self and they include fear, worries, feeling low, social withdrawal, overcontrol, and somatic complaints. By contrast, externalizing problems are predominantly disturbing to others and they involve anger, aggression, misconduct, and undercontrolled behaviors (Wenar & Kerig, 2000).

The risk perspective (Berry, 2006) focuses on the potential stress resulting from the process of migration, entailing, for instance, the loss of social networks, customs, surroundings, and the need to adapt to a new cultural environment (Pantin, Schwartz, Sullivan, Coatsworth, & Szapocznik, 2003; Torres, Driscoll, & Voell, 2012). Within families, a process of asymmetric acculturation may be taking place in which children acquire the receiving country's culture and language much faster than their parents (Kwak, 2003). Together with financial, occupational, and social stressors as a consequence of migration (Leventhal & Brooks-Gunn, 2000), this sets the stage for intergenerational cultural dissonance (ICD; Kane et al., 2016) and stress in immigrant families (Le & Stockdale, 2008). On top of this, the risk perspective emphasizes that immigrants are frequently confronted with prejudice and discrimination which may negatively affect their mental health (Pascoe & Smart Richman, 2009; Schmitt, Branscombe, Postmes, & Garcia, 2014).

In contrast, a resilience perspective (Masten, 2014) emphasizes the healthy developmental trajectories that immigrant youth often display, despite the challenges that the immigration process holds for them and their families (Motti-Stefanidi, Berry, Chryssochoou, Sam, & Phinney, 2012). It is a perspective that highlights the personal, familial, communal, and social resources that immigrant youth draw upon. This notion is also reflected in the so-called "immigrant paradox" (e.g., Fuligni, 2012), holding that immigrant adolescents fare as well, or at times even better, than their non-immigrant peers. This paradox has been explained by pointing to immigrants' strong ethnic support system, sense of family obligations, and academic motivation optimizing the mental health of immigrant adolescents (e.g., Garcia Coll et al., 2012; Van Geel & Vedder, 2011).

The two perspectives are reflected in the mixed results of many former studies on this topic. Several systematic reviews have been conducted. For instance, Stevens and Vollebergh (2008) showed results to vary hugely between studies, with some empirical studies showing more mental health problems in (first and second-generation) immigrant than non-immigrant adolescents, others finding similar levels in both groups, and some showing lower levels of mental health problems in immigrant than in non-immigrant adolescents. An analysis of the studies suggested that mixed findings are due to both the characteristics of immigrant groups and receiving countries. This indicates that understanding the mental health of immigrant children and adolescents is not just a question of a theoretical perspective but is embedded in an understanding of the unique context of specific immigrant groups and individuals (e.g., the values, culture, and the social, political, and economic situation of the country of origin and the receiving country and the social capital of the specific immigrant group) (Berry, 1997).

In their reviews, other authors also acknowledged the importance of this unique context of specific immigrant groups for understanding the mental health of immigrant children and adolescents (Dimitrova, Chasiotis, & Van De Vijver, 2016; Kouider, Koglin, & Petermann, 2014, 2015). However, these authors nevertheless concluded that adolescents with an immigration background, on average, are at increased risk of mental health problems. Kouider and colleagues (2014, 2015) reported immigrant adolescents in Europe and to a lesser extent in American countries as experiencing higher levels of internalizing problems and an equal level of externalizing problems than non-immigrant adolescents. Based on a meta-analysis, Dimitrova and colleagues (2016) came to the partly different conclusion that immigrant adolescents in Northern Europe report more externalizing problems than non-immigrant adolescents, while in pre-adolescent samples in Western Europe internalizing problems were higher in immigrants than in non-immigrants.

Thus, notwithstanding the (at least partial) support for the risk perspective on immigration and adolescent mental health from these overviews of the literature, the overviews also reveal that it is difficult or perhaps even undesirable to draw generalized conclusions about this association. Effects may not only vary with the age group and type of mental health problem, but may also crucially depend upon the context in which immigrant adolescents and their parents grow up in. Immigration is an extremely heterogeneous phenomenon, with different groups of immigrants with a great variety of economic, social, and cultural backgrounds moving into very different countries. In this chapter, we will argue that understanding the mental health of immigrant adolescents demands taking into account aspects of the particular environments in which they live.

An ecological approach to the mental health of immigrant adolescents

The current chapter encourages a multi-level, ecological approach to human development, in which the adolescent experience must be understood within multiple layers of influence, starting from the resources of the individual, through proximal sources of influence, such as the family, school, and peers and including more distal influences, such as the neighborhood, community, and national context and policies. Distal influences such as those occurring at the national, neighborhood, and community level are expected to translate into a variety of changes at the proximal and individual level. However, in order for these distal influences to occur, they need to be perceived, appraised, and negotiated by individuals to be able to become psychologically effective (e.g., Pinquart & Silbereisen, 2004). This implies that interindividual differences in the perceptions and evaluations of changes at distal levels are key to understanding the impact of distal influences on the individual.

In the Integrative Framework for Studying Immigrant Youth Adaptation (IFSIY) (Motti-Stefanidi, Berry et al., 2012), a three-level approach for understanding the adaptation of immigrant adolescents is suggested: the individual level, the interaction level, and the societal level, in which the three levels are interconnected to each other. The framework synthesizes this three-level model with resilience (Masten, 2014) and acculturation (Berry, 1997) approaches to suggest the importance of understanding not only the relevance of multiple levels of influence but also to emphasize the interaction between the young person with each of these layers of influence and the interactions between the levels themselves (Motti-Stefanidi, Asendorpf, & Masten, 2012).

Notwithstanding the former, many studies on immigrant adolescent mental health tend to remain within the more immediate spheres of influence, namely the young person him or herself and their families. Whilst giving rich and valuable data, these studies often neglect the wider context within which the young person is developing. Conceptually, hypothesizing that characteristics at the country level can trickle down to impact on the mental health of the individual adolescent and/or to consider the overall characteristics of the school and not only the young person's perception of it can, at times, seem remote. Yet, a comprehensive understanding of young people's developmental trajectories must incorporate an understanding of multiple layers of impact. In the current chapter, we focus on two specific contexts: the national context and the school context as two critical ecological environments within which the young person is developing.

The impact of the national context on the mental health of immigrant adolescents

The vast majority of research to date has examined immigrant adolescents' mental health in single countries (Dimitrova et al., 2016; Kouider et al., 2014, 2015; Stevens & Vollebergh, 2008). The available internationally comparative studies were mostly conducted in a limited number of (North-Western European) countries (two to five) and focused on non-representative groups of (immigrant and non-immigrant) adolescents. Overall these studies found the mental health problems of immigrant adolescents to vary by the particular receiving country (Geven, Kalmijn, & van Tubergen, 2016; Mood, Jonsson, & Låftman, 2016). Our own study that used representative samples in ten countries revealed that immigrant adolescents reported higher levels of psychosomatic problems, physical fighting and bullying, and lower life satisfaction than non-immigrant adolescents (Stevens et al., 2015). Remarkably, differences in these indicators of mental health problems between immigrant and non-immigrant adolescents did not vary significantly with the receiving country studied, suggesting a general effect of immigration on adolescent mental health in these (mostly North-Western and Southern European) countries. This finding partially contrasts with the results from the meta-analysis conducted by Dimitrova and colleagues (2016) showing that immigrant children and adolescents growing up in particular geographic areas in Europe (Northern and Western Europe) are especially likely to show internalizing and externalizing problems when compared to their non-immigrant peers. Clearly, more research is warranted, not only into investigating whether and to what extent the mental health of immigrant adolescents depends upon certain characteristics of the receiving country, but also upon the specific combination of the characteristics of the receiving country and the immigrant population. In the following we will highlight several examples of why the national context may be important for the mental health of immigrant adolescents.

National-level migration and integration policies

European countries have different policies aimed at the integration of immigrant populations, in terms of family reunion, education, political participation, long-term residence, access to nationality, anti-discrimination, and labor market mobility which are collated in the

Migrant Integration Policy Index (MIPEX). Using this index, European countries can be classified into three policy models (Meuleman, Davidov, & Billiet, 2009). The inclusive model has inclusive policies in all dimensions; the assimilationist model offers relatively easy access to nationality but limited access to the labor market and family reunion, and puts little emphasis on anti-discrimination policies; and the exclusionist model excludes immigrants from most spheres of life and perceives immigrants as "temporary guests." It is likely that these policy models shape the context of the immigrant experience (Borrell et al., 2015). Generally, it is expected that inclusive migration policies will reduce tensions between the receiving society and new groups, while at the same time addressing the feeling among immigrants that they are being discriminated against and oppressed (Hooghe, Reeskens, & Stolle, 2007). However, critics point out that multicultural policy might also lead to cultural and social isolation of immigrant groups and even distrust between groups, because it may encourage (cultural or physical) separation between groups (Barry, 2002). Either way, more positive interethnic relations and fewer perceptions of discrimination are likely to impact upon the lives of both immigrant adults and adolescents directly. Moreover, the stressors immigrant adults face, for instance those related to difficulties in the labor market or prejudices, may also have consequences for their children through problematic family functioning (Lorenzo-Blanco et al., 2017).

These two contrasting perspectives are reflected in the empirical literature. On the one hand, inclusive migration polices have been found to stimulate immigrants' political integration (e.g., political participation and interest, trust in the government) (Jackson & Doerschler, 2016; Koopmans, 2013). Somewhat related to this, multicultural policies and voting rights for foreigners are associated with higher levels of average trust towards strangers in a particular country (Hooghe et al., 2007). On the other hand, while there is some evidence that Muslims are less likely to report discrimination in states with higher multicultural policy orientation (Jackson & Doerschler, 2016), other research indicates that inclusive migration policies are not associated with fewer perceptions of ethnic discrimination (André & Dronkers, 2017) and inclusive migration policies were even associated with fewer interethnic contacts (Koopmans, 2013). Moreover, studies that reveal an association between inclusive migration policies and socioeconomic integration such as unemployment and labor market participation are scarce (Koopmans, 2013). For instance, policies of receiving countries aimed at a better inclusion of immigrants in their society have no effect on the science score of pupils with an immigrant background (Dronkers & De Heus, 2012).

Thus, previous research indicates some positive social effects of inclusive migration policies, although these may also hamper interethnic contact – at least among adults – and may not prevent feelings of discrimination. As such, it remains to be seen to what extent there are associations between migration policies and immigrant mental health, particularly among young people. Among children and adolescents, the scarcity of internationally comparative studies hinders an answer to this research question. As a rough indication of the importance of migration policies for child immigrant mental health, Dimitrova and colleagues (2016) included the MIPEX as a context variable in their meta-analysis. They found that the easier immigrants could reunite with their families and become permanent residents in the receiving country, the fewer their children's internalizing and externalizing problems were respectively. Thus, there is some initial evidence that migration policies may matter for the mental health of immigrant children.

Research focusing on adults is less rare. Although there are some inconsistencies in findings (Levecque & Van Rossem, 2015), overall the literature suggests inclusive migration policies to have positive effects on immigrant health (Giannoni, Franzini, & Masiero, 2016). For instance, research indicates that self-rated health and depression inequalities between immigrants and non-immigrants were stronger in countries with exclusionist and assimilationist policies than in countries with multicultural migration policies, even after adjusting for differences in socioeconomic conditions between these three types of countries (Malmusi, Palència, Ikram, Kunst, & Borrell, 2017). However, migration and integration policies may not only affect immigrant health directly, they may also increase the deteriorating effects of certain risk factors immigrants may be faced with. Notably, Borrell and colleagues (2015) showed that associations between perceived discrimination and self-reported health and depression among adult immigrants were more often found in countries with assimilationist than with inclusive integration policies.

National-level attitudes towards immigrants

Not only migration and integration policies, but also the general public's level of anti-immigrant attitudes may color the immigrant experience in different receiving countries, and as such may impact the mental health of immigrant adolescents. Research on majorities' attitudes towards immigrants has indicated large differences between countries (Coenders, Lubbers, & Scheepers, 2005; Meuleman et al., 2009). Also, it has been substantiated that frequent anti-immigrant attitudes create barriers to full societal participation and may lead to discrimination, with potentially destructive consequences for immigrant adolescent mental health (Schmitt et al., 2014). Thus, the more unfavorable attitudes towards immigrants are in a certain country, the more mental health problems immigrant adolescents may experience.

Again, the lack of large-scale internationally comparative studies on the mental health of immigrant adolescents makes it very difficult to address this research question. Still, there is some indirect empirical evidence to suggest that these attitudes are important for the (mental) health of immigrants. Virta, Sam, and Westin (2004) assessed internalizing problems in Turkish immigrant adolescents in Norway and Sweden. Although the Turkish immigrants in both countries shared a common migration history, Turks in Norway reported more internalizing problems than Turks in Sweden when differences in SES and country of birth were controlled for. These differences were accounted for by the weaker Turkish identity and higher frequency of perceived discrimination of Turkish immigrants in Norway compared to those in Sweden, which may be the result of differences in attitudes toward immigrants in these two countries. Research on this topic among adults is extremely scarce too. One study assessed anti-immigrant attitudes at the community level and found that second-generation immigrants had a higher risk of mortality in communities with greater anti-immigrant prejudice, while such an effect was not found for first-generation immigrants (Morey, Gee, Muennig, & Hatzenbuehler, 2018).

National-level cultural distance

The mental health of immigrant adolescents may not only depend upon structural national characteristics of the receiving country such as migration and integration policies and anti-immigrant attitudes, but the interplay between origin and receiving country characteristics may also be essential for the mental health of immigrant adolescents. In this respect, Berry (2006) claimed that the magnitude of the impact of immigration on mental health may depend on the extent to which the two cultures in contact differ from each other. In this respect the term "cultural distance" has been often used, which is defined as differences between two distinct cultures including economic and socio-cultural aspects (e.g., ethnicity, language) which are associated with differences in values, norms, and habits (Demes & Geeraert, 2015). According to Babiker and colleagues' (Babiker, Cox, & Miller, 1980) classic cultural distance hypothesis, acculturating into a culture highly dissimilar to one's original culture is difficult, stressful, and may lead to alienation. Related to this, it has been suggested that immigrants encountering a culture that is highly dissimilar to that of their country of origin may experience "culture shock," referring to a disorientating experience of suddenly finding that one's culture of origin perspectives and behaviors are not shared by members of the receiving society and that of losing the power of easy communication (Bochner, 2013). These processes of alienation and experiences of "culture shock" may be especially detrimental during adolescence, a period in which adolescents develop their own identity.

Research testing the cultural distance hypothesis again is extremely scarce, especially research focusing on children and adolescents. Several studies have been conducted predominantly among international students in different receiving countries, showing that students that *perceived* a higher cultural distance have a more difficult psychological adaptation (Suanet & Van de Vijver, 2009). However, other studies could not confirm such an association (Nesdale & Mak, 2003). Moreover, recent literature has suggested the use of objective instead of subjective measures to test the cultural distance hypothesis. For instance, Geeraert and Demoulin (2013) argue that the use of subjective measures may be problematic since immigrants who experience more difficulties during the acculturation process may also be more prone to perceive more cultural differences. To our knowledge, only one study tested the impact of objective cultural distance on adult psychological well-being (Kashima & Abu-Rayya, 2014). Their findings revealed that higher levels of cultural distance in two out of four cultural dimensions are associated with lower psychological well-being.

The impact of the school context on the mental health of immigrant adolescents

School is the place where young people spend a significant proportion of their days (Svensson, Stattin, & Kerr, 2011) and professionals at school can function as major socialization agents in their lives (Walsemann, Bell, & Maitra, 2011). Research has focused on a number of different dimensions within the school experience which are likely to impact on young people's well-being and mental health, among both immigrants and non-immigrants. These dimensions include teacher and peer support (Suldo et al., 2009), classroom climate (Samdal, Nutbeam, Wold, & Kannas, 1998), and levels of school pressure and school perceptions (Harel-Fisch et al., 2011).

For immigrant adolescents, the school context may also be significant in many other ways, as it is the place where immigrant young people can learn the cultural values, norms, and behaviors needed for their integration into the receiving society. In school, they form contacts with receiving-society peers, which can either enable and enhance their integration and sense of belonging (D'hondt, Van Houtte, & Stevens, 2015), or can be patterned by discrimination and lead to feelings of rejection and alienation. In addition, in circumstances where immigrant parents are coping with their own immigration stressors (Lorenzo-Blanco et al., 2017), the school context and the adults within it may play a salient role as significant others in the young people's lives (Walsh, Harel-Fisch, & Fogel-Grinvald, 2010), and as institutional representatives of the receiving society (Jasinskaja-Lahti, Liebkind, & Perhoniemi, 2006).

Research has shown the critical role of teacher and peer support in the mental health of immigrant adolescents. For instance, increased teacher support was found to reduce levels of depressive and anxiety symptoms among first generation immigrant youth in the U.S. (Potochnick & Perreira, 2010). Teacher, peer, and parental involvement in school were all found to be significant in predicting psychological well-being among immigrant adolescents in Israel (Walsh et al., 2010). In addition to these general relational measures, immigration related support measures are relevant for understanding immigrant adolescents' mental health. For example, perceived support for integration and inclusion in the school has been associated with higher levels of well-being among immigrant boys and girls (Schachner, Van de Vijver, & Noack, 2018). A particular area of research has been the negative aspect of relations in the school environment, particular focusing on the area of discrimination. Recent research has shown the importance of perceived discrimination both by teachers and by peers in the school context (D'hondt, Eccles, Van Houtte, & Stevens, 2016; Walsh et al., 2018) for the mental health of immigrant adolescents.

Yet, studies on the role of the school context on immigrant adolescent mental health such as those described above have generally taken an individual level perspective (i.e., the perception of the young person of, for instance, the levels of teacher and peer support). In general, few studies have taken a multi-level approach to examine how classroom level support (i.e., an aggregated level of perceived school support) impacts on adolescent mental health (Kidger, Araya, Donovan, & Gunnell, 2012). While an understanding of the individual's perspective of the school context is critical, widening the research goals to see how the school level contributes to immigrant adolescent mental health may be fruitful (Brenick, Titzmann, Michel, & Silbereisen, 2012). Although studies focusing on the latter are scarce, they do indicate the importance of investigating variables on the school level. In our own research, we found that classroom support aggregated on the school level was associated with lower levels of peer violence in both immigrants and non-immigrants (Walsh et al., 2015). Lee and colleagues (2018) found that school-level structural characteristics, such as high levels of school dropout, negatively predict immigrant adolescent school achievements. More research is needed to tease apart the impact of the school context on both the individual and school level, on immigrant adolescent mental health.

Immigrant school composition (ISC) and the mental health of immigrant adolescents

ISC is considered to be the percentage of immigrant adolescents in a school (Agirdag, Demanet, Van Houtte, & Van Avermaet, 2011) and has been suggested as one of the critical factors in understanding levels of mental health among immigrant (and non-immigrant) adolescents (Vervoort, Scholte, &

Overbeek, 2010). The relationship between ISC and different aspects of mental health may be explained through Integrative Threat Theory (Stephan & Stephan, 2000) and Social Identity Theory (Tajfel & Turner, 1979). From these theoretical perspectives, the influx of immigrants in communities and schools is seen to pose fundamental psychological threats, both realistic and symbolic (Stephan, Lausanne Renfro, Esses, White Stephan, & Martin, 2005), to majority groups and may lead to discrimination and prejudice toward the immigrants (Brenick et al., 2012), leading to an internalization of negative perceptions among immigrant youth and intergroup violence (Jackson, 1993). Indeed, studies suggest that in schools with higher percentages of immigrants, the latter perceive discrimination more frequently (Closson, Darwich, Hymel, & Waterhouse, 2014). In turn, greater numbers of immigrant youth in a school may increase their feelings of strength and power which may enable them to fight back or challenge the position of the ethnic majority group and attain greater social dominance (Vervoort et al., 2010). The combination of these two processes can fuel competition and conflicts for social status between immigrant and non-immigrant groups in ethnically mixed schools (Esses, Jackson, Dovidio, & Hodson, 2008), impacting on the mental health of both immigrant and non-immigrant adolescents. An alternative hypothesis has also been formulated, stating that higher percentages of immigrants in a classroom could enable immigrant adolescents to feel a greater sense of connection and belonging within their own ethnic group or the immigrant group in general, while the opposite may be true for non-immigrants (Benner & Crosnoe, 2011). Yet, greater numbers of immigrants in the classroom may make it harder for the immigrant young person to feel a connection to the receiving society, preventing processes of acculturation.

Studies on ISC (or sometimes referred to as ethnic school composition in cases of mixed ethnic groups in a class) have often focused on specific aspects of mental health problems (bullying and fighting) among immigrant and non-immigrant adolescents within the same class. For instance, in our own research on ISC among adolescents in 11 countries (Walsh et al., 2015), we found that a higher percentage of immigrant adolescents in a school was related to more physical fighting and bullying perpetration for both immigrant and non-immigrant adolescents, yet lower levels of victimization for immigrant youth. In contrast, several studies examined the relationship between ISC and internalizing or externalizing problems, and found that in classrooms with higher percentages of immigrants, immigrant adolescents report lower levels of these problems (Geven et al., 2016; Gieling, Vollebergh, & Van Dorsselaer, 2010; Madsen et al., 2016). Many research questions need (further) examination such as whether or not the strength and significance of this association depends on the specific outcomes used, students' ethnicity and country of residence (Geven et al., 2016), the specific operationalization of ISC (size of immigrant or ethnic group, ethnic diversity, see for instance Madsen et al., 2016), or the school climate (Walsh et al., 2015). Additionally, more attention should be paid to potential mediating pathways to test the above suggested opposite pathways in the association between ISC and immigrant adolescent mental health (Geven et al., 2016). Finally, effects of ISC on adolescent mental health may also depend upon the characteristics of the individual immigrant adolescent (e.g., his or her acculturation orientation) (Titzmann & Jugert, 2015) and (other) characteristics of the particular class (e.g., the class climate and classroom level attitudes toward immigrants) (Walsh et al., 2015).

Conclusion

Both the theory and empirical literature on the impact of immigration on the mental health of adolescents indicate that generalized conclusions about this impact are difficult or perhaps even undesirable. In this chapter, we argued that understanding this phenomenon may demand taking into account aspects of the particular environments, specifically the school and national context. In fact, we reasoned, based on available theory and the empirical evidence, that specific school and country characteristics may crucially color the experiences of immigrant adolescents, and as such their mental health. However, the lack of ecologically based empirical studies among adolescents is notable. Given the scarcity of available research, ample research questions still need to be addressed, and some of them are pretty straightforward especially those concerning the impact of the national context. For instance, how important are national level migration and integration policies and attitudes for the mental health of immigrant adolescents? In addition, what might the mediational mechanisms be by which national or school contexts can trickle down to impact on the mental health of immigrant adolescents? How might seemingly distal processes interact with each other? Considering the notion that in order for these distal influences to occur, they need to be perceived and appraised by individuals (e.g., Pinquart & Silbereisen, 2004), how do individual characteristics (e.g., an individual's acculturation orientation, personality characteristics, social support from friends, parents) alleviate or strengthen the school or national-level effects? A more comprehensive understanding of the impact of the multiple levels of context on adolescent immigrant mental health may not only be relevant scientifically, but can also be used to inform policy makers, educators, and counselors working with young immigrant people.

References

Agirdag, O., Demanet, J., Van Houtte, M., & Van Avermaet, P. (2011). Ethnic school composition and peer victimization: A focus on the interethnic school climate. *International Journal of Intercultural Relations, 35*, 465–473.

André, S., & Dronkers, J. (2017). Perceived in-group discrimination by first and second generation immigrants from different countries of origin in 27 EU member-states. *International Sociology*, 32(1), 105–129.

Babiker, I. E., Cox, J. L., & Miller, P. M. C. (1980). The measurement of cultural distance and its relationship to medical consultations, symptomatology and examination performance of overseas students at Edinburgh University. *Social Psychiatry*, 15(3), 109–116.

Barry, B. (2002). *Culture and equality: An egalitarian critique of multiculturalism.* Harvard: University Press.

Benner, A. D., & Crosnoe, R. (2011). The racial/ethnic composition of elementary schools and young children's academic and socioemotional functioning. *American Educational Research Journal*, 48(3), 621–646.

Berry, J. W. (1997). Immigration, acculturation, and adaptation. *Applied Psychology*, 46, 5–34.

Berry, J. W. (2006). Stress perspectives on acculturation. In D. L. Sam & J. W. Berry (Eds.), *Acculturation psychology*. (pp. 43–57). New York: Cambridge University Press.

Bochner, S. (2013). *Cultures in contact: Studies in cross-cultural interaction (Vol. 1).* Oxford, UK: Elsevier.

Borrell, C., Palència, L., Bartoll, X., Ikram, U., Malmusi, D., & health, P. (2015). Perceived discrimination and health among immigrants in Europe according to national integration policies. *International Journal of Environmental Research and Public Health*, 12(9), 10687–10699.

Brenick, A., Titzmann, P. F., Michel, A., & Silbereisen, R. K. (2012). Perceptions of discrimination by young diaspora migrants: Individual-and school-level associations among adolescent ethnic German immigrants. *European Psychologist*, 17(2), 105–119.

Closson, L. M., Darwich, L., Hymel, S., & Waterhouse, T. (2014). Ethnic discrimination among recent immigrant adolescents: Variations as a function of ethnicity and school context. *Journal of Research on Adolescence*, 24(4), 608–614.

Coenders, M., Lubbers, M., & Scheepers, P. (2005). Majorities' attitudes towards minorities in European Union member states: Results from the Standard Eurobarometer 1997-2000-2003 [report 2]. In M. Coenders, M. Lubbers, & P. Scheepers (Eds.), *Majority populations' attitudes towards migrants and minorities* (pp. 279–320). Vienna: European Monitoring. Centre on Racism and Xenophobia.

D'hondt, F., Eccles, J. S., Van Houtte, M., & Stevens, P. A. J. (2016). Perceived ethnic discrimination by teachers and ethnic minority students' academic futility: Can parents prepare their youth for better or for worse? *Journal of Youth and Adolescence*, 45, 1075–1089.

D'hondt, F., Van Houtte, M., & Stevens, P. A. J. (2015). How does ethnic and non-ethnic victimization by peers and by teachers relate to the school belongingness of ethnic minority students in Flanders, Belgium? An explorative study. *Social Psychology of Education*, 18, 685–701.

Demes, K. A., & Geeraert, N. (2015). The highs and lows of a cultural transition: A longitudinal analysis of sojourner stress and adaptation across 50 countries. *Journal of Personality and Social Psychology*, 109(2), 316–337.

Dimitrova, R., Chasiotis, A., & Van De Vijver, F. (2016). Adjustment outcomes of immigrant children and youth in Europe. *European Psychologist*, 21, 150–162.

Dronkers, J., & De Heus, M. (2012). *The educational performance of children of immigrants in sixteen OECD countries.* London: Centre for Research and Analysis of Migration.

Esses, V. M., Jackson, L. M., Dovidio, J. F., & Hodson, G. (2008). Instrumental relations among groups: Group competition, conflict, and prejudice. In J. F. Dovidio, P. Glick, & L. A. Rudman (Eds.), *On the nature of prejudice: Fifty years after Allport* (pp. 225–243). Oxford, UK: Blackwell publishing.

Fuligni, A. J. (2012). The intersection of aspirations and resources in the development of children from immigrant families. In C. García Coll & A. Kerivan Marks (Eds.), *The immigrant paradox in children and adolescents: Is becoming American a developmental risk?* (pp. 61–76). Washington, DC: American Psychological Association.

Garcia Coll, C., Patton, F., Kerivan Marks, A., Domitrova, R., Yang, R., Suarez, G. A., & Patrico, A. (2012). Understanding the immigrant paradox in youth. In A. S. Masten, K. Liebkind, & D. J. Hernandez (Eds.), *Realizing the potential of immigrant youth* (pp. 159–180). Cambridge: University Press.

Geeraert, N., & Demoulin, S. (2013). Acculturative stress or resilience? A longitudinal multilevel analysis of sojourners' stress and self-esteem. *Journal of Cross-Cultural Psychology, 44*(8), 1241–1262.

Geven, S., Kalmijn, M., & van Tubergen, F. (2016). The ethnic composition of schools and students' problem behaviour in four European countries: The role of friends. *Journal of Ethnic and Migration Studies, 42*(9), 1473–1495.

Giannoni, M., Franzini, L., & Masiero, G. (2016). Migrant integration policies and health inequalities in Europe. *BMC Public Health, 16*(1), 463.

Gieling, M., Vollebergh, W. A. M., & Van Dorsselaer, S. (2010). Ethnic density in school classes and adolescent mental health. *Social Psychiatry and Psychiatric Epidemiology, 45*(6), 639–646.

Harel-Fisch, Y., Walsh, S. D., Grinvald-Fogel, H., Amitai, G., Pickett, W., Molcho, M., ... Craig, W. (2011). Negative school perceptions and involvement in school bullying: A universal relationship across 40 countries. *Journal of Adolescence, 34*, 369–652.

Hooghe, M., Reeskens, T., & Stolle, D. (2007). Diversity, multiculturalism and social cohesion: Trust and ethnocentrism in European societies. In K. Banting, T. Courchene, & L. Seidle (Eds.), *Belonging? Diversity, recognition and shared citizenship in Canada* (pp. 387–410). Montreal: Institute for Research on Public Policy.

Jackson, J. W. (1993). Realistic group conflict theory: A review and evaluation of the theoretical and empirical literature. *The Psychological Record, 43*, 395–413.

Jackson, P. I., & Doerschler, P. (2016). How safe do majority group members, ethnic minorities, and muslims feel in multicultural European societies? *Democracy and Security, 12*(4), 247–277.

Jasinskaja-Lahti, I., Liebkind, K., & Perhoniemi, R. (2006). Perceived discrimination and well-being: A victim study of different immigrant groups. *Journal of Community & Applied Social Psychology, 16*(4), 267–284.

Kane, J. C., Johnson, R. M., Robinson, C., Jernigan, D. H., Harachi, T. W., & Bass, J. K. (2016). The impact of intergenerational cultural dissonance on alcohol use among Vietnamese and Cambodian adolescents in the United States. *Journal of Adolescent Health, 58*(2), 174–180.

Kashima, E. S., & Abu-Rayya, H. M. (2014). Longitudinal associations of cultural distance with psychological well-being among Australian immigrants from 49 countries. *Journal of Cross-Cultural Psychology, 45*(4), 587–600.

Kidger, J., Araya, R., Donovan, J., & Gunnell, D. (2012). The effect of the school environment on the emotional health of adolescents: A systematic review. *Pediatrics, 129*, 925–949.

Koopmans, R. (2013). Multiculturalism and immigration: A contested field in cross-national comparison. *Annual Review of Sociology, 39*, 147–169.

Kouider, E. B., Koglin, U., & Petermann, F. (2014). Emotional and behavioral problems in migrant children and adolescents in Europe: A systematic review. *European Child & Adolescent Psychiatry, 23*, 373–391.

Kouider, E. B., Koglin, U., & Petermann, F. (2015). Emotional and behavioral problems in migrant children and adolescents in American countries: A systematic review. *Journal of Immigrant and Minority Health, 17*(4), 1240–1258.

Kwak, K. (2003). Adolescents and their parents: A review of intergenerational family relations for immigrant and non-immigrant families. *Human Development, 46*, 115–136.

Le, T. N., & Stockdale, G. (2008). Acculturative dissonance, ethnic identity, and youth violence. *Cultural Diversity and Ethnic Minority Psychology, 14*, 1–9.

Lee, M., Kim, Y., & Madyun, N. (2018). Do relational and structural characteristics of negative school environments independently predict immigrant adolescents' academic achievement? *Social Psychology of Education, 21*, 539–563.

Levecque, K., & Van Rossem, R. (2015). Depression in Europe: Does migrant integration have mental health payoffs? A cross-national comparison of 20 European countries. *Ethnicity & Health, 20*(1), 49–65.

Leventhal, T., & Brooks-Gunn, J. (2000). The neighborhoods they live in: The effects of neighborhood residence on child and adolescent outcomes. *Psychological Bulletin, 126*, 309–337.

Lorenzo-Blanco, E. I., Meca, A., Pina-Watson, B., Zamboanga, B. L., Szapocznik, J., Cano, M., ... Des Rosiers, S. E. (2017). Longitudinal trajectories of family functioning among recent immigrant adolescents and parents: Links with adolescent and parent cultural stress, emotional well-being, and behavioral health. *Child Development*. Advance online publication. doi: 10.1111/cdev.12914.

Madsen, K. R., Damsgaard, M. T., Rubin, M., Jervelund, S. S., Lasgaard, M., Walsh, S., ... Holstein, B. E. (2016). Loneliness and ethnic composition of the school class: A nationally random sample of adolescents. *Journal of Youth and Adolescence, 45*(7), 1350–1365.

Malmusi, D., Palència, L., Ikram, U. Z., Kunst, A. E., & Borrell, C. (2017). Inequalities by immigrant status in depressive symptoms in Europe: The role of integration policy regimes. *Social Psychiatry and Psychiatric Epidemiology, 52*(4), 391–398.

Masten, A. S. (2014). Global perspectives on resilience in children and youth. *Child Development, 85*(1), 6–20.

Meuleman, B., Davidov, E., & Billiet, J. (2009). Changing attitudes toward immigration in Europe, 2002-2007: A dynamic group conflict theory approach. *Social Science Research, 38*(2), 352–365.

Mood, C., Jonsson, J. O., & Låftman, S. B. (2016). Immigrant integration and youth mental health in four European countries. *European Sociological Review, 32* (6), 716–729.

Morey, B. N., Gee, G. C., Muennig, P., & Hatzenbuehler, M. L. (2018). Community-level prejudice and mortality among immigrant groups. *Social Science & Medicine, 199*, 56–66.

Motti-Stefanidi, F., Asendorpf, J. B., & Masten, A. S. (2012). The adaptation and well-being of adolescent immigrants in Greek schools: A multilevel, longitudinal study of risks and resources. *Development and Psychopathology, 24*(2), 451–473.

Motti-Stefanidi, F., Berry, J. W., Chryssochoou, X., Sam, D. L., & Phinney, J. (2012). Positive immigrant youth adaptation in context: Developmental, acculturation, and social psychological perspectives. In A. Masten, K. Liebkind, & D. Hernandez (Eds.), *Realizing the potential of immigrant youth* (pp. 117–158). Cambridge: Cambridge University Press.

Nesdale, D., & Mak, A. S. (2003). Ethnic identification, self-esteem and immigrant psychological health. *International Journal of Intercultural Relations, 27*(1), 23–40.

Pantin, H., Schwartz, S. J., Sullivan, S., Coatsworth, J. D., & Szapocznik, J. (2003). Preventing substance abuse in Hispanic immigrant adolescents: An ecodevelopmental, parent-centered approach. *Hispanic Journal of Behavioral Sciences, 25*(4), 469–500.

Pascoe, E. A., & Smart Richman, L. (2009). Perceived discrimination and health: A meta-analytic review. *Psychological Bulletin, 135*(4), 531–554.

Pinquart, M., & Silbereisen, R. K. (2004). Human development in times of social change: Theoretical considerations and research needs. *International Journal of Behavioral Development, 28*, 289–298.

Potochnick, S. R., & Perreira, K. M. (2010). Depression and anxiety among first-generation immigrant Latino youth: Key correlates and implications for future research. *The Journal of Nervous and Mental Disease, 198*(7), 470–477.

Samdal, O., Nutbeam, D., Wold, B., & Kannas, L. (1998). Achieving health and educational goals through schools-a study of the importance of the school climate and the students' satisfaction with school. *Health Education Research, 13*(3), 383–397.

Schachner, M. K., Van de Vijver, F. J. R., & Noack, P. (2018). Acculturation and school adjustment of early-adolescent immigrant boys and girls in Germany: Conditions in school, family, and ethnic group. *The Journal of Early Adolescence, 38*(3), 352–384.

Schmitt, M. T., Branscombe, N. R., Postmes, T., & Garcia, A. (2014). The consequences of perceived discrimination for psychological well-being: A meta-analytic review. *Psychological Bulletin, 140*(4), 921.

Stephan, W. G., Lausanne Renfro, C., Esses, V. M., White Stephan, C., & Martin, T. (2005). The effects of feeling threatened on attitudes toward immigrants. *International Journal of Intercultural Relations, 29*, 1–19.

Stephan, W. G., & Stephan, C. W. (2000). An integrated threat theory of prejudice. In S. Oskamp (Ed.), *Reducing prejudice and discrimination* (pp. 23–45). Mahwah, NJ: Lawrence Erlbaum.

Stevens, G. W. J. M., & Vollebergh, W. A. M. (2008). Mental health in migrant children. *Journal of Child Psychology and Psychiatry, 49*(3), 276–294.

Stevens, G. W. J. M., Walsh, S. D., Huijts, T., Maes, M., Madsen, K. R., Cavallo, F., & Molcho, M. (2015). An internationally comparative study of immigration and adolescent emotional and behavioral problems: Effects of generation and gender. *Journal of Adolescent Health*, 57(6), 587–594.

Suanet, I., & Van de Vijver, F. J. (2009). Perceived cultural distance and acculturation among exchange students in Russia. *Journal of Community & Applied Social Psychology*, 19(3), 182–197.

Suldo, S. M., Friedrich, A. A., White, T., Farmer, J., Minch, D., & Michalowski, J. (2009). Teacher support and adolescents' subjective well-being: A mixed-methods investigation. *School Psychology Review*, 38(1), 67.

Svensson, Y., Stattin, H., & Kerr, M. (2011). In-and out-of-school peer groups of immigrant youths. *European Journal of Developmental Psychology*, 8(4), 490–507.

Tajfel, H., & Turner, J. C. (1979). An integrative theory of intergroup conflict. In W. G. Austin & S. Worchel (Eds.), *The social psychology of intergroup relations* (pp. 33–48). Monterey, CA: Brooks/Cole.

Titzmann, P. F., & Jugert, P. (2015). Acculturation in context: The moderating effects of immigrant and native peer orientations on the acculturation experiences of immigrants. *Journal of Youth and Adolescence*, 44(11), 2079–2094.

Torres, L., Driscoll, M. W., & Voell, M. (2012). Discrimination, acculturation, acculturative stress, and Latino psychological distress: A moderated mediational model. *Cultural Diversity and Ethnic Minority Psychology*, 18(1), 17–25.

Van Geel, M., & Vedder, P. (2011). The role of family obligations and school adjustment in explaining the immigrant paradox. *Journal of Youth and Adolescence*, 40, 187–196.

Vervoort, M. H. M., Scholte, R. H. J., & Overbeek, G. (2010). Bullying and victimization among adolescents: The role of ethnicity and ethnic composition of school class. *Journal of Youth and Adolescence*, 39, 1–11.

Virta, E., Sam, L. D., & Westin, C. (2004). Adolescents with Turkish background in Norway and Sweden: A comparative study of their psychological adaptation. *Scandinavian Journal of Psychology*, 45, 15–25.

Walsemann, K. M., Bell, B. A., & Maitra, D. (2011). The intersection of school racial composition and student race/ethnicity on adolescent depressive and somatic symptoms. *Social Science & Medicine*, 72(11), 1873–1883.

Walsh, S. D., De Clercq, B., Molcho, M., Harel-Fisch, Y., Davison, C. M., Madsen, K. R., & Stevens, G. W. J. M. (2015). The relationship between immigrant school composition, classmate support and involvement in physical fighting and bullying among adolescent immigrants and non-immigrants in 11 countries. *Journal of Youth and Adolescence*, 45(1), 1–16.

Walsh, S. D., Harel-Fisch, Y., & Fogel-Grinvald, H. (2010). Parents, teachers and peer relations as predictors of risk behaviors and mental well-being among immigrant and Israeli born adolescents. *Social Science & Medicine*, 70, 976–984.

Walsh, S. D., Kolobov, T., Raiz, Y., Boniel-Nissim, M., Tesler, R., & Harel-Fisch, Y. (2018). The role of identity and psychosomatic symptoms as mediating the relationship between discrimination and risk behaviors among first and second generation immigrant adolescents. *Journal of Adolescence*, 64, 34–47.

Wenar, C., & Kerig, P. (2000). *Developmental psychopathology: From infancy through adolescence*. New York, NY: McGraw-Hill.

Part II

Innovative Methods

Chapter 7

Applying experience-sampling methods to investigate the impact of school diversity on youth development in multicultural contexts

Tiffany Yip, Yuen Mi Cheon, and Alexandra Ehrhardt

As societies become increasingly global, opportunities for multicultural contact also increase. Yet, scholars are just beginning to unpack the developmental impact of multicultural contact on youth development. While demographic shifts can be documented and increases in diversity can be quantified, the developmental significance of multicultural contact requires a focus on the quality and quantity of inter- and intragroup contact (Allport, 1954; Hewstone et al., 2002). Building on developmental theories that emphasize the importance of context for youth development (Bronfenbrenner, 1979; Duncan & Raudenbush, 1999), the current chapter takes a contact-in-context approach (Yip et al., 2019). Instead of conceptualizing and measuring multicultural contact as a static characteristic of the setting, we situate the developmental importance of contact within the specific physical and psychological contexts in which it occurs. As we have noted elsewhere, "diversity is not simply an attribute that exists or fails to exist, it is a psychological experience that results from the interaction of an individual in context" (Yip et al., 2019).

Since youth spend most of their waking time in school contexts, this is our focus of the chapter. While teachers, curricula, academic resources, and school infrastructure have a tremendous impact on youth development, peers become increasingly influential as youth progress through the academic pipeline from preschool through college. In societies that are becoming increasingly multicultural and international, peer diversity is an important mechanism through which societal, neighborhood, and school-level characteristics become proximal and developmentally relevant. To explore the impact of contact-in-context, the chapter focuses on how the application of experience-sampling approaches (where youth are surveyed with intensive repeated measures) has elucidated the importance of peer diversity for youth development. Experience-sampling approaches refer to a category of research methods that involve intensive repeated measures of the same individual over time (Bolger & Laurenceau, 2013). Daily diaries are a popular form of experience sampling that involve taking daily assessments, typically once or twice a day in the morning or evening (Bolger et al., 2003; Bolger & Laurenceau, 2013).

Experience sampling also includes multiple, random, event-contingent, and device-contingent sampling. Random sampling involves completing surveys at intervals unknown to the participant while event-contingent sampling involves completing assessments corresponding with specific events (e.g., student–teacher interaction). Device-contingent sampling can collect physiologic data specific to each device (e.g., heart rate, activity levels). Regardless of the sampling schedule, experience-sampling approaches have a multilevel structure. By taking multiple assessments of peer interactions from the same youth in the same school context, we are also able to assess proximal interpersonal interactions that are embedded at multiple levels (i.e., interactions nested within students who are nested within schools). Multilevel data structures provide the opportunity to model both stable (i.e., school) and dynamic (i.e., social interactions) developmental characteristics as well as the interactions between these.

This chapter reviews research applying experience-sampling methods to the study of peer diversity to illustrate how intensive repeated measures provide unique insight into the influence of peer diversity on youth development by drawing on four experience-sampling studies of ethnic/racial minority youth in New York City, the impact of peer diversity on ethnic/racial identity, psychological outcomes, and academic achievement. Together, these studies illustrate how experience-sampling approaches contribute to existing research on diversity and youth development. The chapter also discusses the limitations and challenges associated with employing experience-sampling approaches with diverse youth. The chapter concludes with recommendations for future research and theory including specific considerations for the research design and implementation phases.

School diversity and youth development

In developed countries, most of youth's waking hours are spent in school contexts. In schools, youth are introduced to social relationships beyond the family, including teachers and peers. While youth's relationships with teachers contribute to their development, their peer relationships become increasingly consequential as they navigate the competing needs of autonomy, belonging, and social identity exploration (Rivas-Drake et al., 2017). The ethnic/racial diversity of peer relationships is associated with important aspects of youth development such as ethnic/racial identity (ERI), psychological adjustment, and academic achievement (Davies et al., 2011; Graham et al., 2014; Rivas-Drake et al., 2017).

Peer ethnic/racial diversity has been depicted at the school or classroom level or by the intra/interracial composition of youth's friendships. Within the classroom, higher levels of ethnic/racial diversity have been linked to less victimization and greater feelings of safety among Latino and African American high school students (Graham et al., 2014), higher levels of teacher-reported academic and social competencies for Native American middle school students (Williams & Hamm, 2018), and middle school students' multiracial identification (Echols et al., 2017). Other studies have focused on the intra/interracial friendship composition with school and classroom settings with mixed results. Some studies find that higher levels of ethnic/racial peer diversity are linked to higher levels of ERI exploration (i.e., the extent to which individuals seek information about their ethnic/racial group or groups) and ERI resolution (i.e., the extent to which individuals feel confident and comfortable about identifying with their ethnic/racial group or groups) among middle school boys (Rivas-Drake et al., 2017). Findings also point to decreased vulnerability (Graham et al., 2014) and higher levels of academic achievement (Kawabata & Crick, 2015) among minority students with more interracial (i.e., cross-race) friendships. On the contrary, middle school African American and Asian American students who only had intraracial (i.e., within race) best friends displayed lower levels of depressive symptoms and higher levels of self-esteem (McGill et al., 2012), and Latinx and Asian American high school students with more intraracial friends had higher levels of ERI belonging (i.e., the extent to which individuals feel that they belong to their ethnic/racial group or groups) and ERI exploration (Kiang et al., 2010).

These studies highlight the important role that classroom, school, and peer network ethnic/racial diversity has on youth development; however, there is much less research focusing on how youth's day-to-day experiences of diversity shape developmental outcomes. Given peer interactions occur and change on a daily basis, intensive repeated measures focusing on daily experiences uniquely elucidate the developmental importance of diversity experiences within classroom and school contexts. Experience sampling methods (ESM) can examine peer diversity with a more micro-level focus on daily dynamics. Taking a person-by-environment approach affords flexibility to investigate how school and peer-level diversity may have a differential impact on youth in the same school or within the same peer network. The developmental meaning and significance of multicultural contact varies not only across youth but also within youth over time.

Using ESM to study youth in multicultural societies

Adolescence and young adulthood are marked by change, growth, and dynamic fluctuations in emotions, thoughts, and behaviors related to different ways of forming an identity. Youth development is informed by active and reciprocal interactions with the environment. As youth act and react to their developmental context (Gauvain, 1995), they are both *shaped by and shape* the environment (Laland et al., 2000). Focusing on a single data point loses the nuance and richness of everyday experiences. Behaviors and experiences of a person that appear to be stable may reveal themselves to be more dynamic across time through the application of intensive repeated measures (Csikszentmihalyi & Larson, 1984). ESM methods are uniquely poised to measure, model, and elucidate these reciprocal dynamics which would otherwise be treated as stable constructs and associations.

Diversity is a psychological experience of an individual resulting from interactions in context (Yip et al., in press). As Lewin (1935) asserted: $B = f$ (PE). A person's behavior in a specific situation (B) is a function of individual dispositions (P) and the immediate environment. Similarly, Bronfenbrenner and Morris (1998) introduced *proximal processes*, the dynamic interactions between an individual and the context. Proximal processes are the mechanism through which development unfolds. Contextual factors, such as societal, neighborhood, and school diversity at the structural level become relevant to youth development only through proximal processes where they encounter *contact in context*. This underscores the importance of momentary and daily interactions (distinguished from stable individual and contextual characteristics) as instrumental places and mechanisms through which diversity becomes relevant to youth development in multicultural societies.

Peer diversity has been frequently operationalized as an interaction between the structural context (e.g., school) and stable characteristics of a person (e.g., race). While stable contextual and individual characteristics are important contributors to youth development, daily experiences are rarely identical even for two individuals who share the same contextual and individual characteristics. For example, individuals may experience different levels and types of contact with peers in their daily lives. Each of these encounters contribute to development in unique ways. Youth may perceive relationships with peers to be generally positive; however, even the most positive relationships encounter daily struggles or disagreements. One-time assessments miss the natural ups and downs of interactions and relationships.

Overview of ESM approaches

ESMs are ideally suited to capture momentary and dynamic processes and experiences. ESM is an umbrella term that refers to research methodologies that intensively and repeatedly measure a person's experience over time in naturalistic settings. Experiences are measured as they occur with little to no time lag between the occurrence of an event and participants' responses, thereby increasing ecological validity (Yip & Douglass, 2013).

Types of ESM designs

ESMs are also referred to as intensive longitudinal methods – measurements of the same person repeatedly over a relatively short period of time, typically within a day, across a few days, a week, or a month (Bolger & Laurenceau, 2013). ESM approaches take repeated measurements within a study period to obtain a sampling of an individual's lived experience. The utility of ESM is exemplified by the diversity of its application. One type of ESM, *random sampling*, sends a predetermined number of random signals to participants throughout the day inquiring about thoughts, behaviors, and/or feelings. This method can gather a representation of physical locations and the presence of other individuals in the setting. A methodological artifact of this approach is that participants report heightened anxiety about random signals at the beginning of the study but acclimate over time (Hektner et al., 2007). Although signals are "random," prompting schedules are selected depending on the research interest. Random sampling provides a representative glimpse into youth's daily lives.

Event sampling takes measurements of predetermined events, such as interpersonal encounters with peers. Participants complete surveys when they encounter the event; thus, event sampling is best suited for research focused on processes and experiences related to specific *events* rather than a representation of everyday experiences. To examine youth's peer diversity experiences, participants could be instructed to complete a survey whenever they are engaged in peer interactions. For optimal results, it is imperative that instructions and definitions of the event of interest are clearly communicated to research participants. While this design does not provide an overall representation of youth's daily lives, it obtains relevant and concurrent information about immediate, event-focused experiences.

Daily diaries are another popular form of ESM, which measures individuals' daily experiences. Daily diaries are typically assessed either once or twice a day, usually at the end of each day before going to bed to capture the day's experiences, or upon waking in the morning to capture initial thoughts or feelings. In some cases, researchers take both a rising morning

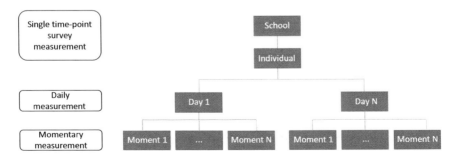

Figure 7.1 Multi-level data structure of ESMs

Table 7.1 Sample data of ESMs

ID	Moment	Day	Gender	School	Variable 1	Variable 2	Variable 3
001	1	1	M	1	3	3.3	0
001	2	1	M	1	2	4.2	1
001	3	1	M	1	3	3.8	1
001	1	2	M	1	0	0.2	0
001	2	2	M	1	1	0.9	0
001	3	2	M	1	1	1.5	0
002	1	1	F	1	5	5.2	1
002	2	1	F	1	4	3.9	1
002	3	1	F	1	5	4.3	1
002	1	2	F	1	0	2.5	0
002	2	2	F	1	0	3.1	1
002	3	2	F	1	1	5.2	0

assessment as well as an evening bedtime assessment, minimizing the influences of retrospective recall biases for the day's events and feelings. Whereas random and event sampling take momentary and *in situ* accounts of experiences, daily diaries depict lived experiences throughout the day with a relatively short time lapse between event and report.

Finally, *device-contingent designs* collect data from devices specifically developed to capture objective information of one's physiology (e.g., blood pressure, heart rate), behaviors (e.g., number of steps taken, performance on cognitive tasks, sleep), environment (e.g., lighting, temperature, noise), and/or space (e.g., location; Bolger & Laurenceau, 2013). Some devices are able to obtain more than one assessment (e.g., sleep and light exposure). One of the strengths of these approaches is passive data collection without active engagement from the participant, omitting concerns about reporting biases. However, the resulting trade-off is that researchers may not be able to associate these data with more psychological processes. Device-contingent designs are sometimes employed in isolation; however, they are often supplemented with self-report accounts provided by the other ESM approaches reviewed above.

Finally, it is worth commenting on how the technology to implement ESM designs has developed exponentially over the years. Just 30 years ago, the first ESM studies were conducted with paper-and-pencil forms and assisted by pagers, watches, and time stamps. In the late 1980s, researchers began to use portable electronic devices and personal digital assistants (PDAs; e.g., Palm Pilots) to integrate the data collection and the prompting device (Feldman Barrett & Barrett, 1989; Yip & Fuligni, 2003). In the early 2000s, as cellular and Wi-Fi technology became more affordable and accessible, researchers adopted mobile phone and tablet technology in combination with online survey programs, SMS messages, or smartphone applications (Killingsworth & Gilbert, 2010; Yip et al., 2013).

The study of peer diversity

In designing an ESM study, an important decision is choosing the frequency and duration of sampling. These decisions should consider the research question, relevant sample characteristics (e.g., sample age, competing demands, participants' schedules), participant burden, and resource availability (e.g., budget, sampling equipment). School-going youth tend to have regular schedules that repeat on a weekly basis and seven data collection days will provide a good representation of adolescents' daily lives. For richer and more reliable data or to capture less frequent events (e.g., academic exam), a researcher might decide to collect data for two or three weeks. A researcher interested in investigating how students' classroom relationship dynamics change throughout a semester may need to collect data for a longer period or sample a week at the beginning and end of the semester. ESM approaches are especially useful for capturing experiences that fluctuate within individuals across time (Bolger & Laurenceau, 2013; Hoffman, 2015). Both quantity and quality of social interactions of youth's peer diversity experiences can be observed, simultaneously giving consideration to stable individual and contextual characteristics (Shelton et al., 2014). A unique strength of ESM approaches is the ability to examine both within-person variations and between-person differences embedded in various layers of environment.

ESM data structure and analytic procedures

ESMs provide rich data. Since the data is collected repeatedly within individuals who are nested within contexts, the data are necessarily multilevel. Individuals' daily experiences are nested within individuals, which are nested within higher levels, such as families, classrooms, schools, and neighborhoods (Figure 7.1). One way to organize such data is in the long format (Table 7.1). This way, both stable individual and contextual characteristics (e.g., gender and school) can be considered simultaneously. This type of data structure elucidates individuals' typical or average experiences, changes or fluctuations in experience over time (relative to one's own average level), changes or fluctuations in experience from one day to the next, and how these processes vary by relatively stable individual differences.

ESM also affords analytical flexibility such as examining within-person variations in daily reports (e.g., how a report on a given day varies from one's own average) and variations in how strongly daily experiences are related to one another (e.g., differences in a person's slope representing the association between two variables; Cham et al., under review). Within-person variations can be addressed by centering each day's response around one's own mean across time (Wang et al., 2017). Variations in how strongly two daily experiences (i.e., peer diversity and anxiety) are related can be considered by employing random intercepts and slopes for these variables in the linear equation. Modeling random intercepts and slopes means that each individual intercept and slope are allowed to vary as a function of individual differences. Next, statistical analyses are conducted to explore whether there is significant variation in individuals' intercepts and slopes. Significant variation in the random intercept indicates that there are individual differences in average levels of anxiety across the youth in the sample, whereas significant variation in the slope indicates that the association between the two daily experiences (e.g., peer diversity and anxiety) varies from one individual to another. In other words, the ability to explore possible individual differences in daily-level associations is a unique analytical strength of ESM designs.

Additionally, the temporal order of each response provides important information since experiences may change over time, and same and next-day associations may be different (e.g., how peer diversity is related to same-day anxiety vs. how peer diversity is related to next-day anxiety). A variable that indicates the temporal order of each response is necessary (e.g., study day, weekday/weekend, morning/evening). It may also be useful to create an additional "lag variable" which shifts the responses for a certain variable by one interval of measurement. To examine a one-day lagged effect, a response from Tuesday can be shifted to align with responses on Wednesday. This newly created lag variable allows researchers to examine the associations between the previous and next day's experiences. Yip et al. (2013) used this technique and found that while yesterday's contact with same-ethnic others was positively associated with today's ERI, yesterday's ERI was not related to next-day's contact with same-ethnic others, suggesting the directionality of development from same-ethnic contact to ERI. In addition to hints about the directionality of developmental processes, lagged effects also provide information about how long a day's or a moment's experience persists.

Multilevel models which take into account the naturally occurring nested nature of ESM designs are best suited for analyses. Multilevel analysis includes statistical models such as hierarchical linear models, general mixed models, and random regression models (Bolger et al., 2003). These methods are suited for analyzing ESM data because they adjust for nested and repeated measurement (Heck & Thomas, 2015; Kreft & De Leeuw, 1998; Luke, 2004; Raudenbush & Bryk, 2002).

Examples of ESM studies focused on ethnicity/race

In this next section, we review the methods and results from four ESM studies focused on the developmental impact of peer diversity. All samples were selected from the larger population of adolescents and young adults in the New York City metropolitan area over a 20-year period beginning in 1998 to the present. The four studies are presented in chronological order, illustrating corresponding advances in data collection methods and technology. For each study, we highlight the ESM method as well as the sample and the primary research question.

Study 1: daily diary study of Chinese adolescents' ethnic identity salience

Study 1 involved a two-week daily diary study of Chinese adolescents and focused on daily experiences of ethnic identity salience. Participants completed paper-and-pencil diaries every night for 14 nights (Yip & Fuligni, 2003). They also completed a demographic survey at the beginning and end of the two-week period. A total of 102 adolescents with a mean age of 16.43 (SD = 1.02) participated. The application of daily diary methods to the study of ERI was novel at the time, and this was the first study to find empirical support for the theoretical notion that feelings of ERI, specifically ERI salience, are dynamic and responsive to daily-level processes.

Study 2: experience sampling study of ethnic identity salience among Asian college students

Study 2 employed another ESM approach, that of experience sampling where participants were randomly prompted six times per day for one week to respond to questions about their immediate context, ERI salience, and mood (Yip, 2005). There was a total of 62 participants in this study and data were collected on electronic Palm Pilot devices. At the time, the use of an electronic hand-held device such as the Palm Pilot was novel because it integrated the signaling and the data collection device. Participants responded to an audible prompt on the Palm Pilot and completed their experience-sampling reports using the Experience Sampling Program (Feldman Barrett & Barrett, 1989) on the same device. The aim of the study was to move beyond daily-level variation in ERI salience and to explore whether salience varied at the level of the specific situation.

Study 3: Youth Experiences Study (YES)

Study 3 employed a combination of random experience sampling and daily dairy designs over three years. A baseline survey was administered to participants during an orientation session in groups of 10–30 students. The survey included questions about demographic information and measures of ERI and psychological well-being. Upon completion of the survey, students were given a cellular phone with access to a web-based survey to respond to questions about their daily experiences every night before going to bed for seven days. All functions on the cellular phone other than access to the study's web survey were blocked. On average, participants completed 4.53 (SD = 1.99, range: 1 to 7) surveys of seven possible in total. Along with the daily diaries, students were also randomly prompted five times each day – a total of 35 signals per week – to provide experience-sampling reports. On average, participants completed 17 (SD = 9, range: 1–34) surveys. Participants' compliance was tracked online every night. At the end of the week participants completed a post-survey, returned the cellular phone, and were compensated. They also completed a follow-up survey six months later.

Study 4: Adolescent Sleep Study

The fourth and most recent study is a four-year longitudinal project, the Adolescent Sleep Study, which includes a daily diary design and incorporates device-contingent sampling with the use of sleep actigraphy. First, baseline surveys were administered before the daily diaries. The survey contained questions about demographic information and measures of ethnic/racial identity, school diversity, discrimination experiences, and various measures of psychological adjustment and academic achievement as overall perceptions. Adolescents were provided with an actigraphy watch to wear for 14 days and were instructed to complete nightly daily diary surveys online using a Wi-Fi or data-enabled tablet each night before going to bed. The actigraphy watch passively detects and records adolescents' daily activities and sleep patterns in one-minute intervals. Along with the sleep data from the actigraphy watch, adolescents also reported on their daily contact with peers, school and academic experiences, psychological adjustment, and sleep experiences. At the end of the week, adolescents completed a post-survey and were compensated. They were also followed up after six months with similar sets of survey questionnaires.

In the following sections, we review how the above and related studies have informed research on the influence of peer diversity on youth outcomes and development, specifically as they relate to multicultural contexts. In turn, we review findings of research employing ESM approaches focused on ERI, psychological adjustment, and academic outcomes.

Peer diversity and ERI

A noteworthy contribution of ESM in understanding peer diversity in multicultural societies is its ability to capture youth's relatively immediate contact experience in context. Dynamic daily interactions provide opportunities for youth to develop their identity. Previous studies have found that in addition to the development of ERI at the individual level, ERI changes, fluctuates, and develops in youth's day-to-day lives (Yip, 2005; Yip & Fuligni, 2003). These findings call for the need to examine how peer diversity experienced as immediate contact in context becomes relevant to youth's ERI development.

Study 1 was the first study to find that youth's feelings of ERI are related to their daily experiences. This study found that ERI was more salient on days in which adolescents participated in ethnic behaviors (e.g., watching ethnic media). Study 2 examined this phenomenon at the situation level and found that important features of the context (e.g., presence of same-ethnic others, use of Chinese language) were associated with elevated salience at the level of the specific situation for Asian college students. Another important contribution of this study was the ability to partition variance in ERI salience attributable to the adolescents' individual characteristics versus the situation. Among the total variance in ERI salience, about two-thirds was attributable to characteristics of the adolescent and the remaining third to situation-level influences. That is, adolescents' person-level characteristics were largely responsible for why the salience of their ERI varied across situations.

Study 3 included a random-sampling design and a daily diary, and the association between the contact with same-ethnic peers and a dimension of ERI called "ethnic private regard" (i.e., feelings about one's own ethnic/racial group) was examined among 132 Asian adolescents in four different high schools (Yip et al., 2013). This study found a positive relationship between contact with same-ethnic peers and ethnic private regard for youths who were highly identified with their ethnic group and who attended predominantly White or ethnically diverse schools. Using the lag variable mentioned earlier, intraracial (i.e., same-ethnic) contact was associated with increased levels of ethnic private regard the next day. However, ethnic private regard was not associated with the following day's contact, suggesting that intraracial peer contact predicts ERI, rather than the other way around. Specifically, contact as measured by *surrounding* same-ethnic peers was more strongly associated with ERI private regard than *interactions* with those peers. In Study 4, consistent results were found among ethnically/racially diverse high school students. On days in which adolescents *interacted* with a higher percentage of same ethnic/racial others, the level of ERI centrality and private regard increased. The associations were stronger among those who were in low rather than high diversity schools. However, with this sample, the associations with the following day's ERI measures were not observed.

ESM has made several contributions to the existing understanding of peer diversity and ERI development, including the moment-to-moment and day-to-day dynamic of peer interactions and ERI development. Distinguishing the relatively immediate impact of different types of contact with same-ethnic peers (i.e., surrounded by vs. interacting with) in youth's daily lives would not be possible with school/classroom-level diversity scores or peer nominations alone. ESM has also provided information about the directionality of the association between contact and ERI. Finally, ESM has added to the understanding of how day-to-day same-ethnic peer contacts interact with relatively stable personal and contextual characteristics such as the overall ERI and school diversity.

Peer diversity and psychological adjustment

Daily peer contact has developmental implications not only for youth's ERI development, but also for psychological adjustment. Youth's mood changes even within one day. Data from Study 3 finds that approximately 41 percent of anxious mood, 45 percent of positive mood, and 38 percent of negative mood is explained by within-person variability, suggesting the importance of context for mood experiences. At the level of the specific situation, same-ethnic/race peer contact was associated with lower levels of anxious mood among ethnic/racial minority youth (i.e., Asian, Asian American, Hispanic, Latinx, Black, African American, or West Indian, American Indian, Native Hawaiian or Other; Douglass et al., 2014). When this association was examined among youth who experienced changes in school diversity level from elementary, to middle, or to high school, this situation-level association was significant only among adolescents who also placed a high importance on their ethnicity/race (i.e., high levels of ERI centrality).

In Study 4, on days in which youth were *surrounded by* a higher percentage of same-ethnic/race others, they experienced heightened levels of ethnic/racial discrimination. However, on days in which youth *interacted with* a higher percentage of same-ethnic/race others, they experienced higher levels of positive mood and life satisfaction. While school diversity was associated with higher levels of anxious mood at the daily level, on days in which youth in diverse schools *interacted with* a higher percentage of same-ethnic/race others they experienced lower level of anxious mood. For those in less diverse schools, anxious mood was generally higher than those in more diverse schools. On days in which they *interacted with* a higher percentage of same-ethnic/race others, their anxious mood increased. As for being *surrounded by* same-ethnic/race others, youth in low diversity schools experienced higher levels of anxious mood than those in high diversity schools both on days in which they *interacted with* a low and high percentage of same-ethnic/race others. In summary, daily experiences of being *surrounded by* (versus *interacting with*) same-ethnic/race others were differentially associated with adolescents' psychological adjustment. Moreover, whereas objective school diversity was positively related to anxious mood, daily reports of anxious mood varied within highly diverse schools depending on whether adolescents interacted with same-ethnic/race others on that day.

These studies expand the current understanding of the association between peer diversity and psychological adjustment. Even within the same school and within the same individual, varying levels of interactions and psychological adjustment were observed across moments and days. There were differences in the level and the degree of associations between daily interactions and psychological adjustment of youth in schools with different levels of diversity. As a result, these findings highlight the critical roles that diversity play in youth's psychological adjustment both at the structural level and within moments and days.

Peer diversity and academic achievement

Academic experiences are another salient sphere of youth's life. In some studies, higher levels of structural diversity at school, measured by Simpson's index (Simpson, 1949), have been found to be associated with higher levels of overall academic competence and motivation to learn (Kawabata & Crick, 2015; Williams & Hamm, 2018) while other studies have found negative associations (Schachner et al., 2018; van Ewijk & Sleegers, 2010). While academic outcomes are most often considered at the person level, academic experiences (e.g., tests, grades, studying) also vary across days. Below, we review some results from our four ESM studies.

In Study 3, contrary to previous findings, structural (i.e., school) level objective and subjective diversity scores were associated with lower academic grades among ethnically/racially diverse youth. However, the ESM data were suggestive of different conclusions. For example, approximately 35 percent of daily reports of highest grade received and 69 percent of daily satisfaction with grades could be explained by within-person variability, suggesting that while there is some stability, there is also day-to-day variability in adolescents' academic satisfaction. On days in which youth interacted with a higher percentage of same-ethnic/race others (adjusting for effects related to being merely surrounded by), they expressed higher satisfaction with their grades. Similar findings were observed in Study 4. At the structural (i.e., school) level, higher levels of objective school diversity were associated with lower academic grades. At the daily level, however, approximately 55 percent of youth's daily school engagement could be explained by within-person variability. On days in which youth interacted with (but not when they were merely surrounded by) a higher proportion of same-ethnic/race others, school engagement was higher. Taken together, interracial contact may promote satisfaction with grades and daily school engagement for diverse youth which may have downstream developmental implications for more higher academic motivation and performance (Fortier et al., 1995).

The impact of school diversity for youth's academic experiences remains equivocal. Based on ESM studies, the structural (i.e., school) level diversity and youth's daily inter- and intra-ethnic/racial interactions may have different associations with youth's academic experiences. The multilevel nature of ESM approaches make it possible to partition daily-level within-person experiences from the structural, school-level effects. Taken together, these findings imply that a deeper investigation into how youth's dynamic daily experiences are related to person-level associations over time may hold the key to resolving these inconsistencies. Thus, the analytical flexibility afforded by ESM has the potential to further unlock and expand the current understanding of the association between peer diversity and academic experiences in multicultural societies.

Limitations and contributions of ESMs

While ESM has contributed to the understanding of youth development in multicultural societies, limitations exist. Due to repeated measurements, ESM is more time-consuming and burdensome for participants, potentially contributing to participant fatigue (Stone & Broderick, 2008). Researchers employ graduated incentive schedules and other techniques to maintain the response quality and compliance over time. Repeatedly asking the same questions may introduce biases and methodological artifacts such as an increased awareness of the phenomenon of interest (e.g., ERI salience) and therefore requiring additional strategies to mitigate such effects. For example, including filler questions about unrelated topics is a popular strategy for detracting the focus from the variables of interest (Yip & Douglass, 2013). For research focused on sensitive topics such as race and diversity, researchers should be mindful of social desirability concerns (Krumpal, 2013) as well as proper ethical treatment of participants' responses. For random sampling designs, signals at inopportune moments may disrupt participants' daily lives, influencing participants' responses or compliance. Furthermore, ESM is not appropriate for research focused on rare phenomena (e.g., death of a loved one, car accidents), which are not likely to be captured in weekly or monthly data collection intervals.

Despite the limitations, ESM approaches address a unique gap in developmental science. ESM approaches measure youth experiences as they occur in naturalistic settings. Data collection with proximal time intervals minimize retrospective recall biases and methodological artifacts (Stone &

Shiffman, 2002). ESM allows researchers to study relationships within and between individuals' everyday behaviors, activities, and perceptions while allowing for the systematic exploration of differences in daily or situation-level processes – an important goal of developmental research. ESM approaches favor the ecological validity of developmentally meaningful experiences in naturalistic settings over experimental manipulations and control of confounding influences. Importantly, ESM techniques uniquely elucidate the day-to-day developmental processes and mechanisms which accumulate over time to explain developmental changes observed between annual/bi-annual surveys.

These methods also capture the significance of everyday experiences. Further, ESM approaches have advanced developmental theory and statistical analyses. For example, using data from Study 4, we proposed a new statistical approach – "slope-as-mediator" (SAM) – to describe daily developmental processes by which *the association between two variables* serves as the mediating mechanism linking person-level change (Cham et al., under review). This is a departure from existing mediational methods which focus on *means-as-mediating pathways*. Adopting this method, we observed that the association between adolescents' feelings of ERI commitment and exploration with anxiety were mediated through the daily-level association between ethnic/racial discrimination and rumination. On average, days in which adolescents reported more ethnic/racial discrimination, they also reported higher levels of rumination. However, adolescents reporting higher levels of ERI commitment (i.e., feelings of clarity and certainty about ethnicity/race in one's life) reported a weaker association between ethnic/racial discrimination and rumination. That is, adolescents with ERI commitment were buffered against the negative impact of ethnic/racial discrimination. In turn, the association between ethnic/racial discrimination and rumination predicted overall levels of anxiety among adolescents. This example illustrates the potential for new and innovative methods of discovery coupling the intensive repeated measures of ESM approaches with cutting-edge analytical tools to unpack how developmental processes unfold over time.

Conclusions and future directions

ESM approaches are increasingly applied to the study of cultural issues such as diversity and identity development (Yip & Douglass, 2013). Applied to the study of developing youth in multicultural societies, ESM approaches have the potential to uniquely elucidate how daily or situation-level processes serve as proximal developmental mechanisms. The enhanced ecological validity of ESM approaches also redirects the sole focus from the developing youth to understanding how youth interact and experience everyday contexts and interactions. In doing so, the developmental context shares the foreground with the developing youth. Together, with rigorous analytical tools, ESM is uniquely able to inform the everyday experiences of youth in multicultural contexts.

References

Allport, G. W. (1954). *The nature of prejudice*. Reading, MA: Addison-Wesley.

Bolger, N., Davis, A., & Rafaeli, E. (2003). Diary methods: Capturing life as it is lived. *Annual Review of Psychology, 54*(1), 579–616.

Bolger, N., & Laurenceau, J.-P. (2013). *Intensive longitudinal methods: An introduction to diary and experience sampling research*. New York, NY: The Guilford Press.

Bronfenbrenner, U. (1979). *The ecology of human development: Experiments by nature and design*. Cambridge, MA: Harvard University Press.

Bronfenbrenner, U., & Morris, P. (1998). *The ecology of developmental processes*. Hoboken, NJ: Wiley.

Cham, H., Yip, T., Wang, Y., & Aytürk, E. (under review). Mechanisms of change via relationships between variables (slope-as-mediator): A multilevel structural equation modeling framework. *Psychological Methods*.

Csikszentmihalyi, M., & Larson, R. W. (1984). *Being adolescent: Conflict and growth in the teenage years*. New York, NY: Basic Books.

Davies, K., Tropp, L. R., Aron, A., Pettigrew, T. F., & Wright, S. C. (2011). Cross-group friendships and intergroup attitudes: A meta-analytic review. *Personality and Social Psychology Review, 15*(4), 332–351.

Douglass, S., Yip, T., & Shelton, N. (2014). Intragroup contact and anxiety among ethnic minority adolescents: Considering ethnic identity and school diversity transitions. *Journal of Youth and Adolescence, 43*(10), 1628–1641.

Duncan, G. J., & Raudenbush, S. W. (1999). Assesing the effects of context in studies of child and youth development. *Educational Psychologist, 34*(1), 29–41.

Echols, L., Ivanich, J., & Graham, S. (2017). Multiracial in middle school: The influence of classmates and friends on changes in racial self-identification. *Child Development, 89*(6), 2070–2080.

Feldman Barrett, L., & Barrett, D. J. (1989). *Experience sampling program*. Boston. MA.

Fortier, M. S., Vallerand, R. J., & Guay, F. (1995). Academic motivation and school performance: Toward a structural model. *Contemporary Educational Psychology, 20*, 257–274.

Gauvain, M. (1995). Thinking in niches: Sociocultural influences on cognitive development. *Human Development, 38*, 25–45.

Graham, S., Munniksma, A., & Juvonen, J. (2014). Psychosocial benefits of cross-ethnic friendships in urban middle schools. *Child Development, 85*(2), 469–483.

Heck, R. H., & Thomas, S. L. (2015). *An introduction to multilevel modeling techniques: MLM and SEM approaches using Mplus*. New York, NY: Routledge/Taylor & Francis Group.

Hektner, J. M., Schmidt, J. A., & Csikszentmihalyi, M. (2007). *Experience sampling method: Measuring the quality of everyday life*. Thousand Oaks, CA: Sage Publications, Inc.

Hewstone, M., Rubin, M., & Willis, H. (2002). Intergroup bias. *Annual Review of Psychology*, 53(1), 575–604.

Hoffman, L. (2015). *Longitudinal analysis: Modeling within-person fluctuation and change.* New York, NY: Routledge.

Kawabata, Y., & Crick, N. R. (2015). Direct and interactive links between cross-ethnic friendships and peer rejection, internalizing symptoms, and academic engagement among ethnically diverse children. *Cultural Diversity and Ethnic Minority Psychology*, 21(2), 191–200.

Kiang, L., Witkow, M. R., Baldelomar, O. A., & Fuligni, A. J. (2010). Change in ethnic identity across the high school years among adolescents with Latin American, Asian, and European backgrounds. *Journal of Youth and Adolescence*, 39(6), 683–693.

Killingsworth, M. A., & Gilbert, D. T. (2010). A wandering mind is an unhappy mind. *Science*, 330(6006), 932.

Kreft, I. G., & De Leeuw, J. (1998). *Introducing multilevel modeling.* Thousand Oaks, CA: Sage.

Krumpal, I. (2013). Determinants of social desirability bias in sensitive surveys: A literature review. *Quality & Quantity*, 47(4), 2025–2047.

Laland, K. N., Kumm, J., & Feldman, M. W. (2000). Gene-culture coevolutionary theory. A test case. *Current Anthropology*, 36(1), 131–156.

Lewin, K. (1935). *A dynamic theory of personality: Selected papers of Kurt Lewin.* New York, NY: McGraw-Hill.

Luke, D. A. (2004). *Multilevel modeling* (Vol. 143). Thousand Oaks, CA: Sage.

McGill, R. K., Way, N., & Hughes, D. (2012). Intra-and interracial best friendships during middle school: Links to social and emotional well-being. *Journal of Research on Adolescence*, 22(4), 722–738.

Raudenbush, S. W., & Bryk, A. S. (2002). *Hierarchical linear models: Applications and data analysis methods* (Second ed.). Newbury Park, CA: Sage.

Rivas-Drake, D., Umaña-Taylor, A. J., Schaefer, D. R., & Medina, M. (2017). Ethnic-racial identity and friendships in early adolescence. *Child Development*, 88(3), 710–724.

Schachner, M. K., Juang, L., Moffitt, U., & van de Vijver, F. J. (2018). Schools as acculturative and developmental contexts for youth of immigrant and refugee background. *European Psychologist*, 23, 44–56.

Shelton, N., Douglass, S., Garcia, R. L., Yip, T., & Trail, T. E. (2014). Feeling (mis) understood and intergroup friendships in interracial interactions. *Personality and Social Psychology Bulletin*, 40(9), 1193–1204.

Simpson, E. H. (1949). Measurement of diversity. *Nature*, 163, 688.

Stone, A. A., & Shiffman, S. (2002). Capturing momentary, self-report data: A proposal for reporting guidelines. *Annals of Behavioral Medicine*, 24(3), 236–243.

Stone, A. A., Broderick, J. E., Schwartz, J. E., & Schwarz, N. (2008). Context effects in survey ratings of health, symptoms, and satisfaction. *Medical Care*, 46(7), 662.

van Ewijk, R., & Sleegers, P. (2010). Peer ethnicity and achievement: A meta-analysis into the compositional effect. *School Effectiveness and School Improvement*, 21, 237–265.

Wang, Y., Cham, H., Aladin, M., & Yip, T. (2017). Parental cultural socialization and adolescent private regard: Exploring mediating pathways through daily experiences. *Child Development*. Advanced online publication. doi: doi:10.1111/cdev.12911.

Williams, J. L., & Hamm, J. V. (2018). Peer group ethnic diversity and social competencies in youth attending rural middle schools. *The Journal of Early Adolescence*, 38(6), 795–823.

Yip, T. (2005). Sources of situational variation in ethnic identity and psychological well-being: A palm pilot study of Chinese American students. *Personality and Social Psychology Bulletin*, 31(12), 1603–1616.

Yip, T., Cheon, Y. M., & Wang, Y. (in press). The diversity paradox: Opportunities and challenges across development. *Research in Human Development*.

Yip, T., & Douglass, S. (2013). The application of experience sampling approaches to the study of ethnic identity: New developmental insights and directions. *Child Development Perspectives*, 7(4), 211–214.

Yip, T., Douglass, S. E., & Shelton, N. (2013). Daily intragroup contact in diverse settings: Implications for Asian adolescents' ethnic identity. *Child Development*, 84(4), 1425–1441.

Yip, T., & Fuligni, A. J. (2003). Daily variation in ethnic identity, ethnic behaviors, and psychological well-being among American adolescents of Chinese descent. *Child Development*, 73(5), 1557–1572.

Yip, T., Cheon, Y. & Wang, Y. (2019). The diversity paradox: Opportunities and challenges across development. *Research in Human Development*, 16(1), 51–75, https://doi.org/10.1080/15427609.2018.1549404

Chapter 8

Immigrant youth adaptation in a multilevel context

Conceptual and statistical considerations

Jens B. Asendorpf and Frosso Motti-Stefanidi

Immigration is not a new phenomenon. However, during the last two decades historically unprecedented and rapid surges of migration have taken place. Currently millions of people live in countries other than the country where either they or their parents were born. Some have voluntarily migrated seeking opportunities for a better life, others have forcibly left their countries fleeing war and devastation. Large numbers of people have crossed international borders and have often settled in countries that were either traditionally the destination of immigrants (e.g., the United States of America, Canada, Australia, Germany), or former colonizing countries (e.g., France, the United Kingdom, the Netherlands, Spain), or they settled in countries that actually used to be the source of immigrants (e.g., Greece and Italy).

As a result, the face of receiving societies has changed. Ethnic diversity has become the rule rather than the exception in these countries. There is an urgent pressure to help these people integrate into receiving societies. The consequences of a failure to integrate them into their new home are undeniably significant both for the well-being of immigrants and for the prosperity and social cohesion of society. To achieve this goal, efforts are geared in particular towards the integration of migrant children and youth, since their present positive adaptation is a forerunner of their future success in highly valued adult developmental achievements, such as work, contributing to the community, and raising a family (Motti-Stefanidi, in press; Motti-Stefanidi & Masten, 2017).

In this context, there is global interest in understanding whether being an immigrant increases the probability that a young person will have difficulties in adaptation or will present mental health problems and in how to best promote their positive adaptation. Thus, during the last two decades we have witnessed a surge in research on immigrant youth adaptation. The ultimate goal of this research is to inform policies and practices that will mitigate any risks to youth who live and grow between two cultures and to promote their integration into the host society (Motti-Stefanidi & Salmela-Aro, 2018).

Immigrant youth are developing individuals. Therefore, developmental systems theory can best guide research on their adaptation (Motti-Stefanidi, in press; Motti-Stefanidi, Berry, Chryssochoou, Sam, & Phinney, 2012; Motti-Stefanidi & Masten, 2017; Suárez-Orozco, Motti-Stefanidi, Marks, & Katsiaficas, in press). However, immigrant youth are also acculturating individuals. They live and grow between at least two cultures, that is, their ethnic and host cultures, which are often embedded in a societal context replete with prejudice and discrimination. Thus, based on core tenets of developmental systems theory, their adaptation needs to be examined in a multilevel context, spanning from the individual to the societal level, and integrating developmental, acculturative, and societal influences. Furthermore, since both their development and acculturation involve change, the focus needs to shift from understanding individual differences in their current adaptation, to understanding variations and change in their long-term adaptation. The conceptual and methodological implications of these two key tenets will be examined and discussed later in the chapter.

Extant research reveals great diversity in immigrant youth adaptation. Some adapt well whereas others falter. This chapter examines immigrant youth adaptation from a risk and resilience perspective. It addresses the question: "Who among immigrant youth do well, concurrently and over time, and why?" The chapter includes two sections which focus on conceptual and statistical considerations when addressing this research question. The first section presents an integrative framework which offers criteria for judging the quality of immigrant youth adaptation and examines, based on core principles of developmental systems theory, their adaptation, development, and acculturation, in a multilevel developmental context integrating acculturation and social psychological concepts and perspectives. The second section presents regression models that respect the nested structure of multilevel data and allow the testing of cross-level effects, which reveal cross-level moderations. By adding age as another level of analysis, these models seamlessly integrate the analysis of developmental changes into the multilevel framework.

A multilevel integrative framework for conceptualizing immigrant youth adaptation

To understand the diversity in immigrant youth adaptation, Motti-Stefanidi and colleagues (Motti-Stefanidi, in press; Motti-Stefanidi et al., 2012a; Motti-Stefanidi & Masten, 2017; see also Suárez-Orozco et al., in press) developed a multilevel integrative framework. This framework was influenced by theory from multiple fields, but especially the following conceptual approaches: Masten's resilience developmental framework (Masten, 2014); Bronfenbrenner's bioecological model of human development

(Bronfenbrenner & Morris, 2006); Berry's cultural transmission model (Berry, Phinney, Sam, & Vedder, 2006); and the three-level model of immigrant adaptation proposed by Verkuyten (2005).

This *integrative* model for conceptualizing immigrant youth adaptation offers *integrated* criteria for judging positive adaptation, encompassing both developmental and acculturation perspectives. The first criterion is their success in normative age-salient developmental tasks, such as doing well in school, having close friends/being liked/being accepted by peers, knowing or obeying the laws of society, civic engagement, development of self-control, and establishment of a cohesive, integrated, and multifaceted sense of identity (Masten, 2014; Motti-Stefanidi & Masten, 2017). These tasks reflect the expectations and standards for behavior and achievement that parents, teachers, and societies set for individuals over the life span in a particular context and time in history. The second criterion is the success of immigrant youth in acculturative tasks. A key acculturative task is the development of cultural competence. Cultural competence involves the acquisition of the knowledge and skills of both ethnic and national cultures (Oppedal & Toppelberg, 2016). Finally, an additional criterion for judging how well they are doing concerns their internal psychological adaptation, which is evaluated mainly by indices of perceived psychological well-being versus distress (Motti-Stefanidi & Masten, 2017).

According to this conceptual developmental model, individual differences in youth's adaptation are the result of continuous interactions that span multiple levels of the developing organism (at many levels of genetic, neurobiological, psychological, and behavioral function) as well as the many other socioecological and environmental systems in which the developing organism is embedded (family, friendships, educational, cultural, healthcare, ecological, and many other interconnected systems) (e.g., Cicchetti & Toth, 2009; Masten & Kalstabakken, in press). How well immigrant youth will adapt to their new situation depends on interactions among many systems over time. Thus, resilient adaptation is dynamic, changing over time, and also distributed through multiple systems that extend beyond the individual person.

Potential predictors of immigrant youth's positive adaptation are examined at multiple levels of context and analysis. Motti-Stefanidi and colleagues' integrative conceptual framework consists of three levels (Motti-Stefanidi et al., 2012a; Motti-Stefanidi & Masten, 2017). The societal level refers to cultural beliefs, social representations, and ideologies, including the acculturation ideology and preferences of receiving societies, as well as to social position variables, such as social class, immigrant status, and ethnicity, that have been shown to have an impact on immigrants' adaptation (García-Coll et al., 1996). The level of interaction is focused on youth's immediate environment, such as the school, the family, and neighborhoods. These contexts constitute their lived space where they are in direct contact with close others (parents, teachers, peers). They are important influences both for immigrant youth's development and acculturation. Some represent the home culture (family, ethnic peers, ethnic group) and others the host culture (school, non-immigrant peers). Finally, the individual level refers to youth's personal attributes, such as their personality, cognition, and motivation, which also have been shown to have an impact on immigrant youth adaptation (Bornstein, 2017).

No precedence is given either to the individual as sole agent, or to society as sole determinant of individual differences in immigrant youth's adaptation. Instead, it is argued that both the individual and society, that is, both sociocultural circumstances and structures, and human agency play a central role in the adaptive processes that lead to the success (or failure) of immigrant youth.

The levels of this integrative model refer to system levels of context. However, the concept of levels can also refer to levels of analysis or scientific explanation. The influence of each of the levels of context (individual, level of interaction, societal) on adaptation can be examined at different levels of scientific explanation. These two conceptions of levels are interrelated, yet distinct. For example, the influence of socioeconomic status (SES), a societal level variable, on adaptation can be examined at the individual level of analysis, by assigning to each study participant a score reflecting the SES standing of the family, or at the level of interaction, by assigning to each school its mean SES score. At the individual level of analysis, students' low SES (after controlling for immigrant status) has been found to predict negatively academic achievement (e.g., Motti-Stefanidi, Asendorpf, & Masten, 2012; OECD, 2010). At the school level of analysis, students were found to perform better in schools with a higher average socioeconomic composition (e.g., Motti-Stefanidi et al., 2012a; OECD, 2010). Such data require the conducting of multilevel statistical analyses because the effects of SES on achievement operate at both the individual and the school level. These methods allow investigators to disentangle individual and group effects on the outcome of interest.

It should be noted that researchers at times confuse psychological mechanisms at different levels when they interpret their data. Consider the classic study by Robinson (1950) on reading ability in the USA in 1930. Across all federal states, the mean reading ability in a state correlated .53 with the percentage of immigrants in the state, that is, the higher the proportion of immigrants in a state, the better the reading ability in this state. This may seem paradoxical; do immigrants read better than non-immigrants? In fact, the opposite was the case; within all states, non-immigrants showed a higher reading ability than immigrants. The correlation at the state level resulted from selective immigration; immigrants selected states with better working opportunities for their residence, and the *non-immigrants* in these states had a higher reading ability. The seemingly paradoxical result was not paradoxical, it was a misinterpretation of the results by confusing the level of contexts (US states in this case) with the level of individuals. The .53 correlation concerned differences between federal states; it is silent about between-person differences (differences between immigrants and non-immigrants in this case).

Robinson (1950) called this confusion the *ecological fallacy* because the "ecological" correlation involving environmental differences is misinterpreted as a correlation involving between-person differences. This mistake is so common – even nearly 70 years after the publication of Robinson's seminal publication – because we intuitively interpret psychological data from the perspective of individual actors and therefore tend to apply this perspective to differences between social contexts.

These multilevel, diverse influences on immigrant youth's adaptation, development, and acculturation result in multiple possible trajectories (Masten & Kalstabakken, in press; Motti-Stefanidi, in press; Motti-Stefanidi et al., 2012b). Two concepts stemming from developmental systems theory are relevant here. The concept of equifinality refers to different adaptation pathways leading to the same or similar outcomes and the concept of multifinality refers to different outcomes among individuals who had similar starting points. For example, Suárez-Orozco, Suárez-Orozco, & Todorova (2010) found five different individual trajectories of academic performance in a longitudinal study of 400 recently arrived young adolescents from five sending origins to the USA. In spite of the challenges these youths faced, some were consistently high achievers, others were consistently low achievers, yet others' declined either slowly or precipitously, and another group of students' academic performance improved over time. Thus, as would be expected on the basis of the multifinality principle (e.g., Cicchetti & Toth, 2009), significant individual variation is observed within immigrant youth in adaptive trajectories, with some beating the odds and doing well.

Statistical analysis of multilevel data

Because a study of immigrant youth adaptation includes data at both the individual level and the level of immediate social context, two statistical problems result. First, if some participants share the same context (e.g., students of the same classroom or adolescents of the same neighborhood), their data can be statistically dependent, that is, participants who share the same context are more similar than participants from different contexts. Although this dependency does not change statistical estimates such as correlations or regression coefficients, their standard errors are underestimated such that all statistical tests are biased (most often they are too liberal such that too many statistically significant findings result). These biases can be easily avoided with procedures that adjust the standard errors such that the statistical tests are unbiased. No multilevel model is required in this case.

Second, often one is interested in effects of higher-order units on lower-order units, for example, effects of the proportion of immigrants in a classroom on immigrants' versus non-immigrants' popularity among their classmate. In this case, two-level regression models can be used where classroom differences in immigrants' popularity are predicted by the proportion of immigrants in each classroom. Multilevel methods also adjust the standard errors such that the statistical tests are unbiased.

In addition, statistical multilevel approaches seamlessly integrate the analysis of developmental changes by including time points as a level of analysis below the individual level (thus, time points are nested in individuals). These changes are analyzed with statistical three-level models where time is nested in individuals, and individuals are nested in contexts. In the following we illustrate each of the three statistical approaches with concrete examples from our research on immigrant youth adaptation.

Adjustment of standard errors

Statistical dependence violates the assumption of most statistical tests that the units of analysis are independently sampled, and thus biases all significance tests. For example, in a study of students sampled in classrooms, the data of all students on a particular outcome can be statistically dependent because they share teachers, classmates, and often also the neighborhood of the school. Any statistical test about group differences, correlations, regressions, paths in structural equation models, and so forth is biased to the extent that classmates are more similar to each other than to students of other classrooms.

This similarity is measured in terms of the *intraclass correlation* (ICC) that compares the variance of higher-order units with the overall variance. The higher the intraclass correlation, the greater the problem of statistical dependency. In a study of students in classrooms, an intraclass correlation of .30 for some outcome variable of interest indicates that 30 percent of the variance in the outcome concerns differences between classrooms whereas 70 percent concerns differences within classrooms (including measurement error); an intraclass correlation of zero indicates that there are no classroom differences in the outcome.

If all classrooms have the same distribution of the outcome variable, the intraclass correlation is zero and statistical dependency is not a problem. If all classmates of each classroom have identical values in the outcome variable, but the outcome is different across classrooms, the intraclass correlation is 1 and the analysis should be done at the classroom level only. In most cases, the intraclass correlation is not large but substantial such that ignoring the nested structure of the data leads to biased significance tests.

This first problem of nested data (often the alternative term *clustered data* is used) can be easily resolved by adjusting the standard errors for the statistical tests. Many statistical packages such as R, SPSS, or MPlus provide simple adjustment procedures for clustered data. It is *not* necessary to conduct a multilevel analysis if one only wants to control statistical dependencies in nested data. This is a particular advantage if the data are analyzed with complex structural equation models at the individual level because multilevel SEMs are highly complex and require large samples of higher-level units (thus, social contexts) for achieving sufficient statistical power for the significance tests. In this case, adjusting the standard errors is an option in most SEM software (for applications, see e.g., Reitz, Asendorpf, & Motti-Stefanidi, 2015; Reitz, Motti-Stefanidi, & Asendorpf, 2016).

Two-level models of individuals in contexts

Often, one is interested in effects of higher-order units on lower-order units (so-called *cross-level effects*). For example, does the difference between immigrant and non-immigrant students' math achievement depend on the teaching style of the math teacher? Teaching style is a variable at the classroom level because all students in the same classroom share it (its intraclass correlation is 1).

Whenever cross-level effects are interesting, *multilevel analysis* is required. If the effects can be described by linear regressions, *multilevel linear regression models* are applied (also called *hierarchical linear models* or *random coefficient regression models*). These are multiple regression models where the regression coefficients obtained at a lower level ("random coefficients") are assumed to vary across higher-order units, and therefore can be regressed at the higher level on characteristics of the higher-order units. "Random" refers in this context to meaningful individual differences, not to measurement error! For example, within each classroom, students' math achievement can be regressed on their math anxiety. Classrooms may vary in the extent to which achievement depends on anxiety, and this variation may be predictable by the teaching style of the math teacher.

Such cross-level effects could be tested without applying multilevel models. One could simply regress within each classroom achievement on anxiety, record the classroom-specific intercepts and slopes, and regress them in a second step on teaching style. However, the advantage of multilevel models is that they simultaneously estimate all effects within one model and weight the lower-order regressions according to their reliability. It is intuitively clear that the within-classroom regressions are better estimated in larger classrooms than in smaller classrooms such that the larger classroom results should get a higher weight in the between-classroom regressions (similar to the weighting of large versus small studies in meta-analysis). Multilevel models include such weighting and have additional advantages from an estimation point of view (see Hox, 2010, for an easily accessible overview).

Here we illustrate the application of multilevel regression models with a study of immigrant youth's adaptation and well-being in Greek schools (Motti-Stefanidi et al., 2012a). We focus only on the question whether immigrant status is a risk factor for academic achievement (grade point average), and whether this risk is moderated by *classroom adversity*, the mean family social adversity (a cumulative risk index) in the classroom. This classroom characteristic is important also because all students were forced by law to attend the nearest school in their neighborhood such that all students in a classroom shared a similar level of family social adversity (an index of the social adversity of their neighborhood). In terms of multilevel analysis, classroom adversity was a variable at Level 2 (classrooms), and we were interested in whether it moderated the prediction of academic achievement from the risk factor immigrant status (immigrant yes/no) at Level 1 (students). Because immigrant status was correlated with individual family social adversity, parental involvement in school issues, and self-efficacy which also correlated with academic achievement, immigrant status was controlled for these three Level 2 covariates.

Although the study was a three-year longitudinal study, in this section we consider only the first wave of data where 1057 students were assessed in 49 classrooms in the first year of middle school. The sample might look very large but it is just sufficient for a two-level analysis where classrooms make up Level 2. In all multilevel analyses, all significance tests refer to the highest level of analysis such that the number of classrooms is the critical one, not the number of students. Hox (2010) proposed a 50/20 rule of thumb for two-level analyses with cross-level effects (50 units at Level 2 along with 20 Level 1 units within each Level 2 unit, thus 1000 Level 1 units). The study by Motti-Stefanidi et al., (2012a) meets this requirement. Studies with much fewer than 50 units at Level 2 run into power problems for all statistical tests, and studies with much fewer than 20 Level 1 units run into power problems for tests of cross-level effects.

The first question in such a two-level analysis is whether the outcome variable varied significantly between classrooms; if not, an ordinary moderated regression analysis would be sufficient. The intraclass correlation for academic achievement was ICC = .09 and significant; thus, 9 percent of the overall variance in achievement was accounted for by classroom differences. Therefore, a two-level analysis was in order that studied the cross-level moderation of the immigrant status effect on achievement by classroom adversity.

Table 8.1 Results of a two-level regression analysis predicting academic achievement from immigrant status and its moderation by classroom adversity

Fixed effects	b	SE	p
Overall intercept	14.28	0.21	0.000
Classroom adversity	−0.41	0.16	0.013
Immigrant status:			
intercept	−0.96	0.30	0.003
classroom adversity	0.55	0.26	0.044

Notes: 1057 students in 49 classrooms. Reported are unstandardized regression coefficients. Immigrant status was controlled for three covariates (see text).

The results are presented in Table 8.1 in terms of unstandardized regression coefficients (see Asendorpf, 2017, for technical details of the analysis). The intercepts and slopes in a multilevel analysis are called *fixed effects* whereas *random effects* refer to the variance components of the analysis which are not of further interest here. In any multilevel analysis, all fixed effects refer to units with zeros in all predictors at all levels. For example, in a longitudinal study where the waves of data assessment are coded as 1, 2, ... all effects are computed for the (non-existing!) Wave 0. Therefore, waves in longitudinal studies should be coded with care (e.g., as 0, 1, 2, ... if one studies a process starting in Wave 0, or by deviations from another psychologically meaningful time point). Often it is useful to grand-mean center all variables such that all effects refer to mean effects. An exception are differences between two alternative groups such as gender or immigrant status because in this case the effects for both groups can be easily computed (the intercept refers to the group coded zero, the intercept plus the group effect refers to the group coded 1).

The intercept $b = 14.28$ in Table 8.1 indicates that the mean academic achievement of Greek students (those with zero immigrant status) was 14.28 on the grading scale 1–20 used in Greece. Its standard error SE refers to the variation of the mean achievement of Greeks in a classroom across classrooms. Its significance p is trivial because all grades are larger than zero anyway; it is reported only for completeness.

Because classroom adversity was standardized across classrooms, the classroom adversity effect $b = -0.41$ indicates that an increase of 1 SD in classroom adversity was associated with a decrease of 0.41 points on the achievement scale. Note that increase and decrease do not refer to changes over time in this cross-sectional analysis. Instead, they refer to differences on the predictor and the outcome scale. The use of increase and decrease is ubiquitous in regression analysis although it can easily lead to causal misinterpretations of merely correlational findings. A more precise interpretation would be in this case that a difference of 1 SD in classroom adversity is accompanied by a difference of −0.41 points in academic achievement. If one were to reverse the direction of prediction by forecasting classroom adversity from classroom achievement, one would find a similarly strong effect (which does not make sense in this case). Both ordinary and multilevel cross-sectional effects based on regressions are only of limited value for causal interpretation.

The immigrant status intercept of $b = -0.96$ in Table 8.1 indicates that the mean achievement of immigrants across classrooms was 0.96 points lower than the achievement of their Greek classmates (thus, the immigrants achieved 14.28 − 0.96 = 13.32 points on average). Thus, immigrants were at risk of low academic achievement even if their higher individual social adversity, the lower school involvement of their parents, and their lower self-efficacy was taken into account. Finally, the classroom adversity effect on the immigrant status effect (the cross-level effect) of $b = 0.55$ indicates that the effect of classroom adversity on achievement was more positive for immigrants.

As in ordinary moderation analysis, it is helpful to visualize this interaction effect with a standard interaction plot where the means in the academic achievement of immigrants and Greeks are plotted for classrooms 1 SD below and 1 SD above the overall mean in classroom adversity (see Figure 8.1). Thus, Greeks achieved better than immigrants only in classrooms/neighborhoods with low social adversity. In highly adverse classrooms/neighborhoods, achievement was low for both immigrants and Greeks.

Three-level models of developmental changes of individuals in contexts

The two-level cross-sectional model discussed in the preceding section can be expanded to a longitudinal model by adding time points (waves of the longitudinal study) at a new lowest level of analysis. Thus time points are nested in individuals who are nested in contexts. Multilevel analyses are extremely flexible concerning the longitudinal design because all available assessments of each individual are used for computing the intercept and slope of this individual's developmental trajectory. Therefore, the number and timing of the assessments can vary from individual to individual, and missing assessments and systematic participant drop-out are automatically taken into account by the estimation procedures. Although longitudinal multilevel regression analysis estimates linear change for each individual such that the individual developmental trajectory is described with an intercept and a slope, nonlinear change can be easily studied by

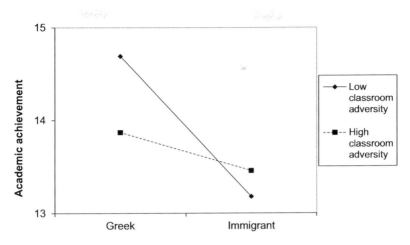

Figure 8.1 Cross-level effect of classroom adversity on the effect of immigrant status on academic achievement
Source: Adapted from Asendorpf, 2017, Figure 8.1, with permission of Springer Nature.

transforming time. For example, quadratic change is studied with the slopes for time squared.

Time can be centered at the first assessment such that the Level 1 intercept refers to Wave 1 of the study, at the midpoint of the observation interval (thus at Wave 2 in the case of three waves), at the mean time of assessment (which is most often somewhat earlier than the midpoint because of participant drop-out), or at the last assessment. Which option one chooses depends on the research question. In risk and resilience research, studies typically center the predictor at time 1 (forward prediction) although it is also possible to center at the last wave if one is interested in predicting antecedents of given outcomes (backward prediction). In addition, in the present case the first wave of assessment was psychologically particularly meaningful because it was scheduled in the first year in middle school. Therefore, Motti-Stefanidi et al., (2012a) centered time at Wave 1.

Table 8.2 presents the results of a three-level analysis with the three waves of assessment (first, second, third year in middle school) at Level 1, students at Level 2, and classrooms at Level 3. Time was centered at Wave 1; the Level 2 predictor immigrant status was centered at Greek students such that all intercepts refer to Greek students, and the three continuous covariates individual social adversity, parental involvement, and self-efficacy were grand-mean centered such that all intercepts refer to average levels in these variables; and the Level 3 predictor classroom adversity was

Table 8.2 Results of a three-level regression analysis predicting initial level and change of academic achievement from immigrant status and its moderation by classroom adversity

	Initial level			Change		
Fixed effects	b	SE	p	b	SE	p
Overall intercept	14.23	0.18	0.000	−0.37	0.07	.001
Classroom adversity	−0.43	0.14	0.004	0.14	0.07	.046
Immigrant status:						
intercept	−1.28	0.25	0.001	.00	.08	.951
classroom adversity	0.45	0.24	0.066	.02	.06	.739

Notes: 1057 students in 49 classrooms assessed in three waves. Reported are unstandardized regression coefficients. Immigrant status was controlled for three covariates (see text).

centered at the mean classroom adversity across classrooms because it was standardized. Table 8.2 is organized similar to Table 8.1 except that each effect is now separately estimated for the initial status and change (slope) of the individual trajectories.

The effects for the initial status closely correspond to those reported in Table 8.1 because both refer to Wave 1 effects. However, they are not identical because the estimations in the three-level analysis take the assessments of all waves into account. The immigrant status effect ($b = -1.28$) was again significant whereas the cross-level effect of classroom adversity on the immigrant status effect ($b = 0.45$) was only marginally significant.

Regarding change, the overall effect of $b = -0.37$ indicates that academic achievement decreased among Greek students by 0.37 points per year (see Table 8.2). This overall decrease was moderated by classroom adversity; in more adverse classrooms/neighborhoods, the slopes were more positive ($b = 0.14$), that is, the decrease was less marked. Therefore, the negative effect of classroom adversity on Greek students in Wave 1 of −0.43 became less negative in Wave 3, namely $-0.43 - 2 \times 0.14 = -0.15$.

Because the immigrant status effect on change and its moderation by classroom adversity were virtually zero (see Table 8.2), the results for overall change and its moderation by classroom adversity applied to immigrants as well. The lack of significant immigrant status effects on change is an important finding because researchers who study only immigrants, without a control group of age-matched non-immigrants, sometimes misinterpreted the decreasing achievement of their immigrant sample as an immigrant-specific effect. Fuligni (2001) actually argued that to elucidate whether a potential decline in immigrant youth's adaptation is the result of acculturation or development one would need to study a third group, consisting of youth who remained in the immigrant's home country. If their adaptation trajectories were stable, the decreases in immigrant youth's adaptation could be attributed to acculturation on the developmental change. Otherwise, the parallel declining paths of the three groups could reflect purely developmental change. In any case, in the Motti-Stefanidi et al., (2012b) study, the decline in achievement was not immigrant specific but typical for all adolescents.

Longitudinal two-level models are very similar to structural equation models (SEMs) with a fixed time schedule for all participants (see e.g., Little, 2013). In these SEMs the individual intercepts and the individual slopes are treated as latent factors of the observed manifest assessments of the dependent variable. The factor loadings for the latent slope factor play the role of the time variable in the Level 1 equation of a multilevel model, and the slope factor plays the role of the slope coefficient in the Level 1 equation (see Hox, 2010, for a detailed description of this equivalence). The only difference between the standard longitudinal two-level model and the standard latent growth curve model is that the error variances in the multilevel model are assumed to be equal; if they are constrained to be equal in the latent growth curve model, the multilevel and the latent growth curve model yield *identical* results. The main advantage of the multilevel approach is that longitudinal models with many levels can be easily studied; the main advantage of the latent growth curve approach is that latent variables and multiple outcomes can be easily studied (see Asendorpf, in press, for a more detailed discussion).

Conclusion

This chapter focused on conceptual and methodological considerations that contribute to a better understanding of the diversity in immigrant youth adaptation. Principles and concepts of developmental systems theory guided the research design and the type of statistical analyses performed to address the research question "Who among immigrant youth adapt well, concurrently, and over time, and why?" Immigrant youth's adaptation was examined in multilevel context, integrating developmental, acculturative, and social psychological perspectives. Furthermore, because immigrant youth change as they develop and acculturate, different pathways of adaptation were examined. Thus, theory on immigrant youth adaptation, development, and acculturation guided the research.

The nested structure of data on immigrant youth adaptation can be respected either by correcting the statistical tests for statistical dependencies of the effects at the individual level within social contexts or by using multilevel analyses if cross-level effects of context characteristics on the effects at the individual level are of interest. These two-level analyses can be expanded to longitudinal three-level analyses where time points are nested in individuals who are nested in social contexts. We encourage researchers on immigrant youth to respect the nested structure of their data and to longitudinally test effects of the social context on the adaptation of both immigrants and non-immigrants.

References

Asendorpf, J. B. (2017). Measuring positive development I: Multilevel analysis. In N. J. Cabrera & B. Leyendecker (Eds.), *Handbook of positive development of minority children and youth* (pp. 35–52). Cham, Switzerland: Springer Nature.

Asendorpf, J. B. (in press). Modeling developmental processes. In J. R. Rauthmann (Ed.), *Handbook of personality dynamics and processes* Amsterdam, NL: Elsevier.

Berry, J. W., Phinney, J. S., Sam, D. L., & Vedder, P. (2006). Immigrant youth: Acculturation, identity, and adaptation. *Applied Psychology*, 55, 303–332.

Bronfenbrenner, U., & Morris, P. A. (2006). The bioecological model of human development. In R. M. Lerner (Ed.), *Handbook of child psychology*. Vol. 1: Theoretical models of human development (6th ed., pp. 793–828). Hoboken, NJ: Wiley.

Bornstein, M. H. (2017). The specificity principle in acculturation science. *Perspectives on Psychological Science*, 12, 3–45.

Cicchetti, D., & Toth, S. L. (2009). The past achievements and future promises of developmental psychopathology: The coming of age of a discipline. *Journal of Child Psychology and Psychiatry*, 50, 16–25.

Fuligni, A. J. (2001). A comparative longitudinal approach to acculturation among children from immigrant families. *Harvard Educational Review*, 71, 566–578.

García-Coll, C., Crnic, K., Lamberty, G., Wasik, B. H., Jenkins, R., Garcia, H. V., & McAdoo, H. P. (1996). An integrative model for the study of developmental competencies in minority children. *Child Development*, 67, 1891–1914.

Hox, J. J. (2010). *Multilevel analysis: Technique and applications* (2nd ed.). New York, NY: Routledge.

Little, T. D. (2013). *Longitudinal structural equation modeling* New York, NY: Guilford Press.

Masten, A. S. (2014). *Ordinary magic: Resilience in development* New York, NY: Guilford Press.

Masten, A. S., & Kalstabakken, A. W. (in press). Developmental perspectives on psychopathology in children and adolescents. In J. M. Butcher (Ed.), *APA handbook of psychopathology*. Vol.2. Child and adolescent psychopathology (pp. 15–36). Washington, DC: American Psychological Association.

Motti-Stefanidi, F. (in press). Resilience among immigrant youth: The role of culture, development and acculturation. *Developmental Review*, 50, 99–109.

Motti-Stefanidi, F., Asendorpf, J. B., & Masten, A. (2012a). The adaptation and well-being of adolescent immigrants in Greek schools: A multilevel, longitudinal study of risks and resources. *Development and Psychopathology*, 24, 451–473.

Motti-Stefanidi, F., Berry, J., Chryssochoou, X., Sam, D. L., & Phinney, J. (2012b). Immigrant youth adaptation in context: Developmental, acculturation, and social-psychological perspectives. In A. S. Masten, K. Liebkind, & D. J. Hernandez (Eds.), *Realizing the potential of immigrant youth* (pp. 117–158). New York, NY: Cambridge University Press.

Motti-Stefanidi, F., & Masten, A. S. (2017). A resilience perspective on immigrant youth adaptation and development. In N. J. Cabrera & B. Leyendecker (Eds.), *Handbook of positive development of minority children* (pp. 19–34). Amsterdam, NL: Springer.

Motti-Stefanidi, F., & Salmela-Aro, K. (2018). Editorial challenges and resources for immigrant youth positive adaptation: What does scientific evidence show us? *European Psychologist, 23*, 1–5.

OECD (2010). *Closing the gap for immigrant students: Policies, practice, and performance.* Paris: Author.

Oppedal, B., & Toppelberg, C. O. (2016). Acculturation and development. In D. L. Sam & J. Berry (Eds.), *Cambridge handbook of acculturation psychology* (2nd ed., pp. 71–92). New York, NY: Cambridge University Press.

Reitz, A. K., Asendorpf, J. B., & Motti-Stefanidi, F. (2015). When do immigrant adolescents feel personally discriminated against? Longitudinal effects of peer preference. *International Journal of Behavioral Development, 39*, 197–209.

Reitz, A. K., Motti-Stefanidi, F., & Asendorpf, J. B. (2016). Me, us, and them: Testing sociometer theory in a socially diverse real-life context. *Journal of Personality and Social Psychology, 110*, 908–920.

Robinson, W. S. (1950). Ecological correlations and the behavior of individuals. *American Sociological Review, 15*, 351–357.

Suárez-Orozco, C., Motti-Stefanidi, F., Marks, A., & Katsiaficas, D. (in press). An integrative risk and resilience model for understanding the adaptation of immigrant origin children and youth. *American Psychologist, 73*, 781.

Suárez-Orozco, C., Suárez-Orozco, M. M., & Todorova, I. (2010). *Learning a new land: Immigrant students in American society.* Cambridge, MA: Harvard University Press.

Verkuyten, M. (2005). *The social psychology of ethnic identity.* New York, NY: Psychology Press.

Chapter 9

The role of comparative research in understanding the diversity of immigrant youth

Alison E. F. Benbow and Lara Aumann

Almost a century of psychological research on acculturation has demonstrated that acculturation is a complicated, multidimensional, and dynamic phenomenon, dependent on multiple processes and many moderating influences at individual, group, societal, and interactional levels (e.g., Arends-Tóth & van de Vijver, 2006; Berry, Kim, Minde, & Mok, 1987; Zick, 2010). This complexity only increases when considering acculturation in youth, because their experiences incorporate the coaction of bio-psycho-social development and cultural change (Benbow & Rutland, 2017; Titzmann & Lee, 2018). How children and adolescents navigate the experience of being part of more than one culture depends in no small part on individual differences such as gender, personality/temperament, motivation, cognitive development, socialization experiences, parental income, and education (Bornstein, 2017; Stürmer & Benbow, 2017). Furthermore, youth acculturation takes place within specific and distinctive contexts, such as families, schools, and peer groups, that are unlike adult contexts and bring their own benefits and challenges (Schachner, van de Vijver, & Noack, 2017; Ward & Geeraert, 2016).

According to the UN, 10 percent of all migrants were youth in 2013, a number that is rapidly increasing. Their reasons for migration are as varied as their personal situations, and include, amongst the most prominent, the search for alternative livelihoods and opportunities in education, employment, marriage, and family reunification, as well as protection from conflict (UN, 2013). In the future it is likely that the effects of climate change will become a further prominent reason for leaving home. Additionally, youth with a migration background – that is youth descended from immigrants – make up substantial percentages of the population of many countries across the globe. In light of the sheer number of youth affected by migration, it is perhaps not surprising that there is a surging interest in gaining a research-based understanding of their acculturation processes. A simple search on the database PsycINFO with the keywords "migrant or immigrant" and "adolescents or teenagers or youth" indicated a fourfold increase of research on immigrant minority youth in the

12 years after 2006 (4746 hits) compared to the same period before 2006 (1203 hits). It is particularly striking that only approximately 10 percent of these studies track acculturating adolescents longitudinally through the developmental and acculturative changes they experience, as only longitudinal studies can disentangle general developmental processes from processes of cultural change. Such clarification is, however, essential to fully understanding acculturating youth (Fuligni, 2001).

Given the described diversity and complexity of youth acculturation, considering acculturating groups instead of acculturating individuals may seem futile at first glance, because by focusing on group averages the group level necessarily masks many of the distinct, heterogeneous, acculturation experiences made by individual group members (Bornstein, 2017). However, it is equally the case that acculturation as a process of cultural change is as much a social psychological phenomenon as it is a phenomenon of individual development and change. The challenge therefore lies in uncovering the social and contextual variables that can explain individual acculturating experiences. Put differently, an understanding of the development of acculturation in young people requires approaches that can identify what is unique, what is group and/or context-specific, and what may be universal about their experiences (Bornstein, 2017; Lerner, 2018).

In this chapter, we will argue that cross-comparative research offers one methodological approach to answering this question. After providing our definition of immigrant youth taking taxonomic distinctions into account, we discuss the relevance of social phenomena in acculturation research. These include social identity processes related to negotiating more than one culture and setting conditions (e.g., reasons why people migrate, the places they migrate to and from, the fit between places; Bornstein, 2017). We give examples from three overarching groups of immigrant youth: immigrant minority youth, diaspora immigrant youth, and refugee children and adolescents. In doing so we will highlight that our knowledge about acculturation is bounded by issues surrounding how acculturation is investigated and the specific context in which it takes place. Building on this overview, we make a case for comparative acculturation research, presenting a definition, outlining key assumptions, and theoretical and methodological considerations in planning such research. We then describe different types of cross-comparative research and their uses, providing examples where possible and delineating strengths and weaknesses of each approach. The chapter ends with some recommendations for future research.

Characteristics of current research on different groups of immigrant youth

In this chapter, we consider *immigrant youth* to be representatives of groups that immigrated to a new country of settlement within the last one or two generations. We thus include the children and grandchildren of new immigrants with children who have themselves immigrated into a country, but do not consider youth from ethnocultural minorities with a shared and longstanding history in their country of residence (who can be considered sedentary rather than migratory). Following established taxonomic descriptions, such as the one put forward by Berry et al. (1987), migrant groups can be further differentiated into those whose acculturation is voluntary (as is the case for economic migrants) or involuntary (as is the case for refugees), as well as those whose settlement is temporary (i.e., due to a work-placement) or permanent (as is likely for second or third generation immigrants). However, research on immigrant adolescents does not cover each of these dimensions in equal detail, with very little research on voluntary, non-permanent migration and youth for example. We therefore limit this section to current research on the acculturation of immigrant minority youth, diaspora youth and refugee youth.

In our definition, *immigrant minorities* include all youth whose family migrated voluntarily, and who plan to stay permanently in the country of settlement. Much research on youth in this category has focused on numerically large immigrant communities in "Western" host countries. Prominent examples include research with Latinx communities in the United States and Turkish immigrant minorities in Germany and the Netherlands (Nguyen & Benet-Martínez, 2013). Unlike immigrant minority youth, *diaspora migrant youth* are returning to the country of their ancestors with which they share a common history, their heritage and/or religious background, and which they feel is their ancestral home (Tsuda, 2009). Well-known examples are found in the resettlement of Russian Ethnic Jews to Israel and of ethnic-German returnees from the former Soviet Union to Germany (Silbereisen, Titzmann, & Shavit, 2014). In contrast, *refugee youth* are representatives of groups who do not migrate voluntarily, but are displaced worldwide because of persecution, war, conflict, or generalized violence (UNHCR, 2018). Research on refugees and asylum seekers often defines the group membership of participants based on their experience of forced migration or their legal status, so that samples are sometimes more diverse in terms of national origin than is the case in other research (Fazel, Reed, Panter-Brick, & Stein, 2012). There are more unaccompanied minors in this group than in the immigrant minority and diaspora youth groups, which tend to migrate in the family unit. Research on refugees is also somewhat more likely to take place outside of "Western" host societies, although this context is predominant even in this group. In terms of absolute numbers, little acculturation research focuses on refugee youth, a somewhat larger amount considers diaspora youth, but the vast majority of research on acculturating immigrant youth considers immigrant minorities (Nguyen & Benet-Martínez, 2013). The groups therefore differ in terms of the size of the actual literature, and empirical knowledge available, about them.

Additionally, research on immigrant youth is also characterized by different prevalent research methodologies. Because refugee migration is involuntary, forced, and traumatic, current research on refugee youth is often qualitative – allowing an approach that is individual, culturally appropriate, accessible, and sensitive. In psychology, such qualitative research explores refugees' subjective and individual experiences of acculturation, without assuming knowledge about this experience a priori. It thus highlights young people's own narratives, providing them with an active voice and the opportunity to participate in shaping the knowledge surrounding their experiences (Doná, 2006). The goal and focus of research on young refugees is frequently to support them, to assess their risk and resilience with regard to mental health, and to influence child-centered programs and policies (e.g., Doná, 2006; Fazel et al., 2012). By contrast, most research on immigrant minority and diaspora youth has been quantitative, with a focus on testing hypotheses about acculturation in a scientifically objective and generalizable manner, usually through the administration of construct-based, reliable, and valid questionnaires. This research tends to have a much more general focus on adolescent acculturation preferences and psycho-socio-cultural adaptation outcomes such as self-esteem, well-being, inter-group attitudes, educational achievement, and cultural competences, such as language use. Each methodological approach has its justification, as well as advantages and disadvantages. The fact that different methods are applied – with different objectives – to separate immigrant youth groups does, however, mean that one source of diversity in findings about these groups may stem from these differences. It also means that findings resulting from these studies are not always easily compared to one another.

Nonetheless, all the research we have reviewed, regardless of group or methodology, would suggest that youth acculturation and adaptation is driven by distinctly social phenomena that play out in different ways for different groups and individuals. Take, for example, the question of preferences in the individual negotiation of the cultures involved in the acculturation process, as conceptualized by acculturation orientations, bicultural competence, or bicultural identity integration (Benbow & Rutland, 2017; Benet-Martínez & Haritatos, 2005; Berry, Phinney, Sam, & Vedder, 2006). This negotiation of host and heritage culture is dependent not only on individual characteristics and motivations, but hinges upon the social interactions cultivated by individuals, as well as the actual and perceived nature of the heritage society of migrants and the host society in which they have settled (Ward & Geeraert, 2016).

Societies differ, for example, in terms of population size and make-up, migration history, laws and policies (generally and with regard to citizenship and migration specifically), political climate (levels of conflict, racism), and with regard to specific cultural qualities, such as values and societal norms. Based on these characteristics different individuals and groups are likely to bring markedly different experiences and expectations to a receiving country and will equally face markedly different conditions when they arrive. For instance, different labor and migration laws in a receiving country may result in a much easier transition into that new culture including access to all institutions for legal economic migrants (and their families) than is afforded to refugees situated in camps with little or no access to the labor market, health care, and educational systems. Considering that the school context and cross-ethnic friendships are known to provide opportunities for interaction and identification with the majority culture (Ward & Geeraert, 2016), it quickly becomes apparent how these different laws limit the options regarding negotiating different cultures. Compared to immigrant minority youth meeting host society peers in school every day, refugee youth in reception camps without the opportunity to come into regular, orderly contact with the majority society (Robila, 2018), are less likely to learn about the host culture and much less able to identify with it.

Moreover, next to objective characteristics of receiving societies and societies of origin, perceptions of these characteristics may also play an important role in decisions to migrate (Mähönen, Leinonen, & Jasinskaja-Lahti, 2013) and reactions to migrants from and in different societies (Verkuyten, Altabatabaei, & Nooitgedagt, 2018). In addition, these perceptions affect individual acculturation preferences, because they guide the interpersonal and intergroup interactions that are possible and likely for immigrant minority youth in a given setting. For instance, diaspora migrants often describe being pulled towards their so-called ancestral homes, because of the privileged conditions and specific rights of immigration afforded to them by these countries (e.g., immediate residence and work permit, Silbereisen et al., 2014). Despite a physical absence that has sometimes spanned generations, this ideal of "returning home" implies an expectation of religious, cultural, and ethnic similarity between these immigrants and the settlement society that is not usual for other immigrant groups. One might assume that this expectation of similarity would lead to higher levels of host–peer relations and host culture identification for diaspora youth than other immigrant youth groups. Research has not found this to be the case, however. In fact, diaspora adolescents are found to be quite similar to other immigrant groups under investigation in terms of acculturative stress, sociocultural adaptation, and cultural identification despite a historic cultural bond with the settlement society (Titzmann & Stoessel, 2014). This may be because diaspora youth are actually well acculturated and established in their country of birth. This affects the real distance between the cultures of the country of birth and the receiving society, which has changed substantially since the time of the original emigration (e.g., Tsuda, 2009). As a consequence, their expectations of cultural closeness may not actually be fulfilled after arrival.

Unfortunately, pre-migration characteristics (such as the cultural, social, regional, and economic background of migrating groups and individuals) are often neglected in research on immigrant minority youth, partly because samples in this group often comprise 1.5 to second generation adolescents, with no direct experience of their familial heritage culture (e.g., Schachner et al., 2017). Research with refugee youth often pinpoints pre-migration traumatic events, but seldom considers other aspects of the heritage culture (Keles, Friborg, Idsoe, Sirin, & Oppedal, 2016). This makes it difficult to assess the meaning of pre-migration setting conditions for acculturating youth, and also highlights that we currently cannot actually disentangle the effects of heritage culture conditions from other influences in the acculturation process (Diehl, Lubbers, Mühlau, & Platt, 2016). More generally, current research on diverse acculturating youth would benefit from a greater integration of the divergent literatures and methodologies discussed above to understand what is unique and what is universal about the acculturation of young immigrants. We now outline, why and how comparative research may help to achieve such an integration.

The case for comparative research

Even the brief literature we have reviewed highlights that our current understanding of acculturation processes in young people is disparate regarding the topics under investigation, the societies in which the research takes place, the types of people who are investigated, as well as the types of theories and methodologies that have been applied at different times in the history of acculturation research. Research is often social psychological in nature focusing on group and context-based explanations of individual acculturation experiences. There is also a clear predominance of research within Western contexts focusing on the conditions within receiving countries over conditions in countries of origin. Participants in such research often come from well-established, voluntary, and permanent migrant groups.

Existing research is often conducted in single contexts and/or with single groups, making it difficult to identify similarities in adaptation and the generality of relationships on the one hand, and group-specific aspects of adaptation and limits of generality on the other (Berry et al., 2006; Slonim-Nevo, Mirsky, Rubinstein, & Nauck, 2009). It is also rarely well-equipped to address the increasing complexity of conditions moderating the acculturation process in modern societies confronted with growing cultural and religious heterogeneity. This is further compounded by the fact that specific conditions are rarely explicitly delineated or measured in current research, making it impossible to pinpoint reasons for the differences that may arise in different groups and societal settings (e.g., Kohn, 1987).

Comparative research, defined here as quantitative research that utilizes *systematically comparable* data from two or more ethnic, national, or immigrant groups, within or between countries, may be a useful approach to understanding the diversity of immigrant youth, because it can establish the generality of research findings and provide evidence for the validity of theories based on single-group studies. In the area of acculturation, comparative studies seek to understand whether acculturation proceeds in similar ways across different setting conditions (i.e., reasons for migrating, societies of emigration and immigration). This approach also makes it possible to understand and highlight country and group-specific differences that might increase or decrease adaptive acculturation outcomes. A comparative framework, comparing acculturating to non-acculturating youth (ideally across time), is also essential to understand the dynamic interplay of general development and acculturation that is a unique and substantive feature of immigrant youth's life experiences and their psycho-socio-cultural adaptation (Titzmann & Stoessel, 2014). Comparative research should therefore give us some indication of underlying mechanisms that can explain why and where some acculturating youth do better than others. However, this can only be achieved if the research is carefully planned and designed as outlined in the next section.

Planning and designing comparative studies

As with any empirical method, the quality of comparative research depends on the rigor with which the scientific principles are applied to its procedures, from the conception of the research question to the interpretation of the research findings. The first step in this process is, as always, to define a research question that can add to a body of knowledge (in this case the diversity of acculturating youth) in a meaningful way. In the case of comparative research this will usually involve some consideration of a unique, group-specific, or universal aspect of migrating youths' acculturation based on a sound understanding of the current research literature. Thus, the comparative researcher will likely derive testable a priori hypotheses based on one, or several, of the theoretical models outlining acculturation conditions, processes, and outcomes (e.g., Arends-Tóth & van de Vijver, 2006; Zick, 2010). For instance, one might decide to investigate the role of pre- and post-migration socio-economic status (SES) of the migrant family on adolescent adaptation, to test the assumption that this variable has a greater impact on psycho-socio-cultural adaptation than acculturation orientations such as integration (Aumann & Titzmann, 2019; Rudmin, Wang, & Castro, 2017). Once the research question has been clearly defined delineating the comparison variables of interest, the ethnic group and the comparison group should be selected accordingly.

In the following steps, a good comparative design will always aim to reduce bias and establish equivalence of methods across comparison groups and contexts as closely as possible (see Matsumoto & van de Vijver, 2011 for a detailed coverage of appropriate cross-cultural research methods in psychology). This is the only way to ensure that differences between comparison groups are not artifacts of methodological weaknesses in the study design (e.g., Kohn, 1987). A clear definition of the immigrant groups under investigation is needed: Are groups based on common ethnicity, common nationality, or other common features (such as shared refugee status or experience of diaspora migration)? The definition of these groups of interest should add enough detail to avoid making group membership a proxy or a mask for other variables such as SES, age, length of residence, generational status, language, education, discrimination, or culture itself (Cauce, Coronado, & Watson, 1998). Choices are therefore necessary regarding the features of the comparison group or groups that should match the chosen immigrant group and those that should vary systematically. In our example above, the question would suggest a comparison between groups varying systematically with regard to high/or low SES before and after migration – factors that might be held constant would probably include age and time since migration/length of stay. Next, specific setting conditions should also be decided: in our example one might try to hold the ethnic group, heritage context, and receiving context constant, so that effects on adaptation can be traced back to the effect of SES alone. If, on the other hand, the question posed were regarding the extent to which migration experience or length of residence affect the acculturation process of adolescents, relatively new arrivals could be compared to more experienced immigrant youth. If the aim were to disentangle acculturative and development-specific processes, native comparison groups might be the medium of choice. Likewise, and as is the case with all good psychological research, sample sizes should be planned a priori and be large enough to have sufficient power to be able to uncover small to medium effect sizes.

Consequently, a considerable amount of planning should be invested to ensure that the measures utilized in the sample are appropriate to address the comparisons under scrutiny. Cultural equivalence must be established: constructs used must not differ in their internal structure or the meaning they are assigned when answered by participants from different comparison groups (e.g., Helms, 1992). This can be achieved, amongst other things, by translating and back-translating reliable and valid questionnaires that have also been extensively discussed with insiders to the culture of interest and adapted to be equally relevant to all participants. Psychometric and scalar equivalence can then be assessed empirically after data collection is completed to further support the validity of assumptions made about the comparisons between groups (Matsumoto & van de Vijver, 2011). If comparative research questions are applied to secondary or archival data, not all desired indicators may be available – in this case other matching procedures, such as propensity scoring, may need to be applied to ensure comparability of the included groups.

Before we turn to a more detailed account of the different types of comparisons addressed by comparative research, a word of caution should be given with regard to the interpretation of the findings of such research. The issue is not so much with findings that highlight similarities across acculturating groups – in this case the research provides evidence for the generality of some principle, mechanism, or process. Rather, it is the differences that are uncovered with comparative research that need to be interpreted with particular care. Such differences are harder to explain and can potentially reproduce and perpetuate ethnic or cultural stereotypes when they (inadvertently) imply cultural hierarchies (!Cauce et al., 1998; Kohn, 1987). For instance, research that compares immigrant youth to native youth may (unintentionally) suggest that the group of natives is the norm from which immigrants deviate in some way. To avoid such biased interpretations it is important that comparative researchers, and acculturation researchers more generally, reflect upon and question the implicit and explicit assumptions they have and are making about the nature of culture (Cauce et al., 1998).

Types of comparisons in comparative research

If universal and unique features of minority and majority settings that support or undermine known acculturation processes are to be uncovered (Berry et al., 2006), decisions have to made about the type (or types) of comparisons that are to be made in the comparative research. These choices will always depend on the purpose of the research and the specific research questions under investigation. The resulting types of comparisons usually vary with regard to the setting (within single or across multiple receiving cultures), the number and type of groups (single or multiple immigrant groups with or without native comparison groups), and the design (cross-sectional or longitudinal). We now outline specific examples of different types of comparisons by research purpose and highlight advantages and disadvantages of each type.

The first type of comparative research that is found in the literature aims for a better understanding of immigrant adaptation to a specific country, for instance to provide insights into epidemiological questions relevant to policy decisions. For this kind of research question it may be sufficient to compare several immigrant and minority groups with native groups within a specific (and therefore consistent) country context. Such research can give information about the importance of various heritage society setting conditions, and/or group characteristics such as cultural distance, and/or individual characteristics for adaptation outcomes. To exemplify: Betancourt et al. (2017) used propensity score matching to compare trauma profiles, mental health needs, and service use across refugee, immigrant, and U.S.-origin children in a large clinical sample. Their research was able to control for potential individual and demographic differences between the groups and thus could identify distinct patterns of trauma exposure, distress symptoms, and service needs for refugee youth. They were able to highlight important lacunae in the current planning and provision of appropriate mental health services to this group.

No matter how well designed, this type of comparative research at the national level cannot, however, speak to country or societal level conditions affecting the acculturation process. These, in turn, may be investigated by comparing a specific group of immigrants (e.g., immigrants from a particular culture) across different national contexts – a second type of comparison often found in the literature. Yagmur and van de Vijver (2012) considered how decisions about heritage culture and language maintenance and of host culture and language adoption differ for Turkish immigrants as a function of the level of pluralism associated with four reception countries: Australia, France, Germany, and the Netherlands (total N = 1085, with at least 265 participants in each country). In a departure from predictions made by interactive acculturation models (e.g., Bourhis, Moise, Perreault, & Senécal, 1997), which would assume an integration stance in pluralist societies, they were able to show that maintenance was lowest and culture adoption highest for Turks in Australia, the most pluralist country with the least pressure to assimilate. This study provides a good example of cross-national comparisons of one cultural group, which can invite further advancement of our knowledge regarding actual, rather than presumed, differences in acculturating societies. However, it still does not fully rule out the possibility that the Turkish migrants under investigation differ in some specific way from each other, for instance regarding individual characteristics, or specific reasons that led them to choose "their" receiving country. Accordingly, we do not know to what extent differences in migrants' integration trajectories across destinations reflect country-specific immigrant selectivity or reception contexts including ethnic boundaries, integration policies, or the broader institutional setting.

If research aims to address such variation at the country level and interactional effects at the group, inter-group, and/or individual level of acculturation conditions, then it needs to define several groups that are matched and systematically varied both within and across different countries – a third type of comparison. Depending on its outlook, generalized statements are then possible across comparative and contextual levels. For instance, Aumann and Titzmann (2018) utilized a cross-national comparative design with two diaspora immigrant samples originating from the former Soviet Union to investigate the acculturation gap that is often found between parents and children in immigrant families. Their research was able to show that parent–child communication suffered through the presence of an acculturation gap in both countries, but that the size of gaps in the ethnic domain differed between Germany and Israel, possibly as a consequence of different pre-migration knowledge and setting conditions in each country. Due to the focus on diasporic families and because there was no native comparison group little can be said with regard to how these processes might generalize (or not) and whether the gaps represent generational processes as well as acculturative processes.

The added advantages of cross-national research that considers separate ethnic groups and native groups – a further type of comparative research – is demonstrated in the following study by Stevens et al. (2015). Their detailed international comparative study of immigration and adolescent emotional and behavioral problems aimed to provide a comprehensive account of these issues in the Western world. To this end, they compared native and migrant adolescents from ten countries in a large-scale, cross-national, representative sample. Alongside variations in national migration policies and attitudes towards immigrants, the authors also gathered information about the generational status of the adolescents, their ethnic background, and various outcome variables including life-satisfaction, psychosomatic complaints, and physical fighting, amongst others. Their results provide compelling overall evidence that immigration to Western receiving societies is a risk factor for the development of adolescent problem behaviors, while highlighting the complex role of gender, generational status, and factors related to the receiving society in these processes. This example of research shows clearly where the strengths of a good cross-comparative design lie: it combines large representative samples with clear predictions about relevant factors across acculturating conditions and speaks to a multitude of outcome measures utilized in other research in this area. However, because it is cross-sectional in nature this study cannot give any information about individual trajectories in the acculturation process and therefore may be susceptible to bias with regard to the finality of the youth's unsuccessful adaptation.

If research wants to uncover processes then it needs to add longitudinal data to the comparative design – resulting in a further type of comparative research. Only research that combines international cross-comparative designs with a longitudinal approach can speak to the question whether effects in adolescent samples stem from individual and group differences in acculturation processes or from different stages of normative development or from an interaction of both. This is because longitudinal studies go beyond documenting differences at a specific point in time to mapping inter-individual differences in intra-individual changes over time (Titzmann & Stoessel, 2014). Since immigrant youth essentially follow a double transition from one culture to another and from adolescence to adulthood, following the trajectories of such youth across stages of development and acculturation may help to understand how it is that they manage to negotiate these transitions. Such longitudinal research could also help to delineate and separate pre-migration and post-migration conditions from age and other cohort effects.

The project "The Impact of Social and Cultural Adaptation of Juvenile Immigrants from the Former Soviet Union in Israel and Germany on Delinquency and Deviant Behavior" by Silbereisen and Fishman (2001–2007) is a prominent example of such research. In their comparative and longitudinal design (four waves spanning six years), they planned the comparison of diaspora migrant adolescents from the former Soviet Union, in Germany and Israel, to immigrant minority and native youth in Germany and Israel. The results from this project are elucidating. For example, most immigrant and native youth showed a similar rate of change in autonomy expectations (Titzmann & Silbereisen, 2012), and were similar in terms of trajectories in depressed mood, but only when the acculturation transition was not recent (Michel, Titzmann, & Silbereisen, 2012). Furthermore, latent growth curve models showed newcomers to have lower levels and more pronounced increases of self-efficacy as compared to experienced immigrant adolescents (Titzmann & Jugert, 2017), while growth mixture modeling was able to uncover distinct inter-individual trajectories and types of cultural identity change (Stoessel, Titzmann, & Silbereisen, 2014). Taken together, research from this project has been able to show that immigrant and native youth are more similar than one might expect, but that the interplay of development and acculturation is nuanced and dependent on outcome measures and moderating variables. Of course the examples provided here are by no means the only examples of comparative acculturation research, but they do serve to illustrate that comparative research can take numerous forms in addressing different (open) questions regarding unique and more general developmental and acculturative processes of diverse immigrant youth.

Concluding comments and directions for future research

We have outlined in this chapter how complex and diverse the experience of immigrant youth are today and how our current understanding of these experiences is unfortunately bound and limited by a research focus that does not often include rigorous cross-comparative designs. It is not our intention to criticize extant research. Far more, we are motivated to caution towards over-interpreting what we know about acculturation in immigrant youth at this moment in time, because we so often focus on very specific and singular instances of acculturation without being able to state exactly what may or may not be generalized from them. Our aim was to show how our understanding can change when we are able to get closer to the complexity experienced by these youth through the methods we apply. We hope that future research will continue to address this challenging issue and would like to give several further recommendations for future research that is well equipped to do justice to diversity. First and foremost, we would like to see more acculturation research in non-Western contexts, as well as research that compares Western and non-Western contexts, because without such research we are missing the biggest part of today's reality of migration. We would also welcome larger-scale research that explicitly compares different types of immigrant groups to each other and to natives in heritage and host countries, as we believe that these types of comparisons are best suited to understanding multiple moderators of acculturation processes. Psychologists have a lot to learn from neighboring disciplines such as sociology in regard to undertaking such large scale international projects, and we believe that more interdisciplinary work would further strengthen our common understanding of acculturating youth. In a related point, and given the difficulty of recruiting from certain samples and the tendency to focus on a limited number of outcomes, we also consider it worthwhile to combine qualitative studies with quantitative comparative approaches to gain a broader understanding of acculturating youth, their psychosocial adaptation, and their need for support. Furthermore, more longitudinal comparative research would help to examine differences in levels and rates of acculturative and developmental change. Finally, we have noted that adolescent development and acculturation is set in contexts such as schools, families, and peers. As yet, there is little research that is cross-comparative at this contextual level, as well as the group and societal levels. The assumptions we have about how these contexts affect acculturation in adolescents may therefore be similarly specific and unable to identify unifying and unique processes. We would therefore encourage researchers to undertake more research that looks specifically at the interactions between contexts at multiple ecological levels of acculturating conditions. Ideally, such research would also make use of appropriate techniques, such as multi-level modeling approaches. We are convinced that by addressing the diversity of life experiences of acculturating youth in this way, we will be able to uncover new and important insights that will help to better understand and appropriately support these youth in successfully negotiating acculturative and developmental demands towards positive outcomes in all contexts.

References

Arends-Tóth, J. V., & van de Vijver, F. J. R. (2006). Issues in conceptualization and assessment of acculturation. In M. H. Bornstein & L. R. Cote (Eds.), *Acculturation and parent-child relationships: Measurement and development* (pp. 33–62). Mahwah, NJ: Erlbaum.

Aumann, L., & Titzmann, P. F. (2018). Acculturation gaps in diaspora immigrant adolescent-mother dyads: The case for a domain-, group- and context-specific view on family adaptation. *International Journal of Psychology*. doi:10.1002/ijop.12524

Aumann, L., & Titzmann, P. F. (2019). Is role redistribution an immigrant phenomenon? A comparative study of family interactions and their implications for the psychosocial development of adolescents in high SES families. *Manuscript in preparation for submission*.

Benbow, A. E. F., & Rutland, A. (2017). Competence matters! Understanding biculturalism in ethnically diverse adolescents. *Journal of Community & Applied Social Psychology*. doi:10.1002/casp.2312

Benet-Martínez, V., & Haritatos, J. (2005). Bicultural identity integration (BII): Components and psychosocial antecedents. *Journal of Personality*, 73(4), 1015–1050. doi:10.1111/j.1467-6494.2005.00337.x

Berry, J. W., Kim, U., Minde, T., & Mok, D. (1987). Comparative studies of acculturative stress. *International Migration Review*, 21(9), 491–511.

Berry, J. W., Phinney, J. S., Sam, D. L., & Vedder, P. (2006). *Immigrant youth in cultural transition: Acculturation, identity, and adaptation across national contexts*. Mahwah, NJ: Lawrence Erlbaum Associates Publishers.

Betancourt, T. S., Newnham, E. A., Birman, D., Lee, R., Ellis, B. H., & Layne, C. M. (2017). Comparing trauma exposure, mental health needs, and service utilization across clinical samples of refugee, immigrant, and U.S.-origin children. *Journal of Traumatic Stress*, 30(3), 209–218. doi:10.1002/jts.22186

Bornstein, M. H. (2017). The specificity principle in acculturation science. *Perspectives on Psychological Science: A Journal of the Association for Psychological Science*, 12(1), 3–45. doi:10.1177/1745691616655997

Bourhis, R. Y., Moise, L. C., Perreault, S., & Senécal, S. (1997). Towards an interactive acculturation model: A social psychological approach. *International Journal of Psychology*, 32(6), 369–386.

Cauce, A. M., Coronado, N., & Watson, J. (1998). Conceptual, methodological, and statistical issues in culturally competent research. In M. Hernandez & M. R. Isaacs (Eds.), *Systems of care for children's mental health. Promoting cultural competence in children's mental health services* (pp. 305–329). Baltimore, MD, US: Paul H Brookes Publishing Co.

Diehl, C., Lubbers, M., Mühlau, P., & Platt, L. (2016). Starting out: New migrants' socio-cultural integration trajectories in four European destinations. *Ethnicities*, 16(2), 157–179. doi:10.1177/1468796815616158

Doná, G. (2006). Children as research advisors: Contributions to a 'methodology of participation' in researching children in difficult circumstances. *International Journal of Migration, Health and Social Care*, 2(2), 22–34. doi:10.1108/17479894200600013

Fazel, M., Reed, R. V., Panter-Brick, C., & Stein, A. (2012). Mental health of displaced and refugee children resettled in high-income countries: Risk and protective factors. *Lancet*, 379(9812), 266–282. doi:10.1016/s0140-6736(11)60051-2

Fuligni, A. J. (2001). A comparative longitudinal approach to acculturation among children from immigrant families. *Harvard Educational Review*, *71*(3), 566–578.

Helms, J. E. (1992). Why is there no study of cultural equivalence in standardized cognitive ability testing? *American Psychologist*, *47*(9), 1083–1101. doi:10.1037/0003-066X.47.9.1083

Keles, S., Friborg, O., Idsoe, T., Sirin, S., & Oppedal, B. (2016). Depression among unaccompanied minor refugees: The relative contribution of general and acculturation-specific daily hassles. *Ethnicity & Health*, *21*(3), 300–317. doi:10.1080/13557858.2015.1065310

Kohn, M. L. (1987). Cross-national research as an analytic strategy: American Sociological Association, 1987 presidential address. *American Sociological Review*, *52*(6), 713–731.

Lerner, R. M. (2018). *Concepts and theories of human development* (4th ed.). New York, NY: Routledge.

Mähönen, T. A., Leinonen, E., & Jasinskaja-Lahti, I. (2013). Met expectations and the wellbeing of diaspora immigrants: A longitudinal study. *International Journal of Psychology*, *48*(3), 324–333. doi:10.1080/00207594.2012.662278

Matsumoto, D., & van de Vijver, F. J. R. (2011). *Cross-cultural research methods in psychology*. New York, NY: Cambridge University Press.

Michel, A., Titzmann, P. F., & Silbereisen, R. K. (2012). Language shift among adolescent ethnic German immigrants: Predictors of increasing use of German over time. *International Journal of Intercultural Relations*, *36*(2), 248–259. doi:10.1016/j.ijintrel.2011.10.002

Nguyen, A.-M. D., & Benet-Martínez, V. (2013). Biculturalism and adjustment: A meta-analysis. *Journal of Cross-Cultural Psychology*, *44*(1), 122–159. doi:10.1177/0022022111435097

Robila, M. (2018). *Refugees and social integration in Europe*. Retrieved from United Nations Department of Economic and Social Affairs (UNDESA) Division for Social Policy and Development:

Rudmin, F., Wang, B., & Castro, J. D. (2017). Acculturation research critiques and alternative research designs. In S. H. Schwartz & J. Unger (Eds.), *The oxford handbook of acculturation and health* (pp. 75–96). Oxford: Oxford University Press.

Schachner, M. K., van de Vijver, F. J., & Noack, P. (2017). Contextual conditions for acculturation and adjustment of adolescent immigrants – Integrating theory and findings. *Online Readings in Psychology and Culture*, *8*(1). doi:10.9707/2307-0919.1142

Silbereisen, R. K., Titzmann, P. F., & Shavit, Y. (Eds.). (2014). *The challenges of diaspora migration: Interdisciplinary perspectives on Israel and Germany. Studies in migration and diaspora*. Farnham: Ashgate Publishing Ltd.

Slonim-Nevo, V., Mirsky, J., Rubinstein, L., & Nauck, B. (2009). The impact of familial and environmental factors on the adjustment of immigrants: A longitudinal study. *Journal of Family Issues*, *30*(1), 92–123.

Stevens, G. W. J. M., Walsh, S. D., Huijts, T., Maes, M., Madsen, K. R., Cavallo, F., & Molcho, M. (2015). An internationally comparative study of immigration and adolescent emotional and behavioral problems: Effects of generation and gender. *Journal of Adolescent Health*, *57*(6), 587–594. doi:10.1016/j.jadohealth.2015.07.001

Stoessel, K., Titzmann, P. F., & Silbereisen, R. K. (2014). Being "them" and "us" at the same time? Subgroups of cultural identification change among adolescent diaspora immigrants. *Journal of Cross-Cultural Psychology, 45*(7), 1089–1109. doi:10.1177/0022022114534770

Stürmer, S., & Benbow, A. E. F. (2017). Psychological foundations of xenophilia: Understanding and measuring the motivational functions of exploratory cross-cultural contact. *Personality and Social Psychology Bulletin, 43*(11), 1487–1502. doi:10.1177/0146167217722555

Titzmann, P. F., & Jugert, P. (2017). Transition to a new country: Acculturative and developmental predictors for changes in self-efficacy among adolescent immigrants. *Journal of Youth and Adolescence, 46*(10), 2143–2156. doi:10.1007/s10964-017-0665-9

Titzmann, P. F., & Lee, R. M. (2018). Adaptation of young immigrants: A developmental perspective on acculturation research. *European Psychologist, 23*(1), 72–82. doi:10.1027/1016-9040/a000313

Titzmann, P. F., & Silbereisen, R. K. (2012). Acculturation or development? Autonomy expectations among ethnic German immigrant adolescents and their native German age-mates. *Child Development, 83*(5), 1640–1654. doi:10.1111/j.1467-8624.2012.01799.x

Titzmann, P. F., & Stoessel, K. (2014). Diaspora migration in Israel and Germany: Unique contexts or examples of a general phenomenon? In R. K. Silbereisen, P. F. Titzmann, Y. Shavit, R. K. Silbereisen, P. F. Titzmann, & Y. Shavit (Eds.), *The challenges of diaspora migration: Interdisciplinary perspectives on Israel and Germany* (pp. 271–288). Burlington, VT: Ashgate Publishing Co.

Tsuda, T. (Ed.). (2009). *Diasporic homecomings. Ethnic return migration in comparative perspective*. Stanford, CA: Stanford University Press.

UN. (2013). *International migration report 2013*. New York, NY: United Nations, Department of Economic and Social Affairs, Population Division.

UNHCR. (2018). *Global trends: Forced displacement in 2017*. Retrieved from The UN Refugee Agency www.unhcr.org/globaltrends2017/

Verkuyten, M., Altabatabaei, H. G., & Nooitgedagt, W. (2018). Supporting the accommodation of voluntary and involuntary migrants: Humanitarian and host society considerations. *Social Psychological and Personality Science, 9*(3), 267–274. doi:10.1177/1948550617737600

Ward, C., & Geeraert, N. (2016). Advancing acculturation theory and research: The acculturation process in its ecological context. *Current Opinion in Psychology, 8*, 98–104. doi:10.1016/j.copsyc.2015.09.021

Yagmur, K., & van de Vijver, F. J. R. (2012). Acculturation and language orientations of Turkish immigrants in Australia, France, Germany, and the Netherlands. *Journal of Cross-Cultural Psychology, 43*(7), 1110–1130.

Zick, A. (2010). *Psychologie der Akkulturation*. Wiesbaden: VS-Verlag.

Part III
Adolescents' Diverse Social Worlds

Chapter 10

Adolescent language brokers

Developmental and familial considerations

Robert S. Weisskirch

Language brokering is when children, adolescents, and adults act as translators or interpreters from the heritage language to the host language on behalf of their parents and other adults (Tse, 1995). Children, adolescents, and adults engage in such activities without formal training and may be considered informal or natural translators (Harris & Sherwood, 1978). Language brokers may translate and interpret items such as notes from school, bills, rental agreements, and immigration papers and in settings such as medical appointments, face-to-face conversations, teacher and parent conferences, and similar items (Dorner, Orellana, & Jiménez, 2008). Given that children often learn the host language more quickly than do adults, language brokering is a common practice among immigrant families (Suárez-Orozco & Suárez-Orozco, 2001). Language brokering is one of many acculturation strategies, cultural and psychological, used by parents and families to navigate and manage the transition to a new culture with a new language and customs (Berry, 2003). These acculturations strategies, noted by Berry (2003), include the attitudes and behaviors utilized for day-to-day intercultural interactions. At the same time, parents also juggle their roles as parents in an acculturative environment in which the power dynamics within the family may shift because of their dependence on children to communicate on behalf of parents or the family. As children move into adolescence, the developmental processes of adolescence unfold and add another layer of complexity for the adolescents, the parents, and for family dynamics (Weisskirch, 2017). Since language brokering may provide an elevated power position within the family for adolescents, family roles may have to be renegotiated for optimal family functioning (Pedersen & Revenson, 2005).

Language brokering and adolescents

Adolescence is typically a time period in which individuals increase their striving for autonomy from parents and individuation (McElhaney, Allen, Stephenson, & Hare, 2009). As a result, adolescents spend less time at home with parents and other family members and increase their time spent with peers. However, with immigration, this developmentally typical trajectory may be compromised as parents' and family acculturation needs for language brokering may take precedence over the individual adolescent's development (Titzmann & Lee, 2018). This pull towards independence from the family of origin can be orthogonal to the parental need for the adolescent to act as a translator.

From the developmental perspective of an adolescent, on a small scale, parents may ask the adolescent to translate a note that came home from school, which may be a relatively minor task for the adolescent. On a larger scale, the adolescent may be asked to translate at a medical appointment for parents, interpreting sophisticated language across two (or more) authority figures or with complicated medical forms. In the former case, the adolescent may not feel especially burdened by the task, and it might be experienced as a typical chore that parents ask of their adolescents. In the latter case, the adolescent may be cognizant that adolescents would not usually be present at a medical appointment of an adult, may be limited in understanding medical terminology and in interacting with medical personnel, and may be privy to aspects of the parents' lives in which he or she would not typically have access. As a consequence, the experience of language brokering might be seen as especially burdensome, and, in particular, as this type of activity occurs again and again – the effects may be cumulative.

On the other hand, adolescents may find language brokering activities to be just part of what one does in an immigrant family (Dorner et al., 2008). The adolescent may benefit from the additional time with parents, and the attention that concentrated time together brings may gain the understanding of their parents, and receive appreciation and praise from parents for the work of language brokering. Past research has indicated that adolescents reported positive relationships with parents when they felt positively about language brokering (Weisskirch, 2017). The cognitive challenge of language brokering may also promote language ability and cognitive processes (Rainey, Flores-Lamb, & Gjorgieva, 2017). The stakes involved with language brokering may also vary from relatively small to much higher stakes for the broker and for the family. In some situations, the outcome of the translating may be relatively low stakes, such as a note from school, where precision in translation may not be critical for understanding and where the information conveyed is relatively understandable for the adolescent. Whereas, in other situations, the stakes may be much higher, such as translating immigration paperwork, which would require greater precision in translating and understanding what is being asked because of the dire potential outcomes for the family. Recently, Anguiano (2018) found that, among U.S. Latino adolescents, those youth who language brokered frequently in high stakes settings (i.e., legal and medical situations) had lower grade point averages (GPAs) and greater perceived stress in comparison to those language brokering in low stakes settings. These findings may indicate that adolescents recognize the potential repercussions of their language brokering, which may then take a psychological and emotional toll on them. The same outcomes may be true when translating a face-to-face conversation in which the information may need contemporaneous translation under the pressure of interacting with two adults, given the relatively high stakes of feedback from adults who possess a level of authority and power over the adolescent. Professional translators undergo years of training and certification of proficiency to engage in successful contemporaneous translating. Adolescent language brokers manage this task from just their lived experience.

Developmental considerations

Developmentally, adolescents also may lack understanding of sophisticated concepts and have uneven language skills in the heritage language, the host language, or both (Reyna & Farley, 2006). Adolescence is typically a time in which individuals increase in their ability to understand abstract concepts (Beck & Riggs, 2014). However, this ability has limits and may still be maturing, hampering an adolescent language broker's ability to provide a complete and accurate interpretation of concepts. At the same time, linguistic skills may also be uneven and may be dependent on when the adolescent language broker immigrated and his or her proficiency in the host language (Edele, Seuring, Kristen, & Stanat, 2015; Scott, Roberts, & Glennen, 2011). Rainey et al. (2017) have noted that language brokering may particularly challenge an adolescent's still developing executive functioning skills in which the broker must shift back and forth from language to language, finding the right word, and suppressing the vocabulary from the other language. Even with language proficiency, adolescents still have limited life experience and may not have encountered specific vocabulary and concepts necessary for accurate translation (Kievit et al., 2017).

Socially, adolescence also is a time in which social and brain changes bring about heightened sensitivity to social cues (Mills, Lalonde, Clasen, Giedd, & Blakemore, 2014). Adolescents' neurocircuitry growth, physiological changes, and social environment make them more aware of and sensitive to feedback from others, such as facial expressions, tone of voice, inclusion and exclusion, and personal validation (Somerville, 2013). Given the heightened social sensitivity, adolescents are, generally, more emotional than are adults or younger children (Larson, Moneta, Richards, & Wilson, 2002). Adolescent language brokers may be more cognizant than older brokers of how the parties involved in brokering react to their brokering and are emotionally responsive to that feedback. That is, when they register that the parties were pleased, they may then feel good about the language brokering experience, but when they feel as though the parties were displeased when brokering, the adolescent is likely to feel profoundly bad. The content of the communication translated may also make a difference. In particular, if the adolescent has to translate negative communication (e.g., problems with immigration paperwork, negative reports about siblings' behavior at school, or negative medical information), they may attribute disappointment with or negative reaction to the information as directed towards them. With developmental sensitivity to these kinds of social interactions, over time, the adolescents' emotional and psychological responsivity may be affected.

Adolescents are also sensitive to social feedback from parents. Indeed, Whittle et al. (2014) found that the frequency of positive parental behavior during early adolescence was associated with development of brain regions implicated in reward processes, emotional reactivity, and regulation. If parents provide praise or positive feedback, for example during language brokering, it may contribute to adolescents' brain development of reward and emotions. Areas of the brain implicated in perspective taking and prosocial behaviors are particularly sensitive during adolescence, which may then lead to greater prosocial behaviors (Tashjian, Weissman, Guyer, & Galván, 2018). When parents regularly provide positive feedback to their adolescent language broker, over time, it may build the adolescent's own behavior to engage in language brokering and other prosocial activities. Moreover, negative criticism from parents is associated with greater negative emotional responses and difficulty regulating negative emotions in adolescents as documented by brain activation and imaging studies (Lee, Siegle, Dahl, Hooley, & Silk, 2015). Over time, parents who are critical of their adolescent language broker or who are demanding of him or her may unintentionally contribute to how the adolescent's brain regulates negative emotional responses. Given that language brokering is a fundamentally social experience, it stands to reason that social sensitivity during adolescence may contribute to outcomes for adolescent language brokers.

Within the family, adolescence is also a time in which adolescents are expected to renegotiate their roles in the family (Granic, Hollenstein, Dishion, & Patterson, 2003). With a pull towards autonomy and individuation, adolescents may seek to distance themselves from parents. Language brokering responsibilities may make this natural pull towards separation more challenging because adolescents are tasked with brokering responsibility and refusal to participate may not be a realistic option (Weisskirch, 2017). The adolescent language broker may feel pressured or burdened by brokering responsibilities (Tse, 1996; Wu & Kim, 2009). In contrast, the broker may feel helpful or empowered by assisting parents. So, as adolescents mature, their experience of language brokering may differ as roles shift within the family, as they become more proficient at brokering, and as regular brokering might be perceived as impinging on their own activities.

Cultural issues

Culturally, for adolescents, language brokering experiences may be emblematic of cultural shifts within the family necessitated by the immigration experience. For the most part, immigrant-sending countries are collectivist in their cultural orientation (Hofstede, 2001). That is, in collectivistic societies, the needs, aspirations, and desires of the family, clan, ethnic group, or society is prioritized over those of the individual. In contrast, many of the immigrant-receiving countries are more individualistic, where individual achievement and accomplishment are prioritized, praised, and desired. Depending on when in their development adolescents emigrated, assuming it was early enough in childhood, they may be growing up in an individualistic-oriented society, absorbing individualistic values, and developing expectations of autonomy and separation from parents and family similar to native-born youth. In contrast, parents who come from a more collectivistic-oriented society than the host society are likely to retain expectations that their children will act concordantly with collectivist values and prioritize family needs, such as language brokering, over more individualistic pursuits (Bacallao & Smokowski, 2007). That is, parents may expect youth to engage in language brokering willingly. As a consequence, there may be added conflict for the parent–adolescent relationship because the parent may expect the adolescent to conform with collectivist cultural values – such as helping the family by language brokering – and the adolescent may expect a more unfettered expectation of less obligation to parents. Over time, as the parent makes solicitations for help and the adolescent responds, there may be a pattern of interacting that affects the adolescent, specifically, as well as the parents and family dynamics overall.

There is some evidence that because adolescents often acculturate at a faster pace than do parents that the acculturation discrepancy (i.e., an acculturation gap) gets compounded into a conflict between parents and their children (Portes & Rumbaut, 1996; Szapocznik & Kurtines, 1993). With greater discrepancy, there is evidence that there may be poor communication, less involvement, and poorer family functioning, which then leads to greater risks for the adolescent such as depression and substance use (Martinez, 2006; Unger, Ritt-Olson, Wagner, Soto, & Baezconde-Garbanati, 2009). Indeed, Schwartz et al. (2016) found that the relationship of parent–adolescent acculturation discrepancy to poor outcomes was mediated by poor family functioning and that it is the loss of heritage cultural retention (including language proficiency) that accounts for the negative outcomes among U.S. Latino adolescents and their parents. Moreover, Titzmann and Gniewosz (2018) found that, among ethnic German adolescents from the former Soviet Union, that those who had better proficiency in German had mothers who reported fewer adaptation problems.

Similarly, those ethnic German families from the former Soviet Union who reported a greater acculturation gap also reported greater family conflict (Titzmann & Sonnenberg, 2016). These findings may support the notion that acculturation dissonance between parents and adolescent may not be the sole antecedent fueling poorer outcomes but rather that lack of heritage cultural retention by the adolescent may be one underlying factor (Telzer, Yuen, Gonzales, & Fuligini, 2016). Wu and Kim (2009), in fact, found that, among Chinese American adolescents, those adolescents who were more Chinese culturally oriented were more likely to feel a sense of efficacy when language brokering for mothers and fathers as explained by their endorsement with traditional, cultural values. In contrast, they also found that those adolescents who were less Chinese oriented felt a sense of burden when language brokering for mothers and for fathers, as explained by a reduced endorsement of heritage cultural values. Similarly, Cila and Lalonde (2015) found that heritage cultural retention, diversity of items translated, and number of people for whom language brokering occurred, among brokering South Asian Canadian adolescents, predicted personal empowerment and family cohesion. Kam, Marcoulides, and Merolla (2017) found that stronger ethnic identity among U.S. Latino adolescents was more likely to predict occasional–moderate language brokering, but that brokering did not predict ethnic-racial discrimination, depressive symptoms, or risky behaviors, indicating that brokering with ethnic identification may not be detrimental. Among former Soviet Union adolescents to the United States, Jones and Trickett (2005) reported that frequency of cultural brokering (i.e., broader tasks than just language brokering) was unrelated to family disagreements, despite the adolescents' greater acculturation. Similarly, there are some cases where heritage cultural retention may not be desirable by the host culture or may be actively discouraged (Schachner, Juang, Moffitt, & van de Vijver, 2018; Ward, 2013). It may be that acculturation dissonance or discrepancy contributes to outcomes of language brokering when family functioning is poor.

Language brokering outcomes

For adolescents, language brokering may have positive or negative outcomes. Some positive outcomes for the individual include increased self-concept or identity as well as academic performance. For example, Weisskirch (2007) found a positive association between self-esteem and frequency of language brokering among U.S. Latino early adolescents. The difficulty of the language brokering activity and positive attitudes toward brokering were related to academic self-concept and peer popularity and confidence in physical appearance, respectively, among U.S. Latino adolescents (Niehaus & Kumpiene, 2014). Diversity of language brokering (i.e., across people, places, and things) has been positively associated with academic performance and, notably, reading scores among U.S. Latino adolescents (Buriel, Perez, De Ment, Chavez, & Moran, 1998; Dorner, Orellana, & Li-Grining, 2007). Acoach and Webb (2004) found that language brokering frequency, among U.S. Latino and Pacific Islander high school students, was positively associated with academic self-efficacy and grade point average. In addition, frequency of language brokering was positively associated with ethnic identity search and belongingness (Weisskirch, 2005) and biculturalism (Acoach & Webb, 2004). Positive feelings about language brokering was also associated negatively with cigarette use among young adolescents (Kam, 2011).

There are also some findings of negative repercussions for individuals as well. For example, frequency of language brokering has been associated with depressive symptoms (Love & Buriel, 2007) and internalizing problems among U.S. and Canadian Asian and Latino adolescents (Hua & Costigan, 2012; Martinez, McClure, & Eddy, 2009). Negative feelings about language brokering were linked to greater depressive symptoms (Kam & Lazarevic, 2014; Kim et al., 2014). Martinez et al. (2009) reported that those adolescents who were in contexts which required a high degree of language brokering engaged in more substance use in comparison to those in low brokering contexts. Those in high brokering contexts also performed worse in school tasks such as homework quality and language arts in comparison to those in low brokering contexts.

Parenting and parent–child relationships and language brokering

From a family systems perspective, immigration is a non-normative event, which requires the family to reorganize itself in order to establish equilibrium and function successfully (Falicov, 2012). Parents may shape the thoughts, feelings, and behaviors of adolescents through interactions and through family relationships as well (Rohner & Britner, 2002). Moreover, language brokering research supports the notion that the way that parents frame brokering activities may have deleterious or salutary effects for the adolescents. More specifically, when parents are appreciative of the work of the language broker, offer praise, and provide positive feedback, among other behaviors, adolescents benefit. For example, Chao (2006) found that frequency of brokering was associated with greater respect for at least one parent among a diverse group of U.S. adolescents. Furthermore, when adolescents feel positively about language brokering, there may be some benefits. Buriel, Love, and De Ment (2006) found that positive feelings about brokering were linked positively to greater parent–child bonding. Frequency of language brokering for the mothers was associated with higher perceptions of maternal sacrifice among Chinese and Korean American adolescents (Shen, Kim, Wang, & Chao, 2014).

Parents who, with their requests for and interactions during language brokering, are demanding or overburden adolescents may unwittingly foment negative outcomes for youth. These negative outcomes may include depressive symptoms, stress, and poorer perceived family relationships. For instance, adolescents' negative feelings about language brokering were predictive of brokers' greater depressive symptoms among Latino and Chinese American adolescents (Kam & Lazarevic, 2014; Kim et al., 2014). In addition, negative feelings about language brokering were found to relate to family-based, acculturative stress (Kam & Lazarevic, 2014). Among Chinese American adolescents, a sense of burden when language brokering predicted depressive symptoms (Kim et al., 2014). Frequency of brokering for both parents among Korean American adolescents related positively to externalizing behaviors (Chao, 2006) and with greater family conflict (Hua & Costigan, 2012). Furthermore, more language brokering about home management issues (i.e., bills, credit cards, insurance forms) was associated with adolescents reporting less parental authority in decision-making and with less parental knowledge about the adolescent's activities, associates, and whereabouts (Roche, Lambert, Ghazarian, & Little, 2015). Frequency of language brokering was associated negatively to acculturation level and positively to acculturative stress (Kam, 2011; Kam & Lazarevic, 2014; Weisskirch & Alva, 2002). For adolescents in settings that require a high amount of language brokering, there was an association with being in that context and lower ethnic identity belonging and ethnic identity search among U.S. Latino adolescents in comparison to those in low brokering contexts (Martinez et al., 2009).

Conclusion

Currently, there is a wave of immigration taking place globally. For many families, this immigration requires adjustments to how families function and familial efforts towards acculturation. In many families, adolescents are solicited by parents to serve as language brokers where they translate and interpret written text, conversations, and media. For many families, language brokering is a necessary psychological and cultural acculturative strategy but consideration should be given to the developmental needs of the adolescent language broker as well (Titzmann & Lee, 2018).

Developmentally, adolescents are typically seeking greater autonomy from parents and family and seek to spend more time with peers. This developmentally appropriate desire may clash with ongoing responsibilities to language broker for parents. Furthermore, adolescents' own cognitive, linguistic, and language skills are still maturing, may be limited, or uneven in some domains, which may compromise their ability to language broker accurately and competently. At the same time, adolescents may also be quite skilled and accurate at translating (Valdés, 2003). Socially, adolescence is also a time of heightened sensitivity to social cues. Adolescents' brains are maturing and are particularly responsive and reactive to feedbacks from others in social interactions and of perceptions in social activities. As a consequence, language brokering may differentially impact adolescents in ways that do not affect younger children and adults. In addition, ongoing language brokering activities may attune the adolescents' emotional responses to others. Hence, developmental issues are important to consider in studying and working with acculturating, immigrant families.

Within the family, parents' interactions with their children may shape the outcomes adolescents experience from language brokering. For some, the outcomes are positive such as increased self-esteem, ethnic identity, or reading scores. For others, the outcomes may be negative such as an increase in depressive symptoms, family conflict, or stress. Cultural issues may play a part in outcomes for adolescents and for family functioning. Adolescents who retain more heritage values may be more syntonic with their parents' expectations and have more salutary experiences with language brokering, whereas those who acculturate quickly and eschew heritage values may feel more burdened by language brokering.

From an interventionist viewpoint, it may be worthwhile to support immigrant families in understanding that adolescents do better when they receive positive feedback from parents for language brokering. In addition, families may also benefit from understanding that new cultural values may push for more autonomy for adolescents than parents might be expecting to grant, and that language brokering activity with supportive feedback can avoid being perceived as burdensome by the adolescents and the resulting negative outcomes. For adolescents, if they are recognized for providing support for their family by language brokering and are taught ways to communicate or to seek outside support when they do feel overwhelmed or stressed with brokering responsibilities, then they are likely to avoid negative outcomes and gain the benefits from being a broker. Adolescents who engage in brokering may develop increased understanding of both cultures, increased proficiency in both languages, and greater maturity from being in situations requiring them to negotiate between adults. These skills may create employment opportunities and be keys towards upward mobility (Morando, 2013).

References

Acoach, C. L., & Webb, L. M. (2004). The influence of language brokering on Hispanic teenagers' acculturation, academic performance, and nonverbal decoding skills: A preliminary study. *Howard Journal of Communications*, 15, 1–19. doi:10.1080/10646170490275459

Anguiano, R. M. (2018). Language brokering among Latino immigrant families: Moderating variables and youth outcomes. *Journal of Youth and Adolescence*, 47, 222–242. doi:10.1007/s10964-017-0744-y.

Bacallao, M. L., & Smokowski, P. R. (2007). The costs of getting ahead: Mexican family system changes after immigration. *Family Relations*, 56, 52–66.

Beck, S. R., & Riggs, K. J. (2014). Developing thoughts about what might have been. *Child Development Perspectives*, 8, 175–179. doi:10.1111/cdep.12082

Berry, J. W. (2003). Conceptual approaches to acculturation. In K. M. Chun, P. Balls Organista, & G. Marín (Eds.), *Acculturation: Advances in theory, measurement, and applied research* (pp. 17–37). Washington, DC: American Psychological Association. doi:10.1037/10472-004.

Buriel, R., Love, J. A., & De Ment, T. L. (2006). The relation of language brokering to depression and parent-child bonding among Latino adolescents. In M. H. Bornstein & L. R. Cote (Eds.), *Acculturation and parent-child relationships: Measurement and development* (pp. 249–270). Mahwah, NJ: Lawrence Erlbaum Associates Publishers.

Buriel, R., Perez, W., De Ment, T. L., Chavez, D. V., & Moran, V. R. (1998). The relationship of language brokering to academic performance, biculturalism, and self-efficacy among Latino adolescents. *Hispanic Journal of Behavioral Sciences*, 20, 283–297. doi:10.1177/07399863980203001.

Chao, R. K. (2006). The prevalence and consequences of adolescents' language brokering for their immigrant parents. In M. H. Bornstein & L. R. Cote (Eds.), *Acculturation and parent-child relationships: Measurement and development* (pp. 271–296). Mahwah, NJ: Lawrence Erlbaum Associates Publishers.

Cila, J., & Lalonde, R. N. (2015). Language brokering, acculturation, and empowerment: Evidence from South Asian Canadian young adults. *Journal of Multilingual & Multicultural Development*, 36, 498–512. doi:10.1080/01434632.2014.953540

Dorner, L. M., Orellana, M. F., & Jiménez, R. (2008). "It's one of those things that you do to help the family": Language brokering and the development of immigrant adolescents. *Journal of Adolescent Research*, 23, 515–543. doi:10.1177/0743558408317563

Dorner, L. M., Orellana, M. F., & Li-Grining, C. (2007). "I helped my mom," and it helped me: Translating the skills of language brokers into improved standardized test scores. *American Journal of Education*, 113, 451–478. doi:10.1086/512740

Edele, A., Seuring, J., Kristen, C., & Stanat, P. (2015). Why bother with testing? The validity of immigrants' self-assessed language proficiency. *Social Science Research*, 52, 99–123. doi:10.1016/j.ssresearch.2014.12.017.

Falicov, C. J. (2012). Immigrant family processes: A multidimensional framework. In F. Walsh (Ed.), *Normal family processes: Growing diversity and complexity* (pp. 297–323). New York, NY: Guilford Press.

Granic, I., Hollenstein, T., Dishion, T. J., & Patterson, G. R. (2003). Longitudinal analysis of flexibility and reorganization in early adolescence: A dynamic systems study of family interactions. *Developmental Psychology*, 39, 606–617. doi:10.1037/0012-1649.39.3.606.

Harris, B., & Sherwood, B. (1978). Translating as an innate skill. In D. Gerver & H. W. Sinaiko (Eds.), *Language interpretation and communication* (pp. 155–170). New York, NY: Plenum Press.

Hofstede, G. (2001). *Culture's consequences: Comparing values, behaviors, institutions, and organizations across nations*. Thousand Oaks, CA: Sage.

Hua, J. M., & Costigan, C. L. (2012). The familial context of adolescent language brokering within immigrant Chinese families in Canada. *Journal of Youth and Adolescence, 41*, 894–906. doi:10.1007/s10964-011-9682-2.

Jones, C. J., & Trickett, E. J. (2005). Immigrant adolescents behaving as culture brokers: A study of families from the former Soviet Union. *The Journal of Social Psychology, 145*, 405–427. doi:10.3200/SOCP.145.4.405-428

Kam, J. A. (2011). The effects of language brokering frequency and feelings on Mexican-heritage youth's mental health and risky behaviors. *Journal of Communication, 61*, 455–475. doi:10.1111/j.1460-2466.2011.01552.x

Kam, J. A., & Lazarevic, V. (2014). The stressful (and not so stressful) nature of language brokering: Identifying when brokering functions as a cultural stressor for Latino immigrant children in early adolescence. *Journal of Youth and Adolescence, 43*, 1994–2011. doi:10.1007/s10964-013-0061-z

Kam, J. A., Marcoulides, K. M., & Merolla, A. J. (2017). Using an acculturation-stress-resilience framework to explore latent profiles of Latina/o language brokers. *Journal of Research on Adolescence.* doi:10.1111/jora.12318

Kievit, R. A., Lindenberger, U., Goodyer, I. M., Jones, P. B., Fonagy, P., Bullmore, E. T., & Dolan, R. J. (2017). Mutualistic coupling between vocabulary and reasoning supports cognitive development during late adolescence and early adulthood. *Psychological Science, 28*, 1419–1431. doi:10.1177/0956797617710785

Kim, S. Y., Wang, Y., Weaver, S. R., Shen, Y., Wu-Seibold, N., & Liu, C. H. (2014). Measurement equivalence of the language-brokering scale for Chinese American adolescents and their parents. *Journal of Family Psychology, 28*, 180–192. doi:10.1037/a0036030

Larson, R. W., Moneta, G., Richards, M. H., & Wilson, S. (2002). Continuity, stability, and change in daily emotional experience across adolescence. *Child Development, 73*, 1151–1165. doi:10.1111/1467-8624.00464

Lee, K. H., Siegle, G. J., Dahl, R. E., Hooley, J. M., & Silk, J. S. (2015). Neural responses to maternal criticism in healthy youth. *Social Cognitive and Affective Neuroscience, 10*, 902–912. doi:10.1093/scan/nsu133

Love, J. A., & Buriel, R. (2007). Language brokering, autonomy, parent-child bonding, biculturalism, and depression: A study of Mexican American adolescents from immigrant families. *Hispanic Journal of Behavioral Sciences, 29*, 472–491. doi:10.1177/0739986307307229

Martinez, C. R., Jr. (2006). Effects of differential family acculturation on Latino adolescent substance use. *Family Relations: An Interdisciplinary Journal of Applied Family Studies, 55*, 306–317. doi:10.1111/j.1741-3729.2006.00404.x

Martinez, C. R., Jr., McClure, H. H., & Eddy, J. M. (2009). Language brokering contexts and behavioral and emotional adjustment among Latino parents and adolescents. *The Journal of Early Adolescence, 29*, 71–98. doi:10.1177/0272431608324477.

McElhaney, K. B., Allen, J. P., Stephenson, J. C., & Hare, A. L. (2009). Attachment and autonomy during adolescence. In R. M. Lerner & L. Steinberg (Eds.), *Handbook of adolescent psychology: Individual bases of adolescent development* (pp. 358–403). Hoboken, NJ: John Wiley & Sons.

Mills, K. L., Lalonde, F., Clasen, L. S., Giedd, J. N., & Blakemore, S. (2014). Developmental changes in the structure of the social brain in late childhood and adolescence. *Social Cognitive and Affective Neuroscience, 9*, 123–131. doi:10.1093/scan/nss113

Morando, S. J. (2013). Paths to mobility: The Mexican second generation at work in a new destination. *The Sociological Quarterly, 54*, 367–398. doi:10.1111/tsq.12019

Niehaus, K., & Kumpiene, G. (2014). Language brokering and self-concept: An exploratory study of Latino students' experiences in middle and high school. *Hispanic Journal of Behavioral Sciences, 36*, 124–143. doi:10.1177/0739986314524166.

Pedersen, S., & Revenson, T. A. (2005). Parental illness, family functioning, and adolescent well-being: A family ecology framework to guide research. *Journal of Family Psychology, 19*, 404–419. doi:10.1037/0893-3200.19.3.404.

Portes, A., & Rumbaut, R. G. (1996). *Immigrant America: A portrait*. Oakland, CA: University of California Press.

Rainey, V. R., Flores-Lamb, V., & Gjorgieva, E. (2017). Cognitive, socioemotional, and developmental neuroscience perspectives on language brokering. In R. S. Weisskirch (Ed.), *Language brokering in immigrant families: Theories and contexts* (pp. 205–223). New York, NY: Routledge/Taylor & Francis Group.

Reyna, V. F., & Farley, F. (2006). Risk and rationality in adolescent decision making: Implications for theory, practice, and public policy. *Psychological Science in the Public Interest, 7*, 1–44. doi:10.1111/j.1529-1006.2006.00026.x

Roche, K. M., Lambert, S. F., Ghazarian, S. R., & Little, T. D. (2015). Adolescent language brokering in diverse contexts: Associations with parenting and parent–Youth relationships in a new immigrant destination area. *Journal of Youth and Adolescence, 44*, 77–89. doi:10.1007/s10964-014-0154-3

Rohner, R. P., & Britner, P. A. (2002). Worldwide mental health correlates of parental acceptance–rejection: Review of cross-cultural and intracultural evidence. *Cross-Cultural Research: The Journal of Comparative Social Science, 36*, 15–47. doi:10.1177/106939702129146316

Schachner, M. K., Juang, L., Moffitt, U., & van de Vijver, F. J. R. (2018). Schools as acculturative and developmental contexts for youth of immigrant and refugee background. *European Psychologist, 23*, 44–56. doi:10.1027/1016-9040/a000312

Schwartz, S. J., Unger, J. B., Baezconde-Garbanati, L., Zamboanga, B. L., Córdova, D., Lorenzo-Blanco, E. I., … Szapocznik, J. (2016). Testing the parent–adolescent acculturation discrepancy hypothesis: A five-wave longitudinal study. *Journal of Research on Adolescence, 26*, 567–586. doi:10.1111/jora.12214

Scott, K. A., Roberts, J. A., & Glennen, S. (2011). How well do children who are internationally adopted acquire language? A meta-analysis. *Journal of Speech, Language, and Hearing Research, 54*, 1153–1169. doi:10.1044/1092-4388

Shen, Y., Kim, S. Y., Wang, Y., & Chao, R. K. (2014). Language brokering and adjustment among Chinese and Korean American adolescents: A moderated mediation model of perceived maternal sacrifice, respect for the mother, and mother–child open communication. *Asian American Journal of Psychology, 5*, 86–95. doi:10.1037/a0035203

Somerville, L. H. (2013). The teenage brain: Sensitivity to social evaluation. *Current Directions in Psychological Science, 22*, 121–127. doi:10.1177/0963721413476512.

Suárez-Orozco, C., & Suárez-Orozco, M. M. (2001). *Children of immigration.* Cambridge, MA: Harvard University Press.

Szapocznik, J., & Kurtines, W. M. (1993). Family psychology and cultural diversity: Opportunities for theory, research, and application. *American Psychologist, 48,* 400–407. https://doi.org/10.1037/0003-066X.48.4.400

Tashjian, S. M., Weissman, D. G., Guyer, A. E., & Galván, A. (2018). Neural response to prosocial scenes relates to subsequent giving behavior in adolescents: A pilot study. *Cognitive, Affective & Behavioral Neuroscience, 18,* 342–352. doi:10.3758/s13415-018-0573-9.

Telzer, E. H., Yuen, C. X., Gonzales, N. A., & Fuligini, A. J. (2016). Filling gaps in the acculturation gap-distress model: Heritage cultural maintenance and adjustment in Mexican-American adolescents. *Journal of Youth and Adolescence, 45,* 1412–1425.

Titzmann, P. F., & Gniewosz, B. (2018). With a little help from my child: A dyad approach to immigrant mothers' and adolescents' socio-cultural adaptation. *Journal of Adolescence, 62,* 198–206. doi:10.1016/j.adolescence.2017.04.005.

Titzmann, P. F., & Lee, R. M. (2018). Adaptation of young immigrants: A developmental perspective on acculturation research. *European Psychologist, 23,* 72–82. doi:10.1027/1016-9040/a000313.

Titzmann, P. F., & Sonnenberg, K. (2016). Adolescents in conflict: Intercultural contact attitudes of mothers and adolescents as predictors of family conflicts. *International Journal of Psychology, 51,* 279–287. doi:10.1002/ijop.12172.

Tse, L. (1995). Language brokering among Latino adolescents: Prevalence, attitudes, and school performance. *Hispanic Journal of Behavioral Sciences, 17,* 180–193.

Tse, L. (1996). Language brokering in linguistic minority communities: The case of Chinese-and Vietnamese-American students. *The Bilingual Research Journal, 20,* 485–498.

Unger, J. B., Ritt-Olson, A., Wagner, K. D., Soto, D. W., & Baezconde-Garbanati, L. (2009). Parent-child acculturation patterns and substance use among Hispanic adolescents: A longitudinal analysis. *The Journal of Primary Prevention, 30,* 293–313. doi:10.1007/s10935-009-0178-8.

Valdés, G. (2003). *Expanding definitions of giftedness: The case of young interpreters from immigrant communities.* Mahwah, NJ: Lawrence Erlbaum Associates Publishers.

Ward, C. (2013). Probing identity, integration and adaptation: Big questions, little answers. *International Journal of Intercultural Relations, 37,* 391–404. doi:10.1016/j.ijintrel.2013.04.001

Weisskirch, R. S. (2005). The relationship of language brokering to ethnic identity for Latino early adolescents. *Hispanic Journal of Behavioral Sciences, 27,* 286–299. doi:10.1177/0739986305277931

Weisskirch, R. S. (2007). Feelings about language brokering and family relations among Mexican American early adolescents. *The Journal of Early Adolescence, 27,* 545–561. doi:10.1177/0272431607302935.

Weisskirch, R. S. (2017). A developmental perspective on language brokering. In R. S. Weisskirch (Ed.), *Language brokering in immigrant families: Theories and contexts* (pp. 7–25). New York, NY: Routledge.

Weisskirch, R. S., & Alva, S. A. (2002). Language brokering and the acculturation of Latino children. *Hispanic Journal of Behavioral Sciences, 24,* 369–378. https://doi.org/10.1177/0739986302024003007

Whittle, S., Simmons, J. G., Dennison, M., Vijayakumar, N., Schwartz, O., Yap, M. B. H., ... Allen, N. B. (2014). Positive parenting predicts the development of adolescent brain structure: A longitudinal study. *Developmental Cognitive Neuroscience, 8,* 7–17. doi:10.1016/j.dcn.2013.10.006.

Wu, N. H., & Kim, S. Y. (2009). Chinese American adolescents' perceptions of the language brokering experience as a sense of burden and sense of efficacy. *Journal of Youth and Adolescence, 38,* 703–718.

Chapter 11

Ethnic majority and minority youth in multicultural societies

Sabahat Cigdem Bagci and Adam Rutland

Today, as a result of significant waves of immigration and globalization, many social environments that surround young people are extremely culturally diverse. Recently collected data demonstrates that not only in the US, but also in various parts of Europe, the White majority status population will become a numerical 'minority' in the future (U.S. Census Bureau, 2011). For example, a study in the UK indicated that the total ethnic minority status population in the country would make up 44 percent of the total population by 2056 (Coleman, 2010). Therefore, how children learn to navigate complex relationships in such super-diverse settings is even more critical now. At the same time, it is crucial to understand the developmental trajectory of the social skills needed to navigate this new social context, since many social skills that develop during this period are known to be influential in later stages of life (Vernberg, Abwender, Ewell, & Beery, 1992; Welsh, Parke, Widaman, & O'Neil, 2001).

On the one hand, multicultural societies offer a number of challenges such as perceived discrimination and intergroup anxiety which often have negative influences on the psychological, social, and academic well-being of group members (Hood, Bradley, & Ferguson, 2017; Schmitt, Branscombe, Postmes, & Garcia, 2014; Verkuyten, 1998). However, it is also the case that such societies provide many benefits for youth, such as the opportunity to expand their sense of self, develop empathy and perspective-taking through cross-group friendships, and learn from other cultures (Paolini, Wright, Dys-Steenbergen, & Favara, 2016; Pettigrew & Tropp, 2008). The current chapter will review theoretical and empirical findings from contemporary social and developmental research which highlights the unique role of multicultural societies in shaping majority and minority children's lives.

Potential challenges of multicultural societies

Imagine that you are surrounded by people from diverse backgrounds and you are the only one from your own ethnic/cultural background. You may not know what to expect, how to respond, and how to communicate with these people coming from a totally different cultural background than yours. Certainly, you may expect to receive some negative treatment towards yourself, even if you do not encounter any. This is the biggest challenge a lot of group members face in everyday intergroup contexts where they meet new people from other ethnic/cultural backgrounds. Hence, at first glance, a multicultural environment may provide a threatening social context where intergroup relations are difficult to initiate and maintain. Such multicultural contexts may increase the perception of discrimination and intergroup anxiety, which in turn do not only lead to more negative intergroup attitudes and behaviors, but also relate to lower psychological and academic outcomes at the individual level. This section will highlight how multicultural social contexts may potentially involve 'dangers' for minority and majority group youth.

Perceived discrimination

In multicultural societies, where social environments such as schools include a variety of ethnic/racial groups that are often visible and where group membership becomes a salient aspect of identities, children and adolescents often experience discrimination. However, increased diversity may not readily translate into a hostile social environment where discrimination is pervasive. Previous research has shown the perception of diversity to be positively associated with the perception of discrimination (Seaton & Yip, 2008), whereas some studies suggested that minorities in desegregated settings may report lower levels of discrimination (Graham & Juvonen, 2002; Postmes & Branscombe, 2002; Verkuyten & Thijs, 2002). Other research studies have shown that increased ethnic diversity has a protective role for ethnic minority youth by relating to greater levels of social satisfaction and feelings of safety (Juvonen, Nishina, & Graham, 2006). These findings indicate that there may be a complex relationship between diversity and perceived discrimination in various multicultural settings.

Discrimination, based on any group membership such as race, ethnicity, gender, or sexual orientation, involves harmful actions towards specific group members because of their group membership (Brown, 2017). Although previous research has shown discrimination to be more common among minority status group children compared to majority status group children (e.g., Verkuyten, 2002; Verkuyten & Thijs, 2002), pervasive discrimination may be part of the social life of majority status group members too (Coker et al., 2009). Recent research has suggested that majority status group Whites have also started to deal with 'reverse racism' which involves racism from minority status group members (Norton & Sommers, 2011). Hence, irrespective of group status, it is important to understand how perceived discrimination is likely to have a detrimental effect on the well-being of all individuals.

Ethnic/racial discrimination during childhood and adolescence often involves negative treatment based on ethnic/racial group in the school or classroom environment. It includes processes such as peer victimization, social exclusion, and name calling, which are known to have adverse effects on group members' well-being in various domains (Seaton, Neblett, Cole, & Prinstein, 2013; Simons et al., 2002; Verkuyten, 2002; Wong, Eccles, & Sameroff, 2003). Empirical evidence demonstrates that perceived discrimination is related to lower self-esteem and psychological resilience (Bagci, Rutland, Kumashiro, Smith, & Blumberg, 2014; Verkuyten, 1998), lower life satisfaction (Seaton, Caldwell, Sellers, & Jackson, 2008; Verkuyten, 2008), and stress, depression, and anxiety-related symptoms (Schmitt et al., 2014). Moreover, when these discriminatory behaviors are faced in the school environment, it may also have detrimental effects on academic outcomes. Previous research revealed that there is a direct negative association between perceived discrimination and academic motivation (e.g., Verkuyten & Thijs, 2004), and the relationship between perceived discrimination and negative school adjustment is found to be mediated by increased stress levels in the school environment (Liebkind, Jasinskaja-Lahti, & Solheim, 2004).

Research also suggests there are a number of moderators of the association between perceived discrimination and well-being. For example, although discrimination may occur among majority group members too in super-diverse social settings, majority group members are less likely to show the negative effects of perceived discrimination in their psychological well-being (Bagci, Rutland, Smith & Blumberg 2014). According to Schmitt and Branscombe (2002), the implications of perceived discrimination may be different for majority and minority status group members. Majority status group members have the structural power in society and therefore perceived discrimination does not necessarily correspond to isolation and stigmatization from society, whereas for the minority status group, who have low power within society, it often means social exclusion and stigmatization from the wider population, which makes perceived discrimination more detrimental for them. Nevertheless, empirical research looking into effects of perceived discrimination among majority youth is scarce, and discrimination towards ethnic majority status youth may be as detrimental as discrimination towards ethnic minority youth where status imbalance is not that salient (such as in low socio-economic schools). Furthermore, the source of discrimination, whether it is from peers or adults, may indicate the extent to which it is detrimental for well-being (Benner & Graham, 2013). Research suggests that discrimination is more harmful when it originates from peers, and group level discrimination rather than personal level discrimination is more prevalent among both minority and majority status adolescents (Verkuyten, 2002). Findings also demonstrate the importance of a positive school racial climate – a positive social atmosphere where diversity is valued – in moderating the effects of perceived discrimination on children's social and developmental outcomes (e.g., Brown, 2015).

An interesting research avenue has shown that lower self-esteem and psychological well-being may not be unconditional consequences of perceived discrimination. A number of studies indicated that perceived discrimination may influence well-being positively, as individuals are likely to attribute failure to external cues and consequently continue to maintain high levels of psychological functioning (Brown, Bigler, & Chu, 2010; Crocker & Major, 1989). Other research has shown that although the direct association between perceived discrimination and psychological well-being is negative, perceived discrimination may contribute to well-being indirectly by promoting ingroup identification. According to the Rejection-Identification Model (Branscombe, Schmitt, & Harvey, 1999), when individuals perceive pervasive discrimination, they respond by forming a strong identity to these negative intergroup experiences. Consequently, such a strong ingroup identification process is likely to be related to higher psychological well-being (Armenta & Hunt, 2009; Branscombe et al., 1999; Schmitt & Branscombe, 2002). Overall, this research literature indicates that perceived discrimination is one potential risk factor for youth development, yet such negative experiences are likely to be attenuated by many individual and social factors.

Intergroup anxiety

A further challenge of multicultural societies is intergroup anxiety, which may be sometimes as detrimental as perceived discrimination among minority and majority group members. Intergroup anxiety is the 'negative feeling or affective state' derived from intergroup interactions (Levine & Hogg, 2010, p. 465) and may be experienced through direct interaction with an outgroup member and as a result of anticipation of a future negative intergroup experience (Stephan, 2014). Previous research has suggested that the structure of the social environment may be a critical aspect of the experience of intergroup anxiety and thus multicultural settings may create stressful intergroup encounters. For example, status differences, competition, and ethnic composition have been indicated to be important in the emergence of intergroup anxiety (Avery, Richeson, Hebl, & Ambady, 2009; Stephan, 2014), which could consequently result in a socially exclusive intergroup setting characterized by high levels of segregation and avoidance of intergroup contact.

Both majority and minority status group youth are likely to experience intergroup anxiety (e.g., Plant & Butz, 2006; Plant & Devine, 2003), and research comparing the experience of intergroup anxiety across majority and minority youth is mixed. For example, Jasinskaja-Lahti, Mähönen, and Liebkind (2011) found that although intergroup anxiety levels were higher among majority group adolescents, it was more strongly related to outgroup attitudes among minority group adolescents. Another study among native and immigrant secondary school students in Italy indicated that intergroup anxiety was equally likely to be a mediator between contact and attitudes among both groups (Vezzali, Giovannini, & Capozza, 2010). Nevertheless, majority and minority group members may hold distinct motivations behind their intergroup anxieties (Tropp, Mazziotta, & Wright, 2016), such that for majority group members intergroup experiences are considered to be stressful because of the fear of 'seeming prejudiced', whereas for minority group members, the real challenge is the potential of being the targets of discrimination (Devine & Vasquez, 1998).

Other empirical research has shown that intergroup anxiety is associated with both negative cognitive and affective responses to outgroup members such as negative stereotypes and attitudes (Pettigrew & Tropp, 2008; Stephan, Stephan, Demitrakis, Yamada, & Clason, 2000; Stephan, Ybarra, & Rios Morrison, 2009), as well as negative contact intentions for future interactions (Hutchison, Fox, Laas, Matharu, & Urzi, 2010; Hutchison & Rosenthal, 2011). Although research on children and youth's intergroup anxiety has been studied relatively less, it has been found that intergroup anxiety is associated with lower levels of self-disclosure (Turner, Hewstone, & Voci, 2007). This suggests that intergroup anxiety may be a major obstacle in multicultural settings leading to less effective communication patterns and avoidance of further cross-ethnic interactions, consequently obstructing the formation of an inclusive social setting.

Beyond its detrimental effects on outgroup attitudes and behaviors, intergroup anxiety is likely to reduce psychological and academic wellbeing of individuals. For example, Mendoza-Denton, Downey, Purdie, Davis, and Pietrzak (2002) demonstrated that race-based rejection sensitivity – 'a cognitive–affective processing dynamic whereby people anxiously expect, readily perceive, and intensely react to rejection in situations in which rejection is possible' (p. 897) – was related to lower levels of belongingness and academic grades among African American university students. Hence, negative expectations and the anticipation of rejection is likely to undermine motivational outcomes, as well as psychological ones (e.g., Reis & Downey, 1999).

A related construct, stereotype threat, is also a common phenomenon, especially in multicultural school settings where group membership may be a salient aspect of school experiences. Stereotype threat, that is, perceived threat based on the knowledge that one is evaluated negatively on the basis of his/her group membership, is known to be related to lower levels of performance on a related task (Steele & Aronson, 1995). The construct has been consistently observed among various groups, such as African Americans performing poorly on academic ability tasks and women performing poorly on mathematical tasks (e.g., Spencer, Steele, & Quinn, 1999; Steele & Aronson, 1995). This shows that anxieties that may stem from the anticipation of future intergroup contact or just the mere recognition that one is compared to other groups may evoke negative feelings and create a stressful environment for certain group members, which may eventually reflect on group members' psychological and academic well-being.

Potential benefits of multicultural societies

Multicultural societies are difficult, but they do not only offer challenging experiences for children and youth: they also offer constructive opportunities for positive psychological and social development. Previous research has provided consistent evidence of children and youth's preference for same-ethnic interactions (Aboud & Mendelson, 1996; McPherson, Smith-Lovin, & Cook, 2001) and shown that cross-ethnic relationships are difficult to initiate, maintain, and become even less common during transition through adolescence (Aboud, Mendelson, & Purdy, 2003; Jugert, Noack, & Rutland, 2011; Kao & Joyner, 2004). Although ethnic diversity increases the chances that one forms more cross-ethnic interactions (Bagci, Kumashiro, Smith, Blumberg, & Rutland, 2014; Quillian & Campbell, 2003), many children are still inclined to choose others with whom they share similarities and common experiences, perhaps because ingroup members provide a more secure environment. Nevertheless, children do engage in positive cross-ethnic interactions in multicultural settings and form friendships that cross ethnic boundaries (Bagci, Kumashiro, Smith & Rutland 2014), and once they are formed, research suggest that cross-ethnic friendships are the best means available to create a socially integrative intergroup context.

Intergroup contact and cross-group friendships

One of the positive features of multicultural societies is that they provide plenty of opportunities to form intergroup relationships. Intergroup contact theory (Allport, 1954; Pettigrew, 1998) suggested that contact between members of different groups is able to reduce prejudice and promote positive intergroup attitudes and behaviors. Empirical research has consistently shown that children's intergroup contact experiences are related to more positive evaluations of the outgroup across different intergroup contexts (see Tropp & Prenovost, 2008). Schools are probably the most convenient social settings to provide such opportunities (Thijs & Verkuyten, 2014; Titzmann, 2014), especially since they encompass many of the contact conditions initially suggested by Allport, including equal status and a cooperative learning environment. Nevertheless, ethnically diverse classrooms may not readily promote integration at the societal level and the potential benefits of multicultural settings may only appear under certain conditions.

Previous research has shown that, like ethnic diversity, intergroup contact per se may not be strong enough to directly change intergroup attitudes (Dovidio, Gaertner, & Kawakami, 2003), although contact has been found to relate to more positive attitudes, even in the absence of positive contact conditions initially proposed by Allport (Pettigrew & Tropp, 2006). Therefore, rather than superficial intergroup encounters that fade away instantly, an established, positive, and reliable cross-ethnic interaction pattern would have stronger effects on intergroup relationships. Pettigrew (1998) suggested that cross-group friendships are of particular importance in changing intergroup relationships, since (a) they involve Allport's contact conditions, (b) they are long-term and stable, (c) they are reciprocated, and (d) they include positivity and intimacy, as well as trust, self-disclosure, and support (e.g., Pettigrew, Tropp, Wagner, & Christ, 2011). Empirical evidence also highlighted the special role assigned to cross-group friendship potential in contact literature (see Pettigrew & Tropp, 2006). Therefore, many research studies have recently started to concentrate on the specific role of cross-group friendships among children and youth, rather than mere intergroup contact.

A further promising finding is that cross-group friendships are supposed to be effective in promoting intergroup relationships for both majority and minority status group children and adolescents, although contact effects among minority group members are usually relatively weaker (Pettigrew & Tropp, 2006; Tropp & Pettigrew, 2005). Some studies did not observe specific differences across status as regards the effects of intergroup contact on race-based exclusionary behaviors (Crystal, Killen, & Ruck, 2008). For example, in a sample of majority and minority youth in Finland, Jasinskaja-Lahti et al. (2011) found that pleasant personal contact experiences, accompanied with positive ingroup norms, were effective in encouraging positive outgroup attitudes among minority as well as majority youth. Other research has shown that cross-ethnic friendships were more effective in improving outgroup evaluations among majority group children, compared to minority status group children (Feddes, Noack, & Rutland, 2009), overall suggesting group status as a potential moderator of cross-group friendships' effects on outgroup attitudes.

Perspective-taking, self-disclosure, and self-expansion

Previous research has distinguished a number of ways through which intergroup contact, in particular cross-ethnic friendships, may promote social integration. While initial studies suggested cognitive mechanisms such as learning from the outgroup as a potential explanatory factor between cross-group friendships and positive outgroup attitudes, more recent research has focused on the affective mediators of intergroup contact (Pettigrew & Tropp, 2008). For example, in a study examining relationships between Asian and White children in the UK, Turner et al. (2007) found that both majority (White) and minority (Asian) status children with cross-group friendships displayed more positive intergroup attitudes. The authors further discovered that cross-group friendships were effective in promoting positive outgroup attitudes through the generation of various interpersonal processes such as self-disclosure. Self-disclosure may be particularly important in the context of intergroup relationships during early adolescence when children start to turn away from their parents and build closer relationships with their peers who now constitute a more important source of self-worth and comfort for them (Fuligni & Eccles, 1993).

Self-disclosure is also critical in cross-ethnic interactions, since it paves the way to the formation of deeper interpersonal processes such as increased empathy and perspective-taking towards the outgroup (Tam, Hewstone, Harwood, Voci, & Kenworthy, 2006). Previous research has shown that cross-group friendships are likely to promote perspective-taking and empathy, and in turn, increased empathy towards the outgroup should promote positive outgroup attitudes and relationships (Pettigrew & Tropp, 2008). Furthermore, cross-group friendships may support the development of more tolerant attitudes among children and adolescents by providing cultural openness (Abbott & Cameron, 2014) and increasing the perceived value of diversity (Tropp & Bianchi, 2006). Intergroup contact and friendships have been also found to be related to the adoption of more tolerant attitudes such as multiculturalism. Accordingly, contact and cross-group friendships lead to the reappraisal of the ingroup whereby individuals get more distant to their ingroup and eventually display a less egocentric and more open view of the world (Deprovincialization Hypothesis, Pettigrew, 1997). Since contact effects do not only concern attitudes and behaviors towards the target outgroup, but often generalize to attitudes towards other groups (even non-contacted) in different contexts, in the long-term, cross-ethnic friendships during childhood and adolescence may lead to the development of important perspective-taking and empathic skills that are transformed into a more open and understanding view of the world in adulthood.

Another process that may emerge as a result of self-disclosure is 'inclusion of the other in the self (IoS)'. Cross-group friendships are likely to foster interpersonal processes between the self and a partner from an outgroup; as a result, children may become more interested in expanding the self and use cross-ethnic relationships as an opportunity to self-expand (Aron, McLaughlin-Volpe, Mashek, Lewandowski, Wright, & Aron, 2004;

Cameron, Rutland, Brown, & Douch, 2006). According to the Self-Expansion Model (Aron & Aron, 1986), individuals have a strong desire to get close to others in order to expand and improve their own self. This need is further characterized by the desire to approach the ones who are dissimilar to us, as a way to gain access to resources that may not be provided by the ones who are similar to us (Paolini et al., 2016). Therefore, against all findings in the friendship literature emphasizing the role of homophily in friendship choices, humans may be more motivated to be attracted to the ones who are different, as a way to contribute to the self. Cross-ethnic friendships, therefore, unlike same-ethnic friendships, are important tools to satisfy this need for self-expansion, providing access to various resources which may be inaccessible without interethnic contact.

Self-disclosure may further enhance other interpersonal mechanisms such as affirmation of ideal-selves – the extent to which cross-ethnic friends are perceived as eliciting the child's ideal self (Bagci, Kumashiro, Rutland, Smith, & Blumberg, 2017). Previous research into interpersonal relationships literature demonstrates that close others are likely to shape one's motivations and aspirations through affirming the ideal-self (i.e., close others supporting the sense an individual has of the ideal person they wish to become), and such a process, in turn, is related to closer relationships and better personal well-being (Michelangelo Phenomenon, Rusbult, Finkel, & Kumashiro, 2009). In a multicultural society, when children's self-esteem declines during early adolescence (Wigfield, Eccles, Mac Iver, Reuman, & Midgley, 1991), affirmation of the ideal-self, especially when it originates from cross-ethnic peers, would be likely to provide outgroup support, encouragement, and opportunity to expand the self in new and desirable directions. This is a critical mechanism that reduces negative expectations from the outgroup and contributes to positive developmental outcomes. Indeed, Bagci et al. (2017) found that for both minority and majority status children recruited from super-diverse London schools, cross-ethnic friendships promoted academic and psychological well-being through increased affirmation of the ideal-self.

Psycho-social benefits of cross-group friendships

Beyond the benefits of cross-group friendships in promoting positive intergroup attitudes through the generation of self-related interpersonal processes, recent research has started to focus on whether children's cross-ethnic friendships in multicultural settings are beneficial for the enhancement of positive social and psychological outcomes. Apart from empathic skills children gain through close cross-ethnic friendships, such friendships do also provide various unique benefits that may not be obtained through same-ethnic friendships. For example, Lease and Blake (2005) found that cross-group friendships are related to increased social competence and popularity. Kawabata and Crick (2008) further indicated that cross-ethnic friendships, but not same-ethnic friendships, were related to social adjustment, assessed by the level of relational inclusion and leadership. This shows that beyond the generation of particular skills such as perspective-taking and empathy, children with cross-ethnic friends are viewed as more skilled and competent than their peers with no such friendships.

Another line of research has indicated that friendships that cross ethnic boundaries are also associated with psychological outcomes among children and youth. For example, Munniksma and Juvonen (2012) studied the role of cross-ethnic friendships on feelings of socio-emotional safety among Latino and White American sixth and seventh grade children attending multiethnic schools, and found that over time children who had more cross-ethnic friends felt safer in the school environment. In a similar vein, Kawabata and Crick (2011) demonstrated that such friendships were able to decrease potential relational victimization among elemantary school children. A further study by Graham, Munniksma, and Juvonen (2014) also showed that cross-ethnic friendships were associated with decreases in perceived vulnerability. This suggests that cross-ethnic friendships may indicate that such children live in a predictable, stable, and thereby safe social environment where the potential dark side of multicultural societies is felt to a lesser degree.

Cross-ethnic friendships do not only have strong direct association with positive developmental outcomes, but they could also function as effective protective mechanisms that could potentially buffer the negative effects of various risk factors in a challenging multiethnic environment. In a study of ethnic minority children, Bagci, Rutland,Smith & Blumberg (2014) investigated whether cross-ethnic friendship quantity and quality would directly increase psychological well-being and resilience and attenuate the negative effects of perceived discrimination on well-being. Findings indicated that cross-ethnic friendships did not only directly relate to both positive developmental outcomes, but they also buffered the negative effects of perceived discrimination on mental health such that the detrimental effects of perceived discrimination emerged only among minority children with lower cross-ethnic friendship quantity.

While these studies in principle show that multicultural settings offer both challenges and benefits, and cross-ethnic friendships may stand as important resources of resilience against these real life challenges, recent research has indicated that they may not unconditionally provide benefits for group members as regards more positive outgroup attitudes, for example if the social context is highly conflictual (Bagci & Çelebi, 2017) or when the quality of cross-ethnic friendships is low (Cernat, 2018). Moreover, in a recent study by Brenick, Schachner, and Jugert (2018), minority youth's friendships with majority group members exacerbated the negative role of perceived discrimination on well-being; this effect was pronounced less among the ones who perceived a more positive racial climate. Overall, this suggests that the benefits of cross-group friendships may also depend on various factors such as the specific intergroup context involved and the quality of relationships.

Confidence in contact model and cross-ethnic friendship self-efficacy

Based on past research highlighting the benefits of cross-group friendships in multiethnic settings, it is critical to explore how and when healthy (i.e., close, positive, stable) cross-ethnic friendships are formed. Previous research has mainly concentrated on opportunities for contact vs. homophily tendencies as preliminary factors behind cross-ethnic friendship formation (McPherson et al., 2001; Quillian & Campbell, 2003; Titzmann, 2014), while other research has focused on specific individual factors such as outgroup orientation and/or environmental factors such as peer norms and perceived contact conditions (Jugert et al., 2011; Tropp, O'Brien, & Migacheva, 2014). Recently, Turner and Cameron (2016) developed an inclusive theoretical model in which children may become 'contact ready' through various situational and contextual factors. The authors suggested that although structural factors such as ethnic diversity is a prerequisite for the formation of cross-group friendships, diversity alone may not necessarily lead to more positive outcomes among children (Brown et al., 2013) and the benefits of multicultural social settings may be only provided if the setting encourages the formation of more stable and positive cross-group friendships. Accordingly, it was suggested that for the promotion of cross-group friendships, children should first acquire confidence in contact, which is described as a state of readiness to engage in successful cross-group friendships (Turner & Cameron, 2016). The authors further proposed a number of situational and individual factors in fostering confidence in contact, including a positive school setting, reduced intergroup anxiety, more positive initial outgroup attitudes and social skills such as empathy and perspective-taking abilities. Such a high level of confidence in contact, in turn, should lead to more benefits from diversity at the intergroup and personal level.

Further empirical research has provided initial evidence for the Confidence in Contact Model. Bagci, Cameron, Turner, Morais, Carby, Ndhlovu, & Leney (forthcoming) introduced a new concept, 'cross-ethnic friendship self-efficacy', by integrating the cross-group friendship literature with Bandura's Self-Efficacy Theory (1986). Accordingly, the formation and maintenance of cross-ethnic friendships in multiethnic settings is contingent upon children's self-efficacy beliefs in forming and maintaining successful cross-ethnic friendships. The original self-efficacy theory assumes that the most critical factor behind performing a specific behavior/action is how much the individual believes he/she can succeed in this behavior/action (Bandura, 1986). Hence, it could be expected that children who actually believe that they could initiate and maintain cross-group friendships would be more likely to engage in actual cross-ethnic friendships.

The authors further investigated the sources of these self-efficacy beliefs and suggested a model in which previously distinguished factors in cross-group friendship formation are integrated. The original Self-Efficacy Theory stated that the most important antecedent of self-efficacy beliefs is past accomplishment (enactive experiences). Accordingly, self-efficacy beliefs about cross-ethnic friendships should be based on whether children had experienced successful interethnic experiences in the past. This has been confirmed in the contact literature showing cross-group friendship habits in childhood are reflected in later stages of life (Stearns, Buchmann, & Bonneau, 2009). A second potential source of self-efficacy beliefs is vicarious experiences; observing other people to successfully perform a behavior increases the belief that one can also succeed in a similar behavior. This corresponds to vicarious and extended cross-group friendships which are likely to promote the formation of direct cross-group friendships (Cameron et al., 2006; Feddes et al., 2009; Turner et al., 2007; Wright, Aron, Mclaughlin-Volpe, & Ropp, 1997). A third source of self-efficacy beliefs from the original theory is social (verbal) persuasion, which highlights the importance of parents and peers in encouraging cross-ethnic friendship formation (e.g., Crystal et al., 2008). A final source of self-efficacy beliefs is physiological states which include negative emotional reactions to intergroup contact such as intergroup anxiety and stress. This has been specifically highlighted in the cross-group friendship literature by consistent empirical findings about the negative role of intergroup anxiety in the formation of cross-ethnic interactions (Page-Gould, Mendoza-Denton, & Tropp, 2008).

Overall, across two studies, Bagci et al. (accepted manuscript) found that cross-ethnic friendship self-efficacy was predicted by all sources of self-efficacy beliefs (except social norms) and in turn self-efficacy was related to greater quality cross-ethnic friendships. Study 2 further incorporated perceived parental quality into this model and demonstrated parental cross-ethnic contact as a further antecedent of children's cross-ethnic friendship self-efficacy (Bagci, Cameron, Turner, Morais, Ndhlovu, & Leney, under review). This shows that, as in Turner and Cameron's (2016) Confidence in Contact Model, cross-ethnic friendships are not just a natural consequence of ethnic diversity; rather they emerge and exist as a function of various complex situational and personal factors in the process. Figure 11.1 depicts the theoretical model of cross-ethnic friendship self-efficacy.

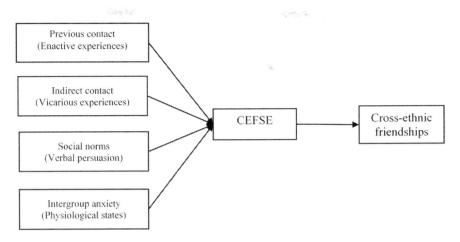

Figure 11.1 Cross-Ethnic Friendship Self-Efficacy Model
CEFSE = cross-ethnic friendship self-efficacy.

Conclusion

Ethnic diversity may not unconditionally provide positive or negative social-developmental outcomes for children and youth. Living in multicultural societies may result in a range of developmental outcomes which are contingent upon whether children transform these characteristics into opportunities or challenges. Such a transformation depends on the combination of a number of personal, situational, and structural processes involved in the setting. Therefore, while ethnic diversity may create an anxiety-provoking and exclusive setting where children and youth experience challenges in the social context, it can also create a unique, positive, and inclusive interethnic environment that could boost children's personal, interpersonal, and social well-being. Under the latter setting, children and youth would be more likely to enjoy schooling experiences and fully benefit from the resources provided by a multicultural setting. Cross-group friendships constitute one potential resource children can rely on, providing unique social skills, such as self-disclosure, empathy, and self-expansion, and enabling children to feel a sense of belonging and safety in a potentially threatening social setting. A number of individual and situational factors are required for the facilitation of cross-group friendships. Importantly, school and family settings are responsible for encouraging a positive and inclusive intergroup setting and cultivating self-efficacy beliefs in children towards forming cross-group friendships, which should eventually equip children with the unique and necessary skills and resources to navigate and succeed in a multicultural society.

References

Abbott, N., & Cameron, L. (2014). What makes a young assertive bystander? The effect of intergroup contact, empathy, cultural openness, and in-group bias on assertive bystander intervention intentions. *Journal of Social Issues, 70*, 167–182.

Aboud, F. E., & Mendelson, M. J. (1996). Determinants of friendship selection and quality: Developmental perspectives. In W. M. Bukowski, A. F. Newcomb, & W. W. Hartup (Eds.), *Cambridge studies in social and emotional development. The company they keep: Friendship in childhood and adolescence* (pp. 87–112). New York, NY: Cambridge University Press.

Aboud, F. E., Mendelson, M. J., & Purdy, K. T. (2003). Cross-race peer relations and friendship quality. *International Journal of Behavioral Development, 27*, 165–173.

Allport, G. W. (1954). *The nature of prejudice*. New York, NY: Addison-Wesley.

Armenta, B. E., & Hunt, J. S. (2009). Responding to societal devaluation: Effects of perceived personal and group discrimination on the ethnic group identification and personal self-esteem of Latino/Latina adolescents. Group Processes & Intergroup Relations, 12(1), 23–39.

Aron, A., & Aron, E. (1986). *Love and the expansion of self: Understanding attraction and satisfaction*. New York: Hemisphere.

Aron, A., McLaughlin-Volpe, T., Mashek, D., Lewandowski, G., Wright, S. C., & Aron, E. N. (2004). Including others in the self. *European review of social psychology, 15*(1), 101–132.

Avery, D. R., Richeson, J. A., Hebl, M. R., & Ambady, N. (2009). It does not have to be uncomfortable: The role of behavioral scripts in Black–White interracial interactions. *Journal of Applied Psychology, 94*, 1382–1393.

Bagci, S. C., & Çelebi, E. (2017). Cross-group friendships and outgroup attitudes among Turkish–Kurdish ethnic groups: Does perceived interethnic conflict moderate the friendship-attitude link? *Journal of Applied Social Psychology, 47*, 59–73.

Bagci, S. C., Kumashiro, M., Rutland, A., Smith, P. K., & Blumberg, H. (2017). Cross-ethnic friendships, psychological well-being, and academic outcomes: Study of south asian and white children in the UK. *European Journal of Developmental Psychology, 14*, 190–205.

Bagci, S. C., Kumashiro, M., Smith, P. K., Blumberg, H., & Rutland, A. (2014). Cross-ethnic friendships: Are they really rare? Evidence from secondary schools around London. *International Journal of Intercultural Relations, 41*, 125–137.

Bagci, S. C., Rutland, A., Kumashiro, M., Smith, P. K., & Blumberg, H. (2014). Are minority status childrens cross-ethnic friendships beneficial in a multiethnic context? *British Journal of Developmental Psychology, 32*, 107–115.

Bagci, S. C., Cameron, L., Turner, R., Morais, C., Carby, A., Ndhlovu, M., & Leney, A. (forthcoming). 'Cross-ethnic friendship self-efficacy': A new predictor of cross-ethnic friendships among children. *Group Processes and Intergroup Relations*.

Bandura, A. (1986). Fearful expectations and avoidant actions as coeffects of perceived self-inefficacy. *American Psychologist, 41*, 1389–1391.

Benner, A. D., & Graham, S. (2013). The antecedents and consequences of racial/ethnic discrimination during adolescence: Does the source of discrimination matter? *Developmental Psychology, 49*, 1602–1613.

Branscombe, N. R., Schmitt, M. T., & Harvey, R. D. (1999). Perceiving pervasive discrimination among African Americans: Implications for group identification and well-being. *Journal of Personality and Social Psychology, 77*, 135–149.

Brenick, A., Schachner, M. K., & Jugert, P. (2018). Help or hindrance? Minority versus majority cross-ethnic friendships altering discrimination experiences. *Journal of Applied Developmental Psychology, 59*, 26–35.

Brown, C. S. (2015). *The educational, psychological, and social impact of discrimination on the immigrant child*. Washington, DC: Migration Policy Institute.

Brown, C. S., Bigler, R. S., & Chu, H. (2010). An experimental study of the correlates and consequences of perceiving oneself to be the target of gender discrimination. *Journal of Experimental Child Psychology, 107*, 100–117.

Brown, R., Baysu, G., Cameron, L., Nigbur, D., Rutland, A., Watters, C., Hossain, R., LeTouze, D., & Landau, A. (2013). Acculturation attitudes and social adjustment in British South Asian children: a longitudinal study. *Personality and Social Psychology Bulletin, 39*(2), 1656–1667.

Brown, J. (2017). Discriminatory experiences of women police. A comparison of officers serving in England and Wales, Scotland, Northern Ireland and the Republic of Ireland. *International Journal of the Sociology of Law, 28*, 91–111.

Cameron, L., Rutland, A., Brown, R., & Douch, R. (2006). Changing childrens intergroup attitudes toward refugees: Testing different models of extended contact. *Child Development, 77*, 1208–1219.

Cernat, V. (2018). When cross-ethnic friendships can be bad for out-group attitudes: The importance of friendship quality. *Journal of Community & Applied Social Psychology, 29*(2), 81–89.

Coker, T. R., Elliott, M. N., Kanouse, D. E., Grunbaum, J. A., Schwebel, D. C., Gilliland, M. J., & Schuster, M. A. (2009). Perceived racial/ethnic discrimination among fifth-grade students and its association with mental health. *American Journal of Public Health, 99*, 878–884.

Coleman, D. (2010). Projections of the ethnic minority populations of the United Kingdom 2006–2056. *Population and Development Review, 36*, 441–486.

Crocker, J., & Major, B. (1989). Social stigma and self-esteem: The self-protective properties of stigma. *Psychological Review, 96*, 608–630.

Crystal, D. S., Killen, M., & Ruck, M. (2008). It is who you know that counts: Intergroup contact and judgments about race-based exclusion. *British Journal of Developmental Psychology, 26*, 51–70.

Devine, P. G., & Vasquez, K. A. (1998). The rocky road to positive intergroup relations. In J. Eberhardt & S. T. Fiske (Eds.), Confronting racism: The problem and the response (pp. 234–262). Newbury Park, CA: Sage.

Dovidio, J. F., Gaertner, S. L., & Kawakami, K. (2003). Intergroup contact: The past, present, and the future. *Group Processes & Intergroup Relations, 6*, 5–21.

Feddes, A. R., Noack, P., & Rutland, A. (2009). Direct and extended friendship effects on minority and majority children's interethnic attitudes: A longitudinal study. *Child Development, 80*, 377–390.

Fuligni, A. J., & Eccles, J. S. (1993). Perceived parent-child relationships and early adolescents orientation toward peers. *Developmental Psychology, 29*, 622–632.

Graham, S., & Juvonen, J. (2002). Ethnicity, peer harassment, and adjustment in middle school, *The Journal of Early Adolescence, 22*, 173–199.

Graham, S., Munniksma, A., & Juvonen, J. (2014). Psychosocial benefits of cross-ethnic friendships in urban middle schools. *Child Development*, 85, 469–483.

Hood, W., Bradley, G. L., & Ferguson, S. (2017). Mediated effects of perceived discrimination on adolescent academic achievement: A test of four models. *Journal of Adolescence*, 54, 82–93.

Hutchison, P., Fox, E., Laas, A. M., Matharu, J., & Urzi, S. (2010). Anxiety, outcome expectancies, and young peoples willingness to engage in contact with the elderly. *Educational Gerontology*, 36, 1008–1021.

Hutchison, P., & Rosenthal, H. E. (2011). Prejudice against Muslims: Anxiety as a mediator between intergroup contact and attitudes, perceived group variability and behavioural intentions. *Ethnic and Racial Studies*, 34, 40–61.

Jasinskaja-Lahti, I., Mähönen, T. A., & Liebkind, K. (2011). Ingroup norms, intergroup contact and intergroup anxiety as predictors of the outgroup attitudes of majority and minority youth. *International Journal of Intercultural Relations*, 35, 346–355.

Jugert, P., Noack, P., & Rutland, A. (2011). Friendship preferences among German and Turkish preadolescents. *Child Development*, 82, 812–829.

Juvonen, J., Nishina, A., & Graham, S. (2006). Ethnic diversity and perceptions of safety in urban middle schools. *Psychological Science*, 17, 393–400.

Kao, G., & Joyner, K. (2004). Do race and ethnicity matter among friends? Activities among interracial, interethnic, and intraethnic adolescent friends. *The Sociological Quarterly*, 45, 557–573.

Kawabata, Y., & Crick, N. R. (2008). The role of cross-racial/ethnic friendships in social adjustment. *Developmental Psychology*, 44, 1177–1183.

Kawabata, Y., & Crick, N. R. (2011). The significance of cross-racial/ethnic friendships: Associations with peer victimization, peer support, sociometric status, and classroom diversity. *Developmental Psychology*, 47, 1763–1775.

Lease, A. M., & Blake, J. J. (2005). A comparison of majority-race children with and without a minority-race friend. *Social Development*, 14, 20–41.

Levine, J. M., & Hogg, M. A. (2010). *Encyclopedia of group processes and intergroup relations (Vol. 1)*. Thousand Oaks, CA: Sage.

Liebkind, K., Jasinskaja-Lahti, I., & Solheim, E. (2004). Cultural identity, perceived discrimination, and parental support as determinants of immigrants' school adjustments. *Journal of Adolescent Research*, 19, 635–656.

McPherson, M., Smith-Lovin, L., & Cook, J. M. (2001). Birds of a feather: Homophily in social networks. *Annual Review of Sociology*, 27, 415–444.

Mendoza-Denton, R., Downey, G., Purdie, V. J., Davis, A., & Pietrzak, J. (2002). Sensitivity to status-based rejection: Implications for African American students college experience. *Journal of Personality and Social Psychology*, 83, 896–918.

Munniksma, A., & Juvonen, J. (2012). Cross-ethnic friendships and sense of social-emotional safety in a multiethnic middle school: An exploratory study. *Merrill-Palmer Quarterly*, 58, 489–506.

Norton, M. I., & Sommers, S. R. (2011). Whites see racism as a zero-sum game that they are now losing. *Perspectives on Psychological Science*, 6, 215–218.

Page-Gould, E., Mendoza-Denton, R., & Tropp, L. R. (2008). With a little help from my cross-group friend: Reducing anxiety in intergroup contexts through cross-group friendship. *Journal of Personality and Social Psychology*, 95, 1080–1094.

Paolini, S., Wright, S. C., Dys-Steenbergen, O., & Favara, I. (2016). Self-expansion and intergroup contact: Expectancies and motives to self-expand lead to greater interest in outgroup contact and more positive intergroup relations. *Journal of Social Issues, 72*, 450–471.

Pettigrew, T. F. (1997). Generalized intergroup contact effects on prejudice. *Personality and Social Psychology Bulletin, 23*, 173–185.

Pettigrew, T. F. (1998). Intergroup contact theory. *Annual Review of Psychology, 49*, 65–85.

Pettigrew, T. F., & Tropp, L. R. (2006). A meta-analytic test of intergroup contact theory. *Journal of Personality and Social Psychology, 90*, 751–783.

Pettigrew, T. F., & Tropp, L. R. (2008). How does intergroup contact reduce prejudice? Meta-analytic tests of three mediators. *European Journal of Social Psychology, 38*, 922–934.

Pettigrew, T. F., Tropp, L. R., Wagner, U., & Christ, O. (2011). Recent advances in intergroup contact theory. *International Journal of Intercultural Relations, 35*, 271–280.

Plant, E. A., & Butz, D. A. (2006). The causes and consequences of an avoidance-focus for interracial interactions. *Personality and Social Psychology Bulletin, 32*, 833–846.

Plant, E. A., & Devine, P. G. (2003). The antecedents and implications of interracial anxiety. *Personality and Social Psychology Bulletin, 29*, 790–801.

Postmes, T., & Branscombe, N. R. (2002). Influence of long-term racial environmental context on subjective well-being in African Americans. *Journal of Personality and Social Psychology, 83*, 735–751.

Quillian, L., & Campbell, M. E. (2003). Beyond Black and White: The present and future of multiracial friendship segregation. *American Sociological Review, 68*, 540–566.

Reis, H. T., & Downey, G. (1999). Social cognition in relationships: Building essential bridges between two literatures. *Social Cognition, 17*, 97–117.

Rusbult, C. E., Finkel, E. J., & Kumashiro, M. (2009). The Michelangelo phenomenon. *Current Directions in Psychological Science, 18*, 305–309.

Schmitt, M. T., & Branscombe, N. R. (2002). The meaning and consequences of perceived discrimination in disadvantaged and privileged social groups. *European Review of Social Psychology, 12*, 167–199.

Schmitt, M. T., Branscombe, N. R., Postmes, T., & Garcia, A. (2014). The consequences of perceived discrimination for psychological well-being: A meta-analytic review. *Psychological Bulletin, 140*, 921–948.

Seaton, E. K., Caldwell, C. H., Sellers, R. M., & Jackson, J. S. (2008). The prevalence of perceived discrimination among African American and Caribbean Black youth. *Developmental Psychology, 44*, 1288–1297.

Seaton, E. K., Neblett, E. W., Cole, D. J., & Prinstein, M. J. (2013). Perceived discrimination and peer victimization among African American and Latino youth. *Journal of Youth and Adolescence, 42*, 342–350.

Seaton, E. K., & Yip, T. (2008). School and neighborhood contexts, perceptions of racial discrimination, and psychological well-being among African American adolescents. *Journal of Youth and Adolescence, 38*, 153–163.

Simons, R. L., Murry, V., Mcloyd, V., Lin, K., Cutrona, C., & Conger, R. D. (2002). Discrimination, crime, ethnic identity, and parenting as correlates of depressive symptoms among African American children: A multilevel analysis. *Development and Psychopathology, 14*, 371–393.

Spencer, S. J., Steele, C. M., & Quinn, D. M. (1999). Stereotype threat and womens math performance. *Journal of Experimental Social Psychology, 35*, 4–28.

Stearns, E., Buchmann, C., & Bonneau, K. (2009). Interracial friendships in the transition to college: Do birds of a feather flock together once they leave the nest? *Sociology of Education, 82*, 173–195.

Steele, C. M., & Aronson, J. (1995). Stereotype threat and the intellectual test performance of African Americans. *Journal of Personality and Social Psychology, 69*, 797–811.

Stephan, C. W., Stephan, W. G., Demitrakis, K. M., Yamada, A. M., & Clason, D. L. (2000). Womens attitudes toward men: An integrated threat theory approach. *Psychology of Women Quarterly, 24*, 63–73.

Stephan, W. G. (2014). Intergroup anxiety: Theory, research, and practice. *Personality and Social Psychology Review, 18*, 239–255.

Stephan, W. G., Ybarra, O., & Rios Morrison, K. (2009). Intergroup threat theory. In T. D. Nelson (Ed.), *Handbook of prejudice* (pp. 43–59). Mahwah, NJ: Lawrence erlbaum Associates.

Tam, T., Hewstone, M., Harwood, J., Voci, A., & Kenworthy, J. (2006). Intergroup contact and grandparent–Grandchild communication: The effects of self-disclosure on implicit and explicit biases against older people. *Group Processes & Intergroup Relations, 9*, 413–429.

Thijs, J., & Verkuyten, M. (2014). School ethnic diversity and students interethnic relations. *British Journal of Educational Psychology, 84*, 1–21.

Titzmann, P. F. (2014). Immigrant adolescents adaptation to a new context: Ethnic friendship homophily and its predictors. *Child Development Perspectives, 8*, 107–112.

Tropp, L. R., & Bianchi, R. A. (2006). Valuing diversity and interest in intergroup contact. *Journal of Social Issues, 62*, 533–551.

Tropp, L. R., Mazziotta, A., & Wright, S. C. (2016). Recent developments in intergroup contact research: Affective processes, group status, and contact valence. In C. Sibley & F. K. Barlow (Eds), *Cambridge handbook of the psychology of prejudice* (pp. 463–481). Cambridge, UK: Cambridge University Press.

Tropp, L. R., O'Brien, T. C., & Migacheva, K. (2014). How peer norms of inclusion and exclusion predict childrens interest in cross-ethnic friendships. *Journal of Social Issues, 70*, 151–166.

Tropp, L. R., & Pettigrew, T. F. (2005). Relationships between intergroup contact and prejudice among minority and majority status groups. *Psychological Science, 16*, 951–957.

Tropp, L. R., & Prenovost, M. A. (2008). The role of intergroup contact in predicting children's interethnic attitudes: Evidence from meta-analytic and field studies. In S. R. Levy & M. Killen (Eds.), *Intergroup attitudes and relations in childhood through adulthood* (pp. 236–248). New York, NY: Oxford University Press.

Turner, R. N., & Cameron, L. (2016). Confidence in contact: A new perspective on promoting cross-group friendship among children and adolescents. *Social Issues and Policy Review, 10*, 212–246.

Turner, R. N., Hewstone, M., & Voci, A. (2007). Reducing explicit and implicit outgroup prejudice via direct and extended contact: The mediating role of self-disclosure and intergroup anxiety. *Journal of Personality and Social Psychology*, 93, 369–388.

US Census Bureau. (2011, August 01). Statistical abstract of the United States: 2012. Retrieved from www.census.gov/library/publications/2011/compendia/statab/131ed.html

Verkuyten, M. (1998). Perceived discrimination and self-esteem among ethnic minority adolescents. *The Journal of Social Psychology*, 138, 479–493.

Verkuyten, M. (2002). Ethnic attitudes among minority and majority children: The role of ethnic identification, peer group victimization and parents. *Social Development*, 11, 558–570.

Verkuyten, M. (2008). Life Satisfaction among ethnic minorities: The role of discrimination and group identification. *Social Indicators Research*, 89, 391–404.

Verkuyten, M., & Thijs, J. (2002). Racist victimization among children in The Netherlands: The effect of ethnic group and school. *Ethnic and Racial Studies*, 25, 310–331.

Verkuyten, M., & Thijs, J. (2004). Psychological disidentification with the academic domain among ethnic minority adolescents in The Netherlands. *British Journal of Educational Psychology*, 74, 109–125.

Vernberg, E. M., Abwender, D. A., Ewell, K. K., & Beery, S. H. (1992). Social anxiety and peer relationships in early adolescence: A prospective analysis. *Journal of Clinical Child Psychology*, 21, 189–196.

Vezzali, L., Giovannini, D., & Capozza, D. (2010). Longitudinal effects of contact on intergroup relations: The role of majority and minority group membership and intergroup emotions. *Journal of Community & Applied Social Psychology*, 20, 462–479.

Welsh, M., Parke, R. D., Widaman, K., & O'Neil, R. (2001). Linkages between childrens social and academic competence. *Journal of School Psychology*, 39, 463–482.

Wigfield, A., Eccles, J. S., Mac Iver, D., Reuman, D. A., & Midgley, C. (1991). Transitions during early adolescence: Changes in children's domain-specific self-perceptions and general self-esteem across the transition to junior high school. *Developmental Psychology*, 27, 552–565.

Wong, C. A., Eccles, J. S., & Sameroff, A. (2003). The influence of ethnic discrimination and ethnic identification on African American adolescents school and socio-emotional adjustment. *Journal of Personality*, 71, 1197–1232.

Wright, S. C., Aron, A., Mclaughlin-Volpe, T., & Ropp, S. A. (1997). The extended contact effect: Knowledge of cross-group friendships and prejudice. *Journal of Personality and Social Psychology*, 73, 73–90.

Chapter 12

A new agenda for examining interethnic interactions amongst youth in diverse settings

Shelley McKeown, Amanda Williams, Thia Sagherian-Dickey, and Katarzyna Kucaba

Young people across the globe are experiencing increasingly ethnically diverse environments – from educational settings and neighbourhoods to online platforms (Unesco World Report, 2009). In the United Kingdom (UK), for example, school statistics demonstrate that 27 percent of pupils in state funded secondary schools in England and Wales are of minority ethnic origin (DfE, 2015) and that neighbourhoods are diversifying (Catney, 2015). The effects of ethnic diversity, however, are hotly contested, demonstrating positive and negative outcomes for both minority and majority group members.

Generally speaking, social psychologists have been mostly concerned with the social effects of racial/ethnic diversity on young people, such as reduced prejudice (Burgess & Platt, 2018) and increased pro-social behaviours (McKeown & Taylor, 2018). Ethnic diversity, however, can have further reaching effects. For example, evidence shows that diversity in the workplace can lead to increased creativity and innovation (Bassett-Jones, 2005) and that ethnic diversity in schools can promote learning outcomes (Denson & Chang, 2009) as well as provide an important stepping stone to positive intergroup relations (Schachner, Juang, Moffitt, & van de Vijver, 2018). At the same time, however, ethnic diversity in school contexts has been found to have negative effects for some youth; in the US, Gurin and colleagues (2002) observed a negative relationship between classroom diversity and self-assessed academic skills for Black students (Gurin et al., 2002). And further, some commentators have argued that ethnic diversity undermines trust and social cohesion (Putnam, 2007). The nature and effects of ethnic diversity, however, are complex and require an integrated approach to truly understand them (Schachner et al., 2018).

Given the contested nature of ethnic diversity and the rise in ethnically motivated hate crimes being observed in contexts such as the UK (TES, 2017), it is vital that we understand how to best promote intergroup relations in diverse settings. One way to do this is through encouraging individuals to engage in meaningful contact with one another, known as the contact hypothesis (Allport, 1954). There is substantial empirical support demonstrating that when positive intergroup interactions occur, under favourable circumstances, prejudice will reduce and this can therefore improve intergroup relations (Pettigrew & Tropp, 2006). We argue, however, that if we are to truly understand how to promote better community relations amongst youth it is vital to consider the complexity of interactions as well as adopt new methods to best capture intergroup behaviours.

In this chapter we first provide definitions of ethnic diversity and interethnic interactions, followed by a brief overview of the research and relevant theories on improving youth intergroup relations in diverse settings through interethnic interactions. We then present what we argue are the current theoretical and methodological limitations of such research. Finally, we end the chapter by proposing a new research agenda that draws on a range of innovative methods and offers new theoretical approaches to studying youth intergroup relations in diverse settings.

Improving intergroup relations in diverse settings through interethnic interactions

Within the broad research literature, there is little consensus on what constitutes ethnic diversity. There is an assumption of an implicit knowledge of the construct, often failing to define it outright. The vernacular definition of ethnic diversity can be understood as dissimilar individuals from a variety of ethnic backgrounds in a specific setting. Measures of ethnic diversity and ethnic segregation, primarily stemming from the geographical, biological, and sociological literatures, are wide-ranging and enable researchers to quantify ethnic diversity. These measures, however, can sometimes be misleading; providing similar numbers for very different context compositions and failing to capture the complexity of the context being studied, requiring researchers to use multiple measures as a consequence.

Further to this, ethnic diversity does not necessarily imply interaction, and whether or not ethnic diversity leads to meaningful intergroup interactions is debatable. For example, some researchers focus on diversity as mere exposure to those from different ethnic groups, some as self-reported perceptions of intergroup interaction that meet the conditions of the contact hypothesis, and others as *observed/reported* friendships (see Hewstone, 2015; McKeown & Dixon, 2017 for more information). The operationalisation of what we understand by diversity, however, is critically important because this impacts on how we understand the downstream consequences of ethnic diversity. Evidence shows that whilst children and young people may be exposed to ethnic diversity in school, through physical co-presence with diverse peers, this may not translate into meaningful contact or friendships (DuBois & Hirsch, 1990). Thus, the success of different interventions and evaluations may be over/underestimated based on the definition of diversity and whether or not this involves meaningful interethnic interactions. In this chapter, we consider both quantity (how often interactions occur) and quality (how positive interactions are) as reflecting what makes a meaningful (or not) interethnic interaction.

People of all ages tend to form close ties to others with whom they share characteristics, befriending people who are similar to them on a number of traits (Kupersmidt, DeRosier, & Patterson, 1995; Schneider, 2000). This is true of young children when it comes to race (McKeown, Williams, & Pauker, 2017) and adolescents in Northern Ireland in relation to ethno-religious identities (McKeown, Cairns, Stringer, & Rae, 2012; McKeown, Stringer, & Cairns, 2015). Although the propinquity hypothesis posits that people tend to become friends not with those who are similar, but with those who are physically close (Festinger, 1954), improved intergroup relations would only occur when superficial contact in a shared environment evolves into meaningful interactions, evidenced through intergroup friendship formation (Echols & Graham, 2013). Understanding how to turn mere exposure into meaningful interactions is therefore vital. Although there are numerous approaches to encouraging interethnic interactions amongst children and adolescents, in this chapter we focus on two of the more popular methods: the contact hypothesis and diversity ideology.

The contact hypothesis

Promoting intergroup contact arguably stands as one of the most utilised means for investigating changes in attitudes and behaviour among youth in diverse and conflict settings. The contact hypothesis (Allport, 1954) posits that positive interaction or contact between members of different social groups under certain conditions (equal status, common goals, cooperation, and authority support) will have the positive effect of reducing prejudice between those groups. Under both experimental conditions and when used as an intervention in real-world settings, when the conditions of the contact hypothesis are met, intergroup contact reduces prejudice and increases positive attitudes (Al Ramiah & Hewstone, 2013; Pettigrew & Tropp, 2006). This is achieved in part because contact fosters empathy, trust, forgiveness, self-disclosure with respect to members of the other group, intentions for further contact, positive behaviour (e.g., Swart, Hewstone, Christ, & Voci, 2011), and anxiety reduction (Turner, West, & Christie, 2013). In their landmark meta-analysis on the role of contact in reducing prejudice, Pettigrew and Tropp (2006) found this link in adolescent samples ($r = -.21$, $k = 114$ samples, $n = 45,602$) and that the effects of contact on prejudice reduction did not significantly vary for adolescent groups compared with children ($r = -.24$, $k = 82$ samples, $n = 10,207$) or university students ($r = -.23$, $k = 262$ samples, $n = 46,553$).

Diversity ideology

Another popular approach to improving intergroup relations in applied settings is to address how diversity is conceptualised – whether differences should be celebrated or ignored. Adopting a multicultural or polycultural approach to diversity that focuses on embracing and celebrating difference can have positive outcomes for young people (Apfelbaum, Pauker, Sommers, & Ambady, 2010; McKeown et al., 2017). Despite some criticisms that multiculturalism might entrench bounded social categories (Brewer, 1997) and promote negative stereotyping (Wolsko, Park, Judd, & Wittenbrink, 2000), multiculturalism has gained popularity in the social psychological literature as a favoured alternative to colour-blind approaches where differences are minimised and ignored (Rosenthal & Levy, 2010). Research has demonstrated that adopting a multicultural approach to difference among Dutch majority adolescents is associated with greater positive evaluation of ethnic minorities, while the same endorsement among the ethnic minority youth is associated with positive ingroup evaluation (Verkuyten, 2005). Further, reading stories to children about embracing and celebrating difference can change behaviour (McKeown et al., 2017) and result in children being more likely to detect racial discrimination and describe events in a way that encourages teacher intervention (Apfelbaum et al., 2010). A growing body of literature demonstrates that how one thinks about diversity and difference can impact on interethnic interactions (Rosenthal & Levy, 2010).

Theoretical limitations of research on youth intergroup interactions

Despite the promises of research on promoting interethnic interactions, there are some limitations when faced with the complexities of real-life contexts where multiple groups are involved and when applied to try to understand observed behaviours (cf. Dixon, Durrheim & Tredoux, 2005a). In order to capture these complexities amongst youth, we argue that a comprehensive social-ecological approach should be applied that considers the wide range of factors that influence youth interethnic interactions.

The social-ecological model (Bronfenbrenner, 1979) argues that humans are bound in social systems and that the individual should be at the centre of the study of human development and behaviour. Demonstrating the importance of a social-ecological approach to understanding complex societal processes, this model is increasingly incorporated across subfields of psychology and in settings of diversity and intergroup conflict (Betancourt

& Khan, 2008; Cummings, Goeke-Morey, Merrilees, Taylor, & Shirlow, 2014). The social-ecological model includes an *individual's* psychological functioning, such as individual differences in personality and political ideology. Surrounding the individual is the *microsystem*, or the everyday influences of family, school, and peer groups; and then the *mesosystem* which incorporates the various sets of relations across the microsystem (e.g., influences across the family, peer, work, and school systems). The next most proximal level is the *exosystem* which is comprised of factors that indirectly influence development (e.g., community health provision, parents' workplace). The *macrosystem* represents the overarching institutional patterns of the culture (e.g., economic, social, educational, legal, and political systems) that shape patterns of social interaction across society. Finally, the *chronosystem* represents the transitions and changes in an individual's life over time which necessitates the collection of longitudinal data, something which is rare within the literature focusing on interethnic relations.

To date, social psychologists examining youth interethnic interactions have tended to focus primarily on the individual or group level, assessing the effects of personality or social attitudes to explain engagement in interactions. With few exceptions (cf. McKeown & Taylor, 2018; Tropp et al., 2016 for work examining school versus peer norm effects on youth attitudes and behaviours) researchers have not yet examined the role that broader social systems may play on both individual and dyadic behaviour. And, whilst there is some research on how different microsystems (e.g., school, family, peers) influence interethnic interactions and on multi-level effects of individuals nested within schools (e.g., Bubritzki et al., 2018) or neighbourhoods (Schmid, Al Ramiah & Hewstone, 2014), to the best of our knowledge little attention has been given to the mesosystem (how different levels of the microsystem interact together), exosystem (i.e., the external systems such as parents' workplace, community health provision), macrosystem (i.e., government policy, subtle messages communicated through the media), or chronosystem (i.e., changes in behaviour over time), and how these systems have influenced youth interethnic interactions. There are, however, some notable exceptions. For example, papers published using the Children of Immigrants Longitudinal Survey in Four European Countries (CILS4EU) dataset have examined the combined effects of school and neighbourhood diversity on youth attitudes (Burgess & Platt, 2018) and on cross-group friendship formation and research using a parent–child survey in Belfast by Merrilees et al. (2018) who examined changes in the individual and context effects of adolescent intergroup contact and attitudes in Northern Ireland (Kruse, Smith, van Tubergen, & Maas, 2016).

We argue that adopting a social-ecological approach to youth interethnic interactions would enable us to better understand the complexity of these social processes as well as to develop theoretical understanding beyond the two-group paradigm. This is important because the nature of identity is complex, with many young people growing up in diverse social environments where majority and minority groups are no longer binary, and identities are contested. Indeed, too often majority voices have dominated research papers and minorities have been lumped together as a large uniform group, when in reality there exists a richness and complexity within this diversity (Jones & Dovidio, 2018). This is problematic because whereas the study of the majority's perspective has focused on the recognition and acceptance of the minority group, there is a need to also include the minority's perspective of the majority, along with recognition and acceptance in the minority group's own right (Shelton, 2000). A social-ecological model of youth interethnic interactions would enable researchers to better examine the facilitating and inhibiting nature of various levels of the social-ecology for a wide range of majority and minority group members. This will require new methods.

Methodological limitations of research on youth intergroup interactions

In our view, the majority of research examining youth interethnic interactions has four main limitations: an over-reliance on (1) experimental/laboratory studies using (2) self-reported measures of interactions collected with cross-sectional samples at (3) single time-points. As mentioned above, the integrity of this area of research is also potentially undermined by a lack of consensus in what is meant by interethnic interactions. We more fully outline our concerns below.

Experimental designs

To date, researchers examining youth's interethnic interactions have relied heavily on experimental and/or cross-sectional designs examining idealised interactions between (sometimes fictitious) dichotomous groups that arguably fail to capture the nature of youth interactions in real world settings. This is particularly true for research involving the contact hypothesis; commentators have argued that there is a gap between "optimal contact" which has proven to be effective in laboratory settings and the type of contact that occurs in everyday life spaces (McKeown & Dixon, 2017).

As a by-product of the over-representation of laboratory-based research in the literature, the testing and building of theory has been developed around adult samples – often first-year female university undergraduates in psychology – in what has been coined WEIRD populations (western, educated, industrialised, rich, democratic; Henrich, Heine, & Norenzayan, 2010), which places the emphasis on the "majority," often at the expense of the "minority" (Shelton, 2000). The downside is that such emphasis assumes that only one group is of interest in a two-group setting, thus limiting our understanding of the perspective of each group in their own right, considering their perspectives, culture, and everyday encountered challenges. There is a need to "check majority privilege" when designing research in "diverse" settings.

Self-report measures

Second, when examining interethnic interactions researchers have relied on self-report measures of attitudes and behaviours. This is problematic for several reasons. Most notably, it is widely acknowledged that self-report measures have an inherent weakness in that they are likely to elicit socially desirable responses. For example, 14 to 16-year-olds demonstrated no evidence of racial outgroup prejudice on explicit attitude measures; however, they did demonstrate a strong pro-White versus Black bias on an implicit measure of racial attitudes (Rutland, Cameron, Milne, & McGeorge, 2005). In addition, responses on self-report measures, including predicting hypothetical future behaviour, are often discrepant with observed behaviour and impossible to verify (Baumeister, Vohs, & Funder, 2007).

Cross-sectional studies at single time points

Finally, whilst self-report measures administered at single time points can provide valuable insights into youth's perceptions of contact, these "snap-shots" of attitudes or behaviour are limited in their ability to examine interethnic interactions over time. Such cross-sectional designs, using single-points of data collection, however, *by definition* fail to capture the complex and dynamic processes underlying intergroup behaviour. For example, children may become more integrated as they spend longer in school (Jugert, Noack & Rutland, 2011) and attitudes may fluctuate depending on external events. Single time-point analysis is unable to capture this complexity.

The overall consequence of the disproportionate focus on self-report measures under experimental (or natural) conditions at a single time-point with cross-sectional samples is that the effects of intergroup interactions may be over or under-estimated, limiting our understanding of everyday influences on youth attitudes and behaviour. To gain insight into what is actually happening in ethnically diverse settings, there is a need to move beyond self-report and study actual behaviour (Baumeister et al., 2007). Happily, researchers are beginning to do just that.

Measuring behaviour in real life contexts

In recent years, researchers have begun to move from self-report and experimental methods toward more novel approaches to capturing behaviour. This research often focuses on people in context, moving us from the individual to the microsystem level in Bronfenbrenner's model (2005). Here, we review some of these approaches as applied to the study of intergroup relations amongst adolescents, focusing specifically on the growing body of research examining micro-ecological behaviour. We also briefly mention the potential of approaches such as social network analysis and the use of new technologies, which are covered in more depth in other chapters in this volume.

Micro-ecological behaviour

A growing number of studies have focused on examining youth intergroup behaviour at the micro-ecological level. That is, "the level at which individuals actually encounter one another in situations of bodily co-presence" (Dixon, Tredoux, & Clack, 2005b, p. 395). To date, the majority of micro-ecological studies have examined race relations in the USA and South Africa through the mapping of seating behaviour in a variety of everyday spaces, although the number of studies using this method within the UK has grown. Below, we review the studies relevant to children and youth.

Typically, micro-ecological research has involved behavioural observation of intergroup interactions through mapping or photography. In one of the first reported micro-ecological studies, Campbell, Kruskal, and Wallace (1966) mapped the racial and gender seating patterns of school children in the USA over the period of a semester. To facilitate this process, observers in the classrooms marked, on a pre-drawn map of the classroom layout, the seating arrangement and race/gender of each person on each seat in the classroom. From this information the authors conducted statistical analysis to examine the levels of segregation in the room. Using the Campbell et al. (1966) aggregation index, which the authors developed, results from this study found that school children remained racially segregated in their seating choice throughout the school year, despite being in a mixed-race environment. Similar patterns of racial segregation have been observed in school settings across the USA (McCauley, Plummer, Moskalenko, & Mordkoff, 2001; Schofield & Sagar, 1977; Silverman & Shaw, 1973).

In a revival of these early studies, micro-ecological research has taken a step forward to examine a greater variety of settings with a range of research techniques. These studies have primarily been conducted amongst university participants in settings including: university lecture theatres and classrooms in South Africa (Alexander & Tredoux, 2010; Koen & Durrheim, 2010), multiethnic cafeterias in the United Kingdom (Clack, Dixon, & Tredoux, 2005), and university dining halls in South Africa (Schrieff, Tredoux, Dixon, & Finchilescu, 2005; Schrieff, Tredoux, Finchilescu, & Dixon, 2010). There are, however, a few studies that have been conducted with children and adolescents in the UK context including schools (McKeown et al., 2015) and community groups (McKeown et al., 2012) in Northern Ireland as well as secondary (Al Ramiah, Schmid, Hewstone, & Floe, 2015; McKeown, in progress) and primary (McKeown et al., 2017) schools in England. Results from these studies show that even in shared spaces, individuals remain clustered in racially or religiously similar groups whilst going about their everyday behaviour.

These studies have produced fascinating results and provide a method by which the complicated processes of real life, everyday contact can be explored. They address inherent problems with the literature by moving beyond idealised conditions of interethnic interactions, simple measures of attitudes, and the focus on prejudice as a primary outcome. There are, however, some limitations of such an approach to examining youth interethnic interactions. First, there is an inherent difficulty in understanding the underlying mechanisms associated with seating behaviour (Orr, McKeown, Cairns, & Stringer, 2011). Second, for the most part seating behaviour has been analysed in isolation from other methods making it difficult to get a comprehensive understanding of interethnic interactions. There are some notable exceptions to this amongst adult samples (e.g., Dixon & Durrheim, 2003; Schrieff et al., 2010) as well as amongst youth samples (Al Ramiah et al., 2015, McKeown, in progress). Despite these limitations, there are some promising avenues for future research that we believe would contribute to a deeper understanding of intergroup interaction behaviour as it occurs in real time. We focus in on two of these avenues next.

One of the ways to further develop this method is to consider how micro-ecological behaviour changes (or not) depending on the context in which the behaviour is occurring. For example, it could be argued that children do not make their friends in the classroom, they do this in the social spaces that make up the wider school context. Therefore, developing an approach in which it would be possible to examine the seating choices of children in the classroom, in the lunchroom, and the social spaces they occupy during breaktime would provide a richer understanding of interethnic interactions. Logistically, this is somewhat difficult to achieve but not impossible. It would require careful preparation in determining the layout of the school being examined, the use of photographs rather than manual observation coding in order to capture dynamism, and the development of appropriate measures that would enable categorisation of spaces into units that would work statistically across the different social spaces being examined.

A second way in which to develop this method further would be to use video-recordings, rather than still images. This would make it possible to determine a more detailed picture of how micro-ecological behaviour develops and changes over time. This is particularly important because we have noted in our own fieldwork that there appears to be a decision-making process when choosing a seat or a social space to inhabit that a still image (often as a final seat selection) does not capture. As such, video-recording seat selection would enable us to examine how a seat appears to be chosen and the ways in which individuals move and change seats. There are, of course, ethical and logistical barriers related to conducting such research with young people and in settings such as schools. Nevertheless, with a rigorous ethical process, careful planning, and consideration of analysis techniques, such an approach would add considerably to our scientific understanding of interaction behaviour and how it manifests in context.

Social network analysis (SNA)

Attempting to move beyond reporting of contact quality and quantity alone, there is a growing literature using SNA as a way to capture youth interactions. SNA enables researchers to inspect positive and negative connections with others (e.g., friendships with and avoidance of others) as well as the effect of contextual and demographic factors on making those connections (Mouw & Etwisle, 2006). It also allows the examination of contact dynamics through longitudinal analysis and disentangling indirect contact links ("friends of friends") and available contact opportunities (i.e., proximity of contact in the direct circle of friends, within peer group, and within broader environment; Wolfer & Hewstone, 2017). It is worth noting, however, that as SNA typically involves participants' self-reported friendships, the extent to which this approach actually captures behaviour could be debated. There are also some ethical considerations associated with using SNA. For example, it is not possible to maintain participant anonymity when using social network data, unless peer names are withheld and only specific social categories are used for identification (e.g., race, ethnicity, gender). And, young people do not always feel comfortable reporting on their friendship networks especially when this involves nominating negative ties. Despite these concerns, SNA offers researchers a tool with which they can examine the predictors and consequences of intergroup friendships.

Using new technologies

Perhaps the most methodologically innovative work happening within the field involves the use of new technologies. Whilst the studies we present below were not conducted with youth samples, we would like to highlight the strength of these studies and their applicability to working with youth in diverse and conflict settings to better understand interethnic interactions.

The first example we would like to draw from is a study by Palazzi et al. (2016) who examined White participant's prejudice towards Black people by examining body movements during intragroup (White–White) and intergroup (White–Black) interactions in addition to implicit and explicit attitudes. In a laboratory setting, White participants were asked to wear a lightweight Shimmer GSR device which measured biometrics (heart rate and emotional arousal) whilst they engaged in two separate video-recorded interactions, one with a White peer and one with a Black peer. The combination of the GSR device and video-recording enabled the researchers to capture a range of body movements including distance and volume. The authors found a range of complex results including that participants who scored higher on implicit prejudice were more likely to maintain distance from outgroup than ingroup members. No relationships, however, were found between the implicit and explicit measures and the biometric data. While this is still a lab-based study with a single data collection point, adapting this approach to capture youth behaviour in various interethnic interaction scenarios would inform understanding as to how social variables may influence subtle non-verbal behaviour, such as body movements.

Chanel Meyers (Meyers & Pauker, in preparation) has provided another example of how new technologies can be adapted for research. Meyers developed a mobile phone app which was used amongst university participants to capture their interethnic interactions by measuring their daily exposure and interactions to racially diverse others. Participants rated how many racially diverse others they saw, how many they interacted with, and whether they engaged in race-related conversations over the course of a week. Those that had more interactions with racially diverse friends reported feeling more comfortable with their race-related conversations. Given the prevalence of mobile phones and their wide use amongst youth, there is a great deal of potential to expand the use of such apps in the future (see also Keil, 2017 for use of mobile phone apps for intergenerational contact).

Our final example comes from the work of John Dixon and colleagues who are currently using GPRS trackers to examine how Protestant and Catholic adults living in religiously segregated areas of Belfast move throughout the city. Whilst the use of GPRS tracking is common outside the psychology literature, it has been rarely applied to studying diverse interactions; through combining this approach with walking interviews, it is possible to capture the nature of how everyday space is negotiated and used (or avoided), which has implications for space and planning. Whilst such research requires careful ethical planning, in terms of consent and the ways in which information is recorded and stored, this approach could be applied to youth to examine how they use and share space with diverse others.

Directions for future research

To date, research has provided much information on how individuals behave in a single controlled setting, such as the research laboratory. With the help of new methodological approaches that often capitalise on emerging technologies, researchers are beginning to examine how behaviour unfolds in everyday life spaces, primarily in the microsystem. There is a need, however, to delve further into Bronfenbrenner's social-ecological model if we are to truly understand the dynamic nature of interethnic interactions, what influences interactions, and what their consequences are. Questions still remain about how the characteristics of the larger social system (macrosystem) influence behaviour observed in the mesosystems and microsystems, as well as how different microsystems interact together (exosystem) to influence behaviour during interethnic interactions. To address such questions, researchers could examine how the same person behaves across different settings (home, school, neighbourhood), or how government policy or social norms serve to influence school or community contexts and corresponding behaviour.

Another point for future research to consider is the reciprocity between individuals and context, for both majority and minority group youth. This is an important direction for further investigation because youth do not exist in isolation and take in social input from a wide range of settings, including subtle and overt cues transmitted back and forth between youth and their parents, teachers, and friends. Further, it is plausible that moving beyond a single-time point of assessment to adopt a longitudinal approach would be insightful to discovering at which point across youth development that different parts of the social-ecology are most predictive of attitudes and behaviours. This is particularly important in interventions designed to improve interethnic relations, so that the longevity of effects can be assessed. Promising interventions for promoting diverse friendships include encouraging interactions under the conditions of the contact hypothesis and indirect forms of contact (Di Bernardo, Vezzali, Stathi, Cadamuro, & Cortesi, 2017), promoting social norms that place value in diversity (McKeown et al., 2017), and having confidence in contact (Turner & Cameron, 2016).

Conclusion

In this chapter we have demonstrated the importance of intergroup contact as a means to promote positive community relations amongst youth in diverse societies. We have also pointed out a range of theoretical and methodological limitations of the research conducted to date on the nature of ethnic diversity and the effects of intergroup contact. We argue that developing new approaches to examine intergroup interactions, across the various social systems which we inhabit, and examining behaviour as it occurs in context are vital if we are to truly understand youth development in multicultural societies. This approach will generate new knowledge that will not only serve to enhance the quality of life for all children and youth, by improving peer relations and corresponding well-being in the short term, but will also ensure the full social and economic participation of future generations in the long term. Information gleaned from more intensive studies that move across the levels of Bronfenbrenner's model will provide important information that more accurately represents how youth negotiate their diverse and dynamic social world. In turn, as researchers and practitioners we will be in a better position to design interventions to encourage these important interactions.

References

Al Ramiah, A., & Hewstone, M. (2013). Intergroup contact as a tool for reducing, resolving, and preventing intergroup conflict: Evidence, limitations, and potential. *American Psychologist*, 68, 527–542. Doi: 10.1037/a0032603

Al Ramiah, A., Schmid, K., Hewstone, M., & Floe, C. (2015). Why are all the White (Asian) kids sitting together in the cafeteria? Resegregation and the role of intergroup attributions and norms. *British Journal of Social Psychology*, 54, 100–124. doi:10.1111/bjso.12064

Alexander, L., & Tredoux, C. (2010). The spaces between us: A Spatial analysis of informal segregation at a South African University. *Journal of Social Issues*, 66, 367–386. doi:10.1111/j.1540-4560.2010.01650.

Allport, G. A. (1954). *The nature of prejudice*. Reading, MA: Addison-Wesley.

Apfelbaum, E. P., Pauker, K., Sommers, S. R., & Ambady, N. (2010). In blind pursuit of racial equality? *Psychological Science*, 21, 1587–1592. doi:10.1177/0956797610384741

Bassett-Jones, N. (2005). The paradox of diversity management, creativity and innovation. *Creativity and Innovation Management*, 14, 169–175. doi:10.1111/j.1467-8691.00337.x

Baumeister, R. E., Vohs, K. D., & Funder, D. C. (2007). Psychology as the science of self-reports and finger movements: Whatever happened to actual behavior? *Perspective on Psychological Science*, 2, 396–403. doi:10.1111/j.1745-6916.2007.00051.x

Betancourt, T. S., & Khan, K. T. (2008). The mental health of children affected by armed conflict: Protective processes and pathways to resilience. *International Review of Psychiatry*, 20, 317–328. doi:10.1080/09540260802090363

Brewer, M. B. (1997). The social psychology of intergroup relations: Can research informpractice? *Journal of Social Issues*, 53, 197–211. doi:10.1111/j.1540-4560.1997.tb02440.x.

Bronfenbrenner, U. (1979). *Making human beings human: Bioecological perspectives on human development*. Thousand Oaks, CA: Sage.

Bubritzki, S., van Tubergen, F., Weesie, J., & Smith, S. (2018). Ethnic composition of the school class and interethnic attitudes: A multi-group perspective. *Journal of*

Ethnic and Migration Studies, *44*, 482–502. doi:10.1080/1369183X.2017.1322501

Burgess, S., & Platt, L. (2018): Inter-ethnic relations of teenagers in England's schools: The role of school and neighbourhood ethnic composition. *CReAM Discussion Paper Series*. Retrieved from www.cream-migration.org/publ_uploads/CDP_07_18.pdf

Campbell, D. T., Kruskal, W. H., & Wallace, W. P. (1966). Seating aggregation as an index of attitude. *Sociometry*, *29*, 1–15. doi:10.2307/2786006.

Catney, G. (2015) Has neighbourhood ethnic residential segregation decreased? In S. Jivraj & L. Simpson (Eds.), *Ethnic identity and inequalities in Britain: The dynamics of diversity* (pp. 109–122). Bristol, UK: Policy Press.

Clack, B., Dixon, J. A., & Tredoux, C. (2005). Eating together apart: Patterns of segregation in a multiethnic cafeteria. *Journal of Community and Applied Social Psychology*, *14*, 1–16. doi:10.1002/casp.787

Cummings, E. M., Goeke-Morey, M. C., Merrilees, C. E., Taylor, L. K., & Shirlow, P. (2014). A social–ecological, process-oriented perspective on political violence and child development. *Child Development Perspectives*, *8*, 82–89. doi:10.1111/cdep.12067

Denson, N., & Chang, M. J. (2009). Racial diversity matters: The impact of diversity-related student engagement and institutional context. *American Educational Research Journal*, *46*, 322–353. doi:10.3102/0002831208323278

Department for Education [DfE] (2015). Schools, pupils and their characteristics. Retrieved 05 July 2015 from www.gov.uk/government/uploads/system/uploads/attachment_data/file/433680/SFR16_2015_Main_Text.pdf.

Di Bernardo, G. A., Vezzali, L., Stathi, S., Cadamuro, A., & Cortesi, L. (2017). Vicarious, extended and imagined intergroup contact: A review of interventions based on indirect contact strategies applied in educational settings. *Testing, Psychometrics, Methodology in Applied Psychology*, *24*, 3–21.

Dixon, J. A., & Durrheim, K. (2003). Contact and the ecology of racial division: Some varieties of informal segregation. *British Journal of Social Psychology*, *42*, 1–23. doi:10.1348/014466603763276090

Dixon, J. A., Durrheim, K., & Tredoux, C. (2005a). Beyond the optimal contact strategy: A reality check for the contact hypothesis. *American Psychologist*, *60*, 697–711. doi:10.1037/0003-066X.60.7.697

Dixon, J. A., Tredoux, C., & Clack, B. (2005b). On the micro-ecology of racial division: A neglected dimension of segregation. *South African Journal of Psychology*, *35*, 395–411. doi:10.1177/008124630503500301

DuBois, D. L., & Hirsch, B. J. (1990). School and neighborhood friendship patterns of Blacks and Whites in early adolescence. *Child Development*, *61*, 524–536. doi:10.1111/j.1467-8624.1990.tb02797.x

Echols, L., & Graham, S. (2013). Birds of a different feather: How do cross-ethnic friends flock together? *Merrill-Palmer Quarterly*, *59*, 461–488. doi:10.13110/merrpalmquar1982.59.4.0461

Festinger, L. (1954). A theory of social comparison processes. *Human Relations*, *7*, 117–140. doi:10.1177/001872675400700202

Gurin, P., Dey, E. L., Hurtado, S., & Gurin, G. (2002). Diversity and higher education: Theory and impact on educational outcomes. *Harvard Educational Review, 72*, 330–360. doi:10.17763/haer.72.3.01151786u134n051

Henrich, J., Heine, S. J., & Norenzayan, A. (2010). The weirdest people in the world? *Behaviour and Brain Sciences, 33*, 61–83. doi:10.1017/S0140525X0999152X

Hewstone, M. (2015). Consequences of diversity for social cohesion and prejudice: The missing dimension of intergroup contact. *Journal of Social Issues, 71*, 417–438. doi:10.1111/josi.12120

Jones, J. M., & Dovidio, J. F. (2018). Change, challenge, and prospects for a diversity paradigm in social psychology. *Social Issues and Policy Review, 12*, 7–56. doi:10.1111/sipr.12039

Jugert, P., Noack, P., & Rutland, A. (2011). Friendship preferences among German and Turkish preadolescents. *Child Development, 82*, 812–829. doi:10.1111/j.1467-8624.2010.01528.x.

Keil, T. (2017). *Capturing everyday contact: Perceptions, experiences and measurement of everyday intergroup contact in public and private settings* (Unpublished doctoral dissertation). University of Exeter, Exeter.

Koen, J., & Durrheim, K. (2010). A naturalistic observational study of informal segregation: Seating patterns in lectures. *Environment and Behaviour, 42*, 448–468. doi:10.1177/0013916509336981

Kruse, H., Smith, S., van Tubergen, F., & Maas, I. (2016). From neighbors to school friends? How adolescents' place of residence relates to same-ethnic school friendships. *Social Networks, 44*, 130–142. doi:10.1016/j.socnet.2015.07.004

Kupersmidt, J., DeRosier, M., & Patterson, C. (1995). Similarity as the basis for children's friendships: The roles of sociometric status, aggressive and withdrawn behavior, academic achievement and demographic characteristics. *Child Development, 66*, 360–375. doi:10.1177/0265407595123007

McCauley, C., Plummer, M., Moskalenko, S., & Mordkoff, J. B. (2001). The exposure index: A measure of intergroup contact. *Peace and Conflict: Journal of Peace Psychology, 7*, 321–336. doi:10.1207/S15327949PAC0704_03.

McKeown, S. (in progress). The diversity effect: Intergroup interactions and the impact of diversity on young people's attitudes and academics. *ESRC Funded research project*

McKeown, S., Cairns, E., Stringer, M., & Rae, G. (2012). Micro-ecological behaviour and intergroup contact. *Journal of Social Psychology, 152*, 340–358. doi:10.1080/00224545.2011.614647

McKeown, S., & Dixon, J. (2017). The 'contact hypothesis': Critical reflections and future directions. *Social and Personality Psychology Compass, 11*. doi:10.1111/spc3.12295

McKeown, S., Stringer, M., & Cairns, E. (2015). Classroom segregation: Where do students sit and what does it mean for intergroup relations? *British Educational Research Journal, 42*, 40–55. doi:10.1002/berj.3200

McKeown, S., & Taylor, L. K. (2018). Perceived peer and school norm effects on youth antisocial and prosocial behaviours through intergroup contact in Northern Ireland. *British Journal of Social Psychology, 57*, 652–665. doi:10.1111/bjso.12257

McKeown, S., Williams, A., & Pauker, K. (2017). Stories that move them: Changing children's behaviour toward diverse peers. *Journal of Community and Applied Social Psychology, 21*, 381–387. doi:10.1002/casp.2316.

Merrilees C.E.,Taylor, L.K., Baird, R., Goeke-Morey, M.C., Shirlow, P., & Cummings E.M. (2018). Neighborhood effects of intergroup contact on change in youth intergroup bias. *Journal of Youth and Adolescence, 47*, 77–87.

Meyers, C., & Pauker, K. (in preparation). Navigating race in a racially diverse environment.

Mouw, T., & Etwisle, B. (2006). Residential segregation and interracial friendship in schools. *American Journal of Sociology, 112*, 394–441. doi:10.1086/506415

Orr, R., McKeown, S., Cairns, E., & Stringer, M. (2011). Examining non-racial segregation: A micro-ecological approach. *British Journal of Social Psychology*, doi:10.1111/j.2044-8309.2011.02080.x.

Palazzi, A., Calderara, S., Bicocchi, N., Vezzali, L., Di Bernardo, G. A., Zambonelli, F., & Cucchiara, R. (2016 September). Spotting prejudice with nonverbal behaviours. In *Proceedings of the 2016 ACM international joint conference on pervasive and ubiquitous computing* (pp. 853–862). ACM.

Pettigrew, T. F., & Tropp, L. R. (2006). A meta-analytic test of intergroup contact theory. *Journal of Personality and Social Psychology, 90*, 751–783. doi:10.1037/0022-3514.90.5.751

Putnam, R. D. (2007). E pluribus unum: Diversity and community in the twenty-first century the 2006 Johan Skytte Prize Lecture. *Scandinavian Political Studies, 30*, 137–174. doi:10.1111/j.1467-9477.2007.00176.x

Rosenthal, L., & Levy, S. R. (2010). The colorblind, multicultural, and polycultural ideological approaches to improving intergroup attitudes and relations. *Social Issues and Policy Review, 4*, 215–246. doi:10.1111/j.1751-2409.2010.01022.x

Rutland, A., Cameron, L., Milne, A., & McGeorge, P. (2005). Social norms and self-presentation: Children's implicit and explicit intergroup attitudes. *Child Development, 76*, 451–466. doi:10.1111/j.1467-8624.2005.00856.x

Schachner, M. K., Juang, L., Moffitt, U., & van de Vijver, F. J. (2018). Schools as acculturative and developmental contexts for youth of immigrant and refugee background. *European Psychologist, 23*, 44–56. doi:10.1027/1016-9040/a000312

Schmid, K., Al Ramiah, A. A., & Hewstone, M. (2014). Neighborhood ethnic diversity and trust: The role of intergroup contact and perceived threat. *Psychological Science, 25*, 665–674. doi:10.1177/0956797613508956.

Schneider, B. (2000). *Friends and enemies: Peer relations in childhood*. New York, NY: Routledge.

Schofield, J. W., & Sagar, H. A. (1977). Peer interaction patterns in an integrated middle school. *Sociometry, 40*, 130–138. Retrieved from www.jstor.org

Schrieff, L., Tredoux, C., Dixon, J. A., & Finchilescu, G. (2005). Patterns of racial segregation in university dining halls. *South African Journal of Psychology, 35*, 433–443. doi:10.1177/008124630503500303

Schrieff, L., Tredoux, C., Finchilescu, G., & Dixon, J. A. (2010). Understanding the seating patterns in a residence-dining hall: A longitudinal study of intergroup contact. *South African Journal of Psychology, 40*, 5–17. doi: 10.1177/008124631004000102

Shelton, J. N. (2000). A reconceptualization of how we study issues of racial prejudice. *Personality and Social Psychology Review, 4*, 374–390. doi:10.1207/S15327957PSPR0404_6

Silverman, I., & Shaw, M. E. (1973). Effects of sudden mass school desegregation on interracial interaction and attitudes in one southern city. *Journal of Social Issues, 29*, 133–142. doi:10.1111/j.1540-4560.1973.tb00107.x

Swart, H., Hewstone, M., Christ, O., & Voci, A. (2011). Affective mediators of intergroup contact: A three-wave longitudinal study in South Africa. *Journal of Personality and Social Psychology, 101*, 1221–1238. doi:10.1037/a0024450

The Times Educational Supplement [TES] (2017). School hate crimes spike following Brexit and Trump votes. TES. Retrieved 07 May 2018 from www.tes.com/news/exclusive-school-hate-crimes-spike-following-brexit-and-trump-votes

Tropp, L. R., O'Brien, T. C., González Gutierrez, R., Valdenegro, D., Migacheva, K., Tezanos-Pinto, P., ... Cayul, O. (2016). How school norms, peer norms, and discrimination predict interethnic experiences among ethnic minority and majority youth. *Child Development, 87*, 1436–1451. doi:10.1111/cdev.12608

Turner, R. N., & Cameron, L. (2016). Confidence in contact: A new perspective on promoting cross-group friendship among children and adolescents. *Social Issues and Policy Review, 10*, 212–246. doi:10.1111/sipr.12023

Turner, R. N., West, K., & Christie, Z. (2013). Out-group trust, intergroup anxiety, and out-group attitude as mediators of the effect of imagined intergroup contact on intergroup behavioral tendencies. *Journal of Applied Social Psychology, 43*, 196–205. doi:10.1111/jasp.12019

Unesco World Report (2009). Investing in cultural diversity and intercultural dialogue. United Nations Educational, Scientific and Cultural Organisation. Retrieved 7 May 2018 from: www.unesco.org/new/en/culture/resources/report/the-unesco-world-report-on-cultural-diversity/

Verkuyten, M. (2005). Ethnic group identification and group evaluation among minority and majority groups: Testing the multiculturalism hypothesis. *Journal of Personality and Social Psychology, 88*, 121–138. doi:10.1037/0022-3514.88.1.121

Wolfer, R., & Hewstone, M. (2017). Beyond the dyadic perspective: 10 Reasons for using social network analysis in intergroup contact research. *British Journal of Social Psychology, 56*, 609–617. doi:10.1111/bjso.12195

Wolsko, C., Park, B., Judd, C. M., & Wittenbrink, B. (2000). Framing interethnic ideology: Effects of multicultural and color-blind perspectives on judgments of groups and individuals. *Journal of Personality and Social Psychology, 78*, 635. doi:10.1037/0022-3514.78.4.635

Chapter 13

Bridging contexts

The interplay between parents, peers, and schools in explaining youth reactions to growing diversity

Marta Miklikowska and Andrea Bohman

Our lives are increasingly marked by diversity. In the U.S., White Americans will compose less than 50 percent of the population by 2044 (Colby & Ortman, 2015) and, in the UK, ethnic minorities will form one-third of the population by 2056 (Coleman, 2010). These trends have been fueled by increases in immigration and in the number of children of immigrant parents (OECD/European Union, 2015). Interacting with people from different backgrounds can be a source of resentment and conflict. Thus, a major challenge of multicultural societies is ensuring positive intergroup relations. This goal is often impeded by negative attitudes. Although they can be held by both majority members and migrants, prejudice of natives bears wide-reaching consequences for lower-status groups, including discrimination and hostility (Brenick, Titzmann, Michel, & Silbereisen, 2012).

The consequences of growing diversity are particularly pertinent for youth. Immigrants to Europe are comparably young, with a median age of 27.9 years (Eurostat, 2016), which implies that the population of youth is becoming more diverse than the adult population (Johnson & Lichter, 2010). In addition, adolescence is a sensitive period for the formation of attitudes, which become harder to change later in life (Rekker, Keijsers, Branje, & Meeus, 2015). Thus, the kind of attitudes young people develop have profound consequences for the cohesion of future societies.

This chapter brings together perspectives from social and developmental research that maps how ethnic majority youth respond to growing diversity. First, we outline recent trends in youth intergroup attitudes. Next, we review research on the role of proximal social contexts, in particular parents and peers, in shaping youth attitudes. We then propose an integrative, ecological perspective that looks at the interrelated effects of parents, peers, and schools. We conclude by discussing how this perspective can inform our attempts to ensure positive relations among youth in a diverse world and push research on the development of prejudice forward.

Growing diversity and youth intergroup attitudes

Group threat theory predicts that with growing diversity majority members perceive an increased threat to their status and resources (Blalock, 1967). This elicits hostility and negative attitudes, particularly among individuals in direct competition with outgroups (Scheepers, Gijsberts, & Coenders, 2002). In this sense, it predicts that the low age of migrants to Europe and the relatively high rates of youth unemployment (Eurostat, 2018) should make intergroup competition particularly salient among young people. More optimistic perspectives suggest that insofar as diversity increases positive encounters, it facilitates positive attitudes. Intergroup contact theory expects positive intergroup contact to enhance empathy, reduce anxiety and feelings of threat, and, ultimately, reduce prejudice (Allport, 1954; Pettigrew, 1998). Although friendships are particularly potent in this regard (Titzmann, Brenick, & Silbereisen, 2015), simply knowing ingroup members who have positive interactions with outgroups can generate positive attitudes (Feddes, Noack, & Rutland, 2009).

Research shows evidence for both of these scenarios. Studies find that younger generations generally display lower prejudice and feelings of threat than older generations (e.g., Ford, 2008). Although educational differences partly account for the cohort differences (Quillian, 1996), it is not too far-fetched to assume that cross-ethnic contact also plays a role (Hewstone, 2015). Indeed, young people in general establish more cross-ethnic friendships than older age groups (Figure 13.1). They also have more opportunities to engage in cross-ethnic friendships than previous generations of youth as diversity facilitates positive intergroup contact (Bagci, Kumashiro, Smith, Blumberg, & Rutland, 2014), although the relationship might not be linear (Moody, 2001) and depend on the target of antipathies (Janmaat & Keating, 2017). Conversely, studies have found that individuals who enter adulthood during high unemployment or immigration waves are particularly negative towards immigrants also later in life (Coenders & Scheepers, 1998). This suggests that intergroup competition during the formative years might trigger feelings of threat and consequently prejudice.

To map youth reactions to growing diversity, we analyzed trends in anti-immigrant attitudes in different age groups for 2002–2016 (Figure 13.2). Results showed that although the period saw several events that could amplify negative attitudes, including large immigration flows and an economic crisis, there are no indications of general increases in prejudice among young people. The lack of a dominating reaction suggests that youth reactions may depend on regional developments (Weber, 2018) and more immediate processes involving proximal social contexts youth are embedded in, such as parents, peers, and schools. Indeed, research on neighborhood effects shows that societal risk factors rarely have direct effects on youth. Instead, they trigger mediatory processes that are more proximal to the child (e.g., parental perceptions) and that influence the child's development (Roosa, Jones, Tein, & Cree, 2003).

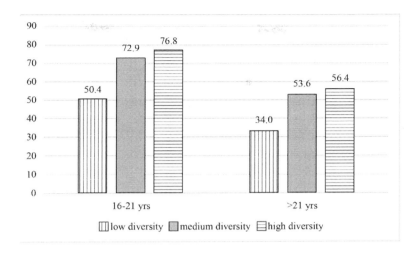

Figure 13.1 Percentage of natives with friends of different race/ethnicity
Source: Data from European Social Survey and OECD including all countries available 2014.

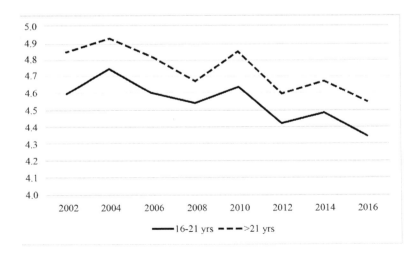

Figure 13.2 Change in anti-immigrant attitudes (index 0–10)
Source: Data from European Social Survey including all countries available 2002–2016.

The role of proximal social contexts in youth intergroup attitudes

A meta-analysis of age-related changes in prejudice has found them in childhood but not in adolescence (Raabe & Beelmann, 2011; but see Miklikowska, 2016, 2017; Van Zalk & Kerr, 2014). This suggests that cognitive processes might primarily drive attitudes of children while youth are more affected by their proximal social environments, such as parents and peers (but see Aboud, 1988; Miklikowska, 2018 for the role of *sociocognitive factors* in youth prejudice).

Social learning and socialization perspectives use direct and indirect teaching to explain how parents and peers socialize youth prejudice. According to Allport (1954), children observe and imitate the labels and associated emotions expressed by parents and peers in order to gain their approval. Initially, this occurs independent of the referent, but with exposure to outgroup members, the labels and emotions become attached to the referent and integrated with the person's personality. Parents are seen as the principal agent of socialization because they provide ingroup identification and norms of appropriate attitudes as well as because they manage children's environments (Grusec, 2011; Reich & Vandell, 2011). They are also attachment figures and children are motivated to affiliate with them and to internalize their values (Bretherton, Golby, & Cho, 1997). Such need for belonging accounts for the social tuning of attitudes (i.e., aligning them with views of those one is motivated to affiliate with) (Sinclair, Dunn, & Lowery, 2005).

Socialization is not the only mechanism explaining prejudice formation. *Intergroup theories* assume that ingroup–outgroup categorization is a major force. According to *intergroup theory of social identity*, group norms held by those youth identify with affect whether youth preference for their own group translates into outgroup prejudice (Nesdale, 2004; Tajfel & Turner, 1986). Given that adolescents are expected to identify more with their peers than with their parents (Berndt, 1979), peers are seen as a main source of intergroup norms. According to *developmental intergroup theory*, prejudice develops when groups become psychologically salient, when children learn to categorize by salient group dimensions, and when they associate negative characteristics with the outgroups (Bigler & Liben, 2006, 2007). Parents and peers can facilitate this process by making certain groups salient, for example by labeling them as "immigrant kids," which increases the likelihood of ethnic categorization (Patterson & Bigler, 2006). They can also influence child perceptions of outgroups through what they say and how they behave toward outgroups. For instance, they can express attitudes that provide clear information about group negative characteristics, such as "immigrants come here to take advantage of our welfare."

Research on the role of parents in youth attitudes

A review of 131 studies on parental bias has shown a significant medium-sized correlation between parent and child ethnic and racial attitudes (for a review see Degner & Dalege, 2013; e.g., Gniewosz, Noack, Wentura, & Funke, 2008; O'Bryan, Fishbein, & Ritchey, 2004).

Longitudinal studies have shown that parental prejudice predicted changes in youth attitudes (Miklikowska, 2016, 2017; Vollerberg, Iedema, & Raaijmakers, 2001). In our research, we showed that attitudes of Swedish majority adolescents with prejudiced parents followed different developmental trajectories than attitudes of youth with less prejudiced parents (Miklikowska, Bohman, & Titzmann, 2019). They displayed higher levels and smaller linear decreases in prejudice from 13 to 17 years of age (Figure 13.3). In this research, we also showed that within-person fluctuations in youth attitudes were not significantly related to within-person fluctuations in parental attitudes, which might be explained by the fact that attitudes undergo few substantial changes in adulthood (Rekker et al. 2015). It suggests that the effects of parents are likely to be a result of a long-term exposure to parental prejudice rather than of short-term fluctuations in parents' attitudes (at least during times of a limited social change).

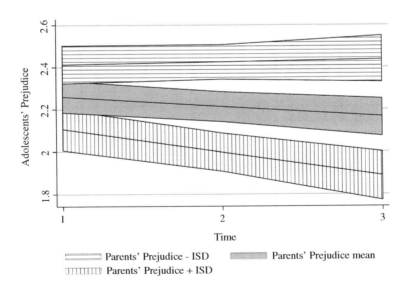

Figure 13.3 The effects of parents' prejudice on the level and change of adolescents' prejudice.

The effects of parents have been shown to be stronger when youth have good relations with them (Miklikowska, 2016; Sinclair, Dunn, & Lowery, 2005), when they accurately perceive parental attitudes (Westholm, 1999), when parents are consistent and similar to each other in attitudes (Jennings, Stoker, & Bowers, 2009; Jugert, Eckstein, Beelmann, & Noack, 2016), and when attitudes are discussed often (Meeusen & Dhont, 2015). These qualifications offer support to social learning and socialization perspectives of how children come to resemble their parents.

Correlations between parent and child attitudes have been shown to increase from childhood to adolescence (Degner & Dalege, 2013). This has been attributed to measures of prejudice being more similar for parents and adolescents than for parents and children. Yet, using the same measures for parents and youth, we found parental attitudes to predict changes in prejudice from mid- to late adolescence, which suggests that with age youth become increasingly similar to their parents Miklikowska et al., 2019.

Tracking American parent–youth pairs 1965–1997, Jennings and colleagues (2009) showed that attitudes acquired from parents in adolescence persisted into adulthood. This is in line with research on attitudinal persistence and impressionable years, where attitudes formed in adolescence are carried on to become more rigid with time (Miller & Sears, 1986; Rekker et al., 2015). However, this result might reflect parental influence in adulthood or adult children's effects on parents. In addition, attributes that parents and youth share may shape their views on new issues (Flanagan & Tucker, 1999). Indeed, there is evidence that parent–child similarity in prejudice might be rooted in the transmission of ideologies (Dhont & Van Hiel, 2012; Meeusen & Dhont, 2015) and personality. For instance, we showed that parental attitudes and home atmosphere were linked to youth empathy which, in turn, predicted their tolerance (Miklikowska, 2017; Miklikowska & Hurme, 2011). Part of parent–child similarity can also be attributed to heritability. In adolescence, however, genetic influences are almost absent while socialization is of paramount importance (Hatemi et al., 2009).

Parents may instill negative attitudes to ensure that their children embrace their ethnic heritage (Munniksma, Flache, Verkuyten, & Veenstra, 2012). If youth have outgroup friends, parents run the risk that youth internalize cultural values of other groups (Vedder, Berry, Sabatier, & Sam, 2009). However, parents are just as likely to teach positive attitudes. We showed that youth with tolerant parents increased in tolerance from early to mid-adolescence (Miklikowska, 2016). In addition, youth attitudes predict changes in parental attitudes (Miklikowska, 2016; Vollerberg et al., 2001). This illustrates that socialization is a bi-directional process and theories of prejudice development should include reciprocal effects.

Research on the role of peers in youth attitudes

Cross-sectional studies have reported peer–child and peer–adolescent similarity in prejudice. For instance, Dutch adolescents' feelings towards ethnic outgroups were associated with the perceived multicultural beliefs of their peers (Thijs, Gharaei, & de Vroome, 2016) and Italian youth prejudice was associated with their peers' attitudes (Kiesner, Maas, Cadinu, & Vellese, 2003). Longitudinal studies have revealed that peers' prejudice at the individual and classroom level predicted changes in youth attitudes (Gniewosz et al., 2008; Miklikowska, 2017; Mitchell, 2018). Our study of Swedish majority adolescents showed that youth with more prejudiced peers displayed a higher level and smaller linear decrease in anti-immigrant attitudes than youth with less prejudiced peers Miklikowska et al., 2019 (Figure 13.4). It also showed that within-person fluctuations in youth attitudes were positively related to fluctuations in peers' attitudes. This result shows the plasticity of youth attitudes and suggests that the creation of a positive atmosphere among youth may produce relatively fast decreases in prejudice. However, it also suggests that youth attitudes, once changed, may relapse easily with changes in the peer context.

Experimental studies have indicated that exposure to peers' opinions can influence youth prejudice. For instance, interactions with fellow classmates trained to convey positive attitudes regarding Afro-Americans resulted in

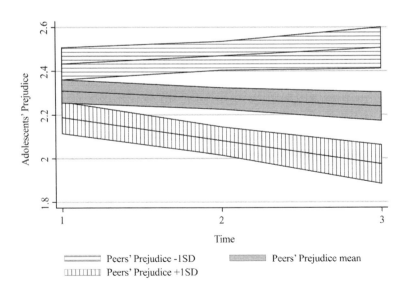

Figure 13.4 The effects of peers' prejudice on the level and change of adolescents' prejudice.

decreases in undergraduates' prejudice (Blanchard, Crandall, Brigham, & Vaugn, 1994). Aboud and Doyle (1996) paired high prejudice children with a low-prejudice friend to talk about their racial attitudes. They showed that high-prejudice children adopted more tolerant attitudes while unbiased children did not adopt their friend's prejudice. This suggests that social influence takes place not only because of imitation or need for approval but that children actively evaluate social cues.

Extensive research on peer ingroup norms has shown that children had more negative attitudes when their ingroup had a norm of exclusion rather than inclusion (e.g., Nesdale & Lawson, 2011; Nesdale, Maass, Durkin, & Griffiths, 2005). For instance, Rutland and colleagues (2005) showed that perceptions of peer norms predicted British majority children's attitudes toward racial and national outgroups. Studies on the Swedish youth peer networks have shown that norms prevalent in the networks predicted changes in adolescents' attitudes towards immigrants (Hjerm, Eger, & Danell, 2018; Van Zalk, Kerr, Van Zalk, & Stattin, 2013). Paluck (2011) showed that the egalitarian attitudes of students trained to confront expressions of prejudice spread to their close friends while their behavior (e.g., signing a gay rights petition) spread even to peers outside of the school. This suggests that peer networks propagate not only attitudes but also norms of behavior, which appear to be more "contagious" than attitudes. Although research shows that youth with low outgroup negativity tend to select peers with similar orientation (Rivas-Drake, Saleem, Schaefer, Medina, & Jagers, 2018), controlling for these selection processes does not annul the effects of peers (Van Zalk et al., 2013).

While the reviewed research shows that peers are important source of attitudes, significant parts of peer influence might actually be caused by underlying influences of parents (Steinberg, 2001), which we discuss in the next section.

Interrelated effects of social contexts on youth attitudes

Parents and peers are not the only proximal social contexts that youth are embedded in, and relationships between various contexts may have important consequences for the development of outgroup attitudes. The ecological developmental model suggests that development is a result of complex links between individuals and multiple, causally interdependent, contexts (Bronfenbrenner, 1979; Reich & Vandell, 2011). The contexts are located in different ecological subsystems, from the proximal social environments of the microsystem, including parents and peers, to the more distal macrosystem, that is, societal norms and laws. The model also includes a mesosystem, which comprises of interactions between individuals and proximal environments as well as direct and indirect links between social contexts, such as interactions between a child's parents and teachers. This cross-context interconnectedness suggests that the mesosystem provides influence beyond that of any individual microsystem (additive and synergistic impact). It also suggests that whether or not individuals develop certain outcomes due to factors present in one environment may be related to the presence of protective or risk factors in other contexts. Indeed, research in other areas has shown that inclusive school norms can buffer the effects of exclusive peer norms on children's aggressive intentions (Nipedal, Nesdale, & Killen, 2010).

The interconnectedness in the mesosystem is to some degree present also in theories of prejudice development. According to social identity theory, the effects of peer norms might be blunted or inhibited when adults who endorse inclusive norms are present or when other social contexts, particularly the school, condemn prejudice (Nesdale, 2004). Similarly, developmental intergroup theory expects parents' and peers' influence to depend on the school environment (Bigler & Liben, 2006, 2007). Children attending ethnically segregated schools are likely to construct ideas about group differences that justify segregation, which become a basis for prejudice. In contrast, children attending ethnically diverse schools are regularly exposed to outgroups, which is theorized to reduce the psychological salience of ethnicity. Although this relationship might be curvilinear (Leszczensky, Flache, Stark, & Munniksma, 2018), it still implies that the school context may moderate other influences. Further, provided that intergroup experiences are positive, diverse settings may increase outgroup liking (McGlothlin & Killen, 2010; for a review see Thijs & Verkuyten, 2014), particularly when they facilitate cross-ethnic closeness and friendships (Bagci et al., 2014; Juvonen, Kogachi, & Graham, 2017). Thus, youth attending diverse schools might rely less on parents' attitudes and more on their own, first-hand experiences.

Research that examines the interplay between proximal contexts is rare but a few recent studies have started filling this gap. McGuire, Rutland, and Nesdale (2015) showed that school norms of inclusion led to more positive attitudes among British majority children even when peers had a norm of exclusion. In this experiment, children knew that their attitudes would not be made known to their peer group. In contrast, when children's attitudes were made known to their peers, the salience of the exclusive peer group norm reduced the positive effects of the school norm. This suggests that school norms might buffer against negative peer norms as long as youth are not answerable for their attitudes to their peer group or, alternatively, when youth are held accountable to their teachers (Nesdale & Lawson, 2011). We showed that, in the Swedish context, ethnically diverse classrooms reduced the effects of parents' prejudice on the level of youth attitudes towards immigrants Miklikowska et al., 2019. Adolescents attending diverse classrooms were less affected by their parents' prejudice than adolescents attending homogenous classes (Figure 13.5). This result suggests that diverse classrooms might offer an alternative source of

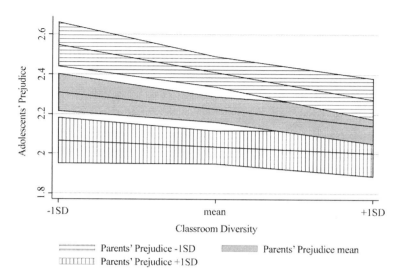

Figure 13.5 The effects of parents' prejudice on the level of adolescents' prejudice depending on classroom diversity.

information about outgroups that runs counter to the possibly prejudiced messages of parents. Alternatively, such classrooms increase the likelihood of cross-ethnic friendships that, in turn, reduce prejudice and account for the buffering role of classroom diversity. This is in line with research showing the lagged effects of parental prejudice to be smaller for youth with high levels of cross-ethnic contact (Miklikowska, 2017; see also Dhont & Van Hiel, 2012; Edmonds & Killen, 2009).

Further, research has shown that parents' and peers' attitudes have consequences for youth intergroup friendships. Smith and colleagues (2014) showed that the more parents cherish traditional values, the more they disapprove of cross-ethnic friendships and the fewer outgroup friends youth make (see also Edmonds & Killen, 2009). In addition, Windzio (2012) showed that parental bias drove even existing friends away from each other. Parents of cross-ethnic friendship dyads were unlikely to be acquainted with each other and this lack of intergenerational closure led to fewer invitations to parties among children. Concerning peers, Tropp and colleagues (2016) found that Chilean adolescents who perceived that their ingroup friends approved of having outgroup friends were more interested in cross-ethnic interactions. Similarly, Hispanic youth perceptions of close friends' comfort with cross-race interactions predicted more favorable attitudes, even when controlling for school diversity and direct friendships (Carlson, Wilson, & Hargrave, 2003).

An integrative ecological perspective on prejudice development also implies that not all proximal environments are equally important, as the influence of one may outweigh the others. Social learning and socialization perspectives identify the parent–child relationship as a major socializing context not only because parents exert a direct influence on children but also because they manage children's and early adolescents' environments (Grusec, 2011; McDowell & Parke, 2009), including their social interactions (Edmonds & Killen, 2009; Reich & Vandell, 2011). Thus, it is possible that apparent peer effects actually reflect (mediate) parents' attitudes, as parents might influence which peers youth associate with (Steinberg, 2001). They might also reflect the influence of parental genes in line with the ideas of active gene–environment correlations, where individuals select what settings they enter based on their genetic predispositions. Consistent with these perspectives, research has shown that parents' attitudes towards racial integration were more strongly linked to youth attitudes than peers' attitudes (Tedin, 1980) and that the lagged effects of parental bias on youth anti-immigrant prejudice were more stable than those of peers (Miklikowska, 2017). Intergroup theories, on the other hand, suggest primacy of peer effects because adolescents spend more time and identify more with their peers (Berndt, 1979). In line with this perspective, a U.S. study shows that with increasing age, children rejected parental messages about racial exclusions but accepted peer norms (Killen, Lee-Kim, McGlothlin, Stangor, & Helwig, 2002).

We compared the effects of parents' and peers' attitudes on the development of attitudes towards immigrants from early to late adolescence Miklikowska et al., 2019. Parents' and peers' direct effects were similar in strength and independent of each other (i.e., no interaction), suggesting that parents and peers exert unique effects on youth attitudes. However, in addition to these direct effects, parental attitudes predicted the kind of peers adolescents associate with (less or more prejudiced) which, in turn, predicted youth attitudes. This indirect effect of parents in combination with their direct influence suggests an overall greater importance of parental bias for youth attitudes. Indeed, the growing importance of peers in adolescence does not necessarily imply detachment from parents (Jager, Yuen, Putnick, Hendricks, & Bornstein, 2015). Quite the contrary, our results suggest that parents are behind-the-scenes power brokers of youth prejudice: they shape attitudes through active socialization and indirect influences via adolescents' selection of more or less prejudiced peers. Further, Tropp et al. (2016) compared the effects of perceived peer and school norms on interethnic experiences of youth. They showed that peers were more influential in the short term but school norms predicted long-term changes in comfort, interest, and quality of cross-ethnic contact. This suggests that at any given point in time, peer norms might be more influential because they hold immediate social consequences, such as peer acceptance or rejection. In the long term, however, stable school norms and parental attitudes might affect youth outgroup attitudes to a greater degree.

Conclusions and future directions

This chapter summarized research on youth reactions to increasing ethnic diversity and the role of proximal social contexts in youth attitudes towards outgroups. It reviewed literature on parent and peer effects which demonstrates that parents and peers who identify individuals by group membership and express negative attitudes towards them perpetuate categories that contribute to negative intergroup relations. Thereafter, the chapter proposed an integrative, ecological perspective to address the interrelated effects of various proximal social contexts on the development of outgroup attitudes. A review of the limited but growing research in this area shows, for example, that schools buffer some of the negative effects of parent and peer prejudice and that part of parental influence is mediated by the effects their attitudes have on the peers youth associate with (i.e., less or more prejudiced).

Taken together, the reviewed research offers a strong argument for addressing parents' and peers' attitudes in anti-prejudice programs, particularly in light of the moderate effect sizes of existing interventions (Beelmann & Heinemann, 2014). It suggests that working with peers might result in faster changes but addressing parental bias might pay off more in the long term. Given that modifying parental prejudice poses an interventional challenge, the reviewed research highlights a couple of alternative, indirect avenues for counteracting its negative effects, namely, cross-ethnic friendships, school diversity, and inclusive school norms.

The reviewed research also supports the need to further map the mesosystem (i.e., links between various proximal contexts; Bronfenbrenner, 1979) in efforts to build more comprehensive theoretical models of how prejudice is formed and perpetuated. Rarely do theories of prejudice integrate various contexts; and research that examines their interrelated effects is even scarcer. As a result, we still know little about the various ways contexts interconnect, about their relative and temporal importance, and about the unique effects they have on prejudice development.

A more integrative, ecological perspective would be fruitful for examining mechanisms that connect different contexts. This involves direct and indirect links (e.g., parents' involvement in creating inclusive school norms and relationships between parents) as well as cross-context communication and knowledge (e.g., communication between parents and teachers and parents' knowledge of their child's intergroup friends). An integrative perspective could also map the degree to which social inputs are conflicting and aligning. Although findings from our own research suggest that there is some degree of convergence between parent and peer context (i.e., that youth with prejudiced parents associate with prejudiced peers and that peers do not moderate the effects of parents), not all youth from prejudiced homes choose prejudiced peers and develop prejudice. Applying the developmental concepts of equifinality and multifinality to the study of prejudice allows for the assumption that many divergent pathways can result in prejudice development even despite the initial absence of risk (i.e., equifinality) that individual starting points that could imply risk (e.g., low empathy or prejudiced parents) may or may not lead to prejudice depending on other factors in the same and other proximal contexts (i.e., multifinality). Research in other areas of development, such as psychopathology, demonstrates that it is useful to study homogeneous subgroups that do not follow average developmental patterns to identify those that might be particularly at risk of developing negative outcomes and, hence, could participate in more tailored interventions. Examining linking mechanisms and alignment of various contexts could also help to identify more factors that counteract the negative effects of parent and peer prejudice. Research on attachment with parents and teachers (Miklikowska & Hurme, 2011; Miklikowska, Thijs, & Hjerm, 2019) and adolescent own characteristics such as empathy (Miklikowska, 2017) shows a few starting points.

An integrative, ecological perspective could further clarify which contexts are more important and when. Our findings of direct and indirect (via peers) parental influences challenge the assumption that parental impact is smaller than that of peers and that this influence decreases during adolescence. Future research should further study the relative effects of contexts paying particular attention to indirect processes (e.g., selection of environments), other developmental stages, and societal changes (e.g., migration crisis).

Finally, an integrative perspective could put the interplay between intraindividual and social processes on the research agenda, further bridging the gap between social and developmental research. Through their own sociocognitive development, youth try to make sense of various inputs and determine which will be influential (Aboud, 1988; Rutland, Killen, & Abrams, 2010). Even young children are active in the process of socialization and can disregard information that is inconsistent with their intergroup attitudes (Bigler & Liben, 1993). Older adolescents are more cognitively equipped to evaluate tolerant and prejudiced perspectives and better able to integrate information into a differentiated picture of others (Miklikowska, 2018; Rutland & Killen, 2015). Studies on adolescent readiness for intergroup contact (Cameron & Turner, 2016) and interplay between contact and youth personality (Vezzali, Turner, Capozza, & Trifiletti, 2017) are good examples of combining individual and contextual conditions. A broader perspective could also incorporate macro-conditions, such as immigration levels and indicators of societal norms. While recent studies show that local and regional conditions can help explain differences in how youth attitudes change over time (Weber, 2018), we need integrative research to understand how such conditions are translated into prejudice. Research on neighborhood effects triggering more proximal processes (e.g., parental perceptions) that influence child development is a good example of incorporating macro-conditions and explaining how their effects reach an individual child (Roosa et al., 2003).

Taking a more integrative perspective poses some challenges. Capturing macro- and proximal processes requires data from various sources and sufficient variation in macro-indicators, which is costly and difficult to anticipate. In addition, the mesosystem concept needs to be translated into measurement strategies that capture actual inter-context experiences. The mesosystem is more than a statistical interaction between characteristics of individual microsystems (i.e., a proxy strategy) and researchers need to design new measures that capture the mechanisms that link various contexts (e.g., cross-context communication and knowledge).

Still, the gains of a broader, unifying framework will outweigh the challenges. Already today, the small but promising literature on the interplay between contexts, including our own research showing the interrelated effects of parents, peers, and school, makes an important contribution to the field. It shows that theory needs to incorporate cross-context experiences in order to explain how prejudice develops. It also shows that we need multi-layer interventions targeting multiple levels of the social ecology. Given the interplay of social contexts, working with a single context (e.g., intergroup contact or school norms) may not reduce prejudice in a substantial and enduring way.

Funding

This research was supported by grants from the Swedish Research Council (dnr 2016-04165), the Swedish Foundation for Humanities and Social Sciences (dnr P16-0446:1), and the Swedish Research Council for Health, Working Life and Welfare (dnr 2016-07177). It was made possible by access to the data from the Political Socialization Program, a longitudinal research program at YeS (Youth & Society) at Örebro University, Sweden. Responsible for the planning, implementation, and financing of the collection of data were professors Erik Amnå, Mats Ekström, Margaret Kerr, and Håkan Stattin. The data collection was supported by grants from Riksbankens Jubileumsfond.

References

Aboud, F. E. (1988). *Children and prejudice*. New York: Blackwell.
Aboud, F. E., & Doyle, A. B. (1996). Parental and peer influences on children's racial attitudes. *International Journal of Intercultural Relations*, 20, 371–383. doi:10.1016/0147-1767(96)00024-7

Allport, G. W. (1954). *The nature of prejudice.* Cambridge, MA: Addison-Wesley.
Bagci, S. C., Kumashiro, M., Smith, P. K., Blumberg, H., & Rutland, A. (2014). Cross-ethnic friendships: Are they really rare? Evidence from secondary schools around London. *International Journal of Intercultural Relations, 41,* 125–137. doi:10.1111/bjdp.12028
Beelmann, A., & Heinemann, K. S. (2014). Preventing prejudice and improving intergroup attitudes: A meta-analysis of child and adolescent training programs. *Journal of Applied Developmental Psychology, 35,* 10–24. doi:10.1016/j.appdev.2013.11.002
Berndt, T. J. (1979). Developmental changes in conformity to peers and parents. *Developmental Psychology, 15,* 608–616. doi:10.1037/0012-1649.15.6.608
Bigler, R.S., Liben, L.S. (1993) A Cognitive-Developmental Approach to Racial Stereotyping and Reconstructive Memory in Euro-American Children. *Child Development, 64,* 1507–1518. doi:10.1111/j.1467-8624.1993.tb02967.x
Bigler, R. S., & Liben, L. S. (2006). Developmental intergroup theory: Explaining and reducing children's social stereotyping and prejudice. *Current Directions in Psychological Science, 16,* 162–166. doi:10.1111/j.1467-8721.2007.00496.x
Bigler, R. S., & Liben, L. S. (2007). Developmental intergroup theory: Explaining and reducing children's social stereotyping and prejudice. *Current Directions in Psychological Science, 16,* 162–166. doi:10.1111/j.1467-8721.2007.00496.x
Blalock, H. M. (1967). *Toward a theory of minority-group relations.* New York: Wiley.
Blanchard, F. A., Crandall, C. S., Brigham, J. C., & Vaugn, L. A. (1994). Condemning and condoning racism: A social context approach to interracial settings. *Journal of Applied Psychology, 79,* 993–997.
Brenick, A., Titzmann, P. F., Michel, A., & Silbereisen, R. K. (2012). Ethnic German immigrant adolescents' perceived discrimination: Individual and school-level associations. *European Psychologist, 17,* 105–119. doi:10.1027/1016-9040/a000118
Bretherton, I., Golby, B., & Cho, E. (1997). Attachment and the transmission of values. In J. Grusec & L. Kuczynski (Eds.), *Parenting and children's internalization of values* (pp. 103–134). New York: Wiley.
Bronfenbrenner, U. (1979). *The ecology of human development: Experiments by nature and design.* Cambridge, MA: Harvard University Press.
Cameron, L., & Turner, R. (2016). Confidence in contact: A new perspective on promoting cross-group friendship among children and *adolescents. Social Issues and Policy Review, 10,* 212–246. doi:10.1111/sipr.12023
Carlson, C. I., Wilson, K. D., & Hargrave, J. L. (2003). The effect of school racial composition on Hispanic intergroup relations. *Journal of Social and Personal Relationships, 20,* 203–220. doi:10.1177/02654075030202005
Colby, S. L., & Ortman, J. M. (2015). *Projections of the size and composition of the U.S. population 2014 to 2016. Current population reports, P25-1143.* Washington, DC: U.S. Census Bureau.
Coenders, M., & Scheepers, P. (1998). Support for ethnic discrimination in the Netherlands 1979–1993: Effects of period, cohort, and individual characteristics. *European Sociological Review, 14,* 405–422. doi:10.1093/oxfordjournals.esr.a01824
Coleman, D. (2010). Projections of the ethnic minority populations of the United Kindom 2006-2056. *Population and Development Review, 36,* 441–486. doi:10.1111/j.1728-4457.2010.00342.x

Degner, J., & Dalege, J. (2013). The apple does not fall far from the tree, or does it? A meta- analysis of parent-child similarity in intergroup attitudes. *Psychological Bulletin*, *139*, 1270–1304. doi:10.1037/a0031436

Dhont, K., & Van Hiel, A. (2012). Intergroup contact buffers against the intergenerational transmission of authoritarianism and racial prejudice. *Journal of Research in Personality*, *46*, 231–234. doi:10.1016/j.jrp.2011.12.008

Edmonds, C., & Killen, M. (2009). Do adolescents' perceptions of parental racial attitudes relate to their intergroup contact and cross-race relationships? *Group Processes and Intergroup Relations*, *12*, 5–21. doi:10.1177/1368430208098773

Eurostat. (2016). Migration and migrant population statistics. Retrieved from http://ec.europa.eu/eurostat/statistics-explained/index.php/Migration_and_migrant_population_statistics

Eurostat. (2018). Retrieved from http://ec.europa.eu/eurostat/statistics-explained/index.php?title=Unemployment_statistics#Youth_unemployment

Feddes, A. R., Noack, P., & Rutland, A. (2009). Direct and extended friendship effects on minority and majority children's interethnic attitudes: A longitudinal study. *Child Development*, *80*, 377–390. doi:10.1111/j.1467-8624.2009.01266.x

Flanagan, C. A., & Tucker, C. J. (1999). Adolescents' explanations for political issues: Concordance with their views of self and society. *Developmental Psychology*, *35*, 1198–1209. doi:10.1037/0012-1649.35.5.1198

Ford, R. (2008). Is racial prejudice declining in Britain? *The British Journal of Sociology*, *59*, 609–636. doi:10.1111/j.1468-4446.2008.00212.x

Gniewosz, B., Noack, P., Wentura, D., & Funke, F. (2008). Adolescents' attitudes towards foreigners: Associations with perceptions of significant others' attitudes depending on sex and age. *Diskurs Kindheits-und Jugendforschung*, *3*, 321–337.

Grusec, J. E. (2011). Socialization processes in the family: Social and emotional development. *Annual Review of Psychology*, *62*, 243–269. doi:10.1146/annurev.psych.121208.131650

Hatemi, P. K., Funk, C. L., Medlad, S. E., Maes, H. M., Silberg, J. L., Martin, N. G., & Eaves, L. J. (2009).Genetic and environmental transmission of political attitudes over a life time. *The Journal of Politics*, *3*, 1141–1156. doi:10.1017/S0022381609090938

Hewstone, M. (2015). Consequences of diversity for social cohesion and prejudice: The missing dimension of intergroup contact. *Journal of Social Issues*, *71*, 417–438. doi:10.1111/josi.12120

Hjerm, M., Eger, M., & Danell, R. (2018). Peer attitudes and the development of prejudice in adolescence. *Socius*, *4*, 1–11. doi:10.1177/2378023118763187

Jager, J., Yuen, C. X., Putnick, D. L., Hendricks, C., & Bornstein, M. H. (2015). Adolescent-peer relationships, separation and detachment from parents, and internalizing and externalizing behaviors: Linkages and interactions. *The Journal of Early Adolescence*, *35*, 511–537. doi:10.1177/0272431614537116

Janmaat, J. G., & Keating, A. (2017). Are today's youth more tolerant? Trends in tolerance among young people in Britain. *Ethnicities*, 1–22. doi:10.1177/1468796817723682

Jennings, M. K., Stoker, L., & Bowers, J. (2009). Politics across generations: Family transmission reexamined. *The Journal of Politics*, *71*, 782–799. doi:10.1017/S0022381609090719

Johnson, K., & Lichter, D. T. (2010). Growing diversity among America's children and youth: Spatial and temporal dimensions. *Population and Development Review*, *36*, 151–176. doi:10.1111/j.1728-4457.2010.00322.x

Jugert, P., Eckstein, K., Beelmann, A., & Noack, P. (2016). Parents' influence on the development of their children's ethnic intergroup attitudes: A longitudinal analysis from middle childhood to early adolescence. *European Journal of Developmental Psychology*, *13*, 213–230. doi:10.1080/17405629.2015.1084923

Juvonen, J., Kogachi, K., & Graham, S. (2017). When and how do students benefit from ethnic diversity in middle school? *Child Development*. doi:10.1111/cdev.12834

Kiesner, J., Maas, A., Cadinu, M., & Vellese, I. (2003). Risk factors for ethnic prejudice during early adolescence. *Social Development*, *12*, 288–308. doi:10.1111/1467-9507.00234

Killen, M., Lee-Kim, J., McGlothlin, H., Stangor, C., & Helwig, C. (2002). How children and adolescents evaluate gender and racial exclusion. *Monographs of the Society for Research in Child Development*, *67*, 1–119. doi:10.1111/1540-5834.00218

Leszczensky, L., Flache, A., Stark, T. H., & Munniksma, A. (2018). The relation between ethnic classroom composition and adolescents' ethnic pride. *Group Processes & Intergroup Relations*, *21*, 997–1013. doi:10.1177/1368430217691363

McDowell, D. J., & Parke, R. D. (2009). Parental correlates of children's peer relations: An empirical test of a tripartite model. *Developmental Psychology*, *45*, 224–235. doi:10.1037/a0014305

McGlothlin, H., & Killen, M. (2010). How social experience is related to children's intergroup attitudes. *European Journal of Social Psychology*, *40*, 625–634. doi:10.1002/ejsp.733

McGuire, L., Rutland, A., & Nesdale, D. (2015). Peer group norms and accountability moderate the effect of school norms on children's intergroup attitudes. *Child Development*, *86*, 1290–1297. doi:10.1111/cdev.12388

Meeusen, C., & Dhont, K. (2015). Parent-child similarity in common and specific components of prejudice: The role of ideological attitudes and political discussion. *European Journal of Personality*, *29*, 585–598. doi:10.1002/per.2011

Miklikowska, M. (2016). Like parent, like child? Development of prejudice and tolerance in adolescence. *British Journal of Psychology*, *107*, 95–116. doi:10.1111/bjop.12124

Miklikowska, M. (2017). Development of anti-immigrant attitudes in adolescence: The role of parents, peers, intergroup friendships, and empathy. *British Journal of Psychology*, *108*, 626–648. doi:10.1111/bjop.12236

Miklikowska, M. (2018). Empathy trumps prejudice: The longitudinal relation between empathy and anti-immigrant attitudes in adolescence. *Developmental Psychology*, *54*, 703–717. doi:10.1037/dev0000474

Miklikowska, M., Bohman, A., & Titzmann, P. (2019). Driven by context? The interrelated effects of parents, peers, and classrooms on development of anti-immigrant attitudes in adolescence. *Developmental Psychology*. doi:10.1037/dev0000809

Miklikowska, M., & Hurme, H. (2011). Democracy begins at home: Democratic parenting and adolescents' support for democratic values. *European Journal of Developmental Psychology*, *8*, 541–557. doi:10.1080/17405629.2011.576856

Miklikowska, M., Thijs, J., & Hjerm, M. (2019). The impact of perceived teacher support on anti-immigrant attitudes from early to late adolescence. *Journal of Youth and Adolescence.* doi:10.1007/s10964-019-00990-8

Miller, S. D., & Sears, D. O. (1986). Stability and change in social tolerance: A test of the persistence hypothesis. *American Journal of Political Science, 30,* 214–236. Retrieved from www.jstor.org/stable/2111302

Mitchell, J. (2018). Prejudice in the classroom: A longitudinal analysis of anti-immigrant attitudes. *Ethnic & Racial Studies.* doi:10.1080/01419870.2018.1493209

Moody, J. (2001). Race, school integration, and friendship segregation in America. *American Journal of Sociology, 107,* 679–716.

Munniksma, A., Flache, A., Verkuyten, M., & Veenstra, R. (2012). Parental acceptance of children's intimate ethnic out-group relations: The role of culture, status, and family reputation. *International Journal of Intercultural Relations, 36,* 575–585. doi:10.1016/j.ijintrel.2011.12.012

Nesdale, D. (2004). Social identity processes and children's ethnic prejudice. In M. Bennett & F. Sani (Eds.), *The development of the social self* (pp. 219–246). East Sussex: Psychology Press.

Nesdale, D., & Lawson, M. J. (2011). Social groups and children's intergroup attitudes: Can school norms moderate the effects of social group norms? *Child Development, 82,* 1594–1606. doi:10.1111/j.1467-8624.2011.01637.x

Nesdale, D., Maass, A., Durkin, K., & Griffiths, J. (2005). Group norms, threat, and children's racial prejudice. *Child Development, 76,* 652–663. doi:10.1111/j.1467-8624.2005.00869.x

Nipedal, C., Nesdale, D., & Killen, M. (2010). Social group norms, school norms, and children's aggressive intentions. *Aggressive Behavior, 36,* 195–204. doi:10.1002/ab.20342

O'Bryan, M., Fishbein, H. D., & Ritchey, P. N. (2004). Intergenerational transmission of prejudice, sex role stereotyping, and intolerance. *Adolescence, 39,* 407–426.

OECD/European Union. (2015). *Indicators of immigrant integration 2015: Settling in.* Paris: OECD Publishing. doi:10.1787/9789264234024-en

Paluck, E. L. (2011). Peer pressure against prejudice: A high school field experiment examining social network change. *Journal of Experimental Social Psychology, 47,* 350–358. doi:10.1016/j.jesp.2010.11.017

Patterson, M. M., & Bigler, R. S. (2006). Preschool children's attention to environmental messages about groups: Social categorization and the origins of intergroup bias. *Child Development, 77,* 847–860. doi:10.1111/j.1467-8624.2006.00906.x

Pettigrew, T. F. (1998). Intergroup contact theory. *Annual Review of Psychology, 49,* 65–85.

Quillian, L. (1996). Group threat and regional change in attitudes toward African-Americans. *American Journal of Sociology, 102,* 816–860. doi:10.1086/230998

Raabe, T., & Beelmann, A. (2011). Development of ethnic, racial, and national prejudice in childhood and adolescence: A multinational meta-analysis of age differences. *Child Development, 82,* 1715–1737. doi:10.1111/j.1467-8624.2011.01668.x

Reich, S. M., & Vandell, D. L. (2011). The interplay between parents and peers as socializing influences in children's development. In P. K. Smith & C. H. Hart (Eds.), *The Wiley-Blackwell handbook of childhood social development* (pp. 263–280). Blackwell Publishing Ltd. https://assets.thalia.media/images-adb/59/f2/59f244cd-c9fb-40ed-b45a-4953d8512213.pdf.

Rekker, R., Keijsers, L., Branje, S., & Meeus, W. (2015). Political attitudes in adolescence and emerging adulthood: Developmental changes in mean level, polarization, rank-order stability, and correlates. *Journal of Adolescence, 41*, 136–147. doi:10.1016/j.adolescence.2015.03.011

Rivas-Drake, D., Saleem, M., Schaefer, D. R., Medina, M., & Jagers, R. (2018). Intergroup contact attitudes across peer networks in school: Selection, influence, and implications for cross-group friendships. *Child Development*. doi:10.1111/cdev.13061

Roosa, M. W., Jones, S., Tein, J.-Y., & Cree, W. (2003). Prevention science and neighborhood influences on low-income children's development. *American Journal of Community Psychology, 31*, 55–72. doi:10.1023/A:1023070519597

Rutland, A., Cameron, L., Milne, A., & McGeorge, P. (2005). Social norms and self-presentation: Children's implicit and explicit intergroup attitudes. *Child Development, 76*, 451–466. doi:10.1111/j.1467-8624.2005.00856.x

Rutland, A., & Killen, M. (2015). A developmental science approach to reducing prejudice and social exclusion: Intergroup processes, social-cognitive development, and moral reasoning. *Social Issues and Policy Review, 9*, 121–154. doi:10.1111/sipr.12012

Rutland, A., Killen, M., & Abrams, D. (2010). A new social-cognitive developmental perspective on prejudice: The interplay between morality and group identity. *Perspectives on Psychological Science, 5*, 279–291. doi:10.1177/1745691610369468

Scheepers, P., Gijsberts, M., & Coenders, M. (2002). Ethnic exclusionism in European countries. Public opposition to civil rights for legal migrants as a response to perceived ethnic threat. *European Sociological Review, 18*, 17–34. doi:10.1093/esr/18.1.17

Sinclair, S., Dunn, E., & Lowery, B. S. (2005). The relationship between parental racial attitudes and children's implicit prejudice. *Journal of Experimental Social Psychology, 41*, 283–289. doi:10.1016/j.jesp.2004.06.003

Smith, S., Maas, I., & Van Tubergen, F. (2014). Parental influence on friendships between native and immigrant adolescents. *Journal of Research on Adolescence, 25*, 580–591. doi:10.1111/jora.12149

Steinberg, L. (2001). We know some things: Parent–Adolescent relationships in retrospect and prospect. *Journal of Research on Adolescence, 11*, 1–19. doi:10.1111/1532-7795.00001

Tajfel, H., & Turner, J. C. (1986). The social identity theory of intergroup behavior. *Psychology of Intergroup Relations, 5*, 7–24.

Tedin, K. L. (1980). Assessing peer and parent influence on adolescent political attitudes. *American Journal of Political Science, 24*, 136–154. Retrieved from www.jstor.org/stable/2110929

Thijs, J., Gharaei, N., & de Vroome, T. (2016). "Why should I?" Adolescents' motivations to regulate prejudice in relation to their norm perceptions and ethnic attitudes. *International Journal of Intercultural Relations, 53*, 83–94. doi:10.1016/j.ijintrel.2016.05.006

Thijs, J., & Verkuyten, M. (2014). School ethnic diversity and students' interethnic relations. *British Journal of Educational Psychology, 84*, 1–21. doi:10.1111/bjep.12032

Titzmann, P. F., Brenick, A., & Silbereisen, R. K. (2015). Friendships fighting prejudice: A longitudinal perspective on adolescents' cross-group friendships with immigrants. *Journal of Youth and Adolescence, 44*, 1318–1331. doi:10.1007/s10964-015-0256-6

Tropp, L. R., O'Brien, T. C., Gutierrez, R. G., Valdenegro, D., Migacheva, K., Tezanos-Pinto, P., … Cayul, O. (2016). How school norms, peer norms, and discrimination predict interethnic experiences among ethnic minority and majority youth. *Child Development, 87*, 1436–1451. doi:10.1111/cdev.12608

Van Zalk, M. H., & Kerr, M. (2014). Developmental trajectories of prejudice and tolerance toward immigrants from early to late adolescence. *Journal of Youth and Adolescence, 43*, 1658–1671. doi:10.1007/s10964-014-0164-1

Van Zalk, M. H., Kerr, M., Van Zalk, N., & Stattin, H. (2013). Xenophobia and tolerance toward immigrants in adolescence: Cross-influence processes within friendships. *Journal of Abnormal Child Psychology, 41*, 627–639. doi:10.1007/s10802-012-9694-8

Vedder, P., Berry, J., Sabatier, C., & Sam, D. (2009). The intergenerational transmission of values in national and immigrant families: The role of zeitgeist. *Journal of Youth and Adolescence, 38*, 642–653. doi:10.1007/s10964-008-9375-7

Vezzali, L., Turner, R., Capozza, D., & Trifiletti, E. (2017). Does intergroup contact affect personality? A longitudinal study on the bidirectional relationship between intergroup contact and personality traits. *European Journal of Social Psychology, 48*, 159–173. doi:10.1002/ejsp.2313

Vollerberg, W. A. M., Iedema, J., & Raaijmakers, Q. A. W. (2001). Intergenerational transmission and the formation of cultural orientations in adolescence and young adulthood. *Journal of Marriage and Family, 63*, 1185–1198. doi:10.1111/j.1741-3737.2001.01185.x

Weber, H. (2018). Attitudes towards minorities in times of high immigration: A panel study among young adults in Germany. *European Sociological Review*. doi:10.1093/esr/jcy050

Westholm, A. (1999). The perceptual pathway: Tracing the mechanism of political value transfer across generations. *Political Psychology, 20*, 525–552. doi:10.1111/0162-895X.00155

Windzio, M. (2012). Integration of immigrant children into inter-ethnic friendship networks: The role of "intergenerational openness". *Sociology, 46*, 258–271. doi:10.1177/0038038511419182

Chapter 14

Understanding the causes and consequences of segregation in youth's friendship networks

Opportunities and challenges for research

Lars Leszczensky and Tobias Stark

How does friendship segregation arise? Preferences, opportunities, and relational mechanisms

Ethnic, racial, and religious segregation are among the most persistent characteristics of youth's friendship networks in modern societies (Leszczensky & Pink, 2015, 2017; Moody, 2001; Quillian & Campbell, 2003; S. Smith, Maas, & van Tubergen, 2014).[1] A natural starting point for understanding the emergence of segregation are individual *preferences*, that is, people's desire to associate with certain people. As social animals, nearly all people have a baseline preference to have some friends instead of no friends at all (Blau, 1977). This tendency especially applies to adolescents, because peers are particularly important at this life stage (Giordano, 2003; Steinberg & Morris, 2001). But what kind of friends do they seek? The most important preference is *homophily*, the preference to associate with people who are similar to oneself (Lewis, 2015; McFarland, Moody, Diehl, Smith, & Thomas, 2014). Similar others tend to understand each other better, can often communicate more easily, and find each other more likeable and predictable (Byrne, 1971). Since race and ethnicity are among the most important determinants of friendship decisions (McPherson, Smith-Lovin, & Cook, 2001), it is not surprising that youth in Western societies report stronger preferences for same-ethnic than for inter-ethnic friends (Phinney, Ferguson, & Tate, 1997; Verkuyten & Kinket, 2000).

The decision to form a friendship, however, is not only affected by one's own preferences but also by preferences of others. An adolescent might desire to befriend a particular classmate, but whether or not this friendship materializes depends on the willingness of the other classmate as well. Surprisingly, this point has been largely neglected in research on intergroup friendships that mainly focused on mutual friendship nominations and overlooked differences in individual preferences. Considering preferences of members of both involved parties does not only complicate matters for friendship-seeking youth, it also illustrates the need for a network perspective when studying friendship formation. For instance, ethnic majority group members may be reluctant to befriend minority group members, but minority groups may likewise prefer friends of their own ethnic group (Smith et al., 2016; Vermeij, van Duijn, & Baerveldt, 2009). In a similar vein, understanding religious friendship segregation requires us to consider the perspectives of members of different religious groups (Leszczensky & Pink, 2017). By focusing on one specific group, research that neglects the network typically fails to map the interplay of preferences of different social groups, which may lead to wrong conclusions.

Besides the preferences of all involved parties, the development of intergroup friendships and thus the emergence of friendship segregation crucially depends on the *opportunities* to meet in- and outgroup members. The composition of important contexts such as schools, neighborhoods, or clubs determines how frequently youth encounter peers of their own or other groups and, accordingly, their chances to befriend them. Thus, relative group size in a given context is one of the most basic features of the opportunity structure (Blau, 1977; Feld, 1982). If there is no Chinese kid in a school, even a kid with strong preferences for Chinese friends will not be able to satisfy this preference. Such opportunity effects contribute to friendship segregation because in most countries ethnic groups are not randomly distributed across schools; instead, ethnic minority groups often are overrepresented in lower educational tracks, and there also is ethnic clustering because of residential segregation (Kruse, Smith, van Tubergen, & Maas, 2016; Mouw & Entwisle, 2006). Also, similar people tend to spend time in similar social contexts (Lomi & Stadtfeld, 2014). For instance, Vermeij and colleagues (2009) found a preference for inter-ethnic friendships (and thus less ethnic segregation) only among Dutch majority group students who lived in more ethnically diverse neighborhoods where they could meet minority friends but not among those living in less diverse neighborhoods (note that Munniksma and colleagues (2017) found a stronger preference for ingroup friends in more ethnically diverse neighborhoods). Inferring preferences without considering the availability of in- and outgroup members as potential friends in a given social context thus may lead to misleading conclusions.

Finally, the opportunity to form friendships is also affected by processes that directly point to social network analysis. *Relational mechanisms* explain how existing relationships affect the creation of new ones (Rivera, Soderstrom, & Uzzi, 2010; Wimmer & Lewis, 2010). Friends of friends tend to become friends as well, and this "triadic closure" can be traced back to both opportunities and preferences (Schaefer, Light, Fabes, Hanish, & Martin, 2010; Stark, 2015). On the one hand, individuals with mutual friends tend to encounter each other, thus having an increased opportunity to spend time together. On the other hand, individuals prefer balanced relations (J. A. Davies, 1963; Heider, 1946), thus desiring good relations with their friends' friends. Valuing balance and symmetry in social relations also makes people more likely to reciprocate friendship; that is, they are likely to consider those as friends who initiate a friendly relationship. Both triadic closure and reciprocity may increase friendship segregation even if individuals hold only weak preferences for ingroup friends because many of these additional friendships will be formed within their own group (Stark, 2015; Wimmer & Lewis, 2010). People can also can differ in their tendency to initiate friendships and their likelihood of being chosen as friends, and group differences in this sociability can also contribute to segregation (Goodreau, Kitts, & Morris, 2009).

Methodological advantages of social network analysis

Measurement

In contrast to traditional self-reported information on the share of friends of different groups, whole network data provide information about relationships between *all* individuals in a given context.[2] Thus, these data do not only identify who is connected to whom but also who is not connected with each other (Marsden, 2011). The latter information is necessary for inferring preferences from friendship connections, because doing so requires us not only to know the number of in- and outgroup friends but also how many in- and outgroup members are actually available. Moreover, relational mechanisms such as reciprocity and triadic closure can only be taken into account if the structure of the whole network is known.

Social network data also provide more accurate information on segregation than self-reports (Kalter, 2015). T. W. Smith (2002) showed experimentally that asking people directly how many inter-racial friendships they have leads to much higher reports of such friendships compared to when friends have to be identified by name. He suspected that direct questions lead to an overreporting of inter-racial friendships, perhaps due to social norms about the desirability of such relationships. T. W. Smith (2002) thus concluded that social network data should be preferred. In whole network studies, adolescents only need to indicate who their friends are; and from these friends' self-reports researchers can infer whether these are same-ethnic or inter-ethnic friendships of their ethnicity. This information is more accurate than asking how many friends of other ethnic groups one has because all friends report their own ethnicity (Kalter, 2015). This advantage is even more relevant when characteristics of friends are considered that cannot easily be observed, such as attitudes or identity (Leszczensky, Stark, Flache, & Munniksma, 2016). Friends' reports about who their friends are can even be used to identify indirect relationships with people from other ethnic groups (Munniksma et al., 2013; Wölfer et al., 2017; Wölfer, Schmid, Hewstone, & van Zalk, 2016).

Disentangling preferences, opportunities, and relational mechanisms

Researchers who want to analyze friendship networks are well advised not to use traditional statistical methods, such as regression analysis or structural equation modeling, because whole network data violate the assumption of independent observations inherent to these models. As illustrated above, friendship choices are not made in a vacuum but depend, for instance, on the choices potential friends have made. Ignoring such dependencies can result in overestimation of central effects, such as homophily (Goodreau et al., 2009; Wimmer & Lewis, 2010).

Sophisticated methods of social network analysis acknowledge the complex interdependencies between network ties by considering and modeling the relationships of all individuals in a given context. This feature is inherent both to cross-sectional models such as exponential random graph models (ERGM, Lusher, Koskinen, & Robins, 2013; Robins, Pattison, Kalish, & Lusher, 2007) and to longitudinal models such as the stochastic actor-oriented model (SAOM, Snijders, van de Bunt, & Steglich, 2010). Both ERGM and SAOM also have the key advantage of being able to disentangle preferences, opportunities, and relational mechanisms (Kalter, 2015; Lewis, 2015). First, by considering the number of available members from different groups in a given context, ERGM and SAOM provide estimates of homophily that are not biased by relative group size. That is, estimates obtained from these models are conditional on opportunity structure; for example, ERGM and SAOM acknowledge that a student with no same-ethnic classmates cannot make ethnically homophilous friendship choices.

Second, by modeling friendship choices of members from different groups, researchers can consider the perspective of different groups as well as the interplay of these perspectives. Thus, researchers can not only study differential preferences for majority and minority group members but also how these preferences interact to form inter-ethnic friendships (see next section). Third, ERGM and SAOM allow us to model relational mechanisms such as reciprocity and triadic closure. These models can thus account for the fact that not all same-ethnic friendships are formed due to a preference for such friendships but also because adolescents reciprocate friendship nominations and become friends with their friends' friends. Finally, SAOM have the additional benefit of allowing us to disentangle selection and influence mechanisms that both can be the cause of the so-called "network autocorrelation," that is the phenomenon that adolescents who are socially related are similar on behavioral (e.g., smoking) or attitudinal (e.g., prejudice) dimensions. SAOM allow us to establish whether observed similarity in friends' attitudes or behavior stems from youth preferring to befriend peers who are similar to themselves or from friends' influencing each other (or both of these processes). This is achieved by modeling the co-evolution of networks and behavior and their reciprocal relationship. Steglich, Snijders, and Pearson (2010) explain the statistical model; various exemplary applications in research on adolescents are discussed in a special issue edited by Veenstra, Dijkstra, Steglich, and Van Zalk (2013).

Key findings on the causes of friendship segregation

There is strong evidence that segregation in friendship networks is at least in part driven by preferences for ingroup friends: even in mixed schools, with vast opportunities to engage in intergroup friendship, ingroup friendships are formed more often than would be expected by chance (Moody, 2001; Quillian & Campbell, 2003). These findings have been backed by studies using state-of-the-art network analyses mentioned in the previous section that adequately accounted for relative group size and relational mechanisms (Leszczensky & Pink, 2015; S. Smith et al., 2014; Vermeij et al., 2009).

Still, even if they are able to account for the opportunity structure and relational mechanisms with the help of social network analysis (SNA), researchers should not hastily conclude that there are strong ingroup preferences. For instance, it has been shown that racial homophily largely is a by-product of more fine-grained ethnic homophily; for example, "Asian" homophily is largely spurious, arising from, for instance, Chinese or Japanese youth befriending peers of the same ethnicity but not of other Asian ethnicities (Wimmer & Lewis, 2010). And such ethnic homophily might in turn be overestimated if alternative mechanisms of friendship formation are not properly accounted for. For instance, if ethnicity is correlated with leisure time behavior or certain opinions, the overrepresentation of same-ethnic friendships might actually be due to homophily (i.e., personal preferences) on this kind of behavior rather than due to ethnic homophily (Stark & Flache, 2012). Such correlations are likely because people who are similar on one dimension tend to be similar on other dimensions as well (Block & Grund, 2014).

Social network studies also stress the importance of considering the perspective of different groups when assessing homophily. For instance, Blacks in the U.S. seem to have stronger ingroup preferences than Whites or Asians (Goodreau et al., 2009; Wimmer & Lewis, 2010); likewise, Turkish and Moroccan minority students in Western Europe appear to have stronger preferences for same-ethnic friends than other ethnic minorities have (S. Smith, 2018). Consistent with these patterns, majority group members seem to have lower ingroup preferences than minority group members (Vermeij et al., 2009).

Further stressing the importance of considering all groups, preference hierarchies also differ between groups. For example, the study by Leszczensky and colleagues (2016) indicates that native youth prefer to befriend ethnic minority classmates with strong rather than weak identification with the ethnic majority group. Jugert and colleagues (Jugert, Leszczensky, & Pink, 2018) found that native youth even appear to be indifferent between fellow native peers and peers with a migration background who identify with the native majority group or have a dual identification. However, they are less likely to befriend peers with a migration background who exclusively identify with an ethnic minority group.

In addition to a preference for ingroup friends, youth can also have a preference against having intergroup friendships. Longitudinal studies found that youth with ethnic prejudice avoid forming friendships or friendly relationships with peers from other ethnic groups (Binder et al., 2009; Stark, Flache, & Veenstra, 2013). A social network studied showed that this is partly due to a relational mechanism: prejudiced youth prefer having friends who do not have outgroup friends. Because people become friends with their friends' friends, these youth are then more likely to form even more ingroup friendships than their less prejudiced peers (Stark, 2015).

There is also clear evidence of how the opportunity structure affects preferences. Controlling for homophily, social network studies found that not only the composition of school classes matters but also the composition of other meeting points, such as the neighborhood (Kruse et al., 2016; Mouw & Entwisle, 2006; Munniksma et al., 2017; Vermeij et al., 2009) or intra-school tracking and extra-curricular activities (Moody, 2001; Schaefer, Simpkins, & Ettekal, 2018). A key finding of network studies in schools is that homophily seems to peak in highly diverse contexts (Moody, 2001). However, a recent study of classrooms in four European countries suggests that the effects of ethnic composition differ for majority (native) and minority (immigrant-origin) group members. Mirroring the findings of Moody (2001), ethnic minority group youth's preference for same-ethnic friends was strongest in ethnically mixed classrooms and less pronounced in classrooms with both low and high ethnic diversity (Smith, McFarland, Van Tubergen & Maas, 2016). For native majority youth, by contrast, the relation between ethnic composition and ethnic homophily is less pronounced. However, native youth's preference for same-ethnic friends was stronger in classrooms in which ethnic minority youth formed dense friendship networks. Ethnic school composition may also affect the extent to which identification-based friendship preferences of ethnic majority and minority group members can be translated into actual friendship choices. For example, ethnic minority youth who do not identify with the majority group may prefer minority to majority group friends. However, they cannot avoid befriending native majority group members if they attend a school with not enough ethnic minority schoolmates to choose from and still want to have some friends (Leszczensky, 2018). Finally, homophily seems to be stronger for relationships that require additional effort such as, for instance, friendships between students who attend different classrooms within the same school (Leszczensky & Pink, 2015) or friendships out of school that need the approval of third parties such as parents (Windzio & Bicer, 2013).

Finally, social network studies have provided evidence that relational mechanisms contribute significantly to segregation. For example, Wimmer and Lewis (2010) showed that the extent of racial homophily is considerably exaggerated if relational mechanisms such as triadic closure are not accounted for. This is because triadic closure intensifies even weak preferences for ingroup friends, which can considerably amplify segregation (Stark, 2015). Likewise, the tendency to form or attract friendships can vary between ethnic groups. For instance, mixed-race college students in the U.S. (Wimmer & Lewis, 2010) and ethnic minority high school students in Germany tend to form more friendships than their peers from the majority group (Stark, Leszczensky, & Pink, 2017).

Key findings on the consequences of friendship segregation

Ethnic segregation means there are few inter-ethnic friendships. This is foremost detrimental to intergroup attitudes as more than 60 years of research on intergroup contact have provided clear evidence that such friendships reduce prejudice (K. Davies, Tropp, Aron, Pettigrew, & Wright, 2011; Pettigrew & Tropp, 2006). A recent network study showed that this is particularly problematic if there is not only a lack of inter-ethnic friendships but also negative relationships between youth of different ethnic groups (Wölfer et al., 2017).

However, this does not mean that existing segregation will prevent future integration. Social network research found that positive attitudes toward intergroup contact promote the creation of intergroup ties and, importantly, adolescents transmit these attitudes to their friends, which can promote intergroup friendships even among those who initially avoid the outgroup (Rivas-Drake, Saleem, Schaefer, Medina, & Jagers, 2018).

Such processes of *social influence* among friends play important roles for many other life domains of youth, ranging from substance abuse to social identification (Brechwald & Prinstein, 2011; Veenstra et al., 2013). Since similar people tend to associate, it is essential to control for selection effects in order to empirically identify social influence mechanisms. As mentioned earlier, this can be achieved by modeling the co-evolution of friendship networks and individual characteristics using SAOM (Steglich et al., 2010). Studies using such models found that adolescents not only befriend peers with similar attitudes toward other ethnic outgroups but are also influenced by their friends' attitudes (Stark, 2015; Van Zalk, Kerr, Van Zalk, & Stattin, 2013).

This feature of SAOM also has made it possible to more rigorously study the long-held argument that friends affect the development of adolescents' ethnic identity. Controlling for friendship selection, research in the United States has shown that ethnic-racial identity development of youth is indeed influenced by friends' ethnic-racial identity (Santos, Kornienko, & Rivas-Drake, 2017). On the other hand, research in European countries has shown that the strength of ethnic minority youth's host country identification is not affected by the level of their friends' identification (Leszczensky, 2018; Leszczensky et al., 2016). Friends can also affect the perception of ethnicity attributed to peers. Using SAOM, Boda (2018) recently showed that friends tend to adopt their friends' judgment of ethnicity of classmates, independently of these classmates' ethnic self-identification.

Besides interethnic attitudes or ethnic identity, friendship segregation can also affect outcomes that are not directly related to ethnicity. One example is adolescents' academic achievement. Longitudinal social network studies have shown that friends affect each other's academic achievement and school-related behaviors (Kretschmer, Leszczensky, & Pink, 2018; Rambaran et al., 2017). A study in Germany found the influence of academic achievement to be stronger among same-ethnic friends than among cross-ethnic friends, and that ethnic minority youth tend to not befriend high achieving peers (Stark et al., 2017). Other research suggests that they will only do so if they can find high achieving peers among their own ethnic ingroup (Flashman, 2012). Such preferences can eventually lead to structural inequality. In many Western countries, students from most minority groups perform less well in school than their majority peers. For members of such disadvantaged groups (e.g., students of Turkish origin in Germany or Latinos in the U.S.), the preference for same-ethnic friends may prevent minority students from gaining access to better performing friends who might help them succeed in school.

Opportunities and challenges for future research

As demonstrated throughout this chapter, SNA helps to facilitate theoretical and empirical innovation by providing insights into the processes underlying the development of social relationships among youth as well as how these relationships in turn shape individual outcomes. While SNA no longer is in its infancy, it is still a relatively young field. We close by pointing to new research questions, methodological challenges and related developments, and the possibility of reducing segregation via network interventions.

New research questions

Precisely because so much progress has been made in the last couple of years, new questions on the causes of segregation have emerged. Disentangling the role of preferences, opportunities, and relational mechanisms remains a key task for further research. Building on the evidence we reviewed in this chapter, researchers now face the task of digging deeper, for example by examining whether preferences or relational mechanisms vary across ethnic groups or whether their importance differs over time as friendship networks emerge and evolve (Lewis, 2015; Rivera et al., 2010). An especially important question for understanding segregation concerns the interplay of the preferences of different groups. For instance, Muslim youth are especially homophilous (Leszczensky & Pink, 2017), but more research is needed to say whether this is due to a genuinely strong ingroup preference, or whether it is rather a reaction to exclusion from the non-Muslim majority group.

Additional effort is also needed to better understand how and why different opportunity structures, both within and out of school, shape preferences. As mentioned above, ethnic friendship segregation is strongest in ethnically diverse schools (Moody, 2001). Other research found that there is more interethnic and also intra-ethnic bullying in ethnically more diverse schools (Tolsma, van Deurzen, Stark, & Veenstra, 2013) and that youth's ethnic identification is heightened in such settings (Leszczensky, Flache, Stark, & Munniksma, 2018). It remains to be studied whether these processes are a direct consequence of ethnic segregation in more diverse schools.

Relatively little research has explored the role of ethnicity in negative interactions, and existing findings are inconsistent and restricted to specific contexts. For example, a recent study found that Hungarian majority youth were more likely to dislike minority (Roma) members than fellow majority members, but minority (Roma) youth did not reciprocate such negative ties (Boda & Néray, 2015). Instead, both minority (Roma) and majority (non-Roma) youth were more likely to bully classmates they perceived to be from the minority group (Kisfalusi, Pál, & Boda, 2018). In contrast, a study in the Netherlands found that ethnicity did not affect who is bullied in a school class, but ethnic minority youth were more often the perpetrators of bullying than their majority group classmates (Tolsma et al., 2013). Moreover, research in the United States has shown that sharing negative relationships with the same network member affects the formation and stability of friendships (Rambaran, Dijkstra, Munniksma, & Cillessen, 2015). Which role ethnicity plays in these processes, however, has not been explored yet.

Methodological challenges and current developments

In spite of its numerous advantages, the study of whole social networks comes at some costs. First, researchers have to pre-define network boundaries that closely resemble the reality of the life of the target group. As youth spend a considerable amount of time in schools, schools are a natural context that might define friendship networks. But even in schools, researchers have to decide whether to focus on the classroom, the grade-level, or other units. This decision is important, as research has shown ethnic segregation to be more pronounced across classrooms than within classrooms (Leszczensky & Pink, 2015; Valente, Fujimoto, Unger, Soto, & Meeker, 2013). Second, each member of the potential network has to be identified upfront so that adolescents can easily nominate their friends in a questionnaire, and so that it is clear who were not chosen even though they were in the given context. This raises ethical questions about gathering information before the students could give their permission and about the collection of data about people who may not give permission at all (Stark, 2018). Third, even though network data provide more objective measures of segregation, for some research questions the perception of inter-ethnic friendships may be more important than the objective reality of such friendships (Zhou, Page-Gould, Aron, Moyer, & Hewstone, 2019).

Also, even when using sophisticated methods of SNA such as ERGM or SAOM, researchers need to be aware of the fact that inferring preferences from observed network patterns still relies on strong assumptions (VanderWeele & An, 2013). For example, these models assume that every member of a network has the same meeting opportunities and is perfectly informed about the relationships and characteristics of everybody else. These assumptions become unrealistic in larger networks or require additional modeling steps that take, for instance, meeting opportunities due to academic tracking in schools into account.

Reducing segregation via network intervention?

Given the persistence of ethnic friendship segregation and its negative consequences of various kinds of individual attitudes and behavior, one of the most pressing questions in ethnically diverse societies is how segregation can be reduced and how positive intergroup relations can be promoted. School-based intervention programs that promote intergroup contact can improve intergroup relations and even reduce ethnic prejudice (Lemmer & Wagner, 2015). However, many of these intervention programs target large groups such as the whole classroom (Stathi, Cameron, Hartley, & Bradford, 2014) and are accordingly complex and expensive to implement. This limits their applicability and potential impact.

SNA provides a potential solution to this problem. So-called "network interventions" either (1) try to change the network structure to reduce segregation or (2) make use of the existing structure to disseminate information or endorse positive behavior change among a large group of people (Valente, 2012). Most interventions aimed at promoting positive relationships between members of different groups are in line with the first type of network interventions, yet very few have explicitly examined the impact of the intervention on the amount of segregation in the network. Using SAOMs, DeLay and colleagues (2016) found that a social-emotional learning intervention reduced ethnic segregation in the friendship networks of participating schools.

The idea of the second type of network intervention is to involve only a few highly influential individuals in the intervention who will subsequently influence their network contacts, who will then influence their own contacts and so on (Valente, 2012). For instance, a recently implemented network intervention successfully reduced social conflict in 56 large schools (with 432 students on average) by training only 20–32 students per school in the intervention program (Paluck, Shepherd, & Aronow, 2016). Other studies have used this approach in an anti-smoking intervention (Steglich, Sinclair, Holliday, & Moore, 2012) or in an intervention aimed at reducing harassment in schools (Paluck & Shepherd, 2012).

The central challenge for the development of effective network interventions is our limited knowledge about who to select as participants for the intervention to make dissemination of the attitude or the behavior most effective. In the search for the most effective "seeds" for behavior change, Paluck and Shepherd (2012) point to "social referents" who can either be widely known adolescents or clique leaders that are more likely to be paid attention to than other peers. Other researchers expect the most popular adolescents to be most influential (Steglich et al., 2012). Little research exists that compares the influence of adolescents in certain positions that may guide future network interventions and it is very likely that who is most influential may vary across domains (Valente, 2012).

Conclusion

Social network analysis has facilitated innovative contributions to our understanding of the causes and consequences of segregation among adolescents. It has illustrated why it is important to simultaneously model the friendship preferences of majority and minority members to understand how they interact in producing segregation. Thereby, it is crucial to account for other factors that affect adolescents' social networks such as meeting opportunities, social influence among friends, and structural factors such as the tendency to become friends with one's friends' friends. The development of various advanced statistical models provides applied researchers with toolkits that allow teasing these factors apart. This relatively recent progress has led to new exciting research questions and exciting ideas for how insights from SNA may guide social interventions to reduce segregation.

Notes

1 Studies in the U.S. tend to focus on racial segregation whereas scholars in Europe tend to study ethnic segregation. Because the assumed fundamental processes are similar, we mostly refer to ethnicity in this chapter.

2 There are two types of social network data with their own type of network analysis (Marsden, 2011; Stark, 2018). We focus mainly on *whole network* data in which all persons in a given social context are interviewed (e.g., a school class). Since the entire network is mapped, these data are particularly well suited to study segregation. This is different in *ego centered* network data, in which participants provide information on their network contacts who typically are not interviewed so that information on the network structure is either lacking or restricted to the perspective of focal actors.

References

Binder, J., Zagefka, H., Brown, R., Funke, F., Kessler, T., Mummendey, A., ... Leyens, J. P. (2009). Does contact reduce prejudice or does prejudice reduce contact? A longitudinal test of the contact hypothesis among majority and minority groups in three European countries. *Journal of Personality and Social Psychology*, 96(4), 843–856.

Blau, P. (1977). *Inequality and heterogeneity: A primitive theory of social structure*. New York: Free Press.

Block, P., & Grund, T. (2014). Multidimensional homophily in friendship networks. *Network Science*, 2(2), 189–212.

Boda, Z. (2018). Social influence on observed race. *Sociological Science*, 5, 29–57.

Boda, Z., & Néray, B. (2015). Inter-ethnic friendship and negative ties in secondary school. *Social Networks*, 43(1), 57–72.

Brechwald, W. A., & Prinstein, M. J. (2011). Beyond homophily: A decade of advances in understanding peer influence processes. *Journal of Research on Adolescence*, 21(1), 166–179.

Byrne, D. E. (1971). *The attraction paradigm*. New York: Academic Press.

Davies, J. A. (1963). Structural balance, mechanical solidarity, and interpersonal relations. *American Journal of Sociology*, 68(4), 444–462.

Davies, K., Tropp, L. R., Aron, A., Pettigrew, T. F., & Wright, S. C. (2011). Cross-group friendships and intergroup attitudes: A meta-analytic review. *Personality and Social Psychology Review*, 15(4), 332–351.

DeLay, D., Zhang, L., Hanish, L. D., Miller, C. F., Fabes, R. A., Martin, C. L., ... Updegraff, K. A. (2016). Peer influence on academic performance: A social network analysis of social-emotional intervention effects. *Prevention Science*. in press. 17(8), 903–913.

Feld, S. L. (1982). Social structural determinants of similarity among associates. *American Sociological Review*, 47(6), 797.

Flashman, J. (2012). Different preferences or different opportunities? Explaining race differentials in the academic achievement of friends. *Social Science Research*, 41(4), 888–903.

Giordano, P. C. (2003). Relationships in adolescence. *Annual Review of Sociology*, 29(1), 257–281.

Goodreau, S. M. S., Kitts, J. A., & Morris, M. (2009). Birds of a feather, or friend of a friend? Using exponential random graph models to investigate adolescent social networks. *Demography*, 46(1), 103–125.

Heider, F. (1946). Attitudes and cognitive organizatione. *Journal of Psychology, 21* (1), 107–112.

Jugert, P., Leszczensky, L., & Pink, S. (2018). The effects of ethnic minority adolescents' ethnic self-identification on friendship selection. *Journal of Research on Adolescence, 28*(2), 379–395.

Kalter, F. (2015). Social network analysis in the study of ethnic inequalities. In R. A. Scott & S. Kosslyn (Eds.), *Emerging trends in the social and behavioral sciences* (pp. 1–15). Hoboken, NJ: Wiley.

Kisfalusi, D., Pál, J., & Boda, Z. (2018). Bullying and victimization among majority and minority students: The role of peers' ethnic perceptions. *Social Networks.* in press. https://doi.org/10.1016/j.socnet.2018.08.006.

Kretschmer, D., Leszczensky, L., & Pink, S. (2018). Selection and influence processes in academic achievement—More pronounced for girls? *Social Networks, 52,* 251–260.

Kruse, H., Smith, S., van Tubergen, F., & Maas, I. (2016). From neighbors to school friends? How adolescents' place of residence relates to same-ethnic school friendships. *Social Networks, 44,* 130–142.

Lemmer, G., & Wagner, U. (2015). Can we really reduce ethnic prejudice outside the lab? A meta-analysis of direct and indirect contact interventions. *European Journal of Social Psychology, 45*(2), 152–168.

Leszczensky, L. (2018). Young immigrants' host country identification and their friendships with natives: Does relative group size matter? *Social Science Research, 70* (1), 163–175.

Leszczensky, L., Flache, A., Stark, T. H., & Munniksma, A. (2018). The relation between ethnic classroom composition and adolescents' ethnic pride. *Group Processes & Intergroup Relations.* in press. 21(7), 997–1013.

Leszczensky, L., & Pink, S. (2015). Ethnic segregation of friendship networks in school: Testing a rational choice argument of differences in ethnic homophily between classroom- and grade-level networks. *Social Networks, 42*(1), 18–26.

Leszczensky, L., & Pink, S. (2017). Intra-and inter-group friendship choices of christian, muslim, and non-religious youth in Germany. *European Sociological Review, 33*(1), 72–83.

Leszczensky, L., Stark, T. H., Flache, A., & Munniksma, A. (2016). Disentangling the relation between young immigrants' host country identification and their friendships with natives. *Social Networks, 44,* 179–189.

Lewis, K. (2015). How networks form: Homophily, opportunity, and balance. In R. A. Scott & S. Kosslyn (Eds.), *Emerging trends in the social and behavioral sciences* (pp. 1–14). Hoboken, NJ: John Wiley & Sons.

Lomi, A., & Stadtfeld, C. (2014). Social networks and social settings: Developing a coevolutionary view. *Kölner Zeitschrift Für Soziologie Und Sozialpsychologie, 66*(S1), 395–415.

Lusher, D., Koskinen, J., & Robins, G. (2013). *Exponential random graph models for social networks. Theory, methods, and applications.* Cambridge: Cambridge University Press.

Marsden, P. V. (2011). Survey Methods for Network Data. In J. Scott & P. J. Carrington (Eds.), *The SAGE handbook of social network analysis* (pp. 370–388). London: Sage.

McFarland, D. A., Moody, J., Diehl, D., Smith, J. A., & Thomas, R. J. (2014). Network ecology and adolescent social structure. *American Sociological Review*, 79(6), 1088–1121.

McPherson, M., Smith-Lovin, L., & Cook, J. M. (2001). Birds of a feather: Homophily in social networks. *Annual Review of Sociology*, 27(1), 415–444.

Moody, J. (2001). Race, school integration, and friendship segregation in America. *American Journal of Sociology*, 107(3), 679–716.

Mouw, T., & Entwisle, B. (2006). Residential segregation and interracial friendship in schools. *American Journal of Sociology*, 112(2), 394–441.

Munniksma, A., Scheepers, P., Stark, T. H., & Tolsma, J. (2017). The impact of adolescents' classroom and neighborhood ethnic diversity on same- and cross-ethnic friendships within classrooms. *Journal of Research on Adolescence*, 27(1), 20–33.

Munniksma, A., Stark, T. H., Verkuyten, M., Flache, A., Veenstra, D. R., & Veenstra, R. (2013). Extended intergroup friendships within social settings: The moderating role of initial outgroup attitudes. *Group Processes & Intergroup Relations*, 16(6), 1–19.

Paluck, E. L., & Shepherd, H. (2012). The salience of social referents: A field experiment on collective norms and harassment behavior in a school social network. *Journal of Personality and Social Psychology*, 103(6), 899–915.

Paluck, E. L., Shepherd, H., & Aronow, P. M. (2016). Changing climates of conflict: A social network experiment in 56 schools. *Proceedings of the National Academy of Sciences of the United States of America*, 113(3), 566–571.

Pettigrew, T. F., & Tropp, L. R. (2006). A meta-analytic test of intergroup contact theory. *Journal of Personality and Social Psychology*, 90(5), 751–783.

Phinney, J. S., Ferguson, D. L., & Tate, J. D. (1997). Intergroup attitudes among ethnic minority adolescents: A causal model. *Child Development*, 68(5), 955–969.

Quillian, L., & Campbell, M. E. (2003). Beyond Black and White: The present and future of multiracial friendship segregation. *American Sociological Review*, 68(4), 540–566.

Rambaran, A. J., Dijkstra, J. K., Munniksma, A., & Cillessen, A. H. N. (2015). The development of adolescents' friendships and antipathies: A longitudinal multivariate network test of balance theory. *Social Networks*, 43, 162–176.

Rambaran, A. J., Hopmeyer, A., Schwartz, D., Steglich, C. E. G., Badaly, D., & Veenstra, R. (2017). Academic functioning and peer influences: A Short-Term Longitudinal Study of network–behavior dynamics in middle adolescenc. *Child Development*, 88(2), 523–543.

Rivas-Drake, D., Saleem, M., Schaefer, D. R., Medina, M., & Jagers, R. (2018). Intergroup contact attitudes across peer networks in school: Selection, influence, and implications for cross-group friendships. *Child Development*, 1–19. early view, https://doi.org/10.1111/cdev.13061

Rivera, M. T., Soderstrom, S. B., & Uzzi, B. (2010). Dynamics of dyads in social networks: Assortative, relational, and proximity mechanisms. *Annual Review of Sociology*, 36(1), 91–115.

Robins, G., Pattison, P., Kalish, Y., & Lusher, D. (2007). An introduction to exponential random graph (p*) models for social networks. *Social Networks*, 29(2), 173–191.

Sanne Smith, Daniel A. McFarland, Frank Van Tubergen, and Ineke Maas (2016). Ethnic Composition and Friendship Segregation: Differential Effects for Adolescent Natives and Immigrants, *American Journal of Sociology* 121, no. 4 (January 2016): 1223–1272. https://doi.org/10.1086/684032

Santos, C. E., Kornienko, O., & Rivas-Drake, D. (2017). Peer influence on ethnic-racial identity development: A multi-site investigation. *Child Development*, 88(3), 725–742.

Schaefer, D. R., Light, J. M., Fabes, R. A., Hanish, L. D., & Martin, C. L. (2010). Fundamental principles of network formation among preschool children. *Social Networks*, 32(1), 61–71.

Schaefer, D. R., Simpkins, S. D., & Ettekal, A. V. (2018). Can extracurricular activities reduce adolescent race/ethnic friendship segregation? In D. Alwin, D. Felmlee, & D. Kreager (Eds.), *Social networks and the life course* (2nd ed., pp. 315–339). Cham: Springer.

Smith, S. (2018). Befriending the same differently: Ethnic, socioeconomic status, and gender differences in same-ethnic friendship. *Journal of Ethnic and Migration Studies*, 44(11), 1858–1880.

Smith, S., Maas, I., & van Tubergen, F. (2014). Ethnic ingroup friendships in schools: Testing the by-product hypothesis in England, Germany, the Netherlands and Sweden. *Social Networks*, 39(1), 33–45.

Smith, S., McMcFarland, D., Maas, I., van Tubergen, F., McFarland, D. A., van Tubergen, F., ... Maas, I. (2016). Ethnic composition and friendship segregation: Differentiaö effects for adolescent natives and immigrants. *American Journal of Sociology*, 121(4), 1223–1272.

Smith, T. W. (2002). Measuring inter-racial friendships. *Social Science Research*, 31(4), 576–593.

Snijders, T. A. B., van de Bunt, G. G., & Steglich, C. E. G. (2010). Introduction to stochastic actor-based models for network dynamics. *Social Networks*, 32(1), 44–60.

Stark, T. H. (2015). Understanding the selection bias: Social network processes and the effect of prejudice on the avoidance of outgroup friends. *Social Psychology Quarterly*, 78(2), 127–150.

Stark, T. H. (2018). Collecting social network data. In D. L. Vannette & J. A. Krosnick (Eds.), *The Palgrave handbook of survey research* (pp. 241–254). Cham, Switzerland: Palgrave Macmillan.

Stark, T. H., & Flache, A. (2012). The double edge of common interest: Ethnic segregation as an unintended byproduct of opinion homophily. *Sociology of Education*, 85(2), 179–199.

Stark, T. H., Flache, A., & Veenstra, R. (2013). Generalization of positive and negative attitudes toward individuals to outgroup attitudes. *Personality and Social Psychology Bulletin*, 39(5), 608–622.

Stark, T. H., Leszczensky, L., & Pink, S. (2017). Are there differences in ethnic majority and minority adolescents' friendships preferences and social influence with regard to their academic achievement?. *Zeitschrift Für Erziehungswissenschaft*, 20(3), 475–498.

Stathi, S., Cameron, L., Hartley, B., & Bradford, S. (2014). Imagined contact as a prejudice-reduction intervention in schools: The underlying role of similarity and attitudes. *Journal of Applied Social Psychology*, 44(8), 536–546.

Steglich, C. E. G., Sinclair, P., Holliday, J., & Moore, L. (2012). Actor-based analysis of peer influence in A Stop Smoking in Schools Trial (ASSIST). *Social Networks*, *34*(3), 359–369.

Steglich, C. E. G., Snijders, T. A. B., & Pearson, M. (2010). Dynamic networks and behavior: Separating selection from influence. *Sociological Methodology*, *40*(1), 329–393.

Steinberg, L., & Morris, A. S. (2001). Adolescent development. *Annual Review of Psychology*, *52*, 83–110.

Tolsma, J., van Deurzen, I., Stark, T. H., & Veenstra, R. (2013). Who is bullying whom in ethnically diverse primary schools? Exploring links between bullying, ethnicity, and ethnic diversity in dutch primary schools. *Social Networks*, *35*(1), 51–61.

Valente, T. W. (2012). Network interventions. *Science*, *337*(49), 49–53.

Valente, T. W., Fujimoto, K., Unger, J. B., Soto, D. W., & Meeker, D. (2013). Variations in network boundary and type: A study of adolescent peer influences. *Social Networks*, *35*(3), 309–316.

Van Zalk, M. H. W., Kerr, M., Van Zalk, N., & Stattin, H. (2013). Xenophobia and tolerance toward immigrants in adolescence: Cross-influence processes within friendships. *Journal of Abnormal Child Psychology*, *41*, 627–639.

VanderWeele, T. J., & An, W. (2013). Social networks and causal inference. In S. L. Morgan (Ed.), *Handbook of causal analysis for social research* (pp. 353–374). Dordrecht: Springer.

Veenstra, R., Dijkstra, J. K., Steglich, C. E. G., & Van Zalk, M. H. W. (2013). Network–behavior dynamics. *Journal of Research on Adolescence*, *23*(3), 399–412.

Verkuyten, M., & Kinket, B. (2000). Social distances in a multi ethnic society: The ethnic hierarchy among Dutch preadolescents. *Social Psychology Quarterly*, *63*(1), 75.

Vermeij, L., van Duijn, M. A. J., & Baerveldt, C. (2009). Ethnic segregation in context: Social discrimination among native Dutch pupils and their ethnic minority classmates. *Social Networks*, *31*(4), 230–239.

Wimmer, A., & Lewis, K. (2010). Beyond and below racial homophily: ERG models of a friendship network documented on Facebook. *American Journal of Sociology*, *116*(2), 583–642.

Windzio, M., & Bicer, E. (2013). Are we just friends? Immigrant integration into high- and low-cost social networks. *Rationality and Society*, *25*(2), 123–145.

Wölfer, R., Jaspers, E., Blaylock, D., Wigoder, C., Hughes, J., & Hewstone, M. (2017). Studying positive and negative direct and extended contact: Complementing self-reports with social network analysis. *Personality and Social Psychology Bulletin*, *43*(11), 1566–1581.

Wölfer, R., Schmid, K., Hewstone, M., & van Zalk, M. (2016). Developmental dynamics of intergroup contact and intergroup attitudes: Long-term effects in adolescence and early adulthood. *Child Development*, *87*(5), 1466–1478.

Zhou, S., Page-Gould, E., Aron, A., Moyer, A., & Hewstone, M. (2019). The extended contact hypothesis: A meta-analysis on 20 years of research. *Personality and Social Psychology Review*, *23*(2), 132–160.

Part IV

Preparing multicultural societies for dealing with diversity inside and outside of schools

Chapter 15

Participatory approaches to youth civic development in multicultural societies

Parissa J. Ballard, Ahna Suleiman, Lindsay Till Hoyt, Alison K. Cohen, Metsehate Ayenekulu, and Genet Ebuy

Civic development refers to the processes by which young people come to see themselves as part of the communities and societies they grow up in. Adolescents today are developing civic attitudes, beliefs, identities, and understanding of social issues in increasingly culturally diverse settings (Vertovec, 2007). Interventions in schools and community organizations working with diverse youth must incorporate strategies to address cultural complexity: a difficult challenge for future research and practice. This chapter focuses on the potential of participatory approaches for civic development and education among diverse youth in multicultural societies.

Civic development in multicultural societies

While the general developmental progression whereby young people expand their social circles to include communities and broader society is somewhat consistent across cultures, the form and shape of civic development is highly dependent on macro- and micro-level contexts in which young people develop (Salamon & Anheier, 1998; Salamon & Sokolowski, 2001). For example, motivations and forms of civic opportunities differ for youth depending on their sociodemographic backgrounds (Ballard, Malin, Porter, Colby, & Damon, 2015; Eckstein, Jugert, Noack, Born, & Sener, 2015; Jensen, 2008). In particular, youth from ethnic/racial minority and immigrant backgrounds may face barriers to full civic participation. Yet, research on civic development of diverse youth lags behind our rapid, ever-changing societies. As many countries become more global and diverse, questions about how to integrate and involve youth in civic life grow. This book tackles a timely question by focusing on civic development in multicultural societies. This chapter presents one type of civic intervention meant to incorporate diverse youth into civic processes in meaningful ways: participatory approaches to civic development.

Participatory approaches to civic development are designed to teach civics through authentic civic experiences. Since such approaches are dynamic and responsive to student needs and individual differences in student learning, they may be particularly suited to multicultural schools and communities that include immigrant, ethnic/racial minority, and other historically marginalized youth.

This chapter will highlight two participatory action approaches: youth participatory action research (YPAR) and action civics (AC). YPAR is an approach to inquiry based on the principles of equity, community-partnership, and respect for youth expertise on issues relevant to their own lives (Ozer, 2016). As an intervention strategy, YPAR is meant to enhance civic development through meaningful civic experiences that build skills and experiences of empowerment. AC is a classroom-based approach to civic education that brings civic lessons to life through youth engagement in communities (Ballard, Cohen, & Littenberg-Tobias, 2016). AC is conceptually similar to YPAR, but more singularly aimed at enhancing civic skills through practice while YPAR aims to build youth research skills and capacity more broadly. YPAR is often targeted at marginalized youth populations across a variety of school and out-of-school contexts while AC is more broadly applied to youth from various backgrounds but targeted in school contexts.

While these approaches differ, YPAR and AC share some common features such as: (1) an emphasis on active participation in communities; (2) some degree of power-sharing between youth and adults; (3) learning and developing skills through practice; (4) a focus on "root causes" of social issues; and (5) a dual emphasis on youth development and systems change. Each of these features is highly relevant in multicultural societies; in particular, striving to help young people understand the "root causes" of social problems that occur in complex sociopolitical contexts is a complicated but promising practice. The following sections will present the theory behind YPAR and AC, evidence of each as an approach to civic development, case studies illustrating YPAR and AC in two different multicultural contexts, and a discussion of benefits and challenges of these approaches in multicultural societies.

Youth-led participatory action research (YPAR)

Theory

YPAR approaches have many goals, uses, and manifestations in practice, and are currently used across fields such as education, public health, and psychology. The core principles of this approach include an iterative integration of research and action that provides youth with training and practice in research skills, strategic thinking, and tactics for influencing change, with intentional youth–adult power sharing (Ozer, Newlan, Douglas, & Hubbard, 2013). Rather than doing research "on youth," a central tenet of YPAR is that youth are valued partners and collaborators in all aspects of the research: identifying the issue, gathering and analyzing the data, developing action plans, and implementing solutions. As a youth-centered version of community-based participatory research, YPAR aims to increase the power of marginalized groups through this iterative cycle of inquiry and action.

YPAR has roots in education and is philosophically based on Paulo Freire's ideas about critical pedagogy. The goal of critical pedagogy is to empower groups from marginalized backgrounds through the awakening of critical consciousness, increasing their understanding of the socioeconomic and historical inequalities that have shaped their oppression (Freire, 1970). YPAR gives young people and adult allies a space to analyze power structures and provoke social change. Because of its emphasis on critical consciousness and social justice, YPAR is an especially promising strategy with young people who experience marginalization (Cammarota & Fine, 2010; Kornbluh, Ozer, Allen, & Kirshner, 2015).

Although YPAR is not exclusively a civic intervention, it can be used to promote civic engagement in multicultural societies. YPAR provides opportunities to: critically analyze structural inequalities; engage in positive, productive work that serves as a counter-narrative to widely held mainstream views of "at risk" youth; learn new skills; and elevate voices that are often silenced (Ozer, 2016). Importantly, YPAR aligns with a "justice-oriented" approach to civic engagement (i.e., collective work towards community betterment while maintaining a critical stance on social issues), which may be especially relevant to marginalized youth compared to traditional routes of good citizenship such as volunteering and participating in local affairs, which more strongly resonate with less marginalized youth (Watts & Flanagan, 2007).

Evidence

Empirical and theoretical studies highlight how YPAR can promote civic development either directly (i.e., civic participation) or indirectly (e.g., decision-making and problem-solving skills, psychological empowerment, or power-sharing with adults). By design, YPAR provides civic and political engagement opportunities (i.e., the "action" in YPAR). YPAR projects may incorporate conversations with school or government leaders, creation of new media to highlight an important issue, presentations to local or regional representatives, or advocacy for youth-specific issues across a variety of settings. For example, the Guatemalan organization, Voces y Manos, used a YPAR approach to identify key issues facing youth in Rabinal, Baja Verapaz, and created a publicly available video: *Voces y Manos*. Through the video, participants presented youth-generated survey data on poverty and disempowerment, collected in local communities, in order to put pressure on elected officials in Guatemala to commit a fund to the Office of Childhood and Adolescence (Ozer & Piatt, 2017). Similarly, in San Diego, California, youth and adults engaged in Youth Engagement and Action for Health (YEAH!), a research and advocacy project aiming to improve access to physical activity opportunities and healthy foods (Ozer & Piatt, 2017). An empirical evaluation of the YEAH! program found that of the 21 groups formed, 20 reported youth engaging with various types of decision makers (e.g., school principals, city council members, parks and recreation officials) and 15 groups reported progress towards system changes as a result of their advocacy (Linton, Edwards, Woodruff, Millstein, & Moder, 2014).

In a clustered-randomized, within-school experimental study testing the effects of participating in a YPAR course on the psychological empowerment of 401 students attending urban public schools in California, YPAR participation was associated with increases in sociopolitical skills, motivation to influence school and community change, and participatory behavior (Ozer & Douglas, 2013). Although few YPAR projects have undergone such rigorous evaluation, several other reports and qualitative data suggest that YPAR promotes self-confidence and critical understanding of the sociopolitical environment, which may help youth researchers see themselves as agents of change in their schools or communities. For instance, a YPAR program with ten high-poverty urban youth in Oakland, California reportedly gave them a sense of civic responsibility and a belief in their ability to make changes in their community (Anyon & Naughton, 2003). Evidence of the benefits of YPAR for developmental outcomes is sparse but points to improvements in strategic thinking, health outcomes, relationships with adults, engagement in school, and a sense of empowerment, efficacy, and perceived control (see Suleiman, Ballard, Hoyt, & Ozer, in press, for a review).

YPAR case study: adolescents 360 Ethiopia

Background

Adolescents 360 (A360) is a four-year project launched in January 2016, funded by the Gates Foundation and the Children's Investment Fund Foundation, and led by Population Services International (PSI). A360 aims to increase contraceptive uptake among 15–19-year-old women in Ethiopia, Nigeria, and Tanzania. Although this began as an adult-driven project with categorical funding focused on contraception, fostering meaningful youth–adult partnerships is one of the key principles of A360. In alignment with the principles of YPAR, a primary goal of the project has been to move from a passive model of youth as sources of data and intervention recipients, towards an engaged model of youth working with adults as partners, advocates, designers, and analysts. By coupling human-centered design (HCD) methodologies with YPAR strategies, youth and adults work as partners in a systematic and cyclical process of reviewing existing evidence, collecting data, advocating for social and policy change, designing and testing prototypes, and vetting and refining intervention approaches. This youth-engaged design process yielded one intervention in each of the three African countries, which will be scaled to national level by project completion in December 2020. In this case study, we will highlight the A360 youth-engaged civic engagement efforts in Ethiopia.

Young people in Ethiopia

There are many compelling reasons to engage the diverse young people in Ethiopia. An estimated 71 percent of the population in Ethiopia is under the age of 30 and 10–24-year-olds constitute 33 percent of the total population (*Ethiopia Demographic and Health Survey 2016*, 2017), thus, Ethiopia is referred to as a country with a "youth bulge." The young people in Ethiopia represent significant ethnic and religious diversity. During the last reported census, more than 80 ethnic groups were documented, with the primary two ethnic groups (Omoro, Amhara) accounting for 61.4 percent of the population, and eight additional groups (Somali, Tigrie, Sidama, Guiagi, Welaita, Hadiya, Afar, Gamo) having populations above one million people (Federal Democratic Republic of Ethiopia Population Census Commission, 2008). The majority of the population are Ethiopian Orthodox Christian (43.5 percent), Muslim (33.9 percent), or Protestant (18.6 percent) (Federal Democratic Republic of Ethiopia Population Census Commission, 2008). Ethiopian adolescents vary on their marital status, level of education, rural versus urban location, source of livelihood, wealth quantile, and exposure to different forms of vulnerabilities such as gender-based violence.

Although there are many issues facing youth in Ethiopia, overall the country has a favorable policy and legal environment to facilitate the development and empowerment of youth. Harmful traditional practices such as child marriage (before 16 years of age) and female genital mutilation and cutting are illegal; performance in primary level girls' education is promising; national women and youth policies are in place; and the health sector is highly committed to address the needs and priorities of young people (Growth and Transformation Plan, 2004). Despite these strong advances, poorer young women (with less educational attainment) are still more likely to marry and bear children earlier, and face a myriad of negative health outcomes as a result (Ethiopia Demographic and Health Survey, 2016). The A360 project was motivated by a strong belief that the diverse young people in Ethiopia (and the other countries) possess unique expertise about the issues that affect their lives and that this expertise is needed to effectively address the challenges they face.

A360 Ethiopia's youth–adult partnership model

Although this project did not involve young people in the selection and identification of the topic, the A360 global initiative did engage youth as co-researchers, co-designers, and co-advocates, and each country's implementation partner, with the support of a YPAR consultant, developed a specific youth engagement plan. As the local implementation partner, PSI/Ethiopia (PSI/ET) led a rigorous recruitment process to hire the youth designers. The required qualifications and experiences were: completion of tenth grade; minimum of two years in youth club activities; conversant in a local language and cultural context of one of the target youth populations; peer facilitation skills; and, in order to successfully engage in the multi-national A360 trainings, strong English comprehension skills. Qualified candidates completed interviews and written English proficiency exams. The original team consisted of 20 youth designers between the ages of 18 and 27 from four diverse regions in Ethiopia – Oromia, Addis Ababa, Afar, and Tigray. In addition to speaking English, the youth designers were fluent in Amharic, Oromigna, Afarigna, or Oromiffa, with five of the designers fluent in multiple languages. Youth designers were hired by PSI/ET through a flexible contract, which allowed them to ebb and flow in their engagement as needed.

Preparing youth designers for civic engagement

The youth designers entered into the project with a diverse range of skills. Many had research methods skills, design backgrounds, or experience facilitating youth development programs; however, none of them had engaged in YPAR. Beginning with the recruitment exam, the young designers were challenged to think about how they could serve as change agents in their communities. In a role-play exercise, one candidate played a religious leader in the community (priest or imam) and the other members were tasked with developing a strategy for convincing the religious leader about the value of using contraception for the community. Another scenario asked candidates to put themselves in the shoes of a girl who lives in a rural region and is given the task of convincing a friend's very protective mother to allow her friend to attend a school event with her. The goal of these scenarios was to identify young people who stepped up to tackle complex social and cultural challenges in sensitive and innovative ways. At the outset, many of the young designers were not aware of the barriers young women faced in accessing contraception.

Once the diverse team of youth was selected, their first activity was to travel to Addis Ababa to attend an intensive two-day training course, facilitated by PSI/ET, in partnership with YPAR and HCD consultants. The training included team-building, research skills, YPAR, ethics, youth–adult partnerships, and a grounding in contraception and the context of the project in Ethiopia. During this time, the youth came to realize the paramount impact that access to contraception could have on the life trajectories of young girls and women in Ethiopia. Following the two-day immersive training, the youth team was joined by a team of 50 adults from the USA, Tanzania, Nigeria, as well as Ethiopia. The training was designed to be inclusive; youth were given platforms to have their voices heard, ask questions, learn from mistakes, and add value to the process. The young designers contributed as equal partners and PSI/ET adopted a successful paradigm shift to facilitate sustained meaningful youth engagement. This meant recalibrating the value of youth insights and expertise and increasing the readiness of adult staff to challenge their own assumptions and system flexibility to accommodate the busy schedules of the young people.

Following the training, during fall 2016, youth and adult teams transitioned to the data collection phase of the project. The teams dispersed to four regions of Ethiopia – Addis Ababa, Afar, Oromia, and Tigray – to conduct research. Through interviews and focus groups they gathered information from 294 people including old and young community members, community influencers, and service providers. The teams then worked together to analyze and synthesize the data. The youth provided critical insights during the data analysis phase that would have likely been misinterpreted or overlooked without their participation. Following data analysis, some of the youth researchers continued to help with the contraception intervention design and prototyping process. The teams tested ten concepts and interviewed 92 people to inform the final contraception intervention model for Ethiopia. The resulting model was named Smart Start, an intervention aimed at newly married couples to help them understand contraception and family planning in the context of financial planning. Community health workers partner with communities to identify eligible couples and provide appropriate and resonant counseling services.

Engaging in social change

Through the YPAR experience, the young designers in A360 built their skills and gained experience as translators, data collectors, and designers. However, the greatest benefit came from seeing themselves as agents of social change. During the first phase of the project, a key official at the Ministry of Health (MOH) requested a presentation from the PSI/ET A360 team to the Ministry leadership. Recognizing the capacity of the young designers, the PSI/ET A360 Project Director proposed that the youth lead the presentation. Unfamiliar with youth engagement, the Ministry official resisted, but the PSI/ET staff and youth designers persisted. After a strong presentation by the young designers, the same Ministry official shared that seeing the youth present reminded him of his own experience as a young person advocating for social change and revitalized his commitment to youth engagement. Based on this experience, the MOH has become a champion of youth engagement and PSI/ET is now being highlighted as a youth engagement leader in the country.

The young designers learned how to communicate effectively with diverse stakeholders, ranging from young people to community members to local officials to members of the MOH. As the youth adult teams worked in the field, the adults recognized that the young designers were very effective at building rapport with parents, young people, and community stakeholders and were able to create new openings for discussing contraception. The young designers also learned how to work as members of a diverse team and how to leverage the principles of HCD to explore a problem from its roots in order to move towards innovative solutions. The young designers (some of whom are still students) not only improved their teamwork and problem-solving skills, but also reported increased confidence working in partnership with adults who have greater experience and expertise. Both youth and adults recognized that the most important insights can come from any member of the team.

Overall, the experiences of the young designers following their participation in A360 suggest the positive impact that engaging in social change had on their personal goals and action. For example, one young designer studying engineering reports that A360 made her aware of social problems and gave her a sense of confidence that she can contribute to social change. As a result, she is actively engaging in different clubs that support community change – specifically focused on advocacy and teaching for parents who plan to force their daughters to drop out of school and enter into early marriage. A second young designer is now working in his own private firm as designer and architect, and also works with a number of organizations to use social media as a platform to advocate for tackling child abuse. A third has embodied the skills she learned in A360 into almost all of her work. As a graduate assistant and teacher at the Mekelle University Department of Psychology, she provides training on HCD, uses HCD principles in her work, and operationalizes the concepts of youth–adult partnership in her classrooms. She was awarded a three-month leadership training by the Young Africa Leaders Initiative as a result of the communication, problem-solving, advocacy, and teamwork skills she honed in A360.

Together, young designers learned how to be part of a solution to social problems and changed their own lives, as well as the lives of others, for the better. The primary goal of A360 was to engage youth in developing the most relevant and impactful contraception intervention. Based on this experience, these young people are now applying YPAR principles to tackle a range of youth issues. Although A360 was not primarily a civic intervention, the YPAR process appears to have provided designers with a powerful experience in civic engagement that built skills, formed relationships, shaped their self-concepts, changed their social environments, and shaped their future trajectories.

Action civics (AC)

Theory

Action civics (AC) is a student-centered, project-based, and participatory approach to civic education. In contrast to YPAR, which is used in a variety of contexts and for many purposes, AC is based in classrooms and is designed explicitly to address curricular needs for civic education. The guiding principles center on collective action, youth voice and agency, and reflection as the key components of high-quality civic education (Gingold, 2013). AC curricular programs arose in response to critiques that civic education in the U.S. had become overly focused on imparting civic knowledge to students. Active, engaging approaches to civic education may promote intrinsic interest and new skills, while also building basic knowledge. In contrast to service-learning oriented approaches, which emphasize the provision of individual services to community organizations, AC programs take a more systemic view of "root causes" of social issues and emphasize collective action to address structural inequalities. In practice, AC is implemented in classrooms through an applied, project-based learning approach, where students learn civics through taking action on an issue in their community (Levinson, 2014).

Evidence

Classroom-based AC programs are fairly new and evaluation research is sparse. To date, there are just over 200 articles that mention the phrase "action civics" in Google Scholar, as compared to over 2000 that mention the phrase "youth participatory action research." Existing evaluations are primarily based on self-reported student civic and academic outcomes (Gingold, 2013) and most often are conducted by AC organizations themselves with the goal of self-understanding and improvement, or have focused on narratives from teachers or other implementers about their experiences teaching action civics (Bass, 2012; Blevins & LeCompte, 2015; Cipparone & Cohen, 2015; Serriere, Mitra, & Cody, 2010). Some work has found that specific AC programs increase students' AC knowledge (knowledge specific to identifying "root causes" of social issues; Ballard et al., 2016; Cohen et al., 2018), civic self-efficacy (Ballard et al., 2016), and preparation for civic action (Cohen et al., 2018).

Case study of AC: Generation Citizen

Background

In the United States, public schools have a mandate to teach civics, but due to the current climate of required standardized testing, civic learning is not often an educational priority (Gould, 2011; Malin, Ballard, Attai, Colby, & Damon, 2014). Although the nature and quality of civic education varies across states and districts in the U.S., in general, schools struggle to provide meaningful civic education that connects to the diverse experiences that young people have in their communities and U.S. society. Further, meaningful civic learning opportunities are unequally distributed across racial, ethnic, and socioeconomic groups (Kahne & Middaugh, 2008; Levinson, 2010), creating a problematic gap in civic preparedness and power across diverse groups in society. Innovative approaches to civic education have arisen to make civic learning more active and to connect students in schools with their communities to learn civics by doing civics.

Generation Citizen (GC) is a youth civic engagement non-profit established in 2008 and now operating in multiple metropolitan areas around the U.S. Its core programming is an action civics model in which trained college student volunteers ("democracy coaches") partner with classroom teachers to deliver a semester-long AC curriculum in school classroom settings (Pope, Stolte, & Cohen, 2011). GC currently offers such programming in several states in the U.S. including California, Texas, Oklahoma, New York, Rhode Island, and Massachusetts. They also have a teacher-led model in which classroom teachers single-handedly implement the curriculum in the states of Massachusetts, New Jersey, and California (Generation Citizen, 2018a). GC serves racially, ethnically, and socioeconomically diverse student populations: the majority of GC participants are students of color and/or attend schools where a high percentage of students qualify for free or reduced-price lunch (i.e., a proxy measure of low socioeconomic status) (Cohen & Chaffee, 2012; Littenberg-Tobias & Cohen, 2016).

Programming

GC's AC approach is action-oriented, community-based, and student-centered (Pope et al., 2011). GC's curriculum has three main stages. In the first stage, students choose an issue. This includes learning about civic structures and democratic processes as well as discussing and building consensus to identify and select an issue to tackle. In the second stage, students learn to take action, which involves researching the chosen issue, analyzing the root causes of that issue, and developing skills to create an action plan. In the third stage, students take action by putting to use the content and skills they learned in the first two phases (Pope et al., 2011). Students implement their action plan – which could involve meeting with decision-makers, writing opinion pieces, designing and circulating petitions, or other activities – then they present their action plans to community leaders and peers at an end-of-semester event called Civics Day. Finally, students reflect on the process and identify strategies for remaining active and engaged citizens.

The curriculum is grounded in what GC calls "the advocacy hourglass," which focuses on systemic change. The hourglass metaphor describes students typically starting with a broad community issue, refining their understanding to identify a more specific area of focus, and then widening their perspective to tackle the issue at hand. In the narrow part of the hourglass process, students must choose a single root cause out of the many potential root causes of the focal issue that they want to tackle. After choosing the root cause, the hourglass begins to widen again: students identify their goal, and then broaden their thinking as they identify multiple targets and multiple tactics that will help them achieve that goal (Generation Citizen, 2018b). For example, three different GC classrooms focused on police brutality as their issue, but each identified different root causes. In Rhode Island, students focused on systemic racism; in Texas students focused on lack of awareness and poor interpersonal skills; and in California, students addressed the negative relationship between the police and residents. This is illustrative of how the advocacy hourglass narrows at the issue identification stage, and can result in divergent broadening after the root causes stage, since each of these different root causes would inspire different approaches to taking action.

Implementation in practice

Across GC projects, students choose a wide variety of issues to tackle, and that range from student bus passes to gang violence to school closings to hunger (Pope et al., 2011). Some projects focus on making change within the school setting, whereas others focus on issues beyond the school. Many classes opt to focus on issues related to safety, but school environment issues and social issues are also common (Ballard et al., 2016). Indicative of these diverse interests, sometimes a classroom will opt to do two different projects if they cannot reach a consensus on a single topic; for example, one classroom tackled both an in-school issue (the cleanliness of school bathrooms) and an out-of-school social issue (a contaminated environmental site in their neighborhood; Cipparone & Cohen, 2015). Learning outcomes, skill building, and civic growth are possible regardless of whether or not the class successfully achieves their action goal; in fact, learning and reflecting upon unsuccessful actions can be just as important as learning from successes, if not more so (Pope et al., 2011).

Action civics in diverse and multicultural classrooms

GC's AC curriculum fosters a democratic classroom climate and working in collaboration with peers, which can facilitate valuable conversations among students from different backgrounds. As one college student volunteer democracy coach shared in an organizational newsletter in June 2015:

> I couldn't wait to hear my students' opinions. But I was surprised to find that they knew little about each other and the issues impacting their community. As we started the curriculum, though, my students learned that some of their classmates faced homelessness.

While classrooms are increasingly multicultural and diverse, simple proximity to peers from diverse backgrounds does not ensure that students know about and become sensitive to the issues faced by others from different backgrounds. As this example points out, structures must be in place for students to feel comfortable with and to have the opportunity to share their own experiences. Curricular approaches such as AC can help schools and classrooms provide such structure and culturally sensitive learning through active civic engagement with diverse others.

Multicultural and diverse classrooms can lead to useful insights that guide students' AC projects. Issues that are experienced by at least some, if not all, members of their community are particularly inspiring to middle and high school students. For example, the same college student volunteer quoted above continued:

> When things got personal, things changed in my classroom. My students became determined to help fix this problem – organizing clothing drives, educating teachers about supporting homeless students, and supplying lists of local resources targeted at homeless youth. This became their issue, because it impacted their community.

In another example, in a Rhode Island middle school classroom, students chose an issue relevant to many in their classroom: the disparities in academic outcomes between White and Latino students. Many students in this classroom had been classified as English Language Learners (Generation Citizen, 2018c). In the U.S., this label is used for students who are non-native English speakers and are still learning English – this often applies to students who are immigrants. In many parts of the U.S., the majority of English Language Learners are Latino. The middle school students' own experiences with the supports that existed for English Language Learners informed the whole class (including those who were never classified as English Language Learners) to tackle the issue of disparities in academic outcomes between White and Latino students. Using the skills gained through AC education, students came up with a plan to reduce these academic disparities by promoting English Language Learner certification for teachers so that they could better support English Language Learner students. The students achieved success when the Providence School Board supported their plan. In both of the above examples (supporting homeless students and English Language Learners), the whole class worked together to support issues experienced by members of minority groups whose needs were not currently being met in their schools. Often minority perspectives can get overshadowed; in these examples (and across many GC classrooms), encouraging students to build a consensus helped foster a supportive classroom climate that led students to choose action projects that directly affected fellow students, especially supporting the experience of minority students, and led to social change.

Beyond the classroom, other students directly tackle issues that arise from living in multicultural *communities*. As an example, many GC projects have focused on interactions between people of color and law enforcement. This is a racially charged issue with many communities of color in the U.S. experiencing disproportionate negative consequences of interactions with law enforcement and heightened negative perceptions of it (Peck, 2015). Through GC, one class of students in Oklahoma chose to address limited communication between law enforcement and residents as their action project. In a newspaper article (Bey, 2016), one student explained that he and his classmates were scared any time they interacted with the police, in part because they saw police officers as different from people like them. They sought to organize an event that would allow law enforcement officers and community residents to interact in a low-stress, social setting, with the goal of working across differences and strengthening social cohesion. In another example, students from one school in Massachusetts talked about their own experiences of being targeted by police based on the color of their skin, connected it to city-level data that spoke to the scale of these experiences, and identified a state bill that would help reduce race-driven traffic stops (Bey, 2016). Another class successfully advocated for the creation of a Youth Advisory Council for their city as a way to increase youth voice and diversify the insights the city government used in developing policies and programs (Huber, 2017). In each of these examples, students' experience with GC gave them the voice, the skills, and the power to tackle complex issues related to racial diversity. Thus, AC can be a powerful participatory approach to civic intervention for youth in multicultural and diverse classrooms, schools, and societies.

Benefits and challenges of participatory approaches to civic interventions in multicultural societies

Participatory approaches to civic development in multicultural societies present both benefits and challenges. YPAR and AC share some important features that position them well as effective civic interventions such as learning and developing skills through practice and a dual emphasis on youth development and systems change. As the case studies illustrated, one major benefit of both participatory approaches is the opportunity to bring together diverse people – with regards to age, social class, and race/ethnicity – in situations with shared goals and structured collaboration. Although exposure to diverse others does not guarantee increased cultural sensitivity, participating actively in projects with shared goals can be a powerful experience in meaningful collaboration across diversity. This idea was evidenced through the example of GC providing a meaningful reason for diverse students to discover the issues facing their peers, and this motivated their civic action.

In particular, striving to help young people understand the "root causes" of social problems that occur in complex sociopolitical contexts is a promising but complicated practice. AC builds this in explicitly, as illustrated by Generation Citizen's advocacy hourglass in which identifying "root causes" is a critical element of the process. As evidenced in the YPAR example, A360 in Ethiopia, youth designers gained deep insights from many community stakeholders in order to uncover the root causes of early and frequent childbearing, and so forming a solution to address one of the underlying causes. The YPAR process gave the youth designers the skills and training necessary for such work, and exposed them to realistic challenges. For example, youth designers had to role play a scenario in which they tried to convince a religious leader in the community about the value of using contraception, which was an important and difficult exercise, given that the issue of contraception is controversial in Ethiopia. Across religious, generational, and gender groups, there are likely many ways to understand the root causes of early and frequent childbearing. Indeed, not all groups may agree that it is a social problem in need of a solution at all. Another challenge to participatory approaches is that they require power-sharing between existing powers (usually adults in professional positions such as teachers, researchers, administrators) and youth. Sharing power is complex and such a change can feel radical to all people involved (see Ozer et al., 2013 for further discussion of power-sharing and other tensions in YPAR). Thus, participatory approaches are promising in providing training and skills to address complex problems, although serious challenges remain.

Conclusion

When considering civic development of youth from diverse backgrounds in increasingly multicultural societies, participatory approaches such as YPAR and AC are promising avenues for meaningfully engaging youth in civic activities to address cultural complexities. Participatory approaches afford developmentally relevant opportunities for youth to use their increasing social awareness, need for autonomy, and critical analysis skills to contribute to their communities and gain new skills (Suleiman et al., in press). Many features of participatory approaches equip young people and their communities for working collaboratively across differences to address social problems and achieve social change. The case studies presented here show how such approaches can: increase youth's collaboration with peers and adults; shape their developmental trajectories, self-concept, and future goals; and build the civic skills needed to understand complex social problems and create social change.

References

Anyon, Y. A., & Naughton, S. A. (2003). *Youth empowerment: The contributions and challenges of youth-led research in a high-poverty, urban community*. Retrieved from https://gardnercenter.stanford.edu/sites/g/files/sbiybj8191/f/Youth%20Empowerment%20Issue%20Brief.pdf

Ballard, P. J., Cohen, A. K., & Littenberg-Tobias, J. (2016). Action civics for promoting civic development: Main effects of program participation and differences by project characteristics. *American Journal of Community Psychology, 58* (3–4), 377–390. doi:10.1002/ajcp.12103

Ballard, P. J., Malin, H., Porter, T. J., Colby, A., & Damon, W. (2015). Motivations for civic participation among diverse youth: More similarities than differences. *Research in Human Development, 12*(1–2), 63–83. doi:10.1080/15427609.2015.1010348

Bass, J. (2012). Engaging students in politics. *ASCD Express, 7*. http://ascd.org/ascd-express/vol7/723-bass.aspx

Bey, D., Generation Citizen, and ROTC period 5 class at Brighton High School. (2016). Search and destroy: Boston high school students push for an end to racial profiling.

Blevins, B., & LeCompte, K. (2015). I am engaged: Action civics in four steps. *Social Studies and the Young Learner, 27*(4), 23–26.

Cammarota, J., & Fine, M. (2010). *Revolutionizing education: Youth participatory action research in motion*. New York, NY: Routledge.

Central Statistical Agency (CSA) [Ethiopia] and ICF. (2016). *Ethiopia demographic and health survey 2016*. Addis Ababa, Ethiopia, and Rockville, MD: CSA and ICF.

Cipparone, P., & Cohen, A. K. (2015). Action civics in fourth grade. *Social Studies and the Young Learner, 27*(4), 11–15. doi:10.1007/BF02043220

Cohen, A. K., & Chaffee, B. W. (2012). The relationship between adolescents' civic knowledge, civic attitude, and civic behavior and their self-reported future likelihood of voting. *Education, Citizenship and Social Justice, 8*(1), 43–57.

Cohen, A. K., Littenberg-Tobias, J., Ridley-Kerr, A., Pope, A., Stolte, L. C., & Wong, K. K. (2018). Action civics education and civic outcomes for urban youth: An evaluation of the impact of Generation Citizen. *Citizenship Teaching and Learning, 13*(3), 351–368.

Eckstein, K., Jugert, P., Noack, P., Born, M., & Sener, T. (2015). Comparing correlates of civic engagement between immigrant and majority youth in Belgium, Germany, and Turkey. *Research in Human Development*, 12(1-2), 44–62.

Ethiopia demographic and health survey 2016. (2017). Rockville, MD. https://dhsprogram.com/pubs/pdf/FR328/FR328.pdf

Federal Democratic Republic of Ethiopia Population Census Commission. (2008). *Summary and statistical report of the 2007 population and housing census: Population size by age and sex.* Addis Ababa, Ethiopia: UNFPA.

Freire, P. (1970). *Pedagogy of the oppressed*, trans. Myra Bergman Ramos (pp. 65–80). New York: Continuum.

Generation Citizen. (2018a). *Where we work*. Retrieved from https://generationcitizen.org/our-programs/where-we-work/

Generation Citizen. (2018b) *Framework for action*. Retrieved from https://generationcitizen.org/our-approach/framework-for-action/

Generation Citizen. (2018c) *Resources for English language learners*. Retrieved from https://generationcitizen.org/story/resources-for-english-language-learners/

Gingold, J. G. (2013). *Assessing action civics: A case-study of the National Action Civics Collaborative (NACC)*. Paper presented at the HGSE Student Research Conference 2013.

Gould, J. (2011). *Guardian of democracy: The civic mission of schools*. Philadelphia, PA, Annenberg Public Policy Center of the University of Pennsylvania.

Growth and Transformation Plan (GTP II) 2015/16-2019/20. (2004). The criminal code of the federal democratic republic of Ethiopia: Proclamation No.414/2004.

Huber, M. (2017, Dec 28th). Bastrop students make history establishing city youth advisory council. *Stateman*.

Jensen, L. A. (2008). Immigrants' cultural identities as sources of civic engagement. *Applied Development Science*, 12(2), 74–83. doi:10.1080/10888690801997069

Kahne, J., & Middaugh, E. (2008). Democracy for some: The civic opportunity gap in high school. Circle Working Paper 59. Medford, MA: Center for Information and Research on Civic Learning and Engagement (CIRCLE).

Kornbluh, M., Ozer, E. J., Allen, C. D., & Kirshner, B. (2015). Youth participatory action research as an approach to sociopolitical development and the new academic standards: Considerations for educators. *The Urban Review*, 47(5), 868–892.

Levinson, M. (2010). The civic empowerment gap: Defining the problem and locating solutions. In L. R. Sherrod, J. Torney-Purta, & C. A. Flanagan (Eds.), *Handbook of research on civic engagement in youth* (pp. 331–361). Hoboken, NJ: John Wiley and Sons.

Levinson, M. (2014). Action civics in the classroom. *Social Education*, 78(2), 68–72.

Linton, L. S., Edwards, C. C., Woodruff, S. I., Millstein, R. A., & Moder, C. (2014). Youth advocacy as a tool for environmental and policy changes that support physical activity and nutrition: An evaluation study in San Diego County. *Preventing Chronic Disease*, 11.

Littenberg-Tobias, J., & Cohen, A. K. (2016). Diverging paths: Understanding racial differences in civic engagement among White, African American, and Latina/o adolescents using structural equation modeling. *American Journal of Community Psychology*, 57(1-2), 102–117.

Malin, H., Ballard, P. J., Attai, M. L., Colby, A., & Damon, W. (2014). *Youth civic development and education: A conference consensus report*. Stanford, CA: Stanford University.

Ozer, E. J. (2016). Youth-led participatory action research: Developmental and equity perspectives. In S. S. Horn, M. D. Ruck, & L. S. Liben (Eds.), *Advances in child development and behavior* (Vol. 50, pp. 189–207). Burlington: Academic Press.

Ozer, E. J., & Douglas, L. (2013). The impact of participatory research on urban teens: An experimental evaluation. *American Journal of Community Psychology, 51* (1–2), 66–75.

Ozer, E. J., Newlan, S., Douglas, L., & Hubbard, E. (2013). "Bounded" empowerment: Analyzing tensions in the practice of youth-led participatory research in urban public schools. *American Journal of Community Psychology, 52*(1–2), 13–26.

Ozer, E. J., & Piatt, A. A. (2017). Youth-led participatory action research (ypar): Principles applied to the us and diverse global settings. In N. Wallerstein, B. Duran, J. G. Oetzel, & M. Minkler (Eds.), *Community-based participatory research for health: Advancing social and health equity* (3rd ed., pp. 95–106). Hoboken, NJ: Wiley.

Peck, J. H. (2015). Minority perceptions of the police: A state-of-the-art review. *Policing: an International Journal of Police Strategies & Management, 38*(1), 173–203.

Pope, A., Stolte, L., & Cohen, A. K. (2011). Closing the civic engagement gap: The potential of action civics. *Social Education, 75*(5), 265–268.

Salamon, L. M., & Anheier, H. K. (1998). Social origins of civil society: Explaining the nonprofit sector cross-nationally. *Voluntas: International Journal of Voluntary and Nonprofit Organizations, 9*(3), 213–248.

Salamon, L. M., & Sokolowski, W. (2001). *Volunteering in cross-national perspective: Evidence from 24 countries*. Baltimore: Johns Hopkins Center for Civil Society Studies.

Serriere, S., Mitra, D., & Cody, J. (2010). Young citizens take action for better school lunches. *Social Studies and the Young Learner, 23*(2), 4–8.

Suleiman, A. B., Ballard, P. J., Hoyt, L. T., & Ozer, E. (in press). Applying a developmental lens to youth-led participatory action research: A critical examination and integration of existing evidence. *Youth & Society*.

Vertovec, S. (2007). Super-diversity and its implications. *Ethnic and Racial Studies, 30*(6), 1024–1054.

Watts, R. J., & Flanagan, C. (2007). Pushing the envelope on youth civic engagement: A developmental and liberation psychology perspective. *Journal of Community Psychology, 35*(6), 779–792. doi:10.1002/jcop.20178

Chapter 16

Teachers' dealings with ethnic diversity

Jochem Thijs and Roselien Vervaet

Schools increasingly serve children from different ethnic backgrounds, and they have the crucial task of promoting positive interethnic relations and preparing future generations for living together. Despite its variation and different labels, a common goal of this so-called ethnic diversity education is to teach students the importance of equality and prevent ethnic prejudice, racism, and discrimination (Portera, 2008; Rosenthal & Levy, 2010; Verkuyten & Thijs, 2013; Zirkel, 2008). As instructors, teachers are clearly implicated in performing this goal. Yet despite the abundant theorizing on ethnic diversity education – in the US (e.g., Banks, 2004; Gay, 2000), but also in Europe (e.g., Arnesen, Allen, & Simonsen, 2009) – there is little systematic empirical knowledge about teachers' individual contributions to it. Even within the same school, what is said and taught about diversity can vary from teacher to teacher (Verkuyten & Thijs, 2013). This variation has potentially important implications for the ways students think and feel about different ethnic groups. Most of the existing studies on teachers' dealings with ethnic diversity have used qualitative methods yielding detailed findings and 'thick descriptions' that are invaluable for understanding the complexities and intricacies of teachers' and students' experiences in specific multi-ethnic contexts (e.g., Baumann, Vertovec, Schiffauer, & Kastoryano, 2004; Gillborn, 1990). Despite their value, however, it is difficult to extrapolate such qualitative findings to other situations, and for more general conclusions about the role of individual teachers, qualitative research approaches should be complemented by quantitative ones.

In this chapter we discuss available quantitative research on teachers' contributions to ethnic diversity education. We focus on teachers in upper elementary and secondary school, as pre-adolescence is an important period for the development of ethnic attitudes and ethnic group relations (Quintana, 1998; Raabe & Beelman, 2011). We begin with a short discussion of some general approaches to diversity education. Then, we address the nature and measurement of teachers' diversity teachings, and the (possible) effects of these teachings on the ethnic attitudes and relations of their (pre) adolescent students. Next, we discuss the additional importance of teacher, school, and classroom conditions, and we end with a conclusion that includes directions for future research.

Approaches to ethnic diversity education

There are different ideological and philosophical approaches to the question of how ethnic diversity should be dealt with (e.g., Rattan & Ambady, 2013). Theorists like Banks (2004), Gay (2000), and Portera (2008) have thought extensively about their application in the domain of education. The *multicultural* approach calls for a recognition and celebration of ethnic and cultural diversity. It argues that prejudice is often rooted in ignorance, and that positive attention for cultural group differences and the (historical) inequalities between groups will increase the understanding and appreciation of ethnic others (Banks, 2004; Rosenthal & Levy, 2010). Banks's (2004) theory is the most elaborate framework within the multicultural approach. Banks identified five dimensions of multicultural education. Content integration refers to the extent to which teachers use examples from different cultures as illustrations in their discipline. The second dimension, the knowledge construction process, describes how teachers help their pupils understand that knowledge is constructed and therefore influenced by the positions of individuals and groups. Prejudice reduction defines strategies to support pupils to develop more democratic attitudes and values. Equity pedagogy, the fourth dimension, exists when teachers take the initiative to improve the academic achievement of pupils from low-status population groups. The last dimension refers to restructuring the organization of a school, creating an empowering school culture, and producing educational equality for pupils from all racial, ethnic, and socioeconomic backgrounds (Banks, 2004).

A possible criticism of the multicultural perspective is that an emphasis on group differences might actually strengthen group boundaries and foster stereotypical thinking. This point is addressed by two other approaches. The *intercultural* approach also tries to stimulate a positive attitude toward cultural diversity but is said to have a less fixed understanding of group differences. It maintains that cultures and cultural identities are dynamic, and that the focus should be on interaction, dialogue, and exchange between people from different ethnic backgrounds (Portera, 2008). Thus, the primary aim of intercultural education is the development of intercultural competence (Barrett, 2013). Still, the exact differences between multicultural and intercultural education are contested and not always clear (Barrett, 2013; Meer & Modood, 2012), and in some countries – like the Netherlands – the terms tend to be used interchangeably. In general, however, multicultural education is more popular in

North America (Kahn, 2008), and intercultural education is more often used in Europe (Portera, 2008). Like the intercultural approach, the *color-blind* approach warns against an emphasis on group differences. Yet this perspective claims that ethnic group differences should be ignored altogether, which means that there is little attention to historical and existing ethnic inequalities (Rosenthal & Levy, 2010; Schofield, 2001). Color-blindness comes in two flavors: value-in-individual differences and value-in-homogeneity. The former stresses that group differences matter far less than people's individual characteristics, but the second emphasizes the importance of common identities that transcend group boundaries (Rosenthal & Levy, 2010). However, finding common ground amidst diversity is not always easy and stressing value-in-homogeneity may take the form of an assimilation approach, which is typically the case in Flanders, the Dutch-speaking part of Belgium (Pulinx, Van Avermaet, & Agirdag, 2017). Research has shown that Flemish school policies tend to focus on assimilation and expect minorities to adapt to and adopt the dominant culture, instead of applying an intercultural or multicultural approach concerning cultural differences (De Wit & Van Petegem, 2000; Pulinx et al., 2017).

Despite their dissimilarities, the different diversity approaches overlap to varying degrees, and there has been discussion on whether interculturalism is not simply an updated version of multiculturalism (Meer & Modood, 2012). Although they advocate different ways of dealing with diversity, all approaches condemn prejudice and discrimination (Rattan & Ambady, 2013). This overlap can make it rather difficult to determine whether specific educational practices should be classified as multicultural, intercultural, or color-blind (or assimilative) and, thus, to systematically compare the effects of the different approaches on students' ethnic attitudes and relations. Moreover, and presumably because of this, there seems to be an imbalance between the extensive theorizing on how students should be taught about diversity, and the number of quantitative empirical tests of different types of diversity education, especially with regards to the role of individual teachers.

Examining ethnic diversity teaching

Most of the quantitative research on ethnic diversity teaching has focused on the evaluation of specific educational programs or classroom interventions based on the global diversity approaches discussed before, indicating that ethnic diversity education has the potential to improve students' ethnic attitudes and intergroup relations (see for reviews, Bigler, 1999; Stephan, Renfro, & Stephan, 2004; Ülger, Dette-Hagenmeyer, Reichle, & Gaertner, 2018). However, a focus on the effects of specific programs, interventions, or curricula implies less attention for the possible contributions of individual teachers. In their recent meta-analysis, Ülger et al.

(2018) concluded that interventions to improve students' out-group attitudes were generally effective when conducted by a trained researcher, but not when carried out by teachers. The authors speculated that this lack of effectiveness 'might be due to a host of variables, such as variation in the quality of teachers' training in the intervention, teachers' understanding of the importance of implementation fidelity, their other demands while presenting the intervention, or their preference to change their delivery to match the audience and their timetable, thus reducing the standardization of delivery' (p. 98). However, although teachers are central to multicultural education programs (see e.g., Stephan et al., 2004), and different policy-driven programs have been developed to improve teachers' diversity attitudes (e.g., Gorski, 2009; Marx & Moss, 2011), research on the effects of diversity interventions typically does not focus on the variation between teachers. Moreover, individual teachers can decide to instruct and educate their students about diversity, also when they do not participate in interventions or when diversity education is not a part of their 'official' school curriculum.

Because interventions and curricula often contain multiple elements, it can be difficult to assess 'what works' in them. These different elements can interact, and the effects of some of them may depend on the presence of the others. For example, research among adults has shown that ethnic majority group members may feel excluded when positive attention for minority group cultures is not accompanied by positive attention for the majority culture, and consequently multicultural messages or interventions may be less effective or even counterproductive (Plaut, Garnett, Buffardi, & Sanchez-Burks, 2011). It is possible to separately evaluate the impact of different components in interventions, but this takes a lot of time and effort.

Both the potential variation between teachers and the multifaceted nature of ethnic diversity education indicate that the research on ethnic diversity interventions and programs should be complemented by quantitative studies that use a variable-centered approach to examine what individual teachers teach about ethnic diversity in their classrooms. As we will see, such research is available, but not all of it has used multiple measures; it has been predominantly conducted in the Netherlands and more recently in Flanders (Belgium). Both countries are interesting cases for studying the effects of ethnic diversity education. Their current levels of cultural diversity are relatively recent and predominantly due to labor migration, followed by migrant family reunification and chain migration processes (Huijnk & Andriessen, 2016; Vanduynslager, Wets, Noppe, & Doyen, 2013). Moreover, despite legal obligations to promote active citizenship and social integration in Dutch students (Onderwijsinspectie, 2006),[1] and, in the case of Flanders, the recent introduction of 'citizenship' courses and the inclusion of curriculum objectives related to respectfully dealing with other cultures (Agirdag, 2016; Colman et al., 2017), there is no structural framework for ethnic diversity education in both countries. Instead, teachers have a lot of autonomy to decide what and how they teach about diversity in the classroom (Bank et al., 2005; Vlaamse Onderwijsraad, 2005).

Differences between teachers

To properly evaluate the role of individual teachers in ethnic diversity education, it is important to use multilevel analysis. Most of the time, whole classrooms and schools rather than individual students are sampled. Because classmates are (partly) exposed to the same influences, there needs to be a correction for the possible interdependencies between data for individual students in the same school environment. Multilevel analysis provides this correction and can examine, for example, how much of the variance in children's perception of multicultural education exists within and between classrooms (Snijders & Bosker, 1999). However, as research typically includes several teachers per school, it can also investigate *between-teacher* variation *within* schools. Agirdag, Merry, and Van Houtte (2016) used this technique to study aspects of multicultural content integration among 706 teachers in 68 primary schools in Flanders. Teachers completed a self-report scale including items like 'In the classroom, I focus explicitly on the topic of ethnic diversity' and 'Ethnic diversity rarely occurs in the course material I use' (reverse coded). The results of the study showed that only a small portion of the variance in multicultural content integration was between schools (5.2 percent), which indicates strong differences between individual teachers (Agirdag et al., 2016).

These results differ somewhat from recent findings by Vervaet, Van Houtte, and Stevens (2018a) who examined 636 teachers in 40 secondary schools in Flanders. Using a self-report scale for multicultural content integration (Banks, 2004), they found that 15 percent of the variance between teachers existed at the school level. Thus, with respect to ethnic diversity teaching, there seems to be more within-school similarity among secondary as compared to primary school children. One reason for this different outcome is that primary school children in Flanders and the Netherlands (grades 1–6) tend to have one teacher (or sometimes two) the whole year round, whereas secondary school children in these countries have different teachers for different subjects. This means that different secondary school teachers often teach the same students. To the extent that they adapt their teaching to these students, and jointly discuss their experiences with them, this can increase the similarity in their approach toward ethnic diversity teaching.[2] More generally, working in the same school can lead to shared work-related values and ideas about education and school (Hargreaves, 1992), and thus to the development of teacher cultures (Van Houtte, 2005).

Effects of teachers' diversity instructions

In considering the effects of teachers' ethnic diversity education on children's interethnic relations, it is useful to make the broad distinction between informational and normative pathways (Verkuyten & Thijs, 2013). Most multicultural or intercultural educational initiatives assume that negative ethnic out-group attitudes and ethnic bias (i.e., a more positive evaluation of the in-group versus the out-group) are due to ignorance or 'faulty' information about cultural others. Hence, acquiring ('correct') *information* about different cultural groups and their experiences is considered of crucial importance (see Nagda et al., 2004; Rosenthal & Levy, 2010). This learning about the out-group can increase understanding and empathy (Hughes, Bigler, & Levy, 2007), result in the discovery of similarities that promote a more inclusive social identity in which 'they are part of us' (Houlette et al., 2004), and lead to a less ethnocentric worldview, implying a more modest in-group evaluation (see Pettigrew, 1998). Next, diversity education can have *normative* effects as it prescribes how diversity should be dealt with. Such effects are particularly relevant in relation to the rejection of prejudice and discrimination. There is a pervasive social norm against (ethnic) prejudice (Crandall, Eshleman, & O'Brien, 2002). Despite their differences, the multiculturalist, interculturalist, and color-blind approaches agree in their endorsement of this norm (Rattan & Ambady, 2013).[3]

Single measure studies

A number of the studies on the effects of teachers' ethnic diversity instructions have used unidimensional measures. Verkuyten and Thijs (2001) conducted a multilevel study in 47 Dutch primary school classrooms (grades 5–6) and found that teachers' self-reported multicultural education was associated with less ethnic bias in native Dutch and Turkish-Dutch children. The self-report measure consisted of four items that loaded on a single factor. However, these items were conceptually different as teachers were asked (1) whether they ever talked about different cultures in class and (2) whether their students did so, (3) whether they discussed discrimination and racism in class, and (4) whether they devoted time to the thought of respect for different cultures and religions. As a result, it is not clear whether the effect of this teaching was driven by the provision of information about group differences or group relation, the transmission of anti-prejudice norms, or both.

Another study asked Dutch secondary school students whether they ever discussed racism and discrimination in class, as well as 'the customs and habits of people from foreign cultures' (Bekhuis, Ruiter, & Coenders, 2013). These student reports were aggregated across classrooms to obtain a classroom-level measure of multicultural education. This measure was found to be unrelated to students' desire to avoid ethnic others (ethnic distance), and another study found that the unaggregated (i.e., student-level) measure was not related to the in-group evaluation of the ethnic majority students (Verkuyten, Thijs, & Bekhuis, 2010). This might suggest that teachers are unimportant for the ethnic attitudes of secondary school children. However, it should be noted that the items used did not directly refer to teachers and that secondary school students have several of them. Moreover, the measure addressed different aspects of ethnic diversity education.

This was not the case in four studies that examined the anti-prejudice component of diversity education in Dutch primary schools. The children in those studies were asked how often their teacher said 'that all cultures should be respected', 'that it is wrong to discriminate', and 'that people from all cultures are equal'. In two of these studies these individual responses were aggregated across students in the same classroom and found to be unrelated to the ethnic bias and out-group attitudes of both ethnic majority and ethnic minority children (Thijs & Verkuyten, 2012), but negatively related to the in-group evaluations of ethnic majority children (Thijs & Verkuyten, 2013). The two other studies examined these perceptions at the individual level and found that ethnic majority children who perceived a stronger teacher norm against prejudice reported more positive attitudes toward ethnic out-groups (Geerlings, Thijs, & Verkuyten, 2017). Taken together, these findings indicate that teachers can make majority children more positive toward their ethnic out-groups if they stress the normative unacceptability of prejudice, but only if these children personally perceive this. Additionally, if students collectively perceive this anti-discrimination norm, majority (but not minority) children may less positively inclined toward their in-group, presumably because they are more likely to regard their group members as prototypical perpetrators of discrimination (see Thijs, 2017).

Multiple measure studies

The number of studies that used multiple measures to assess teachers' ethnic diversity teachings is limited. Multiple measures can be used to relate different perspectives (e.g., those of teachers versus students), but also to examine how different aspects of diversity education complement or rather counteract each other.

The secondary school teachers in the research by Vervaet et al., (2018a, 2018b) completed a self-report scale for multicultural content integration (see Banks, 2004) which consisted of 12 items such as 'During my lessons at this school, I work explicitly on themes about differences between cultures', 'During my lessons at this school, I do not highlight holidays of different religions' (reverse coded), and 'During my lessons at this school, the many different cultures in our society are discussed'. These items loaded on a single factor, and the authors used their mean score to predict the degree of prejudice of native students against ethnic out-groups. However, because secondary school students have different teachers for different subjects, they decided to examine the overall impact of the teachers by aggregating the teacher scores in each school into a measure of multicultural teacher culture. Although there was substantial between-teacher variance (within schools), this aggregation was statistically justified. The main finding of this study was that a more multicultural teacher culture was associated with reduced ethnic prejudice among Flemish pupils, which supports the idea that explicit attention for ethnic and cultural differences can increase students' understanding of and for ethnic others (informational pathway). However, the study also included students' individual perceptions of multicultural teaching – which were assessed with corresponding versions of the teacher items (e.g., 'How many of your teachers at school work explicitly on themes about differences between cultures?') – and it was found that these perceptions mediated the association between multicultural teacher culture and pupils' ethnic prejudice. These findings support the informational pathway and highlight the importance of including pupils' perceptions (Vervaet et al., 2018b).

Kinket and Verkuyten (1999) used two student measures of ethnic diversity teaching in Dutch primary schools and they examined both the original as well as the classroom aggregated versions as simultaneous predictors of children's ethnic attitudes. The first measure involved the degree to which there was attention for cultural differences and discrimination in the classroom, and when aggregated, it had a negative effect on the ethnic bias and a positive effect on the ethnic out-group evaluations of both majority (native Dutch) and minority (Turkish-Dutch) children. Note that this complements the findings of Vervaet et al. (2018b), showing that students' perceptions of diversity teaching are important, but also that shared perceptions can impact children's ethnic attitudes regardless of their personal perceptions. However, minority children's personal perception of attention for discrimination and cultural differences had a positive effect on their out-group evaluations as well. The second measure addressed teachers' behavioral reactions to ethnic bullying, and for this measure, only the original (non-aggregated) version appeared to have effects: both minority and majority children were more positive and less biased toward their ethnic out-group, when they reported that their teacher would stand up against discrimination. In that case, they tended to be more positive about the in-group as well (Kinket & Verkuyten, 1999). These findings provide support for both the informational and normative pathways of ethnic diversity education.

A last study we discuss here does not involve ethnic attitudes, but minority and majority children's perceptions of ethnic discrimination. However, children's experiences of ethnic discrimination are clearly related to the ethnic attitudes in their classrooms (see Thijs, Verkuyten, & Grundel, 2014), and the study nicely illustrates the importance of including multiple measures of diversity teaching. Verkuyten and Thijs (2002) conducted a large scale research in Dutch primary schools (grades 5–6) using classroom-aggregated student perceptions of teachers' attention for discrimination and cultural differences, reactions to ethnic bullying, and teachers' self-reports of the importance they accorded to teaching about discrimination, cultural differences, and respect for other cultures and religions. It was found that children perceived less group discrimination (i.e., discrimination directed at their group in general) if their teacher regarded multicultural education as more important. Moreover, children reported fewer personal experiences with ethnic discrimination in classes where there was a shared perception that teachers and children would stand up against ethnic bullying, which indicates that teachers can improve ethnic relations by instigating an anti-discrimination norm. Yet at the same time, there were stronger reports of personal discrimination from native-Dutch children as well as group discrimination from native Dutch and Turkish-Dutch children in classrooms where students collectively perceived that their teacher paid attention to discrimination and cultural differences. This latter finding can be interpreted as an awareness effect. Learning about cultural differences and discrimination can increase children's ability and motivation to recognize discrimination, and this effect is especially relevant for majority children for whom discrimination is relatively uncommon (Verkuyten & Thijs, 2002).

Conditions of ethnic diversity teaching

Diversity teaching does not take place in a vacuum, and to understand the origins but also the effects of what individual teachers communicate about diversity, it is essential to focus on personal teacher factors as well as school and classroom characteristics.

Teacher factors

As individuals, teachers have their own ideas and preferences, and research has shown that they differ from each other in their beliefs about diversity (Hachfeld et al., 2011), ethnic prejudice (Van den Bergh, Denessen, Hornstra, Voeten, & Holland, 2010; Vervaet et al., 2018a), and their implicit ethnic attitudes (Van den Bergh et al., 2010; Vezzali, Giovannini, & Capozza, 2012). Such individual differences can affect the nature and the frequencies of their ethnic diversity teachings (Gay, 2010). For example, Vervaet and co-authors (2018a) found that ethnically prejudiced teachers in secondary schools were less involved with multicultural teaching than their less prejudiced colleagues. And Hachfeld et al. (2011) showed that German student teachers regarded multicultural teaching as more important if they were less prejudiced and more positive about cultural diversity in their society. However, teacher multi- or intercultural competencies could also play a role (McAllister & Irvine, 2000). A recent Australian study developed and tested an instrument for intercultural understanding in teachers in primary and secondary schools. This instrument contained a subscale for openness to cultural diversity, which was related to subscales for capabilities, such as cultural awareness, interpersonal skills, foreign language proficiencies, and the ability to reflect on one's own cultural background (Denson, Ovenden, Wright, Paradies, & Priest, 2017). The relation between teachers' multi- or intercultural competence and their ethnic diversity attitudes is important, because whereas it might be difficult and perhaps undesirable to change the latter, the former can be trained and developed (DeJaeghere & Cao, 2009).

Individual differences in beliefs, preferences, and competencies could also explain possible differences between ethnic majority versus ethnic minority and younger versus older teachers. For example, research has shown that, compared to their ethnic majority colleagues, ethnic minority teachers have more multicultural competences (McAllister & Irvine, 2000), practice multi-ethnic education to a greater extent (Agirdag et al., 2016), and talk more openly about cultural diversity (Gay, 2010), although they may lack experience and knowledge of other (minority) cultures (McAllister & Irvine, 2000). Likewise, younger teachers tend to have weaker multicultural attitudes (Munroe & Pearson, 2006) and may also have less cultural knowledge and experience (Spanierman et al., 2011).

Additionally, these personal factors might not only explain the difference between teachers' diversity teachings, but also the *effects* of these differences on students' ethnic attitudes and relations. It is reasonable to expect, for example, that teachers' instructions about the value and meanings of cultural differences are more convincing if teachers feel competent and confident in discussing these differences and if they 'believe in what they preach'. However, to date there has been no quantitative research to support (or reject) this claim.

School and classroom characteristics

When the number of ethnic minorities in school increases, the possibility of establishing interethnic contacts and having cross-cultural experiences also grows. This may enhance teachers' multicultural sensitivity and beliefs (Garmon, 2004; Gay, 2010), and research has shown that teachers find it easier to talk about ethnic diversity when more pupils from different cultures are present (Agirdag et al., 2016). Additionally, in multi-ethnic schools and classrooms, ethnic diversity is a part of daily life. This means that there is probably a stronger and more practical need there to pay attention to cultural differences and the problems of prejudice and discrimination. It is also easier to stimulate intercultural dialogue and exchange in these classrooms. In line with these notions, research has shown that multicultural teaching is practiced more in schools with a higher proportion of ethnic minority students (Agirdag et al., 2016; Verkuyten & Thijs, 2013; Vervaet et al., 2018a).

School and classroom ethnic compositions are also related to educational track. For example, in both Flemish and Dutch secondary schools, ethnic minority students are overrepresented in vocational education (Boone & Van Houtte, 2013; Huijnk & Andriessen, 2016), and teachers in this track might therefore have more interethnic contact and cross-cultural experiences. Moreover, these teachers tend to use more interactive forms of learning (Van Maele & Van Houtte, 2011), and this could imply that they talk more about other cultures in their classroom, and use more examples given by their (ethnic minority) students. Accordingly, research has shown that teachers in vocational education practice more multicultural teaching than teachers in academic or technical education (Vervaet et al., 2018a).

Next, the ethnic composition of the schools or classrooms may not only influence the content of ethnic diversity teaching, but also moderate its effects. The nature of this moderation may depend on its specific components. Due to the higher opportunity for contact with ethnic out-group peers, students in ethnically diverse schools may already know much about ethnic diversity and therefore have less need for further learning. Thus, these students may be less affected by what their teacher tells them about different cultures (cf., Bigler, 1999). However, in more ethnically diverse schools, there is also a larger probability of ethnic peer victimization (Thijs et al., 2014), which means that the normative, anti-discrimination component of ethnic diversity teaching is probably most relevant and effective there.

Finally, the religious denomination of schools could play a crucial role. In many countries there are religious (special) schools next to non-religious (or public) ones, and teachers in these various schools may teach different things about ethnic diversity. However, the relation between religious domination and diversity teaching can be complex or ambivalent. Agirdag and colleagues (2016) use a mixed-method study to examine multicultural teaching in Catholic and non-Catholic (state) primary schools in Belgium. Some of the teachers in their study indicated that teaching in a Catholic school provided opportunities to pay more attention to religious differences. Yet, other teachers argued that Catholic structures were largely unsupportive when it comes to multicultural issues. Moreover, teachers in Catholic schools reported less multicultural-content-integration activities than teachers in non-Catholic (state) schools (Agirdag et al., 2016).[4]

Conclusion

In this chapter we discussed the available quantitative research on teachers' contributions to diversity education. This research indicates that there can be individual differences in diversity teaching, even within the same schools, depending on teachers' beliefs, preferences, and competencies. Moreover, these differences can be assessed along multiple dimensions and affect students' ethnic attitudes by providing them with information about ethnic others but also by communicating norms against prejudice and discrimination.

As mentioned, there has been excellent qualitative work on teachers' dealings with diversity, and there will always be a need for qualitative research to obtain an in-depth understanding of the attitudes and behaviors of specific groups of people in particular contexts. Still, we think that the quantitative variable-centered approach discussed has a number of distinct benefits, implying different possibilities for future research. First, focusing on the underlying dimensions of diversity teaching has the distinct advantage that teachers from various contexts can be meaningfully compared. This makes it possible to study ethnic diversity teaching and the effects thereof, even if teachers do not explicitly ascribe to a particular diversity approach and regardless of whether their school has an official diversity curriculum or not. It also allows for comparisons of different teachers in different situations – say, a teacher in the UK who regularly asks her Pakistani-British students to talk about their heritage culture in class, versus a teacher in the Netherlands who celebrates Islamic and Christian feasts with both her Moroccan-Dutch and native Dutch students. As far as we know, there are no good multi-dimensional measurement instruments for making such comparisons. Therefore, developing and testing such instruments is an important task for future research. Ideally, they should contain parallel versions for teachers and students to compare and combine their different perspectives.

Next, a variable-centered approach also allows for a more detailed examination of the informational and normative effects of ethnic diversity education. These different effects may complement each other, but also interact. One possible hypothesis, for example, is that a strong teacher norm against ethnic prejudice and discrimination might be less effective when it is not accompanied by positive attention for cultural differences. In that case, students might develop the 'wrong' motivations to be non-prejudiced. That is to say, they might become excessively concerned with the reactions of others and less focused on the value of ethnic diversity. Eventually this might not reduce prejudice, and even increase it (see Legault, Gutsell, & Inzlicht, 2011).

Finally, combining different dimensions of diversity teaching allows researchers to study and explain both its intended and unintended effects. For instance, one point of criticism on the multicultural approach is that teachers who frequently discuss cultural differences in their classrooms may unintentionally increase children's stereotypical thinking if they do not address the commonalities between cultures, or if they essentialize the differences between them (see Bigler & Liben, 2007). A variable-centered research approach can directly test such claims, and thus provide informed input for discussions about the pros and cons of the different educational approaches toward diversity. We hope that the present chapter inspires researchers to follow this approach to obtain a better understanding of diversity education and its impact.

Notes

1 Until 2006, schools in the Netherlands were legally required to provide multicultural education, but this requirement was changed into the obligation to provide civic education.
2 There are other differences between pre-adolescent and adolescent students which could impact their reactions to diversity education. As there are different contradicting possibilities (e.g., larger independence of teachers with age, but also cognitive development and increased reflection on diversity) which have not been examined yet, we don't discuss them here.
3 The research described in this chapter partly supports the notion that teachers' diversity teachings influence students' diversity attitudes, but all of it used explicit (yet privately reported) measures reflecting the more conscious and deliberate aspects of students' attitudes. It is possible that students' implicit attitudes are less or even not affected by these teachings (see Dunham, Chen, & Banaji, 2013).
4 Religion in itself can also be an important source of group divisions. However, the research on ethnic diversity education has paid little attention to religious diversity.

References

Agirdag, O. (2016). Etnische diversiteit in het onderwijs. In B. Eidhof, M. Van Houtte, & M. Vermeulen (Eds.), *Sociologen over onderwijs. Inzichten, praktijken en kritieken* (pp. 281–308). Antwerpen, Belgium: Maklu.

Agirdag, O., Merry, M. S., & Van Houtte, M. (2016). Teachers' understanding of multicultural education and the correlates of multicultural content integration in Flanders. *Education and Urban Society, 48*(6), 556–582.

Arnesen, A., Allen, J., & Simonsen, E. (2009). *Policies and practices for teaching sociocultural diversity. Concepts, principles and challenges in teacher education.* Strasbourg: Council of Europe.

Bank, F., Bouwer, A., Deng, M., De Laet, A., De Witte, J., Hogendoorn, N., ... Van Crombrugge, H. (2005). *Verscheiden maar toch één. Reflecties over de interculturele vorming van jongeren (DIROO-Academia 6) (No. 6).* Gent/Thorn: Academia Press.

Banks, J. A. (2004). Multicultural education: Historical development, dimensions, and practice. In J. A. Banks & C. A. M. Banks (Eds.), *Handbook of research on multicultural education* (2nd ed., pp. 3–29). San Francisco, CA: Jossey-Bass.

Barrett, M. (2013). Intercultural competence: A distinctive hallmark of interculturalism? In M. Barrett (Ed.), *Interculturalism and multiculturalism: Similarities and differences* (pp. 147–168). Strasbourg: Council of Europe.

Baumann, G., Vertovec, S., Schiffauer, W., & Kastoryano, R. (2004). *Civil enculturation: Nation-state, school and ethnic difference in the Netherlands, Britain, Germany and France*. New York: Berghahn.

Bekhuis, H., Ruiter, S., & Coenders, M. (2013). Xenophobia among youngsters: The effect of interethnic contact. *European Sociological Review*, 29(2), 229–242.

Bigler, R. S. (1999). The use of multicultural curricula and materials to counter racism in children. *Journal of Social Issues*, 55(4), 687–705.

Bigler, R. S., & Liben, L. S. (2007). Developmental intergroup theory: Explaining and reducing children's social stereotyping and prejudice. *Current Directions in Psychological Science*, 16(3), 162–166.

Boone, S., & Van Houtte, M. (2013). In search of the mechanisms conducive to class differentials in educational choice: A mixed method research. *The Sociological Review*, 61(3), 549–572.

Colman, R., De Coster, M., Geysmans, R., Waerniers, R., Mertens, L., Bodart, E., … Hustinx, L. (2017). *Lessenpakket Burgerschap: Basisbegrippen-Globalisering-De Multiculturele samenleving*. Gent: Universiteit Gent.

Crandall, C. S., Eshleman, A., & O'Brien, L. (2002). Social norms and the expression and suppression of prejudice: The struggle for internalization. *Journal of Personality and Social Psychology*, 82(3), 359–378.

DeJaeghere, J. G., & Cao, Y. (2009). Developing U.S. teachers' intercultural competence: Does professional development matter? *International Journal of Intercultural Relations*, 33(5), 437–447.

Denson, N., Ovenden, G., Wright, L., Paradies, Y., & Priest, N. (2017). The development and validation of intercultural understanding (ICU) instruments for teachers and students in primary and secondary schools. *Intercultural Education*, 28(3), 231–249.

De Wit, K., & Van Petegem, P. (2000). *Gelijke kansen in het Vlaamse onderwijs: Het beleid inzake kansengelijkheid*. Leuven, Belgium: Garant.

Dunham, Y., Chen, E. E., & Banaji, M. R. (2013). Two signatures of implicit intergroup attitudes: Developmental invariance and early enculturation. *Psychological Science*, 24, 860–868.

Garmon, M. A. (2004). Changing preservice teachers' attitudes/beliefs about diversity: What are the critical factors? *Journal of Teacher Education*, 55(3), 201–213.

Gay, G. (2000). *Culturally responsive teaching: Theory, practice and research*. New York: Teachers College Press.

Gay, G. (2010). Acting on beliefs in teacher education for cultural diversity. *Journal of Teacher Education*, 61(1–2), 143–152.

Geerlings, J., Thijs, J., & Verkuyten, M. (2017). Student-teacher relationships and ethnic outgroup attitudes among majority students. *Journal of Applied Developmental Psychology*, 52, 69–79. doi:10.1016/j.appdev.2017.07.002

Gillborn, D. (1990). *Race, ethnicity and education: Teaching and learning in multicultural schools*. London: Unwin Hyman/Routledge.

Gorski, P. C. (2009). What we're teaching teachers: An analysis of multicultural teacher education coursework syllabi. *Teaching and Teacher Education*, 25(2), 309–318.

Hachfeld, A., Hahn, A., Schroeder, S., Anders, Y., Stanat, P., & Kunter, M. (2011). Assessing teachers' multicultural and egalitarian beliefs: The teacher cultural beliefs scale. *Teaching and Teacher Education*, 27(6), 986–996.

Hargreaves, A. (1992). Cultures of teaching: A focus for change. In A. Hargreaves & M. Fullan (Eds.), *Understanding teacher development*. London: Cassell and New York: Teachers College Press, 216–240.

Houlette, M. A., Gaertner, S. L., Johnson, K. M., Banker, B. S., Riek, B. M., & Dovidio, J. F. (2004). Developing a more inclusive social identity: An elementary school intervention. *Journal of Social Issues*, 60(1), 35–55.

Hughes, J. M., Bigler, R. S., & Levy, S. R. (2007). Consequences of learning about historical racism among European American and African American children. *Child Development*, 78(6), 1689–1705.

Huijnk, W., & Andriessen, I. (2016). *Integratie in zicht? De integratie van migranten in Nederland op acht terreinen nader bekeken*. The Hague: The Netherlands Institute for Social Research.

Kahn, M. (2008). Multicultural education in the United States: Reflections. *Intercultural Education*, 19(6), 527–536.

Kinket, B., & Verkuyten, M. (1999). Intergroup evaluations and social context: A multilevel approach. *European Journal of Social Psychology*, 29(2-3), 219–237.

Legault, L., Gutsell, J. N., & Inzlicht, M. (2011). Ironic effects of antiprejudice messages: How motivational interventions can reduce (but also increase) prejudice. *Psychological Science*, 22(12), 1472–1477.

Marx, H., & Moss, D. M. (2011). Please mind the culture gap: Intercultural development during a teacher education study abroad program. *Journal of Teacher Education*, 62(1), 35–47.

McAllister, G., & Irvine, J. J. (2000). Cross cultural competency and multicultural teacher education. *Review of Educational Research*, 70(1), 3–24.

Meer, N., & Modood, T. (2012). How does interculturalism contrast with multiculturalism? *Journal of Intercultural Studies*, 33(2), 175–196.

Munroe, A., & Pearson, C. (2006). The Munroe multicultural attitude scale questionnaire: A new instrument for multicultural studies. *Educational and Psychological Measurement*, 66(5), 819–834.

Nagda, B. A., Kim, C. W., & Truelove, Y. (2004). Learning about difference, learning with others, learning to transgress. *Journal of Social Issues*, 60(1), 195–214. https://doi.org/10.1111/j.0022-4537.2004.00106.x

Onderwijsinspectie. (2006). *Toezicht op burgerschap en integratie*. Rijswijk, The Netherlands: GSE.

Pettigrew, T. F. (1998). Intergroup contact theory. *Annual Review of Psychology*, 49(1), 65–85.

Plaut, V. C., Garnett, F. G., Buffardi, L. E., & Sanchez-Burks, J. (2011). "What about me?" Perceptions of exclusion and Whites' reactions to multiculturalism. *Journal of Personality and Social Psychology*, 101(2), 337–353.

Portera, A. (2008). Intercultural education in Europe: Epistemological and semantic aspects. *Intercultural Education*, 19(6), 481–491.

Pulinx, R., Van Avermaet, P., & Agirdag, O. (2017). Silencing linguistic diversity: The extent, the determinants and consequences of the monolingual beliefs of Flemish teachers. *International Journal of Bilingual Education and Bilingualism*, 20(5), 542–556.

Quintana, S. M. (1998). Children's developmental understanding of ethnicity and race. *Applied and Preventive Psychology*, 7(1), 27–45.

Raabe, T., & Beelman, A. (2011). Development of ethnic, racial, and national prejudice in childhood and adolescence: A multinational meta-analysis of age differences. *Child Development*, *82*(6), 1715–1737.

Rattan, A., & Ambady, N. (2013). Diversity ideologies and intergroup relations: An examination of colorblindness and multiculturalism. *European Journal of Social Psychology*, *43*(1), 12–21.

Rosenthal, L., & Levy, S. M. (2010). The colorblind, multicultural, and polycultural ideological approaches to improving intergroup attitudes and relations. *Social Issues and Policy Review*, *4*(1), 215–246.

Schofield, J. W. (2001). The colorblind perspective in school: Causes and consequences. In J. A. Banks & C. A. McGee Banks (Eds.), *Multicultural education. Issues & perspectives* (4th ed., pp. 247–267). New York: Wiley.

Snijders, T., & Bosker, R. (1999). *Multilevel analysis: An introduction to basic and applied multilevel analysis*. London: Sage.

Spanierman, L. B., Oh, E., Heppner, P. P., Neville, H. A., Mobley, M., Wright, C. V., ... Navarro, R. (2011). The multicultural teaching competency scale: Development and initial validation. *Urban Education*, *46*(3), 440–464.

Stephan, C. W., Renfro, L., & Stephan, W. G. (2004). The evaluation of multicultural education programs: Techniques and a meta-analysis. In W. G. Stephan & W. P. Vogt (Eds.), *Education programs for improving intergroup relations: Theory, research, and practice* (pp. 227–242). New York: Teacher College Press.

Thijs, J. (2017). Children's evaluations of interethnic exclusion: The effects of ethnic boundaries, respondent ethnicity, and majority in-group bias. *Journal of Experimental Child Psychology*, *158*, 46–63. doi:10.1016/j.jecp.2017.01.005

Thijs, J., & Verkuyten, M. (2012). Ethnic attitudes of minority students and their contact with majority group teachers. *Journal of Applied Developmental Psychology*, *33*(5), 260–268.

Thijs, J., & Verkuyten, M. (2013). Multiculturalism in the classroom: Ethnic attitudes and classmates' beliefs. *International Journal of Intercultural Relations*, *37*(2), 176–187.

Thijs, J., Verkuyten, M., & Grundel, M. (2014). Ethnic classroom composition and peer victimization: The moderating role of classroom attitudes. *Journal of Social Issues*, *70*(1), 134–150.

Ülger, Z., Dette-Hagenmeyer, D. E., Reichle, B., & Gaertner, S. L. (2018). Improving outgroup attitudes in schools: A meta-analytic review. *Journal of School Psychology*, *67*, 88–103. doi:10.1016/j.jsp.2017.10.002

Van den Bergh, L., Denessen, E., Hornstra, L., Voeten, M., & Holland, R. W. (2010). The implicit prejudiced attitudes of teachers: Relations to teacher expectations and the ethnic achievement gap. *American Educational Research Journal*, *47*(2), 497–527.

Van Houtte, M. (2005). Climate or culture? A plea for conceptual clarity in school effectiveness research. *School Effectiveness and School Improvement*, *16*(1), 71–89.

Van Maele, D., & Van Houtte, M. (2011). Teacher trust in students in technical/vocational schools versus academic schools and the role of teacher perception of students' teachability. In B. R. Curtis (Ed.), *Psychology of trust* (pp. 117–135). Hauppauge, NY: Nova Science Publishers.

Vanduynslager, L., Wets, J., Noppe, J., & Doyen, G. (2013). *Vlaamse migratie- en integratiemonitor 2013*. Brussel, Belgium: Steunpunt Inburgering en Integratie, Studiedienst van de Vlaamse Regering.

Verkuyten, M., & Thijs, J. (2001). Ethnic and gender bias among Dutch and Turkish children in late childhood: The role of social context. *Infant and Child Development*, *10*(4), 203–217.

Verkuyten, M., & Thijs, J. (2002). Racist victimization among children in the Netherlands: The effect of ethnic group and school. *Ethnic and Racial Studies*, *25*(2), 310–331.

Verkuyten, M., & Thijs, J. (2013). Multicultural education and inter-ethnic attitudes. *European Psychologist*, *18*(3), 179–190.

Verkuyten, M., Thijs, J., & Bekhuis, H. (2010). Intergroup contact and ingroup reappraisal: Testing the deprovincialization hypothesis. *Social Psychology Quarterly*, *73*(4), 398–416.

Vervaet, R., Van Houtte, M., & Stevens, P. A. (2018a). Multicultural teaching in Flemish secondary schools: The role of ethnic school composition, track, and teachers' ethnic prejudice. *Education and Urban Society*, *50*(3), 274–299.

Vervaet, R., Van Houtte, M., & Stevens, P. A. J. (2018b). The ethnic prejudice of Flemish pupils: The role of pupils' and teachers' perceptions of multicultural teacher culture. *Teacher College Records*, *120*(5), 1–30.

Vezzali, L., Giovannini, D., & Capozza, D. (2012). Social antecedents of children's implicit prejudice: Direct contact, extended contact, explicit and implicit teachers' prejudice. *European Journal of Developmental Psychology*, *9*(5), 569–581.

Vlaamse Onderwijsraad. (2005). *Beleidsvoerend vermogen van scholen ontwikkelen. Een verkenning*. Antwerpen, Belgium: Garant.

Zirkel, S. (2008). The influence of multicultural educational practices on student outcomes and intergroup relations. *The Teachers College Record*, *110*(6), 1147–1181.

Chapter 17

How to best prepare teachers for multicultural schools

Challenges and perspectives

Sauro Civitillo and Linda P. Juang

Cultural diversity in society is not a new phenomenon, but its nature is rapidly changing around the world. Currently, there are 258 million migrants (i.e., those not living in their country of birth) recorded worldwide, more than ever before (United Nations, 2017). Among refugees specifically, 51 percent are under the age of 18 (UNHCR, 2019). While student populations reflect this global trend of increasing migration-based diversity, teachers and teacher educators remain predominantly homogeneous with an overwhelming presence of members of the dominant culture (Santoro, 2015). For instance, only 7.2 percent of the elementary and secondary school teaching staff in Germany are of migrant background (European Commission, 2016). In stark contrast, 31 percent of school-aged children are of migrant background (Statistisches Bundesamt Mikrozensus, 2016). In the United States, 18 percent of teachers are ethnic minorities while 54 percent of school-aged children are ethnic minorities (U.S. Department of Education, 2016). Thus, the diversity of the educator workforce is not keeping pace with the diversity of the student body. This discrepancy can produce challenges for both students and teachers as they navigate the cultural and pedagogical environment of learning.

Importantly, this growing mismatch between the background and lived experiences of different educational stakeholders represents a potential challenge to effectively teaching diverse students in their classrooms. Not all pre-service teachers may hold positive beliefs about cultural diversity (Glock, Kovacs, & Pit-ten Cate, in press), report high levels of self-efficacy in promoting culturally responsive instructions (Civitillo, Juang, Schachner, & Börnert, 2016; Siwatu, 2011), are comfortable working with minority students (Warren, 2018), and have knowledge of empowering pedagogical approaches in culturally diverse classrooms (Gay, 2000). Initial teacher preparation (ITP) and ongoing professional learning need to provide teachers – independently of their cultural background – with support which is not limited to an isolated learning opportunity (e.g., a single module or an elective course) but a teacher education continuum. There is evidence that teacher training for culturally responsive teaching can be effective, but the evidence is limited (Civitillo, Juang, & Schachner, 2018).

Because of the crucial role of teachers and schools on the social, emotional, and academic development of children and adolescents, many scholars subscribe to the idea that improving ITP empowers students (Gay, 2000; Milner, 2010). Clearly, other important social factors, such as institutional discrimination and poverty, contribute substantially to inequitable educational outcomes (Cochran-Smith & Villegas, 2016) and enlarge the opportunity gap (Gorski, 2017). In addition, teaching universities face a myriad of pressures that influence the way ITPs are designed to include cultural diversity. Unprecedented attention to teacher quality and test-based accountability given by national and international accreditation agencies results from international large-scale assessment investigations such as PISA, all of which raise concerns and increase the pressure related to the quality of preparation of future teachers. However, in the set of ITP professional responsibilities, teacher preparation for meeting cultural diversity in school is often not seen as a priority for educational policymakers.

Nonetheless, in this chapter, we argue that it should certainly be a priority. With increasingly diverse societies around the world, operating within a culturally diverse classroom requires cultural sensitivity and competence on the part of the teacher in order to productively communicate, build relationships with, and teach those who are perceived as culturally different (Barrett, 2018). Therefore, because of the crucial role of ITP in building resilient and well-equipped teachers, in the first part of this chapter we will focus on how ITP should address teacher beliefs about cultural diversity, boost culturally responsive teaching self-efficacy, promote the development of empathy, and support knowledge of pedagogical approaches that have been successful for the needs of culturally diverse students. In the second part of the chapter, we will present guidelines and evaluation questions tailored for use by teacher education institutions to effectively assess the efforts to improve ITP for cultural diversity.

Beliefs about cultural diversity

Research on the bidirectional relationships between teachers' beliefs and practices has rapidly grown in the last two decades. A review of the teacher belief literature (Fives & Buehl, 2012) indicates that beliefs teachers hold towards a certain matter (e.g., cultural diversity in education) have three relevant functions: they act as a filter to knowledge, they influence the framing of a problem or a task, and they guide the teacher's intention and action. The function of beliefs as a filter is particularly relevant in the context of ITP. Beliefs function as a filter in the sense of shaping and interpreting the information teachers receive during all phases of their professional development, determining the knowledge that will later be transferred to their teaching. Thus, ITP is viewed as the principal vehicle to ensure from the very beginning that teachers acknowledge and challenge their own beliefs about cultural diversity in education.

Although beliefs might be relatively stable and resistant to change because the origins of teachers' beliefs are tied to individuals' experiences (e.g., prior school experience, cross-cultural life experiences), it is during ITP that beliefs are more susceptible to change (Milner, 2010). A systematic review of the literature on trainings addressing cultural diversity beliefs with pre-service teachers showed that these trainings can be effective (Civitillo et al., 2018). Two training components seemed particularly beneficial for developing openness and receptivity for diversity: an experiential component, and the opportunity for self-reflection and critical discussion about cultural diversity. However, these trainings differ considerably in terms of content and effectiveness as well as on the way cultural diversity beliefs are operationalized. Moreover, only a few studies reviewed attempted to explore the effects of training on cultural diversity beliefs by also measuring changes in the actual teaching behavior. Therefore, the reported effects of trainings on pre-service teachers need to make sure that changes in beliefs are reflected in effectively teaching diverse students.

Different ideologies derived from the field of social psychology (e.g., color evasiveness[1] and multiculturalism) have been adapted to study teachers' beliefs about cultural diversity. Conceptually, color evasiveness and multiculturalism are not mutually exclusive, in fact, both ideologies arguably advocate for equality. However, empirical research with pre-service teachers has shown that a strong endorsement of color evasive ideology (i.e., ignoring cultural or racial/ethnic differences and pursuing an illusory state of equality) is associated with negative outcomes. In Germany, preservice teachers ($N = 433$) holding beliefs in line with color evasiveness were found to be less willing to adapt teaching to culturally diverse students (Hachfeld, Hahn, Schroeder, Anders, & Kunter, 2015). Likewise, in a sample of 239 U.S. White prospective teachers, greater color evasive beliefs predicted lower levels of cultural diversity awareness (Wang, Castro, & Cunningham, 2014). Thus, counteracting color evasive beliefs can help the recognition of culturally diverse groups, and support the use of culturally responsive teaching.

Pre-service teachers' beliefs are unlikely to be challenged if other significant educational stakeholders (e.g., teacher educators) themselves hold beliefs that are in line with a color evasive ideology or embrace a deficit perspective on diversity. Educational stakeholders with a deficit perspective on diversity are inclined to attribute differences in educational outcomes between majority and minority students to cultural stereotypes, inadequate socialization, or lack of motivation and initiative on the part of the students (Bensimon, 2005). Accordingly, teacher educators who endorse color evasive or deficit-oriented beliefs about cultural diversity were found to be less eager to adopt inclusive teaching practices in universities and ITPs (Aragón, Dovidio, & Graham, 2017). Therefore, in addition to examining pre-service teachers' beliefs, more research is needed to investigate teacher educators' beliefs about cultural diversity, focusing on the effects of different ideologies and deconstructing discourses of deficit regarding diversity.

Culturally responsive teaching self-efficacy

There is an ever-increasing interest about the role of teacher self-efficacy beliefs in the field of teacher education. Grounded in social cognitive theory (Bandura, 1997), self-efficacy beliefs are defined as individuals' perceptions of their capabilities to execute and plan specific behavior. Yet, scant attention has been paid to context and task-specific attributes of teacher self-efficacy. For example, teacher self-efficacy in classrooms and schools with ethnically mixed student bodies could be perceived differently than self-efficacy in schools with a more homogeneous ethnic make-up. Building on culturally responsive teaching (Gay, 2000; Ladson-Billings, 1995), Siwatu (2007) introduced the concept of culturally responsive teaching self-efficacy, partially addressing the context and task-specific issues, by increasing the specificity of teacher self-efficacy. Culturally responsive teaching self-efficacy is the perceived capability to enact the pedagogical principles of culturally responsive teaching. Accordingly, a teacher could feel efficacious when teaching history but less efficacious in the teaching of history regarding marginalized populations or including materials and perspectives that reflect diverse students' cultural backgrounds. Measures of culturally responsive teaching self-efficacy have been adapted to different educational contexts outside of the United States (in Taiwan, Chu, 2013; in Germany, Civitillo et al., 2016), expanding the generalizability of this construct.

Similarly to cultural diversity beliefs, self-efficacy is particularly malleable during ITP. Following Bandura's insights (1997), mastery and vicarious experiences are powerful sources of self-efficacy information and development. For most pre-service teachers, opportunities to practice (mastery experiences) and observe (vicarious experiences) culturally responsive teaching ideally occur during the field experience situated in culturally diverse classrooms. In a mixed-methods study, Siwatu (2011) reviewed the doubts of pre-service teachers who reported low culturally responsive teaching self-efficacy. Participants indicated having few opportunities to practice or observe aspects of culturally responsive teaching during ITP. When these opportunities were offered, they occurred not in their instructional methods courses (e.g., teaching mathematics in the elementary school) but in sporadic classroom discussions. Fitchett and colleagues (2012) developed and tested the effects of a social studies methods course, integrating culturally responsive teaching insights and practical examples of successful culturally responsive instructional planning. At the end of the course, results showed that pre-service teachers were more efficacious in their abilities to teach multicultural social studies content. Thus, also in a method course, a combination of theoretical insights and related practical examples can promote culturally responsive teaching self-efficacy.

Teacher empathy

The development of teachers' empathy is also important for effective teaching in culturally diverse classrooms (Warren, 2014, 2018). Empathy is defined as including both cognitive and affective perspective taking. In other words, teachers engaging in empathy are able to understand children's perspectives within the latter's specific social contexts. Engaging in empathy improves communication between teachers and students in classrooms and, subsequently, how responsive teachers are to culturally diverse students (Warren, 2014, 2018). Teacher empathy is essential for building better student–teacher relationships (Dolby, 2012) by improving the quality of intercultural student–teacher interactions (Peck, Maude, & Brotherson, 2015), so that children feel they are understood and valued.

Empathy is a tool that teachers can use to better understand the students they teach (Warren, 2018). For pre-service teachers, it is useful to learn how empathy informs their professional decisions regarding student learning. More specifically, empathy through perspective taking allows teachers to critique and elaborate on existing knowledge and acquire new knowledge about their students, their students' families, and the specific social context. This knowledge can then guide and inform how the teacher responds to the students, what educational materials they select, and how they structure the students' learning experiences.

Relatedly, a recent study suggests that becoming more familiar with children, for example, staying with them for two years during elementary school instead of just one, is beneficial for children's academic achievement, and especially for children of color and those who show lower academic performance (Hill & Jones, 2018). The findings indicate that the longer period of time spent with the children meant that there was more time for teachers to get to know and work with the child and family, subsequently, in the second year the teacher had more in-depth familiarity and knowledge of the child. Teacher empathy and perspective taking may be the key mechanisms through which familiarity with children is linked to better children's academic performance. Importantly, the study also found that the benefits of longer time spent with children were greater for the less effective (compared to more effective) teachers to improve their teaching.

Pedagogical approaches: culturally responsive teaching

To effectively teach diverse students, the ideological, cognitive, and emotional grounding should be complemented with a mastery of knowledge related to pedagogical principles that account for cultural diversity in education. Born as an outgrowth of multicultural education, culturally responsive teaching (CRT) is a conceptual framework developed in the United States more than 25 years ago. Several scholars from historically underrepresented groups have contributed to the development of CRT (e.g., Gay, 2000; Ladson-Billings, 1995; Nieto, 1992; Paris, 2012). Although there are differences in the way CRT is conceptualized, there is general agreement that it validates students' cultural identities and promotes connections to their multiple cultures. For instance, CRT advocates for including heritage language during teaching instructions and interactions with parents. CRT questions the sole use of standardized testing to assess academic achievement and encourages teachers to employ a plurality of opportunities to demonstrate what students learn. CRT empowers students' sociopolitical consciousness by critically examining school curricula and teaching materials (e.g., books), offering classroom learning occasions that reflect their cultural experiences outside of school. Thus, CRT is a multidimensional construct and encompasses instructional strategies, achievement assessment, as well as curriculum content. The doorway of CRT is establishing positive teacher–student relationships, meaning that teachers consciously pay attention to issues of cultural variations in the relationships with students (Gay, 2000).

A narrative synthesis of qualitative studies has demonstrated that CRT benefits multiple kinds of student achievement across the content areas of history, social studies, as well as subjects often considered culture-free such as mathematics and science (Aronson & Laughter, 2016). Relatedly, more quantitative and longitudinal findings speak in favor of CRT practices for students from various minority and traditionally marginalized groups (Dee & Penner, 2017; Matthews & López, in press). All in all, these results indicate that students' cultural backgrounds should be considered as a resource in teaching and learning rather than as a problem to overcome or ignore. However, much of the existing research on CRT reports evidence from one country, namely the United States. More research is needed to explore and describe how pre-service teachers' exposure to CRT is implemented in ITPs in other major immigrant destinations, across different levels of schooling and subjects.

Furthermore, there is a necessity for translating the insights of CRT scholars into a cohesive representation of teaching and learning practices. Critics to CRT often highlight that it is unclear what CRT means and how it looks in the classroom (Schmeichel, 2012). These critiques provide input for discussion and for conducting more systematic empirical research without dismissing the field of CRT. For example, Powell and colleagues (2016) have recently developed and validated a classroom observation protocol that can be used to assess culturally responsive practices of pre-service and in-service teachers. CRT should not be reduced to a checklist of steps, but this observation protocol can be used in combination with teacher and student self-report measures (e.g., see Civitillo et al., 2019). Capturing CRT through a variety of research methods could support implementation as well as finding obstacles to culturally responsive teaching in ITP.

ITP evaluation framework

Self-evaluations are often the only instrument used to assess the efforts of ITPs to prepare future teachers engaging with culturally and ethnically diverse students. We adopt a framework that has been used to evaluate inclusive initial teacher preparation (Salend, 2010). This evaluation framework, in line with the complexity theory of teacher professional learning (Opfer & Pedder, 2011), highlights the nested nature of organizational levels within ITPs. More specifically, to comprehensively evaluate efforts for developing a coherent teacher preparation for embracing cultural diversity, we should consider demographic characteristics of individual teachers (individual level), learning activities presented to them (activity level), and institutional support for cultural diversity reflected in ITP curricula (institutional level). We thus present and highlight the importance of evaluating three different, albeit related, levels of analysis (individual, activity, and institutional), along with a series of evaluation questions that could be used to carry on a systematic evaluation of ITP for preparing future teachers for diversity (see Table 17.1).

Individual level

In many countries, there is a commitment to training a more culturally and ethnically diverse educator workforce. Recently, the University of Potsdam in Germany has created the Refugee Teachers Programme to prepare refugees who worked as teachers in their home country to teach in German schools (Kubicka, Wojciechowicz, & Vock, 2018). Accordingly, the common perspectives and similar experiences that students and teachers who share the same ethnic minority or migration status, or who are both part of a minority, may be beneficial. For instance, research findings from the USA showed that students with same-ethnic teachers (e.g., African-American) report feeling more cared for, have better student–teacher communication, have better teacher guidance, and also score higher in reading and math, with stronger effects for lower income students (Dee, 2004; Egalite & Kisida, 2018). When there is a higher proportion of

Table 17.1 Evaluation framework with sample evaluation questions for the three levels of initial teaching preparation

	Sample evaluation questions
Individual level	How do demographic characteristics (cultural and ethnic background) of pre-service teachers within ITP reflect the student population within a country?
	What efforts have been implemented and what actions need to be taken by ITP to recruit and retain a culturally and ethnically diverse pool of pre-service teachers and teacher educators?
	What factors are affecting ITP success in the recruitment and retention of a culturally and ethnically diverse pool of pre-service teachers and teacher educators?
Activity level	How is cultural and ethnic diversity framed in coursework and to whom are they offered within ITP?
	How do coursework and field-based experiences provide pre-service teachers opportunities to reflect on their cultural diversity beliefs, foster their empathy and perspective taking, and improve their knowledge of culturally responsive teaching?
	How does service-learning community provide pre-service teachers opportunities to enhance their knowledge of the lives of culturally and ethnically diverse students and families, and broaden their views and understandings?
	What efforts have been implemented and what actions need to be taken to strengthen the collaboration between ITPs, schools, and communities?
Institutional level	How do demographic characteristics (cultural and ethnic backgrounds) of teacher educators within ITP reflect the pre-service teachers and student population within a country? How are ITP's core beliefs regarding cultural diversity transmitted to the ITP curriculum?
	What efforts have been implemented and what actions need to be taken to maintain a conceptual coherence of cultural and ethnic diversity into the ITP curriculum?

ethnic minority teachers in a school district there are fewer suspensions, lower levels of being classified as mildly mentally disabled, and higher levels of enrollment in a gifted program for Latino and African American students (Rocha & Hawes, 2009). When the proportion of the racial/ethnic teacher workforce is similar to the student population there are lower drop-out rates and greater high school graduation rates (Pitts, 2007).

Finally, Black students are three times more likely to be placed in math and reading gifted-education programs if they have a Black teacher rather than a non-Black teacher (Grissom & Redding, 2016). Although supporting diversity in ITP, and successively in the teaching workforce, will not guarantee per se increasing cultural responsiveness in heterogeneous classrooms, some studies do suggest positive academic outcomes when student cultural, ethnic, and migration backgrounds are represented also in teachers. In contrast, two studies in Germany do not find that students of migrant background do better academically if they have teachers of a migrant background (Klein, Neugebauer, & Jacob, 2019; Neugebauer & Klein, 2016).

At the same time, there is a need to generate more knowledge especially around beliefs, empathy, and associated behaviors of ethnic minority pre-service teachers and teacher educators. In fact, the majority of studies focusing on ITP have reported evidence from pre-service teachers who are predominantly members of the dominant culture. One of few exceptions is Bakari's study (2003) in which African American pre-service teachers enrolled in historically Black colleges held more positive beliefs towards teaching African American students than those from predominantly White universities in rural areas of the USA. Cherng and Davis (2017) surveyed a large sample of pre-service teachers from different ethnic backgrounds (N = 2500), finding similar evidence: Black and Latino pre-service teachers reported higher multicultural awareness than White and Asian American teachers. Existing studies cautiously indicate that the diversification of pre-service teachers may be associated with a strong support and commitment to cultural diversity.

Besides devoting efforts to promote greater representations of pre-service teachers from different cultural and ethnic backgrounds in ITP, it is suggested that improving their retention should also be a goal equally important to achieve. In Europe, pre-service teachers with migrant or minority background are more likely to drop out of ITP (European Commission, 2016). Ethnic minority teachers in elementary and secondary schools leave their schools and academic departments at higher rates than ethnic majority teachers (European Commission, 2016). Although there is some evidence that minority in-service teachers face different forms of discrimination based on ethnic origin, language skills, and religious beliefs (Georgi, 2010), it is less clear if similar discriminatory practices can cause pre-service teachers to abandon their studies during ITP. To increase retention rates, research should take into account the experiences, concerns, and issues that ethnic minority pre-service teachers face during ITP (Haddix, 2017). Along the same vein, teacher educators should take the opportunity of the presence of ethnic minority teachers to advance their understanding of factors contributing to their academic persistence and interest in educational careers (Scott & Rodriguez, 2015). Studies of in-service ethnic minority teachers indicate that mentoring and supportive networks from peers and administration can improve retention (for a review, see Achinstein, Ogawa, Sexton, & Freitas, 2010). Importantly, the issue of recruitment along with the graduation and retention of diverse teaching populations and teacher educators is a question that should be asked when evaluating ITP.

Activities level

Coursework

During ITP the number of learning opportunities to prepare for cultural diversity is still scarce. A recent overview of the educational policy of European countries has pointed out that only a relatively small number of ITPs surveyed have included courses on cultural diversity (European Commission, 2017). Moreover, these courses are often elective, in which participants either volunteered or are selected to participate, and thus are offered only to a small number of pre-service teachers. The attendance requirement can indicate how cultural diversity is positioned and reinforced within ITP (Milner, 2010). In addition, pre-service teachers are frequently exposed to one single learning opportunity (Civitillo et al., 2018). This also raises the question of whether completion of a single course on cultural diversity is sufficient, for example, to target and change cultural diversity beliefs. Kumar and Lauermann (2018) found that pre-service teachers who completed more multicultural courses and spent more time in ITP were also more likely to have fewer teacher stereotypical beliefs towards culturally diverse students, less discomfort with student diversity, and less reluctance to implement culturally responsive practices. Yet, it is unclear whether the quantity (number of multicultural courses) may not be enough or more beneficial than just one good coursework (quality), or whether the content or learning methods implemented in a course are the crucial elements for effectiveness.

Field-based experience and community-based learning

Experiential learning in the format of field-based experience and community-based learning is frequently indicated as beneficial in ITP. The benefits derived from pre-service teachers range from helping them to link theoretical insights to teaching practice, to observing other practitioners, to endorsing more positive intergroup attitudes (Salend, 2010). Possible explanations for improving intergroup attitudes might be that contact between groups under certain conditions can improve intergroup relations (Pettigrew & Tropp, 2006). In field-based experiences offered during ITP, however, it is difficult to control for certain moderating factors (i.e., group status, contact quantity) than for other equally valuable aspects of field-based experience (i.e., the valence of the contact or content quality). Given that field-based experiences differed greatly in how they are situated in ITP, it is essential that researchers and teacher educators report in greater detail contextual variables of the field-based experience (e.g., mentoring support, pre- or post-reflections on the experience) that might explain and support their practices. Besides domestic field-based experience, there is also a growing trend of international field-based experiences; that is, gathering experiences associated with the teacher's role in a foreign country. Smolcic and Katunich (2017) reviewed 22 studies published over the past 15 years reporting international cultural immersion field-based experiences in ITP. Collectively, the reviewed studies successively targeted several learning outcomes such as developing an awareness of the role of culture in teaching, socio-political awareness and consciousness, and understanding the process of second language learning. Despite these promising results, the authors note: 'absent from this body of research (i.e., international field-based experience) are the voice and perspectives of the communities of people within which its participants move and learn' (p. 56). This is an important warning for teacher educators that should be considered when planning such international field-based experiences.

Community-based learning, namely being immersed in communities different from one's own and learning how to teach closely with students, is thought to be a meaningful approach for preparing pre-service teachers (Cooper, 2007). In these community-based experiences, pre-service teachers reflect upon, discuss, and negotiate strategies and solutions with other educational stakeholders, including students' families. This, in turn, can help teachers experience and foster a shared and collective responsibility, as well as critically examine teachers' own assumptions and biases (Baldwin, Buchanan, & Rudisill, 2007; Conner, 2010). However, community-based experiences require a consolidated partnership between ITP, school, and community that is often built after a good deal of work, as well as a non-hierarchical interplay between academic, school staff, and community expertise (Zeichner, 2010). Yet, as for field-based experience, the community-based learning needs a research-based approach that makes use of longitudinal and multi-source evaluations to support their effectiveness, involving all educational stakeholders.

Institutional level

Sustaining a radical and durable change in ITP for preparing pre-service teachers to deal with increasing cultural and ethnic diversity requires support and advocacy among teacher educators, administrators, and other institutional personnel. Institutional support and advocacy are reflected in many instances as providing opportunities for professional development for teacher educators, facilitating communications among different departments, as well as creating links with schools and communities. Institutional support and advocacy for cultural diversity shape the core beliefs related to ITP programs that, in turn, reflect the content, delivery, and sequence of the courses and practical teaching experience that make up teacher education (Salend, 2010). ITP programs that have a conceptual coherence and practical coordination are more likely to provide the competencies needed to be a cultural responsive practitioner (Darling-Hammond, 2006). However, creating coherence within ITP is challenging because of often-prevalent individualism and fragmentations, with different departments discretely organized and specialized (Hargreaves & Macmillan, 1994). These common organizational features of ITP can represent important barriers because they convey inconsistent expectations of how prospective teachers should work effectively in culturally diverse schools and classrooms. Therefore, it is important to evaluate whether, within an ITP, there is a shared vision among institutional actors of what the challenges and priorities for teacher preparation are.

While a number of studies have conducted individual and activities level investigations within ITPs, few studies have provided insights into their institutional level. These studies focused on teacher educators' and policymakers' perceptions and preparations for multiculturalism. For example, a study by Goodwin and colleagues (2014) conducted with teacher educators from all over the US showed that minority participants expressed the feeling of being more prepared to handle issues of cultural diversity compared to their counterparts (White teacher educators). In a mixed-methods study conducted in 12 ITPs in Spain, Wassell, Kerrigan, and Hawrylak (2018) investigated teacher educators' conceptions of diversity. Results show that the teacher educators did not mention issues directly connected with diversity such as institutional discrimination and described cultural differences primarily in terms of deficit characteristics. Gorski (2009) reviewed explicit theories and philosophies reported in 45 syllabi from classes on cultural diversity in several ITPs in the US, assessing the ways multicultural education is conceptualized in course descriptions. Most of the syllabi reviewed promoted a deficit perspective on diversity, and dealt only to a small extent with dimensions of systematic oppression, such as racism. Next to examining teacher educators' beliefs and knowledge about cultural diversity, at the institutional level we suggest that research generated by systematically evaluating ITP documents such as course syllabi, degree requirements, and professional standards is likewise important.

Conclusion

In increasingly multicultural societies there is a demand for teachers – regardless of their cultural and ethnic background – to be well-prepared to teach in culturally diverse schools. The question is, how can we best do so? Based on theory and empirical evidence reviewed in this chapter, we argue that ITP should address at least several areas: teacher cultural diversity beliefs, culturally responsive teaching self-efficacy, teacher empathy, and pedagogical approaches effective with culturally diverse students. This is because the cognitive, emotional, and pedagogical components interact with the way teachers in training interpret the information received, derive feelings of efficacy, acknowledge the importance of teacher–student relationships, and shape their teaching. It will also be important to evaluate ITP regarding cultural diversity by assessing who are in these programs (individual level), what learning opportunities are offered (activity level), and how institutional core beliefs shape the content, structure, and implementation of these programs (institutional level). The systematic evaluation of ITPs represents a collective effort and responsibility to form future teacher generations for diversity. While there is still much to be done, we know enough to start somewhere.

Note

1 The original term 'color-blindness' is not used in this chapter to avoid any negative connotation regarding individual differences in visual capabilities.

References

Achinstein, B., Ogawa, R. T., Sexton, D., & Freitas, C. (2010). Retaining teachers of color: A pressing problem and a potential strategy for "hard-to-staff" schools. *Review of Educational Research, 80*, 71–107.

Aragón, O. R., Dovidio, J. F., & Graham, M. J. (2017). Colorblind and multicultural ideologies are associated with faculty adoption of inclusive teaching practices. *Journal of Diversity in Higher Education, 10*, 201–215.

Aronson, B., & Laughter, J. (2016). The theory and practice of culturally relevant education: A synthesis of research across content areas. *Review of Educational Research, 86*, 237–276.

Bakari, R. (2003). Preservice teachers' attitudes toward teaching African American students: Contemporary research. *Urban Education, 38*, 640–654.

Baldwin, S. C., Buchanan, A. M., & Rudisill, M. E. (2007). What teacher candidates learned about diversity, social justice, and themselves from service-learning experiences. *Journal of Teacher Education, 58*, 315–327.

Bandura, A. (1997). *Self-efficacy: The exercise of control*. New York: Freeman.

Barrett, M. (2018). Promoting the intercultural competence of young people in the school context. *European Psychologist, 23*, 93–104.

Bensimon, E. M. (2005). Closing the achievement gap in higher education: An organizational learning perspective. *New Directions for Higher Education, 131*, 99–111.

Cherng, H. Y. S., & Davis, L. A. (2017). Multicultural matters: An investigation of key assumptions of multicultural education reform in teacher education. *Journal of Teacher Education, 70*, 219-236.

Chu, S. Y. (2013). Teacher efficacy beliefs toward serving culturally and linguistically diverse students in special education: Implications of a pilot study. *Education and Urban Society*, 45, 385–410.

Civitillo, S., Juang, L. P., Badra, M., & Schachner, M. K. (2019). The interplay between culturally responsive teaching, cultural diversity beliefs, and self-reflection: A multiple case study. *Teaching and Teacher Education*, 77, 341–351.

Civitillo, S., Juang, L., & Schachner, M. (2018). Challenging beliefs about cultural diversity in education: A synthesis and critical review of trainings with pre-service teachers. *Educational Research Review*, 24, 67–83.

Civitillo, S., Juang, L., Schachner, M., & Börnert, M. (2016). *Validierung einer deutschen Version der "Culturally Responsive Classroom Management Self-Efficacy Scale"* [Validation of the German version of "The Culturally Responsive Classroom Management Self-Efficacy Scale"]. *Empirische Sonderpädagogik*, 8, 279–288.

Cochran-Smith, M., & Villegas, A. (2016). Preparing teacher for diversity and high-poverty schools: A research-based perspective. In J. Lampert & B. Burnett (Eds.), *Teacher education for high poverty schools: Education, equity, economy* (pp. 9–31). Cham: Springer.

Conner, J. O. (2010). Learning to unlearn: How a service-learning project can help teacher candidates to reframe urban students. *Teaching and Teacher Education*, 26, 1170–1177.

Cooper, J. E. (2007). Strengthening the case for community-based learning in teacher education. *Journal of Teacher Education*, 58, 245–255.

Darling-Hammond, L. (2006). Constructing 21st-century teacher education. *Journal of Teacher Education*, 57, 300–314.

Dee, T. S. (2004). Teachers, race, and student achievement in a randomized experiment. *Review of Economics and Statistics*, 86, 195–210.

Dee, T. S., & Penner, E. K. (2017). The causal effects of cultural relevance: Evidence from an ethnic studies curriculum. *American Educational Research Journal*, 54, 127–166.

Dolby, N. (2012). *Rethinking multicultural education for the next generation: The new empathy and social justice*. New York: Routledge.

Egalite, A. J., & Kisida, B. (2018). The effects of teacher match on students' academic perceptions and attitudes. *Educational Evaluation and Policy Analysis*, 40, 59–81.

European Commission. (2016). *Study on the diversity within the teaching profession with particular focus on migrant and/or minority background*. Luxemburg: Publications office of the European Union.

European Commission. (2017). *Preparing teachers for diversity: The role of initial teacher education*. Luxemburg: Publications office of the European Union.

Fitchett, P. G., Starker, T. V., & Salyers, B. (2012). Examining culturally responsive teaching self-efficacy in a preservice social studies education course. *Urban Education*, 47, 585–611.

Fives, H., & Buehl, M. M. (2012). Spring cleaning for the "messy" construct of teachers' beliefs: What are they? Which have been examined? What can they tell us. In K. R. Harris, S. Graham, & T. Urdan (Eds.), *APA Educational psychology handbook* (pp. 471–499). Washington: APA.

Gay, G. (2000). *Culturally responsive teaching: Theory, research, and practice.* New York: Teachers College Press.

Georgi, V. (2010). Lehrende mit Migrationshintergrund in Deutschland: Eine empirische Untersuchung zu Bildungsbiographien, professionellem Selbstverständnis und schulischer Integration [Teachers with migration background in Germany: An empirical study on education biographies, professional self-image and school integration]. Unpublished manuscript, Free University of Berlin, Berlin, Germany.

Glock, S., Kovacs, C., & Pit-ten Cate, I. (in press). Teachers' attitudes towards ethnic minority students: Effects of schools' cultural diversity. *British Journal of Educational Psychology.* Advance online publication.

Goodwin, A. L., Smith, L., Souto-Manning, M., Cheruvu, R., Tan, M. Y., Reed, R., & Taveras, L. (2014). What should teacher educators know and be able to do? Perspectives from practicing teacher educators. *Journal of Teacher Education, 65,* 284–302.

Gorski, P. C. (2009). What we're teaching teachers: An analysis of multicultural teacher education coursework syllabi. *Teaching and Teacher Education, 25,* 309–318.

Gorski, P. C. (2017). *Reaching and teaching students in poverty: Strategies for erasing the opportunity gap.* New York: Teachers College Press.

Grissom, J. A., & Redding, C. (2016). Discretion and disproportionality: Explaining the underrepresentation of high-achieving students of color in gifted program. *AERA Open, 2,* 1–25.

Hachfeld, A., Hahn, A., Schroeder, S., Anders, Y., & Kunter, M. (2015). Should teachers be colorblind? How multicultural and egalitarian beliefs differentially relate to aspects of teachers' professional competence for teaching in diverse classrooms? *Teaching and Teacher Education, 48,* 44–55.

Haddix, M. (2017). Diversifying teaching and teacher education: Beyond rhetoric and toward real change. *Journal of Literacy Research, 49,* 141–149.

Hargreaves, A., & Macmillan, B. (1994). The balkanization of teaching: Collaboration that divides. In A. Hargreaves (Ed.), *Changing teachers, changing times* (pp. 212–240). London: Cassell.

Hill, A. J., & Jones, D. B. (2018). A teacher who knows me: The academic benefits of repeat student-teacher matches. *Economics of Education Review, 64,* 1–12.

Klein, O., Neugebauer, M., & Jacob, M. (2019, July 17). Migrant teachers in the classroom: A key to reduce ethnic disadvantages in school? https://doi.org/10.31235/osf.io/2s8n6

Kubicka, D., Wojciechowicz, A. A., & Vock, M. (2018). Zwischenbericht–Dokumentation zum Projekt "Refugee Teachers Program" [The interim report for the project "Refugee Teachers Program"]. Working Paper, University of Potsdam, Potsdam, Germany.

Kumar, R., & Lauermann, F. (2018). Cultural beliefs and instructional intentions: Do experiences in teacher education institutions matter? *American Educational Research Journal, 55,* 419–452.

Ladson-Billings, G. (1995). Toward a theory of culturally relevant pedagogy. *American Educational Research Journal, 32,* 465–491.

Matthews, J. S., & López, F. (in press). Speaking their language: The role of cultural content integration and heritage language for academic achievement among Latino children. *Contemporary Educational Psychology*. Advance online publication.

Milner, H. R. (2010). What does teacher education have to do with teaching? Implications for diversity studies. *Journal of Teacher Education*, *61*, 118–131.

Neugebauer, M. & Klein, O. (2016). Profitieren Kinder mit Migrationshintergrund von pädagogischen Fachkräften mit Migrationshintergrund? *Kölner Zeitschrift für Soziologie und Sozialpsychologie*, *68*, 259–283.

Nieto, S. (1992). *Affirming diversity: The sociopolitical context of multicultural education*. Longman: White Plains.

Opfer, V. D., & Pedder, D. (2011). Conceptualizing teacher professional learning. *Review of Educational Research*, *81*, 376–407.

Paris, D. (2012). Culturally sustaining pedagogy: A needed change in stance, terminology, and practice. *Educational Researcher*, *41*, 93–97.

Peck, N. F., Maude, S. P., & Brotherson, M. J. (2015). Understanding preschool teachers' perspectives on empathy: A qualitative inquiry. *Early Childhood Education Journal*, *43*, 169–179.

Pettigrew, T. F., & Tropp, L. R. (2006). A meta-analytic test of intergroup contact theory. *Journal of Personality and Social Psychology*, *90*, 751–783.

Pitts, D. W. (2007). Representative bureaucracy, ethnicity, and public schools. Examining the link between representation and performance. *Administration and Society*, *39*, 497–526.

Powell, R., Cantrell, S. C., Malo-Juvera, V., & Correll, P. K. (2016). Operationalizing Culturally Responsive Instruction: Preliminary findings of CRIOP research. *Teachers College Record*, *118*, 1–46.

Rocha, R., & Hawes, D. (2009). Racial diversity, representative bureaucracy, and equity in multiracial school districts. *Social Science Quarterly*, *90*, 326–344.

Salend, S. J. (2010). Evaluating inclusive teacher education programs: A flexible framework. In C. Forlin (Ed.), *Teacher education for inclusion: Changing paradigms and innovative approaches* (pp. 130–140). Abingdon: Routledge.

Santoro, N. (2015). The drive to diversify the teaching profession: Narrow assumptions, hidden complexities. *Race, Ethnicity and Education*, *18*, 858–876.

Statistisches Bundesamt Mikrozensus (2015). Hauptberufliches Bildungspersonal innerhalb und außerhalb früher Bildung, Schulen, und Hochschulen des Mikrozensus 2015. Wiesbaden, Destatis.

Schmeichel, M. (2012). Good teaching? An examination of culturally relevant pedagogy as an equity practice. *Journal of Curriculum Studies*, *44*, 211–231.

Scott, S. V., & Rodriguez, L. F. (2015). "A Fly in the Ointment" African American male preservice teachers' experiences with stereotype threat in teacher education. *Urban Education*, *50*, 689–717.

Siwatu, K. O. (2007). Preservice teachers' culturally responsive teaching self-efficacy and outcome expectancy beliefs. *Teaching and Teacher Education*, *23*, 1086–1101.

Siwatu, K. O. (2011). Preservice teachers' culturally responsive teaching self-efficacy-forming experiences: A mixed methods study. *The Journal of Educational Research*, *104*, 360–369.

Smolcic, E., & Katunich, J. (2017). Teachers crossing borders: A review of the research into cultural immersion field experience for teachers. *Teaching and Teacher Education, 62*, 47–59.

Statistisches Bundesamt. (2016). *Bevölkerung mit Migrationshintergrund – Ergebnisse des Mikrozensus 2015 {Population with immigrant background - Results of the microcensus 2015}*. Wiesbaden, Destatis.

U.S. Department of Education. (2016). *The state of racial diversity in the educator workforce*. Washington, DC: Office of Planning, Evaluation and Policy Development, Policy and Program Studies Service.

UNHCR (2019). *Trends at a glance 2017*. Geneva. Retrieved from: https://www.unhcr.org/globaltrends2017/

United Nations (2018). *Migration*. New York. Retrieved from: https://un.org/en/sections/issues-depth/migration/index.html.

Wang, K. T., Castro, A. J., & Cunningham, Y. L. (2014). Are perfectionism, individualism, and racial color-blindness associated with less cultural sensitivity? Exploring diversity awareness in White prospective teachers. *Journal of Diversity in Higher Education, 7*, 211–225.

Warren, C. A. (2014). Towards a pedagogy for the application of empathy in culturally diverse classroom. *Urban Review, 46*, 395–419.

Warren, C. A. (2018). Empathy, teacher dispositions, and preparation for culturally responsive pedagogy. *Journal of Teacher Education, 69*, 169–183.

Wassell, B. A., Kerrigan, M. R., & Hawrylak, M. F. (2018). Teacher educators in a changing Spain: Examining beliefs about diversity in teacher preparation. *Teaching and Teacher Education, 69*, 223–233.

Zeichner, K. (2010). Rethinking the connections between campus courses and field experiences in college-and university-based teacher education. *Journal of Teacher Education, 61*, 89–99.

Index

Aboud, F. E. 220
academic achievement: acculturation research 147; cross-ethnic friendships 185; ethnic minority teachers 293; friendship segregation 240; immigrant youth adaptation 133, 136–138, 139–141; intergroup anxiety 181, 182; language brokering 168–169; peer diversity 112, 123–124; perceived discrimination 179; stereotype threat 181–182; teacher empathy 289
accommodation 82–83
acculturation 2–3, 41, 74–91, 130, 144–159; asymmetric 92; biculturalism 42; bidimensional framework 24, 26; comparative research 149–156; cultural distance 99; definition of 25; globalization 23, 24–28; immigrant school composition 101; immigrant youth adaptation 131, 132, 140–141; individual experiences of 145, 150; Integrative Framework for Studying Immigrant Youth Adaptation 94; intergenerational conflict 167; language brokering 170; pace 84–86; strategies 163; synchrony 83–84; tempo 80–83, 85–86; timing 77–80, 85–86; *see also* adaptation
Acoach, C. L. 169
action civics (AC) 252, 259–263, 264
Adams, B. G. 27
adaptation 84, 86, 129–143, 147; acculturation discrepancy between parents and adolescents 167; comparative research 152–153; diaspora migrant youth 148; Integrative Framework for Studying Immigrant Youth Adaptation 94; multilevel integrative framework 130–133; statistical analysis of multilevel data 133–141; *see also* acculturation
adolescence: acculturation timing 78; attitudes 213, 216; cultural globalization 30–31; "culture shock" 98; language brokering 163–176; parental influence 218, 225; peer influence 223; youth development 113; *see also* youth
Adolescent Sleep Study 120
Adolescents 360 (A360) project 254–259, 264
advocacy: advocacy hourglass 261, 264; initial teacher preparation 295–296
African Americans: culture 26, 27; ethnic minority teachers 292, 293; peer diversity 112–113, 122; peer influence on attitudes 219–220; race-based rejection sensitivity 181; stereotype threat 181–182; *see also* Black Americans
age 10, 16, 77–78, 264
agency 37, 132, 259
Agirdag, O. 272, 278
Alba, R. 8
Allport, G. W. 182–183, 216
alternating strategy 45–46, 49
Anguiano, R. M. 164–165
anti-immigrant attitudes 97–98, 214–215, 219, 223
anxiety 29, 33, 61; contact hypothesis 198, 214; experience-sampling methods 118, 122–123, 125; intergroup 64, 177, 178, 180–182, 187, 188, 189; perceived discrimination 179; teacher support 100
apps 206
Apriceno, MaryBeth 58–73
Aptekar, S. 12
Arends-Tóth, J. 51
Asendorpf, Jens B. 3, 129–143

Index

Asian Americans: friendship segregation 237; peer diversity 113, 119, 121, 122; polyculturalism 62
assessment 290
assimilation 24, 42, 64, 82–83; acculturation 81; comparative research 153; Flanders 270; national policies 96, 97
asylum seekers 146
attitudes 213–232; acculturation 78, 85, 147; anti-immigrant 97–98, 214–215, 219, 223; contact hypothesis 198; cross-ethnic friendships 184, 186, 187, 239–240; ethnic diversity education 270–271, 274, 275–276, 279, 280n3; friendship choices 236; intergroup anxiety 181; intergroup contact 183, 294; multicultural education 269; parental influence 216, 217–218, 221–222, 223, 224–225; peer influence 219–220, 221, 222, 223–225, 239; polyculturalism 58, 62–65, 66; school diversity 59, 200; self-report measures 202; teachers' 276
Aumann, Lara 2, 144–159
Australia 63, 64–65, 129, 153, 277
Austria 59
autonomy 264–265; adolescence 163, 166, 167; comparative research 155; language brokering 171; peer relationships 112
Ayenekulu, Metsehate 251–267

Babiker, I. E. 98
Bagci, Sabahat Cigdem 3, 177–195
Bakari, R. 293
Ballard, Parissa J. 3, 251–267
Baltes, P. B. 76
Bandura, A. 187, 288
Banks, C. A. M. 60
Banks, J. A. 60, 269
Bekhuis, H. 273–274
Belfast 200, 206
Belgium 270, 271–272, 278; *see also* Flanders
belonging 31, 35, 37, 189; language brokering 169; peer relationships 112; polyculturalism 64; race-based rejection sensitivity 181; school context 99; younger people 16
Benbow, Alison E. F. 2, 144–159
Benet-Martínez, V. 43, 44, 48
Berry, J. W. 81, 98; acculturation 24, 42, 163; cultural transmission model 131; multiculturalism 50; taxonomic descriptions 146
Betancourt, T. S. 153
bias 152, 154, 273
bicultural competence 147
bicultural identity 2, 25, 31, 35, 41–43, 45–46, 48–51, 53–54
bicultural identity integration (BII) 43, 44–45, 48, 147
biculturalism 25, 41–57, 75, 169
bidimensional acculturation framework 24, 26
bidirectional relations 46
Black Americans 61, 62, 122, 196, 237; *see also* African Americans
Blake, J. J. 185–186
blendedness 43, 44, 45
Blumberg, H. 186
Boda, Z. 240
Bohman, Andrea 3, 213–232
Borrell, C. 97
brain processes 165, 166, 170–171
Branscombe, N. R. 179
Brenick, A. 186–187
Bronfenbrenner, U. 114, 130–131, 199, 203, 207, 208
bullying 95, 101, 241, 275, 276

California 60, 254, 260, 261
Cameron, L. 187–188
Campbell, D. T. 203
Canada: acculturation timing 78; ethnic identity 81; language brokering 168, 169; migration to 129
Carby, A. 187–188
Catholic schools 278
Cheon, Yuen Mi 111–128
Cherng, H. Y. S. 293
Cheung, B. Y. 78
children: attitudes 216; parental influence 218; socialization 225
Chile 222
China 63, 64–65
Chinese Americans 43, 119, 168, 170
chronological timing 77–78, 79
chronosystem 200
Cila, J. 168
citizenship 271
civic development 251–267
civic involvement 33, 131
Civitillo, Sauro 3, 285–301
classroom adversity 136–138, 139–140

Coenders, M. 273–274
Cohen, Alison K. 251–267
collectivism 30, 167
Colombia 62–63, 65
color evasiveness 287–288
colorblindness 60, 199, 297n1; ethnic diversity education 270, 273; polyculturalism 64, 65, 68
communication 181
community-based learning 295
comparative research 149–156
competition 214
competitiveness 35–36
Confidence in Contact Model 187
conflict: intergenerational 34, 35–36, 37, 92, 167–168; intergroup 58
contact hypothesis 196–197, 198–199, 207, 214; *see also* intergroup contact
contact-in-context 111, 114
contraception 256–257, 258, 264
Crick, N. R. 186
critical pedagogy 253
cross-sectional studies 202
CRT *see* culturally responsive teaching
Cuban Americans 49, 51
cultural amalgamation 23–24, 28–30, 33, 37
cultural capital 30
cultural competence 131, 147, 286
cultural differences: acculturation 82, 99; essentialist perceptions of 34; ethnic diversity education 275, 276, 277, 279; initial teacher preparation 296; multiculturalism 64, 67, 269, 270, 279
cultural distance 35, 98–99, 153
cultural diversity 1, 271, 277, 285; initial teacher preparation 286, 291–297; multiculturalism 50; teacher empathy 289; teachers' beliefs about 286–288; *see also* diversity
cultural frame switching 44–45
cultural globalization 23–40
cultural heritage *see* heritage culture
cultural identity 2; comparative research 155; cultural amalgamation 29; culturally responsive teaching 290; globalized identity processes 31–32; multicultural identity styles scale 52; polyculturalism 64; psychological well-being 33; self-regulation 48–49; styles 45–46; *see also* identity
cultural immersion 295

cultural intelligence 63
cultural streams: biculturalism 41, 44, 46, 48, 50, 54; cultural globalization 23–37; identity development 48
cultural transmission model 131
culturally responsive teaching (CRT) 285–286, 288–289, 290–291
culture: cultural structures 85; language brokering 167–168, 171; polyculturalism 61–62, 67; *see also* acculturation; cultural differences; cultural diversity; cultural identity; heritage culture; host culture
"culture shock" 75, 98
curriculum 67–68, 271, 290

daily diaries 111–112, 115–116, 119
data analysis: A360 project 257; experience-sampling methods 117–119; statistical analysis 133–141; *see also* methodology; multilevel analysis
data collection 151–152
Davis, A. 181
Davis, L. A. 293
Davis, Rachel J. 41–57
deficit perspective 287–288, 296
DeLay, D. 242
demographic shifts 16, 59, 111
Demoulin, S. 99
Denmark 59
depression 29, 33, 61, 113; acculturation discrepancy between parents and adolescents 167; comparative research 155; impact of national migration policies 97; language brokering 169, 170, 171; perceived discrimination 179; teacher support 100
developmental change: experience-sampling methods 125; immigrant youth adaptation 130, 134, 138–141; language brokering 165–166, 170–171; longitudinal research 156
developmental intergroup theory 216, 221
developmental psychology 76–77
developmental systems theory 130, 131, 133
device-contingent sampling 112, 116
diaspora migrant youth 85, 146, 147, 148–149, 154
Dijkstra, J. K. 237
Dimitrova, R. 93, 95, 97
discrimination 51, 74, 130, 199, 213; anti-immigrant attitudes 97, 98; children 59; ethnic diversity education 270, 273,

274, 275–276, 279; ethnic identity 81; ethnic minority teachers 293; experience-sampling methods 125; impact on mental health 92; institutional 286, 296; intergroup anxiety 181; perceived 96–97, 98, 100, 101, 177, 178–180, 186–187, 275–276; school context 61, 99, 100, 101; *see also* prejudice; racism
diversity 1–2, 60–61, 177, 285; complexification of 7; cross-ethnic friendships 182, 187, 188; demographic shifts 59; diversity ideology 199; dynamic nature of 13; ethnic diversity education 268–284; experience-sampling methods 117, 119–124; growth in 213, 214; as habitual frame of reference 8, 17; impact on youth development 111, 112–113, 119–124, 125–126; influence on attitudes 200, 221–222; interethnic interactions 196–198; migration-driven 16–17; multiculturalism 50; perceived discrimination 178; polyculturalism 62, 64, 68; as psychological experience 114; relational 13; teachers' beliefs about 286–288; youth reactions to 213–232; *see also* cultural diversity; ethnic diversity; superdiversity
Dixon, John 206
Downey, G. 181
Doyle, A. B. 220
Duyvendak, J. W. 8

Eastern Europe 74
Ebuy, Genet 251–267
ecological approach *see* social-ecological approach
ecological fallacy 133
educational tracks 278
Ehrhardt, Alexandra 111–128
Eichas, Kyle 41–57
"emerging adulthood" 31
emotions: language brokering 165–166, 171; parental socialization 216
empathy 58, 184, 186, 273; contact hypothesis 198, 214; cross-ethnic friendships 187, 189; multicultural societies 177; parental influence 218; schools 60; teachers 289, 293
employment 171
English Language Learners 262–263
equifinality 133, 225

equity pedagogy 269
ERGMs *see* exponential random graph models
ERI *see* ethnic/racial identity
Erikson, E. H. 42, 46, 47
ESM *see* experience-sampling methods
Ethiopia 254–259, 264
ethnic diversity 1, 59–61, 112–113, 129, 189, 196–198; *see also* diversity
ethnic diversity education 268–284
ethnic groups: colorblind approach 270; comparative research 151, 154; ethnic diversity education 268; superdiversity research 14
"ethnic protection" 26, 32, 33
ethnic/racial identity (ERI): acculturation 81, 82; biculturalism 52–53; experience-sampling methods 118, 119–122, 125; language brokering 168, 169, 170, 171; peer influence 240; peer relationships 112
ethnic socialization 53, 80, 82
ethnicity: civic development 251; cross-ethnic friendships 148, 182–189, 198, 214–215, 221–222, 224, 235–239; discrimination 178–179; Ethiopia 255; ethnic minority teachers 277, 285, 291–293; experience-sampling methods 119–124, 125; friendship segregation 233–234, 237, 239, 241; immigrant youth adaptation 131; interethnic interactions 196–212; participatory approaches 264; polyculturalism 62, 64; psychological salience of 221; Roma 12; *see also* race
Europe: anti-immigrant attitudes 215; ethnic diversity education 268; ethnic minority teachers 293; friendship segregation 237, 238, 243n1; initial teacher preparation 294; intercultural education 269–270; mental health of immigrants 93, 95; minority youth's host country identification 240; MIPEX 95–96; opinions on migration-driven diversity 16; refugees 12; school diversity 59; superdiversity 18; young immigrants 213, 214
evaluation of initial teacher preparation 291–296
event sampling 112, 115
exclusionist model 96, 97
exosystem 200, 207

experience-sampling methods (ESM) 111–112, 114–126
experimental designs 201–202
exploration 49, 53
exponential random graph models (ERGMs) 236, 242
externalizing problems 92, 93, 95, 97, 101

family: asymmetric acculturation 92; biculturalism 50, 53–54; comparative research 156; cultural amalgamation 29–30; cultural globalization 35–36; familial ethnic socialization 53; "immigrant paradox" 93; immigrant youth adaptation 131–132, 136; language brokering 163–164, 169–170, 171; mental health of immigrants 97; parental income 144; *see also* parents
feedback 166, 171
Ferguson, G. M. 25, 27
field-based experience 294–295
Finland 183
Fishman, G. 155
Fitchett, P. G. 288–289
Flanders 270, 271, 272, 275, 278
forgiveness 198
frame switching 44–45
France 51, 129, 153
Freire, Paulo 253
friendships 15–16, 197; cross-ethnic 148, 182–189, 214–215, 221–222, 224, 235–239; immigrant youth adaptation 131; intraracial and interracial 112–113; multicultural societies 177; polyculturalism 66; promoting diverse 207; propinquity hypothesis 198; segregation 233–248; social network analysis 205
Fuligni, A. J. 140

Gay, G. 269
GC *see* Generation Citizen
Geeraert, N. 99
gender 10, 64, 144, 178
gene-environment correlations 223
Generation Citizen (GC) 260–263, 264
Germany: acculturation discrepancy between parents and adolescents 167–168; comparative research 153; culturally responsive teaching 288; diaspora migrant youth 85, 146, 154, 155; friendship segregation 239, 240; host and heritage identification 84; immigrant minorities 146; migration to 129; Muslims 16–17; Refugee Teachers Programme 291; school diversity 1, 59, 60; social service provision 12; teacher and student diversity 285, 293; teachers' beliefs 276–277, 287; young migrants 16
Gestsdóttir, S. 47
Gibson, M. A. 83
gifted education 292, 293
globalization 2, 23–40
Gniewosz, B. 167–168
Goodwin, A. L. 296
Gorski, P. C. 296
GPRS tracking 206
Graham, S. 186
Greece 59, 129, 136–138, 139
Greenfield, P. M. 82
group threat theory 214
Guatemala 253–254
Gurin, P. 196

Hachfeld, A. 276–277
Hackney 11
Hall, S. M. 17
Haritatos, J. 44
harmony 43, 45
Hawrylak, M. F. 296
heritage culture: acculturation 42, 74–75, 77, 78, 81–82, 84, 86, 147; comparative research 149, 153; ethnic socialization 53, 80; immigrant youth adaptation 132; lack of retention 167, 168; language brokering 171; multiculturalism 41; transnationalism 28
Herskovits, M. J. 24
Hispanics: biculturalism 45, 49, 50, 51; multicultural education 67; peer diversity 122; peer influence 222; *see also* Latinx Americans
homophily 185, 187, 233, 236, 237, 238–239, 241
Hong Kong 32, 33, 64–65
host culture: acculturation 74–75, 78, 79–80, 84, 86, 147; diaspora migrant youth 148–149; identification with 240; immigrant youth adaptation 132
hostility 74–75
hourglass metaphor 261, 264
Hox, J. J. 136
Hoyt, Lindsay Till 251–267
Hungary 241

Hurh, W. M. 75
hybridizing strategy 30, 45–46, 49, 53
Hylland Eriksen, T. 9

ICC *see* intraclass correlation
ideal self 185
identity: acculturation 82, 83, 85; bicultural 2, 25, 31, 35, 41–43, 45–46, 48–51, 53–54, 147; complex nature of 201; "culture shock" 98; development of 48; Erikson's theory 47; global 25, 26; globalized identity processes 31–32; identity confusion 34–35, 37; immigrant youth adaptation 131; intergroup theory of social identity 216; multicultural identity styles scale 52; Rejection-Identification Model 180; social 101, 112, 216, 221, 273; *see also* cultural identity; ethnic/racial identity
IFSIY *see* Integrative Framework for Studying Immigrant Youth Adaptation
"immigrant paradox" 93
immigrant school composition (ISC) 100–102
immigrants: acculturation 74–87, 144–159; adaptation 129–143; anti-immigrant attitudes 97–98, 214–215, 219, 223; biculturalism 42, 51, 53; comparative research 149–156; cultural amalgamation 29; cultural globalization 25, 27–28, 34, 36; current research on 145–149; Europe 213; heritage cultures 41; hostility towards 74–75; language brokering 163; mental health 92–107; polyculturalism 64; student diversity 285; *see also* migration
inclusion of the other in the self (IoS) 184–185
inclusive model 96
India 32, 33–34
individualism 13, 30, 35–36, 167
Indonesia 64–65
inequalities 17, 253, 259, 269, 286
initial teacher preparation (ITP) 285–301
integration 24, 42; bicultural negotiation 44, 53; comparative research 153; cultural 28–30, 33; ethnic diversity education 271; immigrant youth adaptation 129; national policies 95–97; parental attitudes 223; school context 99; self-regulation 49

Integrative Framework for Studying Immigrant Youth Adaptation (IFSIY) 94
Integrative Threat Theory 101
intercultural competence 269, 277
intercultural contact 24, 25, 28; *see also* intergroup contact
intercultural education 269–270, 273
interdisciplinarity 156
interethnic interactions 196–212
intergenerational conflict 34, 35–36, 37, 92, 167–168
intergroup anxiety 64, 177, 178, 180–182, 187, 188, 189
intergroup contact: adolescent readiness for 225; Confidence in Contact Model 187; contact hypothesis 196–197, 198–199, 207, 214; contact-in-context 111, 114; cross-ethnic friendships 239; educational interventions 68; experience-sampling methods 121–124; initial teacher preparation 294–295; intergroup anxiety 180, 182; multicultural societies 178, 182–183; polyculturalism 62, 63, 65–66, 68; school-based interventions 242; schools 58, 60, 121–124; tolerance 184
intergroup theory of social identity 216
internalizing problems 92, 93, 95, 97, 101, 169
intraclass correlation (ICC) 134–135, 136
Iqbal, H. 15–16
ISC *see* immigrant school composition
Israel 85, 146, 154, 155
Italy 12, 129, 181, 219
ITP *see* initial teacher preparation

Jamaica 27, 35–36
Japan 23, 32
Jasinskaja-Lahti, I. 181, 183
Jennings, M. K. 218
Jews 146
Jones, C. J. 168
Josselson, R. 47
Juang, Linda P. 3, 285–301
Jugert, Philipp 1–4, 74–91, 186–187
Juvonen, J. 186

Kam, J. A. 168
Kaspar, V. 81
Katunich, J. 295

Kawabata, Y. 186
Kelley, Robin D. G. 61
Kerrigan, M. R. 296
Kim, K. C. 75
Kim, S. Y. 168
Kinket, B. 275
Korean Americans 170
Kouider, E. B. 93
Kruskal, W. H. 203
Kucaba, Katarzyna 196–212
Kumar, R. 294

labor laws 148
Ladakh 30, 32, 33–34
Lalonde, R. N. 168
language: acculturation 79, 80, 81–82, 83, 85; comparative research 153; culturally responsive teaching 290; heritage culture 75; language brokering 163–176; loss of heritage 86; views on migrants 16
Latinx Americans: acculturation discrepancy between parents and adolescents 167; action civics 262; cross-ethnic friendships 186; ethnic minority teachers 292, 293; friendship segregation 240; language brokering 164–165, 168–169, 170; multicultural education 67; peer diversity 112–113, 122; polyculturalism 62; research 146; *see also* Hispanics
Lauermann, F. 294
Lease, A. M. 185–186
Lee, F. 43
Lee, M. 100
Lee, Richard M. 2–3, 74–91
Leney, A. 187–188
Lerner, R. M. 47
Leszczensky, Lars 3, 233–248
Leu, J. 43
Levy, A. 78
Levy, Sheri R. 58–73
Lewin, K. 114
Lewis, K. 239
Liebkind, K. 181
life paths 32
life satisfaction 95, 122, 154, 179
Linton, R. 24
London 1, 11, 15–16, 50, 185
longitudinal research: acculturation 84, 145; comparative 154–155, 156; culturally responsive teaching 290; friendship segregation 238, 240; immigrant youth adaptation 133, 136–142; interethnic interactions 207; parental influence on youth attitudes 217; peer influence on attitudes 219; polyculturalism 58–59, 60, 62, 63–64, 66; *see also* experience-sampling methods; research
Los Angeles 50

Macau 64–65
macrosystem 200, 207, 220
Magazzini, T. 12
Mähönen, T. A. 181
Malaysia 64–65
Marcoulides, K. M. 168
marginalization 24, 42, 86, 253
Marshall, W. A. 80
Martinez, C. R. 169
Massachusetts 260, 263
Masten, A. S. 130
materialism 35–36
McGuire, L. 221
McKeown, Shelley 3, 196–212
Meca, Alan 2, 41–57
media 1–2; acculturation 78; cultural globalization 25; culture acquisition 53–54; global youth culture 35; heritage-cultural 41
Meissner, Fran 2, 7–22
Mendle, J. 83
Mendoza-Denton, R. 181
mental health 92–107; acculturation 81; ecological approach 94–95; national context 95–99; school context 99–102
Merolla, A. J. 168
Merrilees C. E. 200
Merry, M. S. 272
mesosystem 200, 207, 220–221, 224, 226
methodology: acculturation research 75–76, 147; biculturalism 52; comparative research 151–152; experience-sampling methods 111–112, 114–126; friendship segregation 241–242; innovation 17; polyculturalism 66; social network analysis 235–237; superdiversity research 13, 14; youth interethnic interactions 201–206, 207; *see also* qualitative methodologies; quantitative methodologies; research
Mexican-Americans 51, 80
Mexico 34
Meyers, Chanel 206
Miami 50, 51

micro-ecological behavior 203–205
microsystem 200, 203, 207, 220, 226
migration 1, 41, 129; acculturation 74; complexification of diversity 7; ethnic diversity education 271; national policies 95–97; reasons for 144; social contexts 9; stress of 92; superdiversity research 11–15; views on migrants 16; youth and superdiversity 15–17; *see also* immigrants
Migration Integration Policy Index (MIPEX) 95–96, 97
Miklikowska, Marta 3, 213–232
MISS *see* multicultural identity styles scale
mobile phones 206
mood 122–123
Moody, J. 238
Morais, C. 187–188
morality 36
Moroccans 237
Morris, M. W. 43
Morris, P. 114
motivation 93, 132, 144, 287
Motti-Stefanidi, Frosso 3, 129–143
multi-ethnic youth 2
"multicultural acquisition" 26, 28, 32, 33
multicultural identity styles scale (MISS) 52
multiculturalism 41, 50–51; action civics 262, 263; benefits of 182; critiques of 67, 279; diversity ideology 199; initial teacher preparation 296; multicultural contact 111; multicultural education 60, 269–270, 271, 272, 273–275, 276–278, 279, 296; multicultural societies 177–195, 251–252, 296; policy 96; polyculturalism combined with 65, 67–68; polyculturalism compared to 61, 64; superdiversity research 12; teacher culture 275; teachers' beliefs 276–277, 287
multifinality 133, 225
multilevel analysis: acculturation 75–76, 156; ethnic diversity education 272; experience-sampling methods 118–119, 124; immigrant youth adaptation 130, 132, 133–141; mental health of immigrants 100
Munniksma, A. 186, 234
Muslims: Ethiopia 255; Germany 16–17; homophily 241; national policies 96; Netherlands 60; Paris 51; polyculturalism 62, 63

Native Americans 112–113, 122
Navas, M. 82
Ndhlovu, M. 187–188
Neal, S. 15–16
Nesdale, D. 221
Nesselroade, J. R. 76
Netherlands: bullying 241; civic education 280n1; comparative research 153; ethnic diversity education 271–272, 273–274, 275–276, 279; friendship segregation 234; immigrant minorities 146; intercultural and multicultural education 269; migration to 129; multiculturalism 199; peer influence on attitudes 219; school diversity 59, 60; vocational education 278
network interventions 242–243
New Jersey 260
New York City 50, 112, 119
New York State 260
New Zealand 75, 86
Nieswand, B. 12–13
Noh, S. 81
norms: acculturation 75, 78; anti-prejudice 273, 274, 279; cultural amalgamation 29, 30; cultural distance 98; inclusive 221, 224; intergroup theory of social identity 216; peer 220, 221, 223–224; promotion of diversity 207; school context 99; societal 148
Northern Ireland 198, 200, 204, 206
Norway 59, 98

Oklahoma 260, 263
openness to experience 33
Ozer, Simon 2, 23–40

Palazzi, A. 206
Paluck, E. L. 220, 243
parents: acculturation discrepancy 167–168; cross-ethnic contact 188; ethnic socialization 80; influence on youth attitudes 216, 217–218, 221–222, 223, 224–225; language brokering 163–164, 166, 169–170, 171; parent-child communication 154; *see also* family
Paris 51
participatory approaches 251–252, 264–265; action civics 259–263, 264; benefits and challenges 263–264; youth-led participatory action research 252–259, 263–264

Pearson, M. 237
pedagogy 269, 285
peer influence 219–220, 221, 222, 223–225, 239–240
peer socialization 216
peer support 99, 100
person-environment interactions 46
personality 132, 144, 225
perspective-taking 177, 184, 186; brain processes 166; cross-ethnic friendships 187; school diversity 60; teacher empathy 289
Pettigrew, T. F. 183, 198–199
Pew Foundation 16
Philippines 62–63, 64–65
Pietrzak, J. 181
pluralism 10, 60, 153
police 261, 263
policy: Ethiopia 255; national-level migration and integration policies 95–97, 147–148; polyculturalism 62, 67; post-multicultural politics 15; superdiversity research 11–12
political integration 96
polyculturalism 2, 29, 58–73, 199
Portera, A. 269
post-multicultural politics 15
poverty 286
Powell, R. 291
power-sharing 252, 253, 264
Prashad, Vijay 61
preferences 233–234, 237–238, 241
prejudice 58, 74, 130, 213, 225–226; age-related changes in 216; anti-immigrant 98; Australia 63; children 59; contact hypothesis 196–197, 198–199, 214; developmental intergroup theory 216; ethnic diversity education 268, 270, 273, 274, 279; friendship segregation 238; impact on mental health 92; inter-ethnic friendships 239; intergroup contact 60; intergroup theory of social identity 216; multicultural education 269; multicultural teacher culture 275; negative effects of 61; parental influence 217, 218, 222, 224; peer influence 219–220, 224; school-based interventions 242; self-report measures 202; teachers' beliefs 276–277; theories of prejudice development 221; see also discrimination; racism
proximal processes 114, 214, 216, 226

psychological adaptation 86, 99
psychological adjustment 112, 122–123
psychological risks 32, 34–35
psychological well-being: cross-ethnic friendships 185, 186; cultural distance 99; cultural globalization 33, 34; immigrant youth adaptation 131; intergroup anxiety 181, 182; perceived discrimination 179, 180, 186–187; schools 60; teacher support 100
psychosomatic problems 95, 154
pubertal development 76–77, 79, 80, 83–84, 86
Punjabi youth 83
Purdie, V. J. 181

qualitative methodologies: acculturation research 147; biculturalism 52; comparative research 156; culturally responsive teaching 290; ethnic diversity education 268, 279; polyculturalism 66
quantitative methodologies: acculturation research 147; biculturalism 52; comparative research 156; culturally responsive teaching 290; ethnic diversity education 268, 270–271, 278–279

race: action civics 263; civic development 251; discrimination 178–180, 199; experience-sampling methods 119–124, 125; friendship segregation 198, 233–234, 237, 239; micro-ecological studies 203; parental attitudes 223; participatory approaches 264; peer influence on attitudes 219–220; polyculturalism 62, 64, 67–68; race-based rejection sensitivity 181; self-report measures 202; technology use in research 206; see also ethnic/racial identity; ethnicity
racial diversity 112–113; see also ethnic diversity
racial identity see ethnic/racial identity
racism 74, 148, 261; ethnic diversity education 273; initial teacher preparation 296; "reverse" 178; see also discrimination; prejudice
Rainey, V. R. 165
random sampling 112, 115, 121, 124
RDST see relational developmental systems theory
reading ability 132–133

Index

reciprocity 234–235, 236
Redfield, R. 24
Reese, H. W. 76
reflexivity 14–15
refugees 146, 148, 285; Australia 63; comparative research 149, 153; Eastern Europe 74; Europe 12; language learning 82; qualitative research 147; Refugee Teachers Programme 291
Rejection-Identification Model 180
relational developmental systems theory (RDST) 42, 46–50, 52–54
relational diversity 13
Relative Acculturation Extended Model 82
relative timing 79–80
religion: Ethiopia 255; ethnic diversity education 280n4; friendship segregation 234; religious denomination of schools 278
remote acculturation 25, 26–27, 28, 36, 37
research 9, 17–18; acculturation 75–76, 80, 84, 86, 144–159; comparative 149–156; cultural globalization 36; culturally responsive teaching 290–291; ethnic diversity education 273–280; friendship segregation 240–243; initial teacher preparation 293, 295, 296; mental health of immigrants 93, 101–102; multi-site 53; polyculturalism 61–65, 66; pubertal development 76–77; research questions 150–151; three waves of 10–15; youth interethnic interactions 199–208; youth-led participatory action research 252–259, 263–264; *see also* longitudinal research; methodology; qualitative methodologies; quantitative methodologies
resilience: cross-ethnic friendships 186; immigrant youth adaptation 130, 131; perceived discrimination 179; resilience perspective 92–93, 94
"reverse racism" 178
Rhode Island 260, 261, 262
risk perspective 92, 93
Robinson, W. S. 132–133
Roma 12, 241
Rosenthal, Lisa 2, 58–73
Ruiter, S. 273–274
Rutland, Adam 3, 177–195, 220, 221

Sagherian-Dickey, Thia 196–212
Sam, L. D. 98

SAOMs *see* stochastic actor-oriented models
Schachner, M. K. 186–187
Schmitt, M. T. 179
Schneider, J. 1
Scholten, P. 12
schools 58–61; acculturation 144; action civics 259–263; bullying 241; comparative research 156; cross-ethnic friendships 148, 187, 189; ethnic composition 196, 277–278; experience-sampling methods 117; friendship segregation 234, 238, 241, 242; immigrant youth adaptation 131, 135–138; impact of diversity on youth development 111, 112–113, 119–124, 125–126; inclusive norms 221; influence on attitudes 200, 221–222; intergroup contact 182–183; mental health of immigrants 99–102; micro-ecological behavior 203–205; norms 223–224; perceived discrimination 179–180; polyculturalism 63, 66–68; popularity of immigrants 134; teachers and ethnic diversity education 268–284; *see also* academic achievement
Schwartz, Seth J. 41–57, 167
seating behavior in schools 203–205
segregation 16, 221, 233–248; ethnic 81; intergroup anxiety 180; measures of 197; schools 58, 203; United States 59
self-concept 35, 82, 168
self-control 131
self-disclosure 181, 184–185, 189, 198
self-efficacy: acculturation 82; action civics 259; comparative research 155; cross-ethnic friendships 187–189; immigrant youth adaptation 136, 138; language brokering 169; teachers 285, 288–289
self-esteem 33, 113, 147; cultural integration 29; language brokering 168, 171; multicultural societies 185; perceived discrimination 179, 180
self-evaluation 79, 291–296
self-expansion 185, 189
self-regulation 47, 48–49
self-report measures 202, 273, 274–275
SEMs *see* structural equation models
separation 24, 42, 166, 167
SES *see* socioeconomic status
sexual orientation 64, 178
Shepherd, H. 243

Silbereisen, R. K. 155
Simpson, E. H. 123
Singapore 11
Siwatu, K. O. 288
sleep 120
Smith, P. K. 186
Smith, S. 222
Smith, T. W. 235
Smolcic, E. 295
SNA *see* social network analysis
Snijders, T. A. B. 237
social adversity 136–138, 139–140
social capital 93
social change 257–259, 261, 262–263, 265
social class 131, 264; *see also* socioeconomic status
social cognitive theory 288
social cohesion 196
social competence 185–186
social cues 165–166, 170–171, 220
social-ecological approach 130–131, 199–201, 203, 207, 220–221, 224–225
social exclusion 59, 179
social identity 112, 216, 273
social identity theory 101, 221
social justice 64, 253
social learning 216, 218, 223
social network analysis (SNA) 205; friendship segregation 234, 235–243, 244n2; network interventions 242–243
social psychology 149, 196, 199, 200, 287
social referents 243
social skills 177, 186, 187, 189
socialization 144, 216, 218, 223, 225; deficit perspective 287; ethnic 53, 80, 82; school context 99
socio-cognitive factors 216, 225
socio-cultural adaptation 86
sociocultural context 26, 30, 31, 32
socioeconomic status (SES) 132, 150, 151; *see also* social class
South Africa: cultural globalization 25–26, 27, 30; micro-ecological research 203; polyculturalism 61–62
Soviet Union, former: acculturation discrepancy between parents and adolescents 167–168; diaspora migrant youth 85, 146, 154, 155; host and heritage identification of migrants 84
Spain 129, 296

standard errors 133, 134–135
Stark, Tobias 3, 233–248
statistical analysis 133–141
Steglich, C. E. G. 237
stereotype threat 181–182
stereotypes 287; comparative research 152; intergroup anxiety 181; multiculturalism 60, 67, 199, 269, 279; teachers' beliefs 294
Stevens, Gonneke W. J. M. 3, 92–107, 154
Stevens, P. A. 272
stigmatization 179
stochastic actor-oriented models (SAOMs) 236, 239–240, 242
Stoessel, K. 84
Stokes, B. 16
stress 33, 75; diaspora migrant youth 148; language brokering 164–165, 170, 171; of migration 92; perceived discrimination 179
structural equation models (SEMs) 141, 236
Suárez-Orozco, C. 133
Suárez-Orozco, M. M. 133
substance use 167, 169, 239
Suleiman, Ahna 251–267
superdiversity 1, 7–22, 177; as malleable concept 8–10; as post-multiculturalism concept 19n3; three waves of research 10–15, 18; youth and 15–17; *see also* diversity
Suzuki, L. K. 82
Sweden: mental health of immigrants 98; parental influence on attitudes 217; peer influence on attitudes 219, 220; school diversity 59, 221
Switzerland 59
synchrony 85–86

Taiwan 288
Tanner, J. M. 80
teachers: beliefs of 276–277, 286–288; culturally responsive teaching 285–286, 288–289, 290–291; empathy 289; ethnic diversity education 268–284; Generation Citizen 260; individual differences between 272, 276–277, 278–279; initial teacher preparation 285–301; mental health of immigrants 99, 100
teaching styles 135
technology 117, 205–206
Texas 51, 260, 261
Thailand 30, 36

Thijs, Jochem 3, 268–284
Titzmann, Peter F. 1–4, 74–91, 154, 167–168
Todorova, I. 133
tolerance 60, 184, 218, 220, 225
Toronto 50, 81
tourism 25
transition timing 78–79
transnationalism 28
triadic closure 234–235, 236, 239
Trickett, E. J. 168
Tropp, L. R. 198–199, 222, 223
trust 196, 198
Turkish immigrants 146, 237, 240; comparative research 153; ethnic diversity education 273, 275, 276; mental health of immigrants 98
Turner, R. N. 184, 187–188
two-level regression models 134, 135–138

Ülger, Z. 270–271
Umaña-Taylor, A. J. 53
unemployment 96, 214
United Kingdom (UK): cross-group friendships 184; cultural globalization 30; ethnic diversity education 279; ethnic minorities 177, 213; micro-ecological research 203–204; migration to 129; peer norms 220; school diversity 59, 196
United Nations (UN) 144
United States: action civics 259, 260–263; biculturalism 51; comparative research 153; cross-ethnic friendships 186; cultural globalization 27, 30, 34; culturally responsive teaching 290; culture acquisition 53–54; ethnic diversity education 268; ethnic minority teachers 285, 291–292, 293; friendship segregation 239, 241, 243n1; immigrant minorities 146; initial teacher preparation 296; language brokering 168–169; micro-ecological research 203; migration to 129; minority groups 41; parental influence 218; peer influence 223, 240; polyculturalism 62–65; reading ability of immigrants 132–133; school diversity 59, 60, 196, 285; teachers' beliefs 287; White majority status 177, 213; youth-led participatory action research 254
universities 63–64

values 148; acculturation 74, 78, 84; biculturalism 50; cultural amalgamation 29–30; cultural distance 98; individualistic 167; mental health of immigrants 93; multicultural education 269; retention of heritage 171; school context 99, 272; traditional 222; U.S. culture acquisition 54; Western 35–36
van de Vijver, F. J. R. 51, 153
Van Houtte, M. 272
Van Zalk, M. H. W. 237
Veenstra, R. 237
Verkuyten, M. 131, 273, 275, 276
Vermeij, L. 234
Vertovec, S. 7, 9–10, 12
Vervaet, Roselien 3, 268–284
Vincent, C. 15–16
Virta, E. 98
vocational education 278
Voces y Manos 253–254
Vollebergh, W. A. M. 93
voting rights 96

Wallace, W. P. 203
Walsh, Sophie D. 3, 92–107
Ward, C. 45, 49, 52, 75, 86
Wassell, B. A. 296
Webb, L. M. 169
Weingrod, A. 78
WEIRD populations 201
Weisskirch, Robert S. 3, 163–176
Wessendorf, S. 11
West, A. L. 43–44, 49
West Indians 122
Western culture 26, 34, 35–36
Westin, C. 98
White Americans 62, 186, 237, 262
Whittle, S. 166
Williams, Amanda 196–212
Wimmer, A. 239
Windzio, M. 222
women: Ethiopia 255, 256–257; polyculturalism 64; stereotype threat 181–182
Wu, N. H. 168

Yagmur, K. 153
Ye, J. 11
YES *see* Youth Experiences Study
Yip, Tiffany 3, 111–128

youth 15–17, 18; acculturation research 144–159; comparative research 149–156; cultural globalization 27–28, 30–32; culture acquisition 53–54; current research on 145–149; friendship segregation 233–248; immigrant youth adaptation 129–143; impact of diversity on youth development 111, 112–113, 119–124, 125–126; interethnic interactions 196–212; majority and minority 177–195; mental health of immigrants 92–107; polyculturalism 58–59, 65–66; reactions to diversity 213–232; *see also* adolescence

Youth Engagement and Action for Health (YEAH!) 254

Youth Experiences Study (YES) 120

youth-led participatory action research (YPAR) 252–259, 263–264

Zambia 25, 30, 34, 36

Zamboanga, B. L. 50